TRANSNATIONALISATION OF SOCIAL RIGHTS

TRANSNATIONALISATION OF SOCIAL RIGHTS

Andreas Fischer-Lescano
Kolja Möller
(eds.)

intersentia
Cambridge – Antwerp – Portland

Intersentia Ltd
Sheraton House | Castle Park
Cambridge | CB3 0AX | United Kingdom
Tel.: +44 1223 370 170 | Fax: +44 1223 370 169
Email: mail@intersentia.co.uk
www.intersentia.com | www.intersentia.co.uk

Distribution for the UK and Ireland:
NBN International
Airport Business Centre, 10 Thornbury Road
Plymouth, PL6 7 PP
United Kingdom
Tel.: +44 1752 202 301 | Fax: +44 1752 202 331
Email: orders@nbninternational.com

Distribution for Europe and all other countries:
Intersentia Publishing nv
Groenstraat 31
2640 Mortsel
Belgium
Tel.: +32 3 680 15 50 | Fax: +32 3 658 71 21
Email: mail@intersentia.be

Distribution for the USA and Canada:
International Specialized Book Services
920 NE 58th Ave. Suite 300
Portland, OR 97213
USA
Tel.: +1 800 944 6190 (toll free) | Fax: +1 503 280 8832
Email: info@isbs.com

Transnationalisation of Social Rights

ISBN 978-1-78068-396-6
D/2016/7849/51
NUR 828

Copy-editing: Chris Engert

British Library Cataloguing in Publication Data. A catalogue record for this book is available from the British Library.

CONTENTS

LIST OF CONTRIBUTORS

Maria Backhouse holds a PhD in sociology (Freie Universität Berlin) and works as a senior researcher at the Arnold-Bergstraesser-Institute (ABI), Freiburg. Recent publications: "Green grabbing – The case of palm oil expansion in so-called degraded areas in the eastern Brazilian Amazon", in: Kristina Dietz, Bettina Engels, Oliver Pye and Achim Brunnengräber (eds), *The Political Ecology of Agrofuels*, (London: Routledge, 2015), pp. 167–185.
maria.backhouse@uni-jena.de

Jairo Baquero holds a PhD in sociology (Freie Universität Berlin) and currently serves as Principal Professor of Sociology at the School of Human Sciences, Universidad del Rosario (Colombia). Recent publications: "The Intersection of race, Class, and Ethnicity in Agrarian Inequalities, and the Social Resistance of Peasants in Colombia", *Current Sociology*, 63(7), pp. 1017-1036.
jairo.baquero@fu-berlin.de

Sérgio Costa is Professor of Sociology at the Freie Universität Berlin, spokesperson of the Research Network on Interdependent Inequalities in Latin America (desiguALdades.net) and editor of the book series Entangled Inequalities, Routledge. Most recent publication: "The global constitutionalization of human rights: Overcoming contemporary injustices or juridifying old asymmetries?", *Current Sociology*, 64(2), pp. 311–331 (with G.L. Gonçalves).
sergio.costa@fu-berlin.de

Sebastian Eickenjäger is a research assistant at the Centre of European Law and Politics (ZERP) at the University of Bremen. Recent publication: "Non-financial Reporting for Business Enterprises: An Effective Tool to Address Human Rights Violations?", in: Nora Markard/Kerstin Blome/Hannah Franzki/ Andreas Fischer-Lescano/Stefan Oeter (eds.), *Contested Collisions* (Cambridge: Cambridge University Press, 2016, forthcoming).
eickenj@uni-bremen.de

Andreas Fischer-Lescano is Professor of Public Law, European Law and International Law at the University of Bremen. He is editor of Germany's leading critical law journal *Kritische Justiz*. Recent publications: "A 'non-violent' force?",

(2015) 26 *Law and Critique*, pp. 267-280; "Critical Systems Theory", (2012) 38 *Philosophy & Social Criticism*, pp. 3–23.
fischer-lescano@zerp.uni-bremen.de

Guilherme Leite Gonçalves is Professor of Sociology of Law at Rio de Janeiro State University. Recent publications: "The Global Constitutionalization of Human Rights: Overcoming Contemporary Injustices or Juridifying Old Asymmetries?", (2016) *Current Sociology*, 64(2) (with Sérgio Costa); *The Refuge of Expectations. Essay on Legal Certainty*, (Italian title: *Il Rifugio delle Aspettative. Saggio sulla Certezza del Diritto*), (Lecce: Pensa Multimedia, 2013).
guilherme.leite@uerj.br

Alexandra Kaasch is Junior Professor in Transnational Social Policy at Bielefeld University. She is co-editor of the journal *Global Social Policy*. Recent publications: *Transformations in Global and Regional Social Policies* (2014) (Basingstoke: Palgrave Macmillan, 2014), edited with Paul Stubbs; *Shaping Global Health Policy*, (Basingstoke: Palgrave Macmillan, 2015); *Global Social Governance – Agency and Structures*, (Oxford: Oxford University Press, 2015), edited with Kerstin Martens.
mail@alexandra-kaasch.de

Ibrahim Kanalan holds a PhD in law and is a post-doctoral researcher at the Chair of Public Law and Public International Law and at the Centre for Human Rights Erlangen-Nürnberg (CHREN), University of Erlangen-Nuremberg. Recent publications: "Extraterritoriale Staatpflichten jenseit der Hoheitsgewalt", (2014) 52 *Archiv des Völkerrechts*, pp. 495–521; *Die universelle Durchsetzung des Rechts auf Nahrung gegen transnationale Unternehmen*, (Tübingen: Mohr Siebeck, 2015).
Ibrahim.Kanalan@fau.de

Steffen Kommer holds a PhD in law and is a judge at the administrative court in Bremen (Verwaltungsgericht Bremen). Recent publication: *Menschenrechte wider den Hunger. Das Recht auf Nahrung zwischen Wissenschaft, Politik und globalen Märkten*, (Baden Baden: Nomos, 2016).
steffen.kommer@gmx.de

Georg Lohmann is Professor emeritus of Practical Philosophy at the Otto-von-Guericke University Magdeburg. Recent publications: Arnd Pollmann and Georg Lohmann (eds), *Menschenrechte. Ein interdisziplinäres Handbuch*, (Stuttgart: Metzler, 2012); "Human Dignity and Socialism", in: Marcus Düwell, Jens Braarvig, Roger Brownsword and Dietmar Mieth (eds), *The Cambridge Handbook of Human Dignity: Interdisciplinary Perspectives*, (Cambridge: Cambridge University Press, 2014), pp. 126–134; "Menschenrechte und

transnationale Demokratisierungen. Überforderungen oder Erweiterungen der Demokratie?", in: Michael Reder and Mara-Daria Cojocaru (eds), *Zukunft der Demokratie*, (Stuttgart: Kohlhammer, 2014), pp. 64–77.
Georg.Lohmann@ovgu.de

Stefan Lorenzmeier is "*Akademischer Rat*" (senior lecturer) at the University of Augsburg's Law Faculty. He is the author of numerous publications on European and Public International Law. Recent publications include: "Public Law and Solidarity in Germany", (2014) 26 *European Review of Private Law*, pp. 137-210, "Allocation of Water Resources and Public International Law", in: Vasilka Sancin and Masa Kovic Dine (eds), *International Environmental Law: Contemporary Concerns and Challenges in 2014*, (Ljubljana: GV založba, 2014), pp. 411–427, and *Contemporary Issues of Human Rights Protection in International and National Settings*, with Vasilka Sancin, eds. (Baden Baden: Nomos, 2016).
stefan.lorenzmeier@jura.uni-augsburg.de

Kolja Möller is a Post-Doctorate at the Cluster of Excellence "Normative Orders", University of Frankfurt. Recent publications: "A Critical Theory of Transnational Regimes: Creeping Managerialism and the Quest for a Destituent Power", in: Kerstin Blome, Andreas Fischer-Lescano, Hannah Franzki, Nora Markard and Stefan Oeter (eds), *Contested Collisions: Interdisciplinary Inquiries into Norm Fragmentation in World Society*, (Cambridge: Cambridge University Press, 2015). *Formwandel der Verfassung. Die postdemokratische Verfassheit des Transnationalen*, (Bielefeld: Transcript, 2015).
kolja.moeller@uni-bremen.de

Judith Schacherreiter is a lawyer at Knoetzl Haugeneder Netal Rechtsanwälte GmbH and an external lecturer at the University of Vienna, Department of Comparative, Uniform and Private International Law. Recent publications: *Das Landeigentum als Legal Transplant in Mexiko. Rechtsvergleichende Analysen unter Einbezug postkolonialer Aspekte*, (Tübingen: Mohr Siebeck, 2014); "Propertization as a Civilizing and Modernizing Mission. Land and Human Rights in the Colonial and Postcolonial World", in: Nikita Dhawan (ed), *Decolonizing Enlightenment: Transnational Justice, Human Rights and Democracy in a Postcolonial World*, (Leverkusen: Barbara Budrich Publishers, 2014), pp. 227–242.
judith.schacherreiter@univie.ac.at

Eva Senghaas-Knobloch is a social scientist and Professor for Work Sciences (retired), Senior Researcher, University of Bremen, artec – Research Center for Sustainability Studies, Recent publications: "Mindfulness: A Politically Sensitizing Concept. Care and Social Sustainability as Issues", in: Guido Becke

(ed), *Mindful Change in Times of Permanent Reorganization: Organizations, Institutional and Sustainability Perspectives*, (Heidelberg: Springer Verlag, 2014), pp. 191–208. "Die Lücke der Rechtsbefolgung in der sozialen Dimension der Globalisierung", in: Torsten Meireis (ed), *Gewalt und Gewalten. Zur Ausübung, Legitimität und Ambivalenz rechtserhaltender Gewalt*, (Tübingen: Mohr Siebeck, 2012), pp. 321–342.
esk@artec.uni-bremen.de

Anne Trebilcock is retired Legal Adviser and Director of Legal Services, International Labour Organization (UN Specialized Agency) and is now associated with the Institut für Arbeitsrecht, University of Göttingen and the Centre de droit international, University of Paris Nanterre-La Défense. Recent publications: *Research Handbook on Transnational Labour Law*, (co-ed. with Adelle Blackett, (Cheltenham: Edgar Elgar Publishing, 2015)), *Droit international social*, (co-ed. with J.-M. Thouvenin, (Brussels: Bruylant, 2013)), and "Les visages de la nouvelle gouvernance économique mondiale: la dimension sociale," in: R. Chemain (ed), *La Refondation du système monetaire et financier international: évolutions règlementaires et institutionelles*, (Paris: Pédone, 2011).
annetrebilcock@gmail.com

LIST OF ABBREVIATIONS

ACAMURI	*Asociación Campesina del Municipio de Riosucio* – Peasant Association of the Riosucio Municipality
ACCU	*Autodefensas Campesinas de Córdoba y Urabá* – Peasant Self-Defence Forces of Córdoba and Urabá
AIDS	Acquired Immune Deficiency Syndrome
AMIS	Agricultural Market Information System
ARC	Accounting Regulatory Committee
ATCA	Alien Tort Claims Act
BRD	Butt Rot Disease
CEACR	Committee of Experts on the Application of Conventions and Recommendations
CEDAW	Convention on the Elimination of All Forms of Discrimination against Women
CESCR	Committee on Economic, Social and Cultural Rights
CFS	Committee on World Food Security
CJIP	Commission of Justice and Peace NGO
CONLACTRAHO	*Confederación Latinoamericana y del Caribe Trabajadoras del Hogar* – Latin American Domestic Workers' Associations and their Regional Network
CRC	Committee on the Rights of the Child
CRSR	Convention Relating to the Status of Refugees
CSO	Civil Society Organisations
CSR	Corporate Social Responsibility
ECB	European Central Bank
ECHR	European Convention on Human Rights
ECOSOC	Economic and Social Council of the United Nations
ECS	Economic, Cultural and Social
ECtHR	European Court of Human Rights
EFA	Education for All
EPZ	Export Production Zones
ESC	Economic, Social and Cultural
ETO	Extra-territorial Obligations
EU	European Union
EZLN	*Ejército Zapatista de Liberación Nacional*
FAO	Food and Agriculture Organization

FARC	*Fuerzas Armadas Revolucionarias de Colombia* – Revolutionary Armed Forces of Colombia
FIFA	*Fédération Internationale de Football Association*
FLOOR	Financial Assistance, Land Policy, and Global Social Rights
FPIC	Free, Prior Informed Consent
G8	Group of Eight: currently the Group of Seven (G7), following the suspension of Russia: Canada, France, Germany, Italy, Japan, Russia (suspended *sine die*), the United Kingdom, the United States, and the European Union
G20	Group of Twenty: Argentina, Australia, Brazil, Canada, China, France, Germany, India, Indonesia, Italy, Japan, Republic of Korea, Mexico, Russia, Saudi Arabia, South Africa, Turkey, United Kingdom, United States – and the European Union
GA	General Assembly
GC	General Comment
GNI	Gross National Income
GNP	Gross National Product
GRI	Global Reporting Initiative
GSF	Global Strategic Framework for Food Security
HfA	Health for All
HIV/AIDS	Human Immunodeficiency Virus/Acquired Immune Deficiency Syndrome
HLPE	High Level Panel of Experts
IAASTD	International Assessment of Agricultural Knowledge, Science and Technology for Development
ICC	International Criminal Court
ICCPR	International Covenant on Civil and Political Rights
ICESCR	International Covenant on Economic, Social and Cultural Rights
ICJ	International Court of Justice
ICLS	International Conference of Labour Statisticians
ICSID	International Center for Settlement of Investment Disputes
IDWN	International Domestic Workers Network
IEA	International Energy Agency
IEEP	Institute for European Environmental Policy
IFAD	International Fund for Agricultural Development
IFC	International Finance Corporation
IFI	International Financial Institutions
IFPRI	International Food Policy Research Institute
IHL	International Humanitarian Law

ILC	International Law Commission
ILO	International Labour Organization
ILS	International Labour Standards
ILUC	Indirect Land Use Changes
IMF	International Monetary Fund
INCRA	*Instituto Nacional de Colonização e Reforma Agrária*
IOE	International Organisation of Employers
ISO	International Organization for Standardization
ITLOS	International Tribunal for the Law of the Sea
ITUC	International Trade Union Confederation
IUF	International Union of Food and Allied Workers
LDCs	Least Developed Countries
LFRA	*Ley Federal de la Reforma Agraria*
LIFDC	Low-Income and Food Deficit-Countries
MDGs	Millennium Development Goals
MEP	Member of The European Parliament
MNC	Multinational Corporations
NAFTA	North American Free Trade Agreement
NATO	North Atlantic Treaty Organization
NCP	National Contact Point
NGO	Non-governmental Organisation
OCABA	*Organización Campesina del Bajo Atrato* – Peasant Organisation of Lower Atrato
OECD	Organisation for Economic Co-operation and Development
PBI	Peace Brigades International
PICT	Project on International Courts and Tribunals
RED	Renewable Energy Directive
SBDW	Standard Bidding Documents for the Procurement of Works
SEPPIR	*Secretaria Especial de Políticas de Promoção da Igualdade Racial*
SEWA	Self-Employed Women's Association
SNA	System of National Accounts
UDHR	Universal Declaration of Human Rights
UEFA	Union of European Football Associations
UK	United Kingdom
UN	United Nations
UN HLTF	United Nations High-Level Task Force on Global Food Security
UNCTAD	United Nations Conference on Trade and Development
UNESCO	United Nations Educational, Scientific and Cultural Organization

UNGC	United Nations Global Compact
UNGC COP	United Nations Global Compact Communication on Progress
UNICEF	United Nations Children's Fund
UNRISD	United Nations Research Institute for Developing Nations
US/USA	United States of America
USD	US Dollars
VCLT	Vienna Convention on the Law of Treaties
VGGT	Voluntary Guidelines on the Responsible Governance of Tenure
WBGU	*Wissenschaftlicher Beirat der Bundesregierung Globale Umweltveränderungen* – German Advisory Council on Global Change
WFP	World Food Programme
WHO	World Health Organization
WIEGO	Women in Informal Employment: Globalizing and Organizing
WTO	World Trade Organization
WWF	World Wildlife Fund
WWII	World War Two/Second World War

CHAPTER 1
INTRODUCTION

Andreas Fischer-Lescano and Kolja Möller

The transnationalisation of law and of social rights challenges our understanding of law, society and the state. Facing the recent social and economic crisis in world society, this volume scrutinises both the potentials and the boundaries of de-coupling the notion of "social rights" from the nation-state and of transferring it to the transnational sphere. "Transnationalisation"[1] is an encompassing process which affects national, supranational, international and global law. The seminal works by Boaventura de Sousa Santos,[2] Gunther Teubner,[3] Sally Falk Moore[4] and others provide profound insights into the emerging global legal pluralism and the inter-legality of fragmented clusters of law. The best example for this stems directly from the juridical sphere: courts at different levels increasingly engage in a dialogue across borders.[5] Or think of recent conflicts about austerity programmes and investment protection. The countries affected often invoke international law – such as the UN Covenant on Economic, Social and Cultural Rights or the European Social Charter – when they resist the attempts of multinational companies or creditors to implement

---

1 For a comprehensive overview, see Jean L. Cohen, *Globalization and Sovereignty. Rethinking Legality, Legitimacy and Constitutionalism*, (Cambridge: Cambridge University Press, 2012), p. 21 *et seq.* The seminal point of reference for this debate is Philip C. Jessup's *Transnational Law*, (New Haven CT: Yale University Press, 1956).

2 Boaventura de Sousa Santos, "Beyond Neoliberal Governance: The World Social Forum as Subaltern Cosmopolitan Politics and Legality", in: Boaventura de Sousa Santos and César A. Rodríguez-Garavito (eds), *Law and Globalization from Below: Towards a Cosmopolitan Legality*, (Cambridge: Cambridge University Press, 2005), p. 29 *et seq.*

3 Gunther Teubner, Constitutional Fragments: Societal Constitutionalism and Globalization, (Oxford: Oxford University Press, 2012).

4 Sally Falk Moore, *Law as a Process: An Anthropological Approach*, (London-Boston MA: Routledge & K. Paul), 1978.

5 Anne-Marie Slaughter, "A Global Community of Courts", (2003) 44 *Harvard International Law Journal*, p. 191 *et seq.*

measures which serve their interests.[6] In this situation, we need to establish a more process-oriented notion of the transnational in order to grasp the multiple and often transversal chains of legal communication which cannot be slavishly tied to a distinct level of juridical and political decision-making.

However, there is another reason for drawing on the notion of transnationalisation. The legal dynamics that we are facing are part of a historical shift to world society.[7] The evolution of social communication does not stop at national borders. Social systems, such as the economy, the sciences and politics, all tend to transcend territorial boundaries. The economic system, in particular, with its cognitive expectation structure and strong pressures to adapt, plays the role of a forerunner. Echoing this line of thought, we contend that it is absolutely necessary to scrutinise how legal communication interacts with other social systems and – most notably – with the colonising tendencies of the economic system and the struggles that try to re-embed it. Accordingly, we follow an agenda that integrates legal, sociological and political perspectives. Transnational law may not be a matter of legal discourse alone, but – as the sociological backgrounding of the contributions to the volume show – amounts to an interdisciplinary research field.

Not least, such a notion of transnationalisation seems promising because of the ongoing developments in international law. Since the 1990s, we can observe that international law undergoes a tendency to fragmentation. Accordingly, it cannot be reduced to either a dualistic interplay between international law and national law, or to the monistic supremacy of international law. The increasingly prevalent trend consists in the emergence of transnational legal regimes in subject areas as diverse as the economy, the environment, health, *etc.*[8] The report of the International Law Commission on "The Fragmentation of International Law" had turned special attention to this circumstance:

> "What once appeared to be governed by 'general international law' has become the field of operation for such specialist systems as 'trade law', 'human rights law', 'environmental law', 'law of the sea', 'European law' and even such exotic and highly specialized knowledge as 'investment law' or 'international refugee law', etc. – each possessing their own principles and institutions. The problem, as lawyers have seen it, is that such specialized law-making and institution-building tends to take place

---

6 See Andreas Fischer-Lescano, Human Rights in Times of Austerity Policy: The EU Institutions and the Conclusion of Memoranda of Understanding, (Baden-Baden: Nomos Verlag, 2014).

7 Niklas Luhmann, "The World Society as a Social System", (1982) 8 *International Journal of General Systems*, p. 131 *et seq*.

8 Andreas Fischer-Lescano and Gunther Teubner, "Regime-collisions: The Vain Search for Legal Unity in the Fragmentation of Global Law", (2004) 25 *Michigan Journal of International Law*, p. 999 *et seq*; Kerstin Blome, Andreas Fischer-Lescano, Hannah Franzki, Nora Markard and Stefan Oeter (eds), *Contested Collisions: Interdisciplinary Inquiries into Norm Fragmentation in World Society*, (Cambridge: Cambridge University Press, 2015).

> with relative ignorance of legislative and institutional activities in the adjoining fields and of the general principles and practices of international law. The result is conflicts between rules or rule-systems, deviating institutional practices and, possibly, the loss of an overall perspective on the law."[9]

In our view, this perspective must be extended: the different regimes are entangled in broader processes of transnationalisation and they revolve around the dynamics of the respective social systems. But, most importantly, the emerging legal regimes bring to the fore different types of rationalities and also entail different layers of law and judicial *fora*. This is another reason why the concern with transnationalisation is the starting point of this book: Instead of meticulously discerning different levels of legalisation, the contributions are all engaged in elucidating linkages, in shedding light on new types of conflicts or showing how transnational legalisation plays out at local level.

I. SOCIAL RIGHTS AND MARKET-LIBERAL DOMINANCE

The process of transnationalisation is characterised by large asymmetries. In particular, it is the global economy – which has seen a strong tendency to dis-embed itself in the last decades – which assumes a powerful role.[10] This is also reflected in the legal field. In the meantime, a dense network of transnational economic law exists which privileges free-trade and investment protection. Third world approaches to international law (TWAIL) have again and again pointed out the most important fact, that the Eurocentric vision of international law,[11] which ignores these asymmetries in the history of international law, fails to commemorate the colonialist, imperialist and racist heritage of the international system. Authors such as Antony Anghie,[12] Upendra Baxi,[13] José-

9 See, for example, UN General Assembly, "Fragmentation of International Law: Difficulties Arising from the Diversification and Expansion of International Law", (Report of the Study Group of the International Law Commission: Finalized by Martti Koskenniemi), (13 April 2006) UN Doc A/CN.4/L.682, available at: http://legal.un.org/ilc/documentation/english/a_cn4_l682.pdf, as corrected (11 August 2006) UN Doc. A/CN.4/L.682/Corr.1.

10 See Claire A. Cutler and Stephen Gill (eds), *New Constitutionalism and World Order*, (Cambridge: Cambridge University Press, 2015); Kolja Möller, *Formwandel der Verfassung: Die postdemokratische Verfasstheit des Transnationalen*, (Bielefeld: Transcript, 2015).

11 James Thuo Gathii, "International Law and Eurocentricity", (1998) 9 *European Journal of International Law*, p. 184 *et seq.*

12 Antony Anghie, *Imperialism, Sovereignty, and the Making of International Law*, (Cambridge: Cambridge University Press, 2005).

13 Upendra Baxi, *The Future of Human Rights*, 3rd ed., (New Delhi: Oxford University Press, 2013).

Manuel Barreto,[14] B.S. Chimni,[15] Makau Mutua,[16] Obiora Okafor,[17] Sundhya Pahuja,[18] Balakrishnan Rajagopal,[19] Shalini Randeria[20] and others, have all shaped our understanding of these hegemonic forces.

With these approaches of TWAIL, we share the aim to re-embed the economy and re-foster counter-movements that assure claims to social justice and re-distribution. In the nation-state era, social rights played a crucial role in countering the destructive forces of nascent market economies.[21] They were considered a tool which could bring about a humanisation of the economy, involving welfare schemes, democracy at the workplace, and even equality of men and women. It is one of our central concerns in this volume to discuss the possible avenues to renew the legacy of social rights in the light of transnationalisation. Clearly, the challenge is far more complex: While social rights could traditionally refer to the state on a clearly demarcated territory as its organising entity, the fragmented structure of world society is marked by new types of contradictions and conflicts in which the traditional division between labour and capital is just one among many others. Nowadays, we are facing a severe environmental crisis due to climate change, unsustainable modes of production and standards of living. And we witness sharp tensions between the urge towards modernisation and the claim to secure traditional and communal forms of living. It is not by accident that the human-rights discourse has entered a stage of "third generational human rights" which emphasises the right to development and environmental rights.[22]

---

14 José-Manuel Barreto, Human Rights from a Third World Perspective: Critique, History and International Law, (Cambridge: Cambridge University Press, 2013).

15 B.S. Chimni, "Capitalism, Imperialism, and International Law in the Twenty-first Century", (2012) 14 *Oregon Review of International Law*, p. 17 *et seq.*

16 Makau Mutua, "Savages, Victims and Saviors: The Metaphor of Human Rights", (2001) 42 *Harvard International Law Journal*, p. 201 *et seq.*

17 Obiora Chinedu Okafor, "Poverty, Agency and Resistance in the Future of International Law", in: Richard Falk, Balakrishnan Rajagopal and Jacqueline Stevens (eds), *International Law and the Third World*, (London: Routledge, 2008), p. 95 *et seq.*

18 Sundhya Pahuja, "The Poverty of Development and the Development of Poverty in International Law", in: European Society of International Law (eds.), *Select Proceedings of the European Society of International Law*, 3/2010 (2012), p. 365 *et seq.*

19 Balakrishnan Rajagopal, "Right to Development and Global Governance", (2013) 35 *Human Rights Quarterly*, p. 893 *et seq.*

20 Shalini Randeria, "Legal Pluralism, Social Movements and the Post-Colonial State in India: Fractured Sovereignty and Differential Citizenship Rights", in: Boaventura de Sousa Santos (ed), *Another Knowledge is Possible: Beyond Northern Epistemologies*, (London: Verso Books, 2007), p. 41 *et seq.*

21 See the seminal analysis in: Thomas H. Marshall, *Citizenship and Social Class and Other Essays*, (Cambridge: Cambridge University Press, 1950).

22 See Manfred Nowak, *CCPR Commentary*, 2nd ed. (Kehl am Rhein: N.P. Engel, 2005), Art. 1, note 15.

II. THE DIMENSIONS OF TRANSNATIONAL SOCIAL RIGHTS

Notwithstanding all these complexities, this book draws on the legacy of social rights and aspires to be an *aggiornamento*. It refers to social rights as an overarching instrument and even as a political agenda. In this sense, it uses the term "social rights" not as something which is simply identical with the already existing regime of social human rights in international law. It alludes to the historical legacy and even to the normative desiderates that were once associated with the struggle for social rights as well. Accordingly, transnational social rights entail three dimensions:

1. *Social Rights and Welfarism*: The concept of social rights had its heyday with the establishment of national welfare-state regimes. In this perspective, social rights are not restricted to a definite set of rights relating to social-security schemes, working conditions *etc.*, but rather as a counterforce which should perform a double function: on the one hand, social rights should provide for a re-distribution of wealth and a correction of market failures. But they were not simply meant to correct negative externalities. On the other hand, they should deliver a material basis for negative and participatory rights and should implement participatory rights in other social spheres, most prominently in the economy. Nowadays, in times of a "transnational social question", the pressing challenge consists in the transnationalisation of this endeavour.[23]

2. *Social Rights as Societal Rights*: At the very minimum, the notion of social rights evokes a non state-centric understanding of law. While liberal private law theory draws a clear distinction between public and private law, the demand for social rights undermines this diametric distinction. Accordingly, public law should be seen as a means for the self-organisation of a broader public sphere which is sensitive not only to the state institutions but also to societal structures. And, *vice versa*, private law should be "socialised", in the sense that it must be responsive to claims for justice and democracy, by inserting the necessary "drops of socialist oil".[24] It is especially this "societal" drift which seems to be a starting-point for confronting the emerging liberal private law regime at transnational level with the force of a social law.

3. *Social Rights and/as Economic, Social and Cultural Rights (ESCR):* The evolution of social rights is already part of the UN Human Rights System.[25] In the Universal Declaration of Human Rights of 1948 and in the International

23 Thomas Faist, "The Transnational Social Question", (2009) 24 *International Sociology*, p. 7 *et seq*.

24 Otto von Gierke, writing on the occasion of the development of the German Civil Code in the nineteenth century in *Die soziale Aufgabe des Privatrechts* ("The Social Function of Private Law") (1889), reprinted in 1946, p. 28 *et seq*.

25 Matthew C.R. Craven, The International Covenant on Economic, Social and Cultural Rights: A Perspective on its Development, (Oxford: Clarendon, 1998).

Covenant on Economic, Social and Cultural Rights (ICESCR) (1966), we find a long list of social rights, such as the right to social security, health, food and education. And we face a series of attempts to strengthen these parts of international human rights law – be it via ratification and reporting procedures or via individual complaint-mechanisms before the UN Committee on Economic, Social and Cultural Rights which the recent adoption of the Optional Protocol to the International Covenant on Economic, Social and Cultural Rights has established.[26] The question remains as to how the emergence of "social human rights" within the framework of the UN can take on a broader notion of social rights, and in what way it has the capacity to embody and renew its broader programmatic and normative implications.

Bearing in mind these three tenets, it becomes clear that the debate on the future of social rights cannot be reduced either to a mere bemoaning of the decline of the welfare state under the auspices of global neo-liberalism or to a rather naïve praise of "corporate social responsibility" agreements in multinational companies or to a managerial discourse about the ICESCR. A transnational social rights agenda will only succeed in challenging the vast problems of world society when it relates to the different sites of struggle. It has to be *specific* with regard to the concrete scopes for legal enforcement and judicial doctrine. But it must also constitute a *broader horizon* which opposes market liberal dominance at transnational level in order to be effective.

III. THE ORGANISATION OF THIS VOLUME

This book proceeds in three steps. The first part ("*Transnational Social Rights in Context*") discusses the basic challenges of a transnational social rights agenda. In their contribution, the editors focus on the question of how social conflicts and transnational legalisation are related. By drawing on a framework that combines insights from systems theory and critical legal theory, they establish a new perspective on the transnationalisation of social rights, analyse various concrete conflicts, and discuss avenues of reform with regard to the social human rights regime. However, the question remains as to what foundational normativity is at stake in the claim to transnational social rights. Georg Lohmann elucidates

---

26 See, most recently, Eibe Riedel, Gilles Gaccia and Christophe Golay (eds), *Economic, Social, and Cultural Rights in International Law: Contemporary Issues and Challenges*, (New York: Oxford University Press, 2014); see, also, Craven, note 25 above; John Squires, Malcolm Landford and Bret Thiel, *The Road to a Remedy: Current Issues in the Litigation of Economic, Social and Cultural Rights*, (Sydney: Australia Human Rights Centre, 2005); Margot E. Salomon, *Global Responsibility for Human Rights: World Poverty and the Development of International Law*, (Oxford: Oxford University Press, 2007); Aiofe Nolan (ed), *Economic and Social Rights after the Global Financial Crisis*, (Cambridge: Cambridge University Press, 2014).

the philosophical background of the basic conceptional issues, such as "Human Dignity" or "Duty" and "Right". His analysis is geared towards a normative re-construction of the human rights regime. The first section closes with a contribution of Alexandra Kaasch, who gives an encompassing overview of the different layers and arenas of transnational social rights.

The second part of the book ("*Foundations, Institutions and Enforcement Structures*") is concerned with the legal mechanisms that are characteristic of transnational social rights. In his contribution, Stefan Lorenzmeier turns to a discussion of the legal enforcement mechanisms and engages – using the example of the right to food – with debates about the judicial enforceability of transnational social rights. Ibrahim Kanalan and Sebastian Eickenjäger's contribution is concerned with the hotly debated issue of binding multinational companies to social human rights standards. They extend the perspective to formally private arenas and scrutinise the role of the so-called "horizontal effect" of human rights. Finally, Eva Senghaas-Knobloch focuses on the International Labour Organization and its endeavours to integrate "informal work", such as care work or undocumented work, within its framework. Her analysis shows that the ILO provides an already established legal and institutional framework which is sensitive to the current social transformations.

The contributions in the last part of the book ("*Transnational Struggles*") endeavour to scrutinise their respective subjects areas and the concerned legal norm (the right to food, the right to land, and cultural rights) by applying a methodology that is sensitive to the process of transnationalisation and the interplay of different legal regimes. They all elucidate how social transformations and the claim to social rights mutually instigate each other. The former ILO advisor Anne Trebilcock reveals the interlinkages between the different legal arenas. Transnational social rights may not be an issue for a sole legal regime, but, instead, as Trebilcock shows with regard to the right to food, rely on a highly complex interplay between different institutional settings. In his contribution, Steffen Kommer not only focuses on the "right to food" as the most basic social right, but also contextualises his reasoning with regard to the ongoing food crisis and the rise of agroenergy markets. Although Judith Schacherreiter and Guilherme Leite Gonçalves' text, as well as the contribution by Maria Backhouse, Jairo Baquero Melo and Sérgio Costa examine two different cases from Mexico, Colombia and Brazil, they both share a common starting-point: It is widely acknowledged that cultural rights can also be considered as social rights. But this may come at the price of internal tensions in the social-rights regime. Backhouse, Baquero and Costa show how the cultural bias tends to distort the claims of minorities in the Brazilian case, while Schacherreiter and Leite de Gonçalves touch upon the issue of land rights and the arising tensions between customary law, international and national law.

PART I

TRANSNATIONAL SOCIAL RIGHTS IN CONTEXT

CHAPTER 2
THE STRUGGLE FOR TRANSNATIONAL SOCIAL RIGHTS

Andreas FISCHER-LESCANO and KOLJA MÖLLER

I. THE TRANSNATIONAL SOCIAL QUESTION

Financial crises, food crises, environmental crises, migration crises: world society is facing dramatic challenges. These crises are both interconnected and rife with contradictions. While the Euro zone bailout fund is leveraged with roughly a trillion euro, nobody seems willing to put up the 13 billion dollars which, according to UN calculations, would be necessary to relieve world hunger. *Deutsche Bank*, a German high-street bank, generated a benefit of 4 billion euro in 2014; meanwhile more than 1.3 billion people around the world live in poverty, on less than 1.25 US dollars per day. Refugees find themselves in a particularly precarious situation. In 2014, there were more than 50 million displaced persons, a situation the UN High Commissioner for Refugees attributes to urbanisation, food and water insecurity, as well as shortages of raw materials. These global problems, he says, "are increasingly inter-related, exacerbating conflict and combining in other ways that oblige people to flee their homes".[1]

These trends point to one conclusion: the "social question" is now firmly a *transnational* social question.[2] Societal conflict lines no longer run primarily along national borders. The global economy, global politics, transnational law, and global scholarship and science all contribute, in their own way, to the formation of zones of social exclusion. The axes of disadvantage can intersect and be exacerbated. The existing transnational power structures are both complex and merciless. Those worst affected do not even have – or are denied – access to the very means for sheer survival. Nation states no longer possess

1 António Guterres, "Forced Displacement: Responding to the Challenge of the Next Decade, Statement to the Berlin Symposium for Refugee Protection", June 2011, available at: www.unhcr.org/4c1737c09.html.

2 Thomas Faist, "The Transnational Social Question", (2009) 24 *International Sociology*, p. 7 *et seq*.

adequate solutions to these problems. Nor do they remain the only important players in this field. Sociologists and political scientists accept that the state is just "one of the actors" when it comes to global social policy, and acknowledge that non-state actors such as international organisations and global social movements have now firmly gained entrance to the "contested terrain" of emerging global governance.[3] It is on this contested terrain that the debates on the crises facing world society are played out. It is here, for instance, that political scientists are making the link between climate change and global social policy.[4] The interdisciplinary research group FLOOR (Financial Assistance, Land Policy, and Global Social Rights) explores the possibility of securing a global system of guaranteed basic income.[5] Philosophers study the requirements of global justice and put forward the charge that "our failure to make a serious effort toward poverty reduction may constitute not merely a lack of beneficence, but our active impoverishing, starving, and killing of millions of innocent people by economic means".[6]

Law, too, is itself a contributor to this state of affairs. Transnational law paved the way for and enabled the various crises. The global players of industry have long had a hand in shaping transnational law. Transnational corporations operate in global markets, bolstered by international contracts based upon the so-called *lex mercatoria*, the self-regulating law of global commerce. They have developed techniques to ensure that the law remains in their service, and have shaped a world that corresponds to their own vision. Huge international law firms offer the legal know-how required to assert and secure a company's interests. Judicial forums have been installed at the World Trade Organization (WTO) and at the World Bank, in which the law of free trade and the rights of private investors are both enforced and re-inforced. To leave transnational legal policy to the global players and limit ourselves to mitigating the consequences of globalisation in national welfare states is to address merely the symptoms, while failing to tackle the root of the problem. This is why we need to look for new ways to renew the promise of global social justice. In a bid to establish the relevant necessary steps, we will examine four distinct issues: (1) What are the

3 Bob Deacon, *Global Social Policy and Governance*, (London-Thousand Oaks CA, SAGE Publications, 2007), p. 15.

4 Ian Gogh, "Climate Change and Sustainable Welfare: An Argument for the Centrality of Human Needs", (2014) *NEF Working Paper.*

5 Ulrike Davy, "The Rise of the Global Social: Origins and Transformations of Social Rights under UN Human Rights Law", (2013) 3 *International Journal of Social Quality*, p. 41 *et seq*; Benjamin Davy and Sony Pellissery, "Climate Change and Global Social Policy", (2011) 11 *Global Social Policy*, p. 106 *et seq*; see, also, the homepage of the research group FLOOR: www.floorgroup.raumplanung.tu-dortmund.de/joomla.

6 Thomas Pogge, "Priorities of Global Justice", in: David Held and Anthony McGrew (eds), *The Global Transformations Reader*, (Cambridge: Polity Press, 2003), p. 548; Simon Caney, "Global Poverty and Human Rights: The Case for Positive Duties", in: Thomas Pogge (ed), *Freedom from Poverty as a Human Right*, (Oxford: Oxford University Press, 2007), p. 275 *et seq*.

central characteristics of the global crises? (2) What role does transnational law play? Should we turn to the law at all, or is it an instrument of domination with which it is too perfidious even to engage? (3) What is the current state of transnational social rights? Where can they be found? (4) Which concrete legal and political mechanisms can be used in order to challenge the course of neo-liberal globalisation?

A. THE COUNTER-HEGEMONIC AGENDA

Ever since the 1980s, a neo-liberal trend has dominated the development of transnational law. This development can be seen in the international institutions of the global economy, such as the WTO and the International Monetary Fund (IMF). This trend pushes for the liberalisation of the markets and protects the global players – not social rights.[7] Yet, there are an increasing number of groups that seek to counter neo-liberal norms with an agenda of transnational social rights. Brazilian farm workers invoke social human rights as they call for land reform as a necessary pre-condition for food sovereignty and a life without poverty.[8] German students have instigated court proceedings against the introduction of university tuition-fees, relying on the obligation contained in the International Covenant on Economic, Social and Cultural Rights (ICESCR) to ensure access to higher education "by every appropriate means, and in particular by the progressive introduction of free education". Anti-racist networks are demanding social rights for illegalised immigrants. "Nomadic universities", networks of academics and other temporary university employees, are calling for a charter of social rights, including the right to a basic income, the right to cross-border mobility, and the recognition of common goods such as natural resources or social infrastructure as "Commons" which should not rely on private property rights.[9] In December 2011, the International University College of Turin launched an initiative towards a "European Charter of the Commons", with a particular focus on strengthening the global protection of communally-held resources, such as water, through a process of "globalisation from below".

All of these movements rely on the central idea of human rights: that every human being – regardless of where he or she is from – has the right to rights.[10] The call for "transnational social rights" is increasingly central to the

7 David Kennedy, "Law and the Political Economy of the World", (2013) 26 *Leiden Journal of International Law*, p. 7 *et seq.*

8 See, also, *Dejo Olowu*, "Conceptualising a Rights-based Approach to Poverty Alleviation in Africa", (2003) 43 *The Indian Journal of International Law*, p. 67 *et seq.*

9 See the Universidad Nómada, *Manifesto of the Commons: Towards a New Charter of Social Rights*, 22 May 2011, available at: www.universidadnomada.net/spip.php?article372.

10 As discussed by Hannah Arendt in: *The Origins of Totalitarianism*, (New York: Harcourt, Brace and Company, 1951), p. 294.

activities of globalisation critics. They are based upon the understanding that rights must be realised by "fighting for the democratisation of transnational institutions".[11] Thereby, they use the label "transnational social rights", broadening the traditional understanding of social rights to one which also includes environmental rights, migrant rights and the right to a guaranteed basic income. The framework as a whole can also be seen as a project in which seemingly independent or distinct discussions find a common thread, which serves to offer them a joint foundation and the potential for combined action. This is because these various initiatives are concerned not solely with countering the globalisation of capital, of the markets and of goods with a globalisation of social rights.[12] Transnational social rights, as a whole, are moving towards a counter-hegemonic agenda, one which relies on rights which *already* exist.

The transnational framework is not intended to distract from the political decision-making of national governments or communes. What it does do, however, is shift the perspective. Antonio Negri and Michael Hardt express this best when they write that globalisation is not just one thing, but a collage of disparate processes. Our political task, they argue:

> "is not simply to resist these processes but to reorganize them and redirect them towards new ends. The creative forces of the multitude that sustain Empire are also capable of autonomously constructing a counter-Empire, an alternative political organization of global flows and exchanges."[13]

Based upon the appeal of a "counter-empire", a transnational legal policy is called for, one which focuses on social and ecological justice, and which explores how the potential of world society could be used to establish alternatives to the existing socio-economic conditions.

B. JURIDICO-POLITICAL STRUGGLES

Following on from the series of questions posed at the beginning of this chapter, we wish to put forward four overarching theses with regard to the transnational constellation.

---

11 Thomas Seibert, "Globale Soziale Rechte in der Konvergenz von politischer Aktion und Philosophie", (2008) 41 *Kritische Justiz*, p. 337.

12 See, for example, the platform available at: www.globale-soziale-rechte.de.

13 Michael Hardt and Antonio Negri, *Empire*, (Cambridge MA: Harvard University Press, 2000), p. xv.

1. The social question traverses borders. In other words, it is a transnational social question:

Solving the twenty-first century social question cannot be achieved by addressing only the contradictions within nation states. Even the development of social rights within nation states often relies on factors and institutions outside the control of the political institutions. The causes of the present financial crisis, climate change and the global food crisis all lie within world society. It is at this level that we must tackle them.

2. World society is determined by new contradictions, collisions, and fragmentations. Transnational law forms part of this contradictory system, and is, as such, part of the problem:

Huge corporations have long been operating on transnational terrain, in which transnational law plays a central role. The law provides neo-liberal ideas with a secure legal foundation, corporations with a global playing-field, and investors with the safeguarding of their property. To the state, it offers legitimacy for military action. Moral appeals and non-committal political announcements are not enough to deal with the flagrant dangers inherent to an unfettered global economy, with multi-national corporations, or with fundamental socio-economic conflicts.

3. Transnational social rights can lead to the formation of a counter-law. This counter-law should ensure that the global social order is determined by world society itself, instead of by those who profit, economically and politically, from globalisation.

The social human rights of the UN Covenants together with the European Social Charter and the Core Labour Standards of the International Labour Organization (ILO) already provide a body of transnational social rights. These *can* act as a starting point in the struggle for law. The goal must actually be to redeem the promises of social and ecological security, democratic participation and involvement, which are contained in these documents.

4. There are many juridico-political arenas in which the strengthening of transnational social rights is needed.

Within the state, efforts must be made to ensure that transnational social rights are binding before the courts. This will bolster the monitoring procedure of the UN Covenants and the ILO. In addition, the Social Charter must attain a central role at European level. A European social union must replace the current economically driven European organisation. At transnational level, not only international organisations such as the UN and the WTO, but also non-governmental organisations and transnational corporations, must be obliged to uphold transnational social rights.

II. THE TRANSNATIONAL CONSTELLATION

The word "globalisation" is often invoked to refer to a number of phenomena, such as the growth in transnational economic relations and the increasingly important role of international institutions, as well as the interdependence of nation states. As a result, the debate on globalisation often remains superficial, merely scratching the surface of the issues, without actually addressing the underlying structures that are shaping the transition to a world society. The transnational constellation is not just the manifestation of international state co-operation and world trade. A more far-reaching change of perspective is required in order to understand fully the root causes of globalisation. The increasing connectivity of social relationships around the world in the most diverse sections of society means that the phenomena of globalisation extend far beyond the transborder, capitalist, global economy. Its processes are not limited to business and politics but also exert influence in the fields of religion, art, and education, as well as in technology and risk regulation, transnational public spheres and cyberspace. While the international system of states nonetheless remains important, it no longer enjoys the absolute primacy that it did before. World society is a society both without a head and without a centre. Centralised zones of political decision-making within various similarly structured states are now things of the past. A highest point of decision-making in a unitary nation state no longer exists.

Within this complex world society, the creditworthiness of states is determined by the rapid risk assessments of rating agencies, the Organisation for Economic Co-operation and Development (OECD) reports put national education systems under pressure to adapt, and oppositional movements turn to social networks to topple authoritarian regimes. This de-centralisation and differentiation of world society are Janus-headed phenomena, offering new opportunities and changing power structures while simultaneously evoking great risks. This poses the transnational social question. In the last years, it has primarily been the big players of the global economy and financial markets, who have feathered their own nests at the expense of the environment and social justice. Yet global science and technology also generate new risks to health and to the environment. Different social sectors tend to maximise their own forms of logic and impose them on their social environments. The WTO, the World Bank and the *lex mercatoria* are among those that have assumed a dominant role within this transnational constellation in their attempt to universalise their free-market liberal Esperanto.[14] In doing so, they hope to assert their interests, their way of thinking and their rules on all other social spheres. The systematic

---

14 Martti Koskenniemi and Päivi Leino, "Fragmentation of International Law? Postmodern Anxieties", (2002) 15 *Leiden Journal of International Law*, p. 578.

desire for power is evidenced by the important roles played by politico-economic institutions such as the WTO and the IMF, which form the regulative framework for the global relations of production.

The political institutions, however, are not the only ones growing in the process of global governance; they are joined by legal institutions. Legal norms and the reach of courts are expanding into more and more aspects of society. It seems that there are no limits to what can be considered and decided as a legal question. States have set up courts such as the European Court of Human Rights (ECtHR), regional human-rights courts, the International Tribunal for the Law of the Sea (ITLOS), the International Criminal Court (ICC) as well as the monitoring bodies of universal human rights treaties; the United Nations has established *ad hoc* criminal tribunals, and the international community has permitted the prosecution of international crimes in East Timor and elsewhere before so-called hybrid courts. National courts are included into this system of world courts,[15] such as when US courts hear compensation cases arising from grave human-rights violations in South America or a Dutch court orders Shell Nigeria to compensate Nigerians for oil pollution damage caused by third-party sabotage in Nigeria.[16]

These forums are also on the rise outside the state-created system of global jurisdiction: transnational corporations assert the *lex mercatoria* through privately established courts of arbitration.[17] International judicative and quasi-judicative bodies, such as the World Bank's International Center for Settlement of Investment Disputes (ICSID), are on their way to becoming world courts.[18] It is clear that law has long been transnational, affording rights to, and imposing duties on, individuals, states and transnational corporations.[19] The only way to ensure that this transnational law upholds basic social and environmental justice is – as Otto von Gierke put it – to allow the necessary "drops of socialist oil" to filter through the legal system.[20]

---

15 See George Scelle's theory of "dédoublement fonctionnel" in: idem, *Précis de droit des gens*, Vol. I, (Paris: Recueil Sirey, 1932), p. 54 *et seq*; on this, see Antonio Cassese, "Remarks on Scelle's Theory of 'Role Splitting' (dédoublement fonctionnel) in International Law", (1990) 1 *European Journal of International Law*, p. 210 *et seq*.

16 See, also, note 66 below.

17 Claire Cutler, "Legal Pluralism as the 'Common Sense' of Transnational Capitalism", (2013) 3 *Oñati Socio-Legal Series*, p. 719 *et seq*.

18 For a powerful critique, see Ibironke Odumosu, "The Law and Politics of Engaging Resistance in Investment Dispute Settlement", (2007) 26 *Penn State International Law Review*, p. 25 *et seq*.

19 See, most recently, Sally Engle Merry, "Firming up Soft Law", in: Terence C. Halliday and Gregory Shaffer (eds.),*Transnational Legal Orders*, (Cambridge: Cambridge University Press, 2015), p. 374 *et seq*.

20 Otto von Gierke, writing on the occasion of the development of the German Civil Code in the 19th century in *Die soziale Aufgabe des Privatrechts*, ("The Social Function of Private Law") (1889), reprinted in 1946, p. 28 *et seq*.

The complexity of the transnational constellation is brought sharply into focus by the response to the global food crisis, within which we see various crisis points collide with devastating effects. In 2009, shortly before the G20 states gathered for their summit in Pittsburgh, Olivier De Schutter, the former United Nations Special Rapporteur on the Right to Food, issued a statement in which he called on the G8 and G20 states not to limit their discussions to the financial and economic crisis, but to strive also to reach agreements on fighting global hunger, stating:

> "Just like the collapse of large banks, widespread hunger entails systemic risks."[21]

This is, indeed, the case. Since 2008, we have seen, parallel to the global financial crisis, an intensified worldwide food crisis. The explosion in food prices led to an extra 40 million people going hungry in 2008 alone, bringing the number of people worldwide who are living in hunger to over one billion. More people die each day from hunger than in all the military flashpoints around the world combined. A report of the World Bank of 2011[22] made clear that the huge increase in the number of people living in hunger is largely due to the commodification of food production, food price fluctuations, and the economic crisis. The 82 states then classified as Low-Income Food-Deficit Countries, *i.e.*, countries which depend on food imports in order to meet their own demand, were affected particularly badly by the crisis.

The food crisis is not, however, merely a crisis of supply. We are also noticing a crisis in climate, which is rendering entire regions unsuitable for farming. A closer look at the economic structure of the agricultural sector confirms that the current food crisis will not simply lead back to the ostensibly older phenomenon of malnutrition. The unfolding of events is now shaped by global speculation on food products and by the major agricultural companies. "Agribusiness", which incorporates huge agricultural companies such as Monsanto, concentrates on industrial growth and the development of monocultures at the expense of ecological structures and smallholders.

Such firms sell their patented, genetically engineered seeds and matching pesticides at high prices to farms. If a farmer suffers a crop failure and subsequently cannot afford the newest plant technology, he or she goes bankrupt. Farmers who do not subscribe to seed-buying from such large companies are often sued if patented plants are found growing in their fields, even if the land was cross-contaminated through no fault of the farmer. Big companies often

---

21 Olivier De Schutter, "The global food crisis is not over", 26 June 2009, available at: www.ohchr.org/EN/NewsEvents/Pages/DisplayNews.aspx?NewsID=8991&LangID=E.

22 World Bank, *Poverty Reduction and Equity Group*, August 2011, p 1, available at: http://siteresources.worldbank.org/INTPOVERTY/Resources/335642-1210859591030/FPW_August2011.pdf.

obtain large tracts of land in the Global South, striking deals with the relevant governments and driving small farmers from their holdings.[23] This land is generally used to grow monocultures such as soya, which is shipped back to the company's home country to be used as fodder or as palm oil, which is used in the production of so-called "agrofuel". This practice of land expropriation is now known as "land grabbing".[24]

During the 1990s, foreign direct investment in agriculture amounted to an annual average of 600 million USD; between 2005 and 2007 this rose to an average of 3 billion USD.[25] This structural change is leading to an increased globalisation of the agricultural industry, a process dominated by large transnational companies. It is estimated that roughly 50 million hectares of land are affected, in Latin America, Asia, and Africa. These land deals are about more than just profit, they are also made with an eye to geo-strategic interests and spheres of influence. The climate crisis and population growth in many parts of the world has turned the issue of nutrition into a geo-strategic question of power. Thus, agribusinesses often co-operate with the governments of the countries in which they are based, including the governments of states in the Global South, in order to secure a competitive advantage in the approaching fight for food supplies.

The phenomenon is best evidenced by the case of Madagascar, where the South Korean firm Daewoo sought to obtain 1.3 million hectares of land. According to the NGO *Grain*, the land was to be used solely for the cultivation of maize and palm oil for export back to South Korea. Madagascar belongs to the poorest third of the world and is plagued with malnutrition and poverty. The land grabbing resulted in a severe setback for the country's already ailing food supply system. The Madagascan government backed the deal with Daewoo but was subsequently toppled by widespread protest against Daewoo's land acquisition. The new government was able to revoke the deal, and the Daewoo Corporation has, for the time being, withdrawn from the transaction.

What is driving these scandalous developments which are exacerbating the food crisis and expropriating whole sections of the population? This question brings us back to the UN Rapporteur's appeal to the G20 states. The NGO *Grain* points to a direct link to the crisis in the financial markets:

---

23 See the critique of investor protection in international law by Sundhya Pahuja, *Decolonising International law, Development, Economic Growth and the Politics of Universality*, (Cambridge: Cambridge University Press, 2011), p. 95 *et seq*; see, also, Saskia Sassen, "Land Grabs Today: Feeding the Disassembling of National Territory", (2013) 10 *Globalizations*, p. 25 *et seq*.

24 See Steffen Kommer, Chapter 9 in this volume.

25 Olivier De Schutter, Special Rapporteur on the Right to Food, *Report: Agribusiness and the Right to Food*, A/HRC/13/33, 22 December 2009, at para. 6.

> "Given the current financial meltdown, all sorts of players in the finance and food industries – the investment houses that manage workers' pensions, private equity funds looking for a fast turnover, hedge funds driven off the now collapsed derivatives market, grain traders seeking new strategies for growth – are turning to land, for both food and fuel production, as a new source of profit."[26]

The interplay between these two phenomena is instantly clear. The economic crisis has shown financial products to be extremely risky, and so the search begins for "future-proof" investment options as an alternative to capital markets. It becomes apparent that agricultural land is being imbued with a new significance: it is being transformed into a commodity and recast as a whole new economic sector. Its attractiveness as an investment rises with the threat of climate change, which is posed to reduce the amount of land available. More frequent extreme weather conditions will see entire tracts of land sink into the sea. The greenhouse effect will be amplified though the expansion of industrial agriculture which relies on the use of chemicals and the depletion of natural resources. The dynamics of the financial, food, and climate crises are gradually combining to form a global social crisis.[27] These developments will also have consequences for migration patterns; the World Bank identifies high food prices as a significant trigger for the movement of refugees. The World Bank also points out that an effective response to these crises cannot be found within the individual sectors and calls, instead, for "an integrated agricultural, food security, poverty, and climate agenda".[28]

III. EMANCIPATION THROUGH TRANSNATIONAL LAW?

But doesn't the Global North simply fashion transnational law in its own image? Isn't transnational law simply a more or less subtle way for industrialised nations to keep the Global South in a state of dependence?

A. DIALECTICS OF TRANSNATIONAL LAW

Like all law, transnational law always plays a part in the formation of alienated social relations and, as such, is part of the problem. In a world shaped by political emergencies, and economic and environmental crises, law does not always make the world a more just place. A common critique posits that modern law is an

---

26 Grain, *Grabbing for Land*, 18 January 2009, available at: www.grain.org/article/entries/753-grabbing-land-for-food.

27 For these linkages, see Anne Trebilcock, Chapter 8 in this volume.

28 World Bank, note 22 above, p. 1.

instrument of domination. This line of argument is particularly pertinent when it comes to the transnational constellation. The law constructs a veil of equality and thus obscures the reality of socio-economic inequality. And no one can say that *everyone* has the same access to legal procedures. Who can match the resources of transnational companies or the giant factories of advocates known as international law firms? How many people have the requisite know-how to bring a case before the International Court of Justice? The idealistic belief in civilising the world through law may seem naïve if one fails to take into account the simple fact that the very starting point for this juridico-political struggle is rife with inherent inequalities. The law merely provides a liberal smokescreen to obscure the inherent injustice of global power relations.

The fact that even human rights can be instrumentalised is the central tenet of critical theories of law. At the global level, too, it is clear that this poses a virulent risk: the economic instrumentalisation of human rights is particularly evident in the lending policies of the IMF and the World Bank. In the main, the buzzwords "human rights" and "good governance" denote a particular borrower's economic policy orientation: the protection of liberal human rights, the investors' property rights, and the patent rights of transnational companies.[29] As well as serving the crystallisation of economic property relations, human rights are also invoked in the context of security policy. Thus, in the case of so-called "humanitarian interventions", we see human rights being re-framed as an interventionary norm. The vague nature of human rights allows for "interpretation by special interests" according to their own purposes, while re-interpretations of human rights are employed to legitimise violence.

All of this, however, is just one side of the story. One can also point to the way in which NGOs and other networks are articulating their concerns through the language of human rights and thereby drawing attention to injustice in the transnational public sphere. The socialisation of transnational law has nothing to do with a new vein of juridical socialism. It is concerned not with the legal interpretation of socialism, but with interpreting transnational law in a socialist way. In the words of Friedrich Engels and Karl Kautsky, social and democratic demands must be formulated "as legalistic demands within a program".[30] The struggle for transnational social rights is able to represent an emancipatory project if we express social claims in the form of legal demands, and, in this spirit, re-interpret and re-organise existing rights.

As far as human rights policy is concerned, the above shows the contradictory and paradoxical way in which the law is hauled back and forth between domination and emancipation. This ambivalent quality of law gives rise to a number of warnings. Why should the subalterns turn to the law when it represents

---

[29] David Schneiderman, *Constitutionalizing Economic Globalization: Investment Rules and Democracy's Promise*, (Cambridge-New York: Cambridge University Press, 2008).

[30] Friedrich Engels and Karl Kautsky, "Juristen-Sozialismus", printed as "Juridical Socialism", in: (1977) 7 *Politics and Society*, p. 203 *et seq.*, at 219.

the very tool which guarantees the existing societal order,[31] and which maintains the essential structures that facilitate the re-occurrence of acts of domination?

As far back as the 1920s and 1930s, this was the central question of the critical legal theories emerging from the Frankfurt School. The works of Franz L. Neumann and Otto Kirchheimer, in particular, offer important insights relating to the transnational constellation. Kirchheimer and Neumann provided devastating portrayals of how law worked and its capacity for instrumentalisation. Both take as their starting point the idea that modern law develops into an autonomous social form. Neumann described the law as being only relatively independent.[32] Law is embedded in social relations. Here, Neumann recognised that the reference to its economic embeddedness is not sufficient in order to describe the function of law. He saw that the law is related to politics and academia, too. Political, religious and intellectual structures as well as family structure are all realities that affect the law, just as the economy does.

Otto Kirchheimer's analyses of juridification similarly address this treatment of law as an autonomous force which is independent of other societal spheres, and meticulously describe the processes of juridification that expand to furthest corners of society:

> "In all fields of endeavor things are turned into law."[33]

Everything is subjected to legal discourse: from administration, the principles of business and economics, worker co-determination and the education system, to issues of family and private life. Discourse theory took on these ideas and interpreted them as the colonising tendencies of functional systems. The existing colonisation through law turns all social problems and conflicts into legal questions.[34] World society's most complicated conflicts are given legal hearings, translated into legal terminology and often unrecognisably transformed into conflicts of principles; there is no longer any issue of world society that cannot be decided in the language of law, the programme of law and the code of law. The key players in this fundamental juridification are the transnationally operating courts, élite lawyers, law firms, transnational companies, and NGOs. All are engaged in stabilising societal structures through the legal structure.

---

31 Otto Kirchheimer, "Reichsgericht und Enteignung: Reichsverfassungswidrigkeit des Preußischen Fluchtliniengesetzes?", (1930), in: Otto Kirchheimer, *Von der Weimarer Republik zum Faschismus: Die Auflösung der demokratischen Rechtsordnung*, edited by Wolfgang Luthardt, (Frankfurt aM: Suhrkamp Verlag, 1976), p. 77 *et seq*., at 78.

32 Franz L. Neumann, The Rule of Law: Political Theory and the Legal System in Modern Society, (Leamington Spa: Berg Publishing, 1986).

33 Otto Kirchheimer, "The Socialist and the Bolshevik Theory of the State", in: idem, *Politics, Law, and Social Change: Selected Essays of Otto Kirchheimer*, edited by Frederic S. Burin and Kurt L. Shell, (New York-London: Columbia University Press, 1969), p. 3 *et seq*., at 7.

34 Jürgen Habermas, *The Theory of Communicative Action*, Vol. II, (Boston MA: Beacon Press, 1987), p. 362 *et seq*.

In extreme cases, fundamental questions are no longer decided in democratically organised forums, but, instead, in an expertocratic way before the world's courts, be it by national Constitutional Courts, regional Courts or the International Court of Justice (ICJ).[35] Kirchheimer was the first to describe the subtle mechanisms of the legal structure in terms of its tendency to subjugate, alienate and determine social relations. His conclusions also offer an important impetus for a transnational legal policy. He did not call for de-juridification, something that would have been too simple as well as unrealistic. He realistically assessed the chances of an alternative legal policy by combining Karl Marx's analyses with a movement towards politicisation. From Marx, he adopted the observation that social relations undergo a differentiation, and that one section can follow its self-referential expansionary tendencies to the detriment of other sections of society. Thus, Marx's economic analysis that the economy produces an autonomous commodity form is extended by Kirchheimer to law and legal structure. He combines this Marxist analysis with a critical legal perspective, which reveals the political moment within law's autonomy. He holds in contempt those petty practitioners of the law who believe that law is divorced from politics and that identifying the objective law is a purely scientific exercise. He sees legal decisions not as a mathematical calculation, but as the product of legal and political conflicts. If we accept the diagnosis of juridification, it follows that there are consequences for the form that these conflicts take: in the juridified society, they always relate to law and the legal code.

Through Kirchheimer, one can demonstrate how the law, which, at first glance, only seems to function in a mechanical and technical way, can – itself – be internally re-politicised.[36] A considered understanding of transnational social rights requires one to "bring to light power relations"[37] and confront the established and employed techniques of domination; only then can strategies of resistance be identified, invented or strengthened. Since "[t]he element of strife and of struggle [...] is an integral part of [the law], and has been from the

---

35 On the relationship between law and politics at global level, see the International Court of Justice, *Advisory Opinion on the Legal Consequences of the Construction of a Wall in the Occupied Palestinian Territory*, 9 July 204, ICJ Reports, p. 136 *et seq.* (155, para. 41).

36 On this kind of link between analysis and scope for politicisation in Kirchheimer, see Gunther Teubner, "Man schritt auf allen Gebieten zur Verrechtlichung: Rechtssoziologische Theorie im Werk Otto Kirchheimers", in: Marcus Lutter, Ernst C. Stiefel and Michael Hoeflich (eds), *Der Einfluß deutschsprachiger Emigranten auf die Rechtsentwicklung in den USA und in Deutschland*, (Tübingen: Mohr Siebeck, 1993), p. 505 *et seq.* Parallels to this challenging model based upon Kirchheimer's analysis can be found in the materialist theory of law in the work of Evgeny Pashukanis. See Evgeny Pashukanis, *Law and Marxism: A General Theory*, (London: Pluto Press, 1978).

37 Michel Foucault, "The Subject and Power", (1982) 8 *Critical Inquiry*, p. 777 *et seq.*, at 780.

first",[38] the law is a battleground for the "civil war of 'language' with itself".[39] This opens the way for world society to re-appropriate the law and allows for the re-socialisation of the juridification process, thus reclaiming the arenas of transnational law from the technocrats.

B. TRANSNATIONAL JURIDIFICATION

This kind of re-appropriation of the law has yet to be achieved. While world society has gone through an intensive juridification, transnational law is predominantly geared towards those interested parties within the functional systems. As far back as 1971, the sociologist Niklas Luhmann put forward the "speculative hypothesis" that law would see a move from normative expectations (politics, morality, law) to cognitive expectations (economy, science, technology):

> "At the level of global society, this means that norms (in the form of values, stipulations, goals) will no longer pre-programme recognition patterns; rather, and in stark contrast, the problem of learning adaptation will gain structural primacy, so that the structural conditions for learning within each social system must be supported through normatisation."[40]

In other words, the functional systems – primarily the economy – manage to procure everything that they require from world society – including law.

In order to be in a position to suggest effective changes, it is important to establish which legal, economic and political factors allowed for the emergence of financial market capitalism – from the watered-down capital requirements of the Basel Committee on Banking Supervision to the structural adjustment programmes of the IMF. What the public debate on managers' bonus packages overlooks is that the current economic crisis is part of a development that began in the 1970s with the collapse of the Bretton Woods system of internationally fixed exchange rates. Only since then have we witnessed the triumphant march onward of neo-liberalism and the extreme pressure thereby exerted on social rights. In international political economy, this epoch – in which the global economic players provide their own neo-liberal legal norms – will be seen as

---

38 Rudolph von Jhering, *The Struggle for Law*, originally printed by Callaghan and Co., 1915, p 138.

39 This formulation in Jean-François Lyotard, *The Differend: Phrases in Dispute*, (Minneapolis MN: University of Minnesota Press, 1988) (Theory and History of Literature Vol. 46, 1988, §198, p. 141).

40 Niklas Luhmann, "Die Weltgesellschaft", (1971) 57 *Archiv für Rechts- und Sozialphilosophie*, p. 313 *et seq.*, English translation gathered from Andreas Fischer-Lescano and Gunther Teubner, "Regime-collisions: The Vain Search for Legal Unity in the Fragmentation of Global Law", (2004) 25 *Michigan Journal of International Law*, p. 999, at 1000, translated by Michelle Everson.

one of market-liberal constitutionalism.[41] The global economic order primarily protects the rights of private industry.

The path towards this market-liberal dominance was not a straightforward one. The global economic crises prior to the Second World War and the failure of the supply-orientated economic doctrine resulted in calls for a socially orientated regulatory system coming even from those who had previously supported the capitalist economic order: the Atlantic Charter drawn up by Roosevelt and Churchill in 1941, the 1944 Declaration of Philadelphia of the International Labour Organization, the Charter of the United Nations from 1945, and the Universal Declaration of Human Rights from 1948, were the first to formulate – with the claim of universal application – the idea of social human rights and an international system geared towards social objectives.[42]

Of the many forms of capitalism, the epoch of embedded liberalism in Western nations is distinguished by economic regulation that is demand-orientated, and which stimulates growth through public institutions and wage increases. This economic appeasement policy is supplemented by corporatist arrangements and social compromises between the *bourgeois* and the subaltern classes.[43]

At international level, this period corresponded with increasing law-making under the framework of the United Nations. The Universal Declaration of Human Rights (1948), the International Covenant of Civil and Political Rights (ICCPR) (1966) and the ICESCR (1966) all three emerged in this period. The latter bears witness to the fact that the increased significance of social rights on a national scale at the time was also borne out on an international scale. The ICESCR secures the right to social security, the right to freedom of association, and the right to strike.

The so-called Bretton Woods Institutions exert their influence over the sphere of international economic regulation. The International Monetary Fund and the World Bank safeguard the system of fixed exchange rates and, in doing so, rule out – officially at least – currency speculation and high-risk financial transactions.[44]

This model plunged into crisis in the early 1970s, and the system of fixed exchange rates was abandoned and replaced by a floating exchange rate system.

41 Stephen Gill, "Constitutionalizing Inequality and the Clash of Globalizations", (2002) 4 *International Studies Review*, p. 47 *et seq.*

42 Benjamin Davy, Ulrike Davy and Lutz Leisering, "The Global, the Social and Rights. New Perspectives on Social Citizenship", (2013) 22 *International Journal of Social Welfare*, issue supplement 1, p. 1 *et seq.*

43 Wolfgang Abendroth, "Zum Begriff des demokratischen und sozialen Rechtsstaates im Grundgesetz der Bundesrepublik Deutschland", (1954), in: *Gesammelte Schriften Band 2*, (Hannover: Offizin Verlag, 2008), p. 338 *et seq.*, especially at 354.

44 A watering-down of this attitude has been evident since the 1960s. See Duncan Wood, *Governing Global Banking: The Basel Committee and the Politics of Financial Globalisation*, (Aldershot-Burlington VT: Ashgate Publishing, 2005), p. 32.

Only since then has it been possible to speculate on fluctuating exchange rates, which has since allowed banks to expand their activities in the area of financial and exchange rate speculation.

Neo-liberal economic policy was in line for a change. The IMF and the World Bank acquired a new role: ensuring stable conditions for speculation. The establishment of the WTO in 1995 provided a legal framework for the liberalisation of world markets. It aimed to contribute to "the substantial reduction of tariffs and other barriers to trade and to the elimination of discriminatory treatment in international trade relations" (WTO-Agreement).

This market-liberal constitutionalism is the product of the one-sided configuration of a transnational law that legally guarantees the transactions of the global economy. It also involves a de-democratisation of decision-making processes.[45] This democratic deficit mainly arises from the elimination of the public spheres open to democratic participation and the establishment – in their place – of private institutions without democratic legitimacy. Under this new arrangement, corporate freedom and corporate property rights are removed from democratic and public supervision. These neo-liberal norms are bolstered by a system of global jurisdiction, which sees transnational institutions install their own jurisdictions and dispute resolution procedures, such as the WTO arbitration procedure.

This leads to legal mechanisms that are difficult to change, and whose market-liberal viewpoint excludes alternative paths of politico-economic development. Instead of being subject to democratic decision-making processes, the economic and societal order is safeguarded by a less than transparent process of juridification hatched in the back rooms of international diplomacy and corporations.

While the winners in the global economy have long taken control of the legal machinery and thus created the perfect conditions for their own interests to flourish, attempts to introduce a sense of social and environmental responsibility to the system remain all too rare. As yet, there have been no radical changes in thinking on the scale necessary to bring about a lasting socialisation of neo-liberal excesses.

If the diagnosis is correct that the process of globalisation has given free rein to the economic system, it seems flawed to expect the remedy to come from a kind of national *résistance*. We would be better advised to pinpoint elements of an alternative juridico-political approach that have the potential to re-arrange the unfettered transnational system in a social and ecological way.

Two examples demonstrate the need to extend the fight for social rights beyond the constraints of the nation state:

---

45 See Kolja Möller, *Formwandel der Verfassung. Die postdemokratische Verfasstheit des Transnationalen*, (Bielefeld: Transcript, 2015); Colin Crouch, *Post-Democracy*, (Cambridge-Malden MA: Polity Press, 2004).

1. *The World Trade Organization: AIDS Medicines and the Right to Health*

WTO law primarily supports the liberalisation of world markets, a position which leads to a number of negative consequences. But in the dispute between Brazil and the US over patent protection for AIDS medicines a political struggle around the WTO's essential commitments took place. It escalated in 2001, with the US claiming that Brazilian law was too lenient regarding the production of generic medicines and was thus violating the patent rights of US pharmaceutical companies. The US commenced proceedings against Brazil before the WTO arbitration panel, which had to decide between the social right to health and the economic right to patent protection. The US, however, had under-estimated the forces that it would be up against. From the US perspective, there could not have been a worse time to initiate proceedings relating to patent protection for AIDS medicines before the WTO. A special session of the UN General Assembly focusing on HIV/AIDS was scheduled to begin just a few months after the start of the WTO proceedings. Such special sessions, which focus on issues of the utmost importance, are relatively rare, requiring years of preparation and involving players from both national and civil society spheres. Before long, there was a widespread public outcry surrounding the fact that US economic policy was denying appropriate treatment to people suffering from AIDS. Keen to harness this public sentiment, Brazil managed to get a resolution passed at the next sitting of the UN Commission on Human Rights: Resolution 2001/33 was passed with 52 votes out of 53 – the US abstaining – and called on states:

> "[t]o ensure that their actions as members of international organizations take due account of the right of everyone to the enjoyment of the highest attainable standard of physical and mental health."

The resolution made fairly plain reference to the simmering conflict around the Brazilian AIDS programme, and served as a diplomatic barometer for the pressure mounting against the US government. This explains why, on the first day of the UN's special session, the US announced that it was withdrawing the WTO complaint in favour of negotiations with Brazil. From a US perspective, the proceedings also had a counter-productive effect within the WTO system, as it led to the so-called Doha Compromise (2001), which provided for exceptions from WTO obligations for developing countries.

2. *The Centre for Settlement of Investment Disputes (ICSID): Bolivia and the Right to Water*

Another example is provided by the protests by residents of the Bolivian town of Cochabamba against high water prices and poor water quality following the privatisation of the water supply. Public pressure eventually led to the government reversing the privatisation, to wit, re-nationalising the "public" utility. This prompted the company in question, Aguas del Tunari, a subsidiary of the US firm Bechtel, to bring the Bolivian government before the ICSID in an attempt to force them to uphold the contracts.[46] The case posed the fundamental question of whether the property rights of Aguas del Tunari could trump the rights to food, to freely enjoy natural resources, and to one's own means of subsistence as guaranteed by the ICESCR. Civil societal pressure which pitted property rights against social counter-rights led to an out-of-court settlement, and exposed the contradiction of world society. This is much more than a collision between national regulation and the norms of globalisation. At heart, the conflict represents the tension between profit-driven private business and access to public goods. This tension, prevalent in national law, is also evident in transnational law, as two different normative regimes collide – WTO law and the law of the ICESCR. What happened after the ICSID proceedings reveals the socio-structural conflict at play. Not only were Bolivia's water laws amended, but its new 2009 Constitution also guarantees the right to access to water and stipulates that access to water may not be the object of concession or privatisation. It shows that intervention was required to prevent democratic and social rights from being trounced by global norms, and demonstrates how successful civil-society protests can be.

IV. TRANSNATIONAL SOCIAL RIGHTS

The category of transnational social rights unites three strands of rights that have been separated in conventional legal discourse. Transnational social rights combine *liberal*, *social* and *political* human rights. The fact that these rights would be amalgamated in this way is far from self-evident, due to a pervasive tendency to treat liberal human rights and social rights as two distinct categories, and, in turn, to separate both groups from the category of democratic rights. Liberalism has been particularly effective at giving priority to liberal human rights at the expense of political and social interests. Over time, this has weakened social rights and prevented them from achieving their democratic potential.

A. THE INDIVISIBILITY OF HUMAN RIGHTS

Initially, social and liberal human rights were conceived of as one. This is evident from the Universal Declaration of Human Rights, proclaimed by the UN General

46 ICSID, *Aguas del Tunari S.A.* v. *Republic of Bolivia*, (ICSID Case No. ARB/02/3).

Assembly on 10 December 1948, which reflected the prevailing conceptions of rights immediately after World War II. Along with the usual liberal rights, such as freedom of expression, the prohibition of torture and the right to bodily integrity and effective legal protection, it also included social rights, such as the right to social protection, work, health and food, within the catalogue of human rights.

A tendency to separate these categories of rights emerged with the adoption of the two international covenants in the 1960s, wherein social rights are textually split from liberal human rights: the ICCPR ratified by 168 states, and the ICESCR with 164 parties. This division is echoed at European level. While the European Convention on Human Rights (ECHR) focuses on liberal human rights, social rights are relegated to the European Social Charter.

The main result of this division was that the two categories of rights were not made equally enforceable. The liberal human rights are safeguarded by the European Court of Human Rights (ECtHR), while the social rights are protected only by a committee, which does not even have the power to hear individual complaints. Finally, some attempts are under way to introduce a complaint mechanism into the context of the ICESCR. An optional protocol to this effect was drawn up by the General Assembly in 2008 and entered into force in May 2013.[47] Since then, those whose rights have been violated are able to make a submission to the Committee, which can then make the appropriate recommendations to the state in question.

The separate institutional handling of the two categories of rights shows that, while liberal human rights are conceived of as "hard" actionable rights, social rights are often reduced to the status of non-actionable "non-rights", which robs them of their normative clout.

Slowly, however, the debate is picking up speed. The 1993 Vienna Conference on Human Rights made a significant contribution to the idea of the indivisibility of human rights. Many states ratified both UN Covenants in the wake of the conference. The current status of ratifications indicates that liberal and political human rights *and* social human rights can claim to be valid right across cultural boundaries. Both the Vienna Declaration – adopted at the end of the Vienna Conference in June 1993 – and the United Nations Millennium Declaration explicitly stress the indivisibility of human rights, with the Millennium Declaration going so far as to set out the goal, in paragraph 19, "[t]o halve, by the year 2015, the proportion of the world's people whose income is less than one dollar a day and the proportion of people who suffer from hunger".

The concepts of the indivisibility of human rights and the inter-dependence of liberal, political and social rights are now once again finding favour. This

---

47 Optional Protocol to the International Covenant on Economic, Social and Cultural Rights (UN GA Res. A/RES/63/117 from 10 December 2008); available at: http://treaties.un.org/Pages/ViewDetails.aspx?src=TREATY&mtdsg_no=IV-3-a&chapter=4&lang=en.

viewpoint sees social, political and liberal rights as simply various manifestations of human rights, and not as categorically separate entities.

This typology of human rights is therefore not limited to liberal rights; instead, it can be thought of as being three-dimensional. The (liberal) human rights of the first dimension include defensive and freedom-orientated rights, such as the right to life and to personal freedom. The (social) rights constituting the second dimension are, to a large extent, codified in the ICESCR.[48] These are joined by the third group of rights to political participation and collective rights, such as the rights to development, peace, solidarity and the right to share in the common heritage of mankind.[49] These three dimensions are different forms of human rights. They are interwoven with one another and cannot be categorically divided. Only together can they fulfil their purpose: namely, to enable individual and collective self-constitution.

Other recent codifications of fundamental and human rights re-inforce this conception of indivisible human rights. The Charter of Fundamental Rights of the EU – which became incorporated into primary law following the Treaty of Lisbon – encompasses social as well as liberal rights. The same is true for the Banjul Charter of the African Union and the American Convention on Human Rights. Specialised agreements such as the Convention on the Rights of the Child and the Convention on the Rights of Persons with Disabilities include both liberal and social rights.

Even where there is no such immediately apparent merging of social and liberal rights, the categorical separation of the groups cannot be maintained; the two sets of rights are mutually dependent. The liberal rights have a social dimension, and the social rights have a liberal dimension. The social right to health is not limited to basic claims to health-care – it includes liberty rights which protect the individual against state interference. Relevant state interference could consist of permitting the use of dangerous technologies or breaches of bodily integrity through irreversible surgical measures carried out on intersexual children. The liberal right to free choice of employment brings with it the obligation to provide for fair and reasonable allocation of jobs. Liberal property rights can give rise to social security entitlements, while the right to human dignity combined with the principle of social justice and the welfare state leads to an entitlement to the guarantee of the socio-cultural basic income.

---

48 Manoj Sinha, "New Dimension of International Human Rights Law, with Special Reference of Economic Rights", (2009) 6 *Soochow Law Journal*, p. 65 *et seq.*

49 To the gender-related questions in relation with those third-generation rights, see Celestine Nyamu, "How should Human Rights and Development respond to Cultural Legitimization of Gender Hierarchy in Developing Countries", (2000) 41 *Harvard International Law Journal*, p. 381 *et seq*; see, also, Mosope Fagbongbe, "The Future of Women's Rights from a TWAIL Perspective", (2008) 10 *International Community Law Review*, p. 401 *et seq.*

Similarly, there is no clear delineation between political and social human rights. The fundamental right to worker co-determination, for example, is derived from human dignity, general personality rights and the free choice of profession. These liberal rights give rise to an employee's entitlement to contribute to the governing of his or her own professional environment. The fundamental right to co-determination is therefore not only a social right which is derived from liberal rights, but is also a political right since it establishes the entitlement to democratic participation in business life. The sociologist Thomas H. Marshall pointed out that the social right to freedom of association, for example, also counts as one of the political participation rights that transfer the status as citizen into the industrial sphere, giving rise to the notion of industrial citizenship.[50] Major features of industrial democracy arose through the interpretation of liberal and social human rights.

While the principle of transnational social rights puts emphasis on a combined approach to liberal, political and social human rights, it is possible to identify five distinct kinds of social rights within this approach:[51]

1. liberal human rights with a social component (e.g., free choice of profession) and social human rights with a liberal component (e.g., the right to health);
2. political human rights with a social component (e.g., the right to co-determination) and social human rights with a political component (e.g., the right to strike);
3. equality rights which provide social entitlements to inclusion;
4. rights to social security, which can range from social support to health and environmental protection; and
5. social objectives, such as the goals of social progress and international peace set out in the preamble of the UN Charter.

All of the five elements of this typology have the potential to establish subjective entitlements, *i.e.*, individual social rights that can be enforced in courts. The discovery that social rights exist in current international law leads us directly to the most important point of debate: What are the required conditions to turn subjective rights into concrete enforceable entitlements?

B. OBJECTIONS

Conservative lawyers argue against unlocking the potential of transnational social rights for a number of reasons. Four main objections are generally presented.

---

50 Thomas H. Marshall, *Citizenship and Social Class and Other Essays*, (Cambridge: Cambridge University Press, 1950).

51 See, also, the typology used by Karl-Jürgen Bieback, in "Soziale Rechte", (2010) 43 *Kritische Justiz*, p. 230 *et seq.*

1. *Vagueness*

It is often claimed that social rights are too vague and too ill-defined to establish concrete rights and duties. This was the approach taken, for example, by a German administrative court in refusing to recognise the substantive content of a number of norms from the ICESCR. Students who tried to rely on the Covenant to fight against university fees in Nordrhein-Westfalen in Germany in 2007 were blocked from doing so by the court, which stated:

> "the text of the treaty ... lacks the necessary exactness for a legal norm ... The normal requirements of certainty and precision relating to international treaties cannot be applied here. Due to its political nature and its character as the product of diplomatic compromise, the law of international treaties is often vaguely worded, and occasionally not at all intended to regulate a real life situation, but instead deliberately uses language to cover up the fact that precisely nothing is, in fact, meant to be regulated."[52]

This attempt to erode social rights was subsequently rejected by a higher court, which recognised in its decision that the ICESCR can indeed establish norms and is not merely a political declaration of will.[53] This makes it clear that "vagueness" is, in itself, a vague criterion. All legal norms are vague. The central task of the law is to convert inexactness into exactness, in other words, to determine indeterminable issues. The uncertainty of the law is the starting-point for every legal dispute, which involves pitting two competing interpretations of the law against each other to see which will prevail. Legal norms, particularly human-rights norms, are always in need of concretisation. Take, for example, the first provision of the German Basic Law: "Human dignity shall be inviolable." This provision is no less in need of concretisation than the social ICESCR-guaranteed right at stake in the case of the university fees, which states that:

> "with a view to achieving the full realization of this right [to education] ... [h] igher education shall be made equally accessible to all, on the basis of capacity, by every appropriate means, and in particular by the progressive introduction of free education."

2. *Progressive Realisation*

Social rights are often guaranteed only on condition of feasibility. Article 2 (1) of the Convention on Social and Political Rights obliges a state to do no more than "take steps [...] to the maximum of its available resources, with a view

52 Higher Administrative Court of Münster, *Deutsches Verwaltungsblatt* 2007, 1442.
53 Federal Administrative Court, *Official Series*, 134, 1 *et seq.*

to achieving progressively the full realization of the rights recognized in the present Covenant by all appropriate means, including particularly the adoption of legislative measures". The fact that social rights are to be progressively realised does not mean, however, that it is impossible to substantiate these rights. The Committee on Economic, Social and Cultural Rights, the monitoring body of the ICESCR, thus differentiates between the obligations of states to respect, to protect and to fulfil rights. It argues that progressive realisation, as set out in Article 2 (1) of the Convention, is proof that the Convention represents more than a non-binding list of aims. As Eibe Riedel correctly notes, Article 2 (1) of the Covenant "places an unequivocal legally-binding duty on all State Parties, the intensity of which is balanced against the objective situation in which State Parties find themselves".[54] This duty can establish a prohibition on retrogressive measures, for example, the prohibition on the introduction of university fees, but can also lead to a duty to improve the situation progressively, which could entail a duty to abolish such fees gradually.

3. *Resource Dependence*

The argument based upon the resource-dependent nature of social rights and the need for democratic decisions on the distribution of limited resources has had a significant influence on international law practice. It is indeed the main reason for the reluctance on the part of states when it comes to establishing monitoring bodies for the enforcement of social rights. This approach disregards, however, that political and liberal human rights also depend on resources. This is all the more true if the right requires legal mechanisms to be set up. The establishment of the system of patent protection in order to uphold liberal property rights, for example, entails significant costs. The World Bank estimates the costs of enforcing a WTO-compliant intellectual property right in developing countries at around 1.5 million to 2 million USD per country and warns that:

> "Given other pressing needs in education, health, and policy reform, it is questionable whether the least-developed countries would be willing to absorb these costs, or indeed whether they would achieve much social payoff from investing in them. Moreover, note that poor countries are extremely scarce in trained administrators and judges, suggesting that one of the largest costs would be to divert scarce professional and technical resources out of potentially more productive activities."[55]

---

54 Eibe Riedel, "Measuring Human Rights Compliance, The ISBA Procedure as a Tool of Monitoring", in: Andreas Auer, Alexandre Flueckiger and Michel Hottelier (eds), *Les Droits de l'homme et de la Constitution: Études en l'honneur du Professeur Giorgio Malinverni*, (Geneva: Schulthess, 2007), p. 251 *et seq.*, at 256.

55 World Bank Global Economic Prospects 2002: "Making Trade Work for the World's Poor", (Washington DC: World Bank, 2002), p. 136 *et seq.*

There is a further flaw in the argument that the actionability of social rights would lead to immense costs, in that there are lots of social rights that do not lead to an entitlement to services. They often have more in common with classic defensive rights. If the right to water is violated by environmental pollution, what is required is not some cost-intensive service, but, instead, a mere omission, just as with liberal rights. And where social rights *do* give rise to entitlements, granting these entitlements does not necessarily result in a burden on state finances. The fair distribution of available natural resources such as land and water, the recognition of the traditional usage rights of indigenous peoples or other local communities, or the permission to produce generic medicines despite existing patents, all represent rights that do not entail increased costs to the state. The actionability of social rights does not mean that the court will never take financial considerations into account – quite the opposite. This is why the Committee on Economic, Social and Cultural Rights leaves a certain amount of discretion when it comes to the allocation of resources. The burden of proof rests on the state if it cites "resource constraints" as an explanation for its failure to fulfil its obligations. In practice, the Committee applies the following criteria to the legality of any retrogressive steps taken by a state: the country's level of development, the severity of the alleged breach of rights, the country's current economic situation, and the existence of other serious claims on the state party's limited resources; for example, resulting from a recent natural disaster or from recent internal or international armed conflict.[56]

4. *Judicial Enforceability*

The final objection to social rights holds that, for structural reasons, it is generally not feasible to conceive of social fundamental rights in the same way as directly enforceable rights, such as liberty rights.[57] This argument challenges the justiciability of social rights as such, and generally takes one of two forms. The first one voices doubts about the applicability of such a right, and questions whether the norm has the structural capacity to oblige the addressee to take a particular course of action. The second one posits that such rights represent a duty imposed by international law that is binding on states, but that this does not empower an individual to have recourse to international law in order to claim the right. Both points are important fields of legal and political debate in the battle to determine whether norms may be enforced or whether these provisions will be rendered toothless.

---

56 UN Committee on Economic, "Social and Cultural Rights, An Evaluation of the Obligation to take Steps to the 'Maximum of Available Resources' under an Optional Protocol to the Covenant", 10 May 2007, E/C.12/2007/1, para. 10.

57 See, for example, Wolfgang Rüfner, "§40 Leistungsrechte", in: Detlef Merten and Hans-Jürgen Papier (eds), *Handbuch Grundrechte II*, (Heidelberg: CF Müller, 2007), para. 53.

A look at the European Social Charter demonstrates the fate that awaits social rights when this battle is not fought to the end. For example, the Charter guarantees the right to strike, a right not limited to union-led wage-based strikes. The German approach, which forbids so-called "political strikes", therefore represents a breach of the Charter. German courts, however, have been reluctant to apply the Charter, despite the fact that Germany has ratified it. The reason given for this reluctance is that the Charter's provisions are to be seen as aims that all state parties should strive to achieve. The prevailing legal opinion in Germany maintains that the word "aims" implies that the Charter is not intended to establish subjective rights.

There is good reason to reject this approach, a view shared by the European Committee of Social Rights, the treaty's monitoring body.[58]

The EU Charter of Fundamental Rights presents a similar situation. This Charter introduced a differentiation between "'real' rights" and "principles". The official clarification given is that "'real' rights" are to be treated as "subjective rights", while "principles" need only to be generally observed. Here, in the small print, we see another attempt to weaken social rights – the principles are largely made up of social rights – by framing them in terms of vague concepts, instead of actionable rights.[59]

The enforceability question is also debated with reference to the justiciability of these rights in international forums. As mentioned, states have, to date, been extremely reluctant to allow for individual or collective complaint procedures before both the ICESCR and the European Social Charter. In both cases, the legal and political debate must focus on working towards strengthening these rights. There is nothing in the structure of social, liberal or social-liberal rights that can justify the different way in which these norms are treated.

There is no principled distinction between social human rights and liberal/political human rights. Nor are social rights any less binding. Transnational social rights are equal to, overlap, and cannot be divided from, liberal and political rights. Without the right to self-constitution, *i.e.*, the right to a guaranteed basic income, and without the rights to environmental protection and migration, political and liberal human rights would be rendered hollow.

Liberal and political human rights cannot adequately deal with the problems of people living in refugee camps or people who have lost their livelihoods due to environmental disasters. Social rights are thus a necessary addition to – and not the opposite of – liberal and political rights. All three dimensions rely upon

58 Tino Frieling and Roland Czycholl, "Auswirkungen der Europäischen Sozialcharta auf das Arbeitskampfrecht. Das Streikrecht aus Art. 6 Abs. 4 ESC als vorrangige gesetzgeberische Entscheidung", (2011) *Zeitschrift für europäisches Sozial- und Arbeitsrecht*, p. 322 *et seq*.

59 Thomas Giegerich, "Steuern Völker- und Europarecht die Globalisierung 'im Geiste der Brüderlichkeit'?", in: Thomas Giegerich and Andreas Zimmermann (eds), *Wirtschaftliche, soziale und kulturelle Rechte im globalen Zeitalter*, (Berlin: Duncker & Humblot, 2008), p. 7 *et seq*., at 26 *et seq*.

each other. They are indivisible. The co-originality of political, liberal and social rights is essential for the self-determination of individuals.[60] This indivisibility also means that there are no rights without social rights. Transnational law is social, or it isn't law at all.

V. ARENAS OF TRANSNATIONAL LEGAL POLICY

There are three different arenas where transnational social rights must be strengthened: (A) at global level, the main challenge is to find a timely solution to the threats to social rights posed, not by states, but by transnational corporations. At European level (B), we have to make sure that a social Europe becomes a reality. This is of utmost importance with regard to the strengthening of transnational social rights: a social union which resists the temptation to establish imperial and exploitative (transnational) relations, could be a powerful resource which promotes social rights. Lastly, we must ensure that (C) states and the political organisations of global governance are held to the standard of the emancipatory ideal.

A. TRANSNATIONAL SOCIAL RIGHTS AND TRANSNATIONAL CORPORATIONS

A crucial element of contemporary legal policy is to ensure that transnational corporations are bound to respect social human rights.[61]

The fact that Deutsche Bank can, on the one hand, speculate on crop failures, food scarcities and hunger-related deaths while, on the other, it can issue enthusiastic declarations relating to the UN Global Compact Initiative on upholding human rights is evidence of the complexities of transnational legal policy. How can private companies be bound to uphold transnational social rights? How can the concept of human rights for corporations move from being a mere marketing instrument to becoming actionable legal obligations? We urgently need to find answers to the new kinds of risks that social rights face *not* from global politics, but from transnational corporations.

But what obligations – if any – does international law impose on transnational corporations? For decades, the steadfast position was that international law is a legal order both for and by states. The authors and addressees of this law were therefore states, and not individuals or corporate entities. Yet the transnational constellation of global communication, as well as global social systems of

60 Jürgen Habermas, trans. William Rehg, "Remarks on Legitimation through Human Rights", (1998) 24 *Philosophy and Social Criticism*, p. 157 *et seq.*, at 161.

61 See Ibrahim Kanalan and Sebastian Eickenjäger, Chapter 6 in this volume.

business, science and technology, all raise the question of how international law – and particularly human rights – respond to these all-encompassing processes of transnationalisation. As far back as 1934, Hans Kelsen recognised that:

> "[t]o the extent that international law penetrates areas that heretofore have been the exclusive domain of national legal orders, its tendency toward directly authorizing and obligating individuals must increase."[62]

Calls for direct obligations to be placed on non-state actors are still, however, met with stiff resistance. It is extremely difficult for the victims of violations of transnational social rights to have their rights enforced. This is made shockingly clear in the case of violations of social human rights relating to the right to food. Oil drilling in the Niger Delta has caused extensive environmental pollution. Consortia of transnational corporations headed by the British/Dutch oil company Shell have devastated huge tracts of land, collaborated in the execution of human-rights lawyer Ken Saro-Wiwa and his supporters, and violated the social rights of the Ogoni people. In 2011, the United Nations Environment Programme published an extensive report detailing the contamination caused by oil exploration and production in the Ogoniland of Nigeria.[63]

The oil drilling is a violation of the right to food as well as the collective right to the protection of the natural environment. This protection is one of the key concerns – indeed, the core ecological demand – of transnational social rights. This is due to the fact that environmental rights are rights that are closely linked to human rights. Courts often read ecological concerns into liberal and social human rights, a phenomenon known as the "environmentalisation of human rights". In this way, the European Court of Human Rights has developed the environmental components of the European Convention on Human Rights based upon the right to life and the right to privacy. Similarly, the UN Human Rights Committee interprets the ICCPR in such a way as to include ecological human rights.

The environmental leaning is particularly important when it comes to social human rights. The right to an adequate standard of living, including adequate nutrition, clothing, accommodation and health, contained in the ICESCR also encompasses the right to stable environmental conditions to enable human existence. The UN Committee on Economic, Social and Cultural Rights thus found that these two norms could be read as establishing a right to water.[64]

All of these fundamental norms are directed, in the traditional way, at states. These rights impose three legal obligations on states: (1) the duty to respect

62 Hans Kelsen, *Pure Theory of Law*, (Oakland CA: University of California Press, 1978), p. 327.

63 United Nations Environment Programme, Environmental Assessment of Ogoniland, Nairobi 2011.

64 UN Committee on Economic, Social and Cultural Rights, General Comment 15, 2002, E/C.12/2002/11 from 20 January 2003.

obliges all states to refrain from violating these rights; (2) the duty to protect obliges all states to protect against violations of these rights by third parties; and (3) the duty to fulfil obliges states to ensure that these rights are enforced, which includes their taking active measures to do so.

However, this triad of duties cannot directly impose any obligations on the transnational corporation Shell. The powerlessness of transnational law when it comes to the human rights obligations of transnational corporations is evidenced by the fact that, to date, there has been no final court judgment against Shell. The proceedings in the Netherlands are still ongoing, as Shell has appealed against a judgment of the District Court of The Hague which granted compensation to the victims.[65]

The jurisdiction of national courts also presents problems, as this requires a legal connection to the state in which the court is sitting, *i.e.*, that the corporation, the victim, or the place in which the crime was committed has a connection to the state in question. This is often difficult to achieve in the case of human rights violations. A certain amount of legal creativity is required if, for example, a Nigerian victim of a crime that took place in Nigeria wishes to take a foreign subsidiary of a transnational corporation to court. The US legal system offers quite a lot of scope in cases such as these. In the US, corporations involved in grave violations of human rights may be brought before courts even if there is no immediate connection between the violation and the US. It was for this reason that lawyers taking a case relating to the killing of Ken Saro-Wiwa initiated proceedings before a New York court. When, in June 2009, the court declared the compensation claim admissible, Shell agreed to a settlement with the victims in the region of 15 million USD.[66] Apart from this case, which made use of the opportunity presented by the US legal system, there is little scope at global level to seek a judgment against Shell.

Judgment on the issue has been handed down only to the state of Nigeria, in a case before the African Commission on Human and Peoples' Rights relating to violations of the right to food. In its decision, the Commission stressed the importance of the right to food in the human rights system, finding that:

> "the minimum core of the right to food requires that the Nigerian Government should not destroy or contaminate food sources. [...] The Government has destroyed food sources through its security forces and State Oil Company; has allowed private oil companies to destroy food sources; and, through terror, has created significant obstacles to Ogoni communities trying to feed themselves."[67]

---

65 District Court of The Hague, C/09/337050 / HA ZA 09-1580, judgment of 30 January 2013.

66 US District Court Southern District of New York, *Wiwa* v. *Shell Petroleum*, 96 Civ. 8386, Settlement of 8 June 2009.

67 African Commission on Human and Peoples Rights, *SERAC, Center for Economic and Social Rights* v. *Nigeria*, October 2001, ACHPR/COMM/A044/1, para. 65 f.

The crux of this decision from the African Commission was the involvement of the Nigerian state in violations of social rights.

But what *concrete* human rights obligations exist for transnational corporations?

Thus far, attempts have failed to formulate a draft on the responsibility of corporations under international law and on a declaration of a code of social responsibility with universal applicability and direct effect.[68] Currently, the concept of voluntary codes does have some traction. While these voluntary declarations are problematical, they do at least represent a start. One should not be too quick to reject categorically the legal applicability of such declarations just because they are voluntary in nature. Law is not limited to what states, themselves, set out. Legal norms can also be formed in society. To see the concept of law as being too closely linked to the state is to overlook the unique nature of social norms.

The struggle for law has always entailed debate on the significance of certain symbolic texts. Even the idea that the constitution could have a binding effect on politics was established only after a legal debate. Even the *Magna Carta* was not initially conceived of as a justiciable document.

In a similar way, transnational social and democratic legal policy will have to work to transform these voluntary declarations into binding transnational social rights. The future obligations on transnational corporations to uphold human rights might take a multi-dimensional form, encompassing binding fundamental rules, incentives and voluntary initiatives. There is certainly no shortage of initiatives to create such norms. The following initiatives are of particular importance: (1) The United Nations Global Compact (UNGC): a public-private initiative of the UN, which aims to establish ten universal principles, including that business should respect the protection of human rights. (2) In May 2010, the UNGC came to an agreement with the Global Reporting Initiative to monitor the ten principles by means of the "G3 Guidelines". This will, for the first time, provide guidelines for a monitoring mechanism. (3) The International Organization for Standardization (ISO) should also be mentioned in this context. In May 2010, it adopted the draft ISO 26000 on Social Responsibility. This ISO norm makes a significant contribution to the standardisation of the human rights obligations of companies. (4) The ILO Core Labour Standards also provide for binding human rights obligations on companies. The Declaration on Fundamental Principles and Rights at Work of June 1998 sets out universal fundamental principles for corporations operating internationally, such as the ban on child labour. (5) Finally, reference must be made to the OECD Guidelines

---

68 See Ronen Shamir, "Corporate Social Responsibility: A Case of Hegemony and Counter-hegemony", in: Boaventura de Sousa Santos and César A. Rodríguez-Garavito (eds), *Law and Globalization from Below: Towards a Cosmopolitan Legality*, (Cambridge: Cambridge University Press, 2005), p. 92 *et seq.*

for Multinational Enterprises, a code of conduct for responsible worldwide corporate behaviour.

A common feature of all these efforts is that they are stated in terms of recommendations, attempts to standardise, or voluntary commitments, and thus are not declared as law in a formal sense. This does not, however, exclude the possibility that the legal character of these rules can emerge as a result of the struggle to determine their substance.[69] The legally binding nature of these rules may also emerge with the help of national law. A common litigation strategy of transnational lawyer groups is to hold companies accountable to their Codes of Conduct. Voluntary standards can often be enforced in accordance with competition or consumer laws, where they include relevant representations to the consumer. Thus, a corporation's non-adherence to its own codes can be enforced before courts in the country of the corporation's headquarters.

These are the tentative first steps in the attempt to "get serious" about the human rights obligations of transnational corporations. Transnational social rights that place obligations on corporations can develop out of the complex interplay between various state and non-state systems. In his report from 2008/2009, John Ruggie, the former UN Secretary-General's Special Representative for Business and Human Rights, referred to precisely this multi-dimensional aspect. Ruggie sees complementary responsibilities in terms of human rights, and categorises these interconnected duties into a three-pillar system. His "*protect, respect and remedy*" framework encompasses, apart from the state duty to protect against human rights violations, a corporate responsibility to respect human rights, *i.e.*, a direct duty, aimed at corporations, to act with due diligence to avoid infringing upon the rights of others. Added to this is the right of access to judicial and non-judicial remedies. Thus, alongside the traditional state obligations, he sets out a distinct corporate responsibility, which he says has acquired near-universal recognition. He states:

> "By near-universal is meant two things. First, the corporate responsibility to respect is acknowledged by virtually every company and industry CSR initiative, endorsed by the world's largest business associations, affirmed in the Global Compact and its worldwide national networks, and enshrined in such soft law instruments as the ILO Tripartite Declaration and the OECD Guidelines. Second, violations of this social norm are routinely brought to public attention globally through mobilized local communities, networks of civil society, the media including blogs, complaints procedures such as the OECD NCPs [...] This transnational normative regime reaches not only Western multinationals, which have long experienced its effects,

69 On the emergence of binding legal rules in the field of the *lex mercatoria*, see Moritz Renner, "Occupy the System! Societal Constitutionalism and Transnational Corporate Accounting", (2013) 20 *Indiana Journal of Global Legal Studies*, p. 941 *et seq.*

but also emerging economy companies operating abroad, and even large national firms."[70]

Ruggie goes into more detail on this corporate responsibility in his final report of 2011, in which duties to adhere to certain due diligence standards are placed on corporations in order to guarantee human rights.[71]

Ruggie's work has, however, been criticised for not going far enough. Indeed, efforts must be made, particularly in the area of social rights, to ensure that it is not just defensive rights that exist against transnational corporations, but that corporations can also be obliged to take certain positive steps.[72] In the above-mentioned example of patents for medicines, it is easy to imagine situations in which the patent holder could be obliged to allow for the production of generic drugs or be obliged to make lifesaving medicines available.

What does this mean for the enforcement of transnational social rights regarding corporations? It is clear that defensive as well as positive rights should be demanded from corporations. Political human rights should also be developed in the same way so that the idea of participation can be applied against corporations as well. The Aarhus Convention set up innovative participation and control structures in relation to corporations and environmental issues. Strengthening the rules on co-determination in transnational corporations thus remains a central task.

In all of these areas, it is essential to open up access to judicial avenues. The Ruggie report sets out the right to greater access to effective judicial and non-judicial remedies for victims, and refers to the UN General Assembly's "Basic Principles and Guidelines on the Right to a Remedy and Reparation for Victims of Gross Violations of International Human Rights Law and Serious Violations of International Humanitarian Law". The General Assembly declared that these principles emanate from customary international law. The question remains, however, as to whether or not public international law as it currently stands provides for a duty to compensate. If rights violations can be attributed to a corporation, are they obliged to compensate the victims? Conservative international lawyers flatly deny the existence of *any* individual right to compensation under international law. Yet there is no settled prevailing opinion on the matter. A further question relates to which transnational social rights are included in these basic principles and guidelines, *i.e.*, whether the latter apply only to "gross violations" of human rights. Restrictive answers to this question

70 John Ruggie, Report of the Special Representative of the Secretary-General on the Issue of Human Rights and Transnational Corporations and other Business Enterprises 2009, para. 47.

71 John Ruggie, "Guiding Principles on Business and Human Rights: Implementing the United Nations 'Protect, Respect and Remedy' Framework", 21 April 2011, A/HRC/17/31.

72 For recent attempts to draft an international convention concerning human rights and business, see Ibrahim Kanalan and Sebastian Eickenjäger, Chapter 6 in this volume.

refer to the drafting history of the principles. During negotiations, the term "gross violations" was understood as referring only to crimes in the category of genocide and slavery. But states decided against such a narrow interpretation. Instead, it was made clear that systematic violations would also trigger the legal obligation to provide compensation. The task here is to ensure that as many kinds of violations as possible are included in this system of compensation.

Of more fundamental importance, however, is the dispute over whether the right to the legal proceedings and compensation set out by Ruggie also applies in cases of the violations of rights by private persons and corporations. Here again, the restrictive view argues that the principles are directed solely at states. This claim is not, however, supported by the wording of the principles, which stipulate the duty to:

> "Provide those who claim to be victims of a human rights or humanitarian law violation with equal and effective access to justice, as described below, irrespective of who may ultimately be the bearer of responsibility for the violation."[73]

It is certainly possible that even those violations of transnational social rights that are caused by private parties could trigger a claim to an adequate, effective and prompt remedy. In short, based upon these principles and guidelines, it is possible to extrapolate from the existing law an obligation on corporations to compensate victims where the former have violated transnational social rights.

B. THE EUROPEAN SOCIAL UNION

The European Union is a forceful example for a transnational polity that is highly juridified and even vested with parliamentary institutions. This affects not only the European continent. The EU and the Eurozone is an integrated market that establishes relations of economic exchange to the rest of the world. And, in international institutions such as the WTO, the EU acts as a unitary polity. For the strengthening of transnational social rights, it is absolutely crucial that such regional actors promote social rights instead of echoing the market-liberal and imperial dominance that we have already pointed out. This is why the quest for a social Europe attains a huge importance with regard to the overall project.

Not least, the turn towards austerity policies that the Union has seen in the last years is an important example in order to elucidate the devastating effects of neglecting social rights: the social and democratic deficit of the EU is one of the main reasons why the European competitive order is increasingly plagued by crisis. There is no economic stability without social stability. Financialisation and massive wage restraint have led to economic imbalances. The riots and unrest that we have seen spreading through Europe over the last years are a

---

73 UN GA, A/RES/60/147, 21 April 2008, Guidelines, No. 3) c).

reaction to these imbalances, which leave many Europeans with no prospects. In the Parisian *banlieues*, young people, in particular, are protesting against social stigmatisation, while, in the latest occupations at *Puerta del Sol* in Madrid, well-educated students and graduates are drawing attention to their lack of prospects and demanding a *democracia real*. They call for "a Europe of the citizens and not of the markets. We are not commodities in the hands of politicians and bankers".[74]

The lack of European harmonisation in social and economic policies has exacerbated the crisis. The increasingly precarious job markets play a central role here. Minimum social standards have been lowered while the low-wage sector and atypical forms of employment flourish. Even beyond socio-political considerations, the urgent question now is whether or not a social union which protects minimum wages and income can be established, which could, in turn, help to prevent future imbalances. To date, a Europeanisation of social rights is difficult to discern. In contrast, the jurisprudence of the European Court of Justice, the European Commission and of most of the Member States is agreed that Europe is principally a sphere of economic competition, not a sphere of social justice.

But the crisis in the European competitive order extends beyond the socio-economic dimension in that it is closely linked to the crisis of European democracy. The latter arises out of a growing sense of alienation between the majority of EU citizens and the political and economic élite.

This is also reflected in the EU's approach to international trade policies and regional co-operation. While it tries to establish free-trade agreements with the US and Canada, it is not willing to implement fair trade, based upon asymmetrical trade relations, with the Global South.[75] It still echoes the chants of free trade. And not least of all, it attempts to shield its borders against refugees by implementing new police and security apparatuses. Clearly, the current state of the Union is neither committed to social rights nor to an awareness of Europe's colonial past.

As the EU's situation intensifies, the question must be asked: Will the EU deepen its market-liberal constitution and set up increasingly authoritarian means of regulation, or will it face the crisis by prioritising social rights, democracy and economic re-distribution?

A European social union can only be achieved if we make a great effort to transform the market-liberal legal structure into one that guarantees democratic and social rights. This will require institutional reforms as well as pressure from civil society.

Two issues could be of particular significance when it comes to the Europeanisation of social rights. The strengthening of the European Social

---

74 See www.democracyrealya.es.

75 See Steffen Kommer, Chapter 9 in this volume.

Charter and the establishment of a "social" EU citizenship by means of a minimum income system.

1. The *strengthening of the European Social Charter and the establishment of a European court of social rights* could act as a counter development to market-liberal single market integration. With the adoption of the Social Charter, the majority of the Council of Europe agreed on a catalogue of social rights, precisely those social rights that the European Court of Justice categorises as being subordinate to economic fundamental freedoms: the rights to strike and to demonstrate, and the right to collective bargaining.

In a whole series of judgments from the 1970s and 1980s onwards, the ECJ developed a market-liberal leaning. Recent examples of this tendency can be found in the Court's jurisprudence in the decisions in the *Laval*, *Viking*, *Luxembourg* and *Rüffert* cases.[76] In the *Laval* and *Viking* cases, the Court found that strike and protest actions against wage dumping represented violations of fundamental freedoms. In the matter of *Luxembourg*, the ECJ found Luxembourg's laws protecting workers were not in conformity with EU law. The decision in the *Rüffert* case found that, when awarding contracts, the German state of Lower Saxony was not permitted to set minimum wage limits.

In each of these cases, the Court asserted that the four economic freedoms of the single market – the free movement of goods, people, services and capital – are more important than collective bargaining autonomy and the right of trade unions to strike. It seems that the *effet utile* of European law has long become an *effet néolibéral*, which cossets the European competitive order against calls for social justice.[77]

While the European Charter of Fundamental Rights has become binding with the entry into force of the Treaty of Lisbon, it remains unlikely that the ECJ will revise its single market leaning at any time in the near future. There is nothing to suggest that this might change significantly in the near future. The outlook is all the more gloomy given that the social rights set out in the Charter are largely categorised as "principles", thus deliberately rendering the enforceability of such rights uncertain.

It would be a real breakthrough for social rights in Europe if the EU itself were obliged to adhere to the European Social Charter, given that the Charter is an international treaty that forms part of the law of the European Council and has been signed and ratified by 27 European states (but not by all the EU Member States). As it currently stands, the treaty is of meagre significance.

---

76 Decisions of the European Court of Justice: *Viking* – C-438/05 of 11 December 2007, *Laval* – C-341/05 of 18 December 2007, *Rüffert* – C-346/06 of 3 April 2008 and *Luxembourg* – C-319/06 of 19 June 2008.

77 Christoph Schmid, "From *Effet Utile* to *Effet Néolibéral*: A Critique of the New Methodological Expansionism of the European Court of Justice", in: Rainer Nickel (ed), *Conflict of Laws and Laws of Conflict in Europe and Beyond*, (Oslo: Arena, 2009), p. 421 *et seq.*

Apart from the required ratification, there is no reason why the rights contained in the Charter could not be relied upon in court or invoked to establish an individual or collective complaint procedure. The EU should sign up to the European Social Charter, a move which would significantly bolster the Charter's status. A judicial forum under the framework of the Charter – a "European Court of Social Rights" – could supplement the network of existing European courts. Such a court could be established in complementarity to the European Court of Human Rights in Strasbourg. Alternatively, the monitoring of the Social Charter could be entrusted to the Strasbourg court. Both approaches would fulfil the same purpose: there is a need for a court which – unlike the ECJ/CJEU – does not give priority to upholding the principles of the single market, but, instead, aims to ensure that social rights finally become a central concern in Europe. This is not about legal chicaneries or jurisdiction tricks; it is simply a question of where and how the collision between social democracy and market-liberal economy can be articulated by law, but without priority rules automatically relegating social guarantees to the status of second-class rights.

2. If the observation is correct that securing a minimum standard of subsistence is crucial for inclusion and democratic participation, then this brings with it direct consequences for a socio-legal policy in Europe. The goal is to *establish a social EU citizenship by way of a nuanced system of guaranteed basic income.* Precarity and a lack of prospects have an exacerbating effect on Europe's crises: wage levels and purchasing power plummet while financial insecurity makes it more difficult for people to participate in democratic processes or to have a hand in shaping the future. The sociologist Pierre Bourdieu thus found that such increasingly precarious conditions gave rise to a new form of domination.[78] The right to a basic income could represent an important antidote to the fundamental insecurity felt by people in Europe. In this vein, the Committee on Employment and Social Affairs of the EU Parliament called on the Member States to provide for minimum-income schemes in order to "prevent poverty and social exclusion".[79]

In the report, the Committee finds that "social assistance in most Member States is already below a level which makes poverty a risk", *i.e.*, under 60 per cent of the national average income. Thus, the Committee calls for a differentiated minimum income for everyone in Europe based upon the income levels of the particular state. This social security system should guarantee a minimum income, while minimum wages should be introduced to combat wage dumping. The call for a minimum income is thus framed in terms of a fundamental entitlement. The system would not represent charitable hand-outs, but would,

---

78 Pierre Bourdieu, "Prekarität ist überall" (Precarity is everywhere), in: idem, *Gegenfeuer. Wortmeldungen im Dienste des Widerstands gegen die neoliberale Invasion*, (Konstanz: UVK, 1998), p. 96 *et seq.*

79 Report on Promoting Social Inclusion and Combating Poverty, Including Child Poverty in the EU, Committee on Employment and Social Affairs, A6–0364/2008 at 2 (a).

instead, ground actionable legal claims. The demand for a legally-enforceable minimum income in accordance with the economic situation of each country could inject new energy into the struggle for social rights in the European Union.[80]

The European Court of Justice, in a series of decisions on single-market integration and cross-border mobility, has found that all EU citizens – regardless of their nationality – should have access to social entitlements in their country of residence.[81] This lays the foundations for a form of EU citizenship, which would need to be attuned accordingly in a system of minimum income and expanded to include minimum wages and economic participation. We must aim to create a social EU citizenship that entails more than just cross-border mobility and anti-discrimination rights. This would guarantee a minimum level of subsistence, which could form the basis for further calls for co-determination rights and economic democratisation.

C. INSTITUTIONS OF TRANSNATIONAL SOCIAL RIGHTS

The question remains: In which forums can transnational social rights be enforced? The answer depends on whether the aim is of national, regional or worldwide enforceability.

National infrastructure has an important role to play in the enforceability of transnational social rights. It is not just the US legal system that allows for fundamental human rights to be enforced in a de-centralised manner – *i.e.*, before national courts. Through "role splitting",[82] national court decisions can write transnational legal history. National courts represent more than just an important addition to international institutions; they can – in themselves – drive the enforcement and strengthening of transnational social rights. In the *Pinochet* case, for instance, Spanish and British courts made a significant contribution to the protection against the arbitrary use of state power. In numerous cases, US courts – against the interests of US foreign policy – are playing a leading role in the enforcement of transnational law.

The existing regional and global forums for the protection of human rights must also be strengthened. This applies, first and foremost, to judicial practice. Here, pressure must be applied to ensure that national courts are obliged to take the statements of these and similar bodies into account. The organs of the

---

80 This could be linked with a model of different social corridors within the EU. See Klaus Busch, "The Corridor Model – Relaunched", Working-Paper, International Policy Analysis, (Berlin: Friedrich Ebert Foundation, 2011).

81 See Dawid Friedrich, Patrizia Nanz and Kerstin Blome, "Free Movement and the Emergence of European Social Citizenship", (2012) 41 *Österreichische Zeitschrift für Politikwissenschaft*, p. 383 *et seq.*

82 See note 15 above.

International Labour Organization that monitor observance of core labour standards must be strengthened, as must the complaint procedure of the OECD relating to adherence to the OECD Guidelines for multinational enterprises.

Non-state actors must, to a greater degree, be brought into the system of global jurisdiction. Transnational corporations as well as international organisations such as the United Nations and NATO must be subjected to the jurisdiction of human-rights forums. The same is true for transnational corporations.

VI. THE POLEMICS OF TRANSNATIONAL SOCIAL RIGHTS

The right to a minimum basic income, participation rights, the right to an undamaged environment, and the right to freedom of movement: all of these refer to the law of world society as we know it, while simultaneously suggesting an alternative. The promise of transnational social rights lies not in an elaborate blueprint for a better world order; instead, it is confined, at least for the moment, to the modest demand of allowing the inherent contradiction(s) in transnational law to emerge, so that the critical appropriation of human rights can find a way to gain traction in the arena of legal and political debate. We can use the language of human rights in order, finally, as Theodor Adorno put it, "to put a spark to all this antiquated mustiness, which may even blow it apart".[83]

Transnational social rights are thus directed in a polemical way against the existing system of rights. We thereby enter a conflict of laws. Without *pólemos*, that is, without a fight, without argument, without dissent, a new and different world will remain out of reach. Transnational social rights gently endeavour to achieve the coarsest demand: the ideal of emancipation.

---

83 Theodor W. Adorno and Hellmut Becker, "Education for Maturity and Responsibility", (1999) 12 *History of the Human Sciences*, pp. 21–34, at 24.

CHAPTER 3
NORMATIVE PERSPECTIVES ON TRANSNATIONAL SOCIAL RIGHTS

Georg LOHMANN

INTRODUCTION

The various modes of globalisation have made us conscious of the fact that the inequalities in life chances and increasing poverty are now the problems of a global society. The struggles against discrimination, exclusion and other forms of injustice can no longer solely be aligned within the respective state borders, but must, in order to be successful, (also) be conducted transnationally and globally. Social struggles emerge around concrete and local experiences of injustice. But then, the normative demands and justifications have to address the transnational roots of these injustices, and national actors tend to turn into international actors. Therewith, the framework of social struggles and of normative justification changes. The field ranges from voluntary, humanitarian aid to moral demands of global social justice and the enforcement of transnational social rights. Social rights, which traditionally protect and defend the life chances of citizens in a domestic frame, now need be conceived as transnational social rights and need transnational orientations and justifications. This chapter seeks to determine, from a philosophical point of view, which conceptual and argumentative problems can be found in these normative perspectives.

I. CONCEPTIONAL AND SYSTEMATIC CLARIFICATIONS

A. "TRANSNATIONAL SOCIAL RIGHTS" AS HUMAN RIGHTS

I would like to understand "transnational social rights" as *human rights*. Frequently, human rights are seen – unfortunately, particularly by moral philosophers – as purely "moral rights" which merely correspond to "moral obligations" for all. This is, in many ways, not just one-sided, but will frequently lead to false and distorting considerations and conclusions. Human rights, properly understood, have three dimensions, which cannot be reduced to one another: a moral, a legal, and a political-historical dimension.[1] They are motivated by historical processing of experiences of grave injustices and crimes against humanity; since the Second World War, international (political-given, legally-constituted and morally-justifiable) human rights, have been accredited in the same way to every human being in virtue of his or her human dignity.[2] Thus, philosophical reflections on human rights should not only methodically emanate from the legal (national and international) human-rights documents, but must also track each other's separate considerations in political and moral terms.

Human rights are "*global*" or "transnational" in two ways:

1) all human beings are bearers of these rights; and
2) corresponding duties have a transnational broadcast, *i.e.*, the bearers of the corresponding duties cannot merely be identified in the national, but must also be identified in the international or "global" realm. It remains unclear who, exactly, is backing the corresponding obligations: every single human being, all states, or staggered, multi-level subsidiary obligors?

Human rights are formulated in lists of rights, which traditionally can be differentiated in three or four substantial groups of *individual liberal rights, political and legal participatory rights, and social rights of participation.*[3] In spite of this substantial differentiation, all the groups belong together and are "universal, indivisible, interdependent and interrelated".[4] The concrete list of social human rights can both vary according to the conception of human rights and between one document and another (see, in particular, the *Universal Declaration of Human Rights* (UDHR), Articles 22–27, and, further, the *International Covenant on Economic, Social and Cultural Rights* (ICESCR).

---

1 Samantha Besson, "The Law in Human Rights Theory", (2013) 7 *Zeitschrift für Menschenrechte*, p. 120 *et seq*; see, already, Georg Lohmann, "Menschenrechte zwischen Moral und Recht", in: Stefan Gosepath and Georg Lohmann (eds), *Philosophie der Menschenrechte*, (Frankfurt aM: Suhrkamp Verlag, 1998), pp. 62–95.

2 For this differentiated and complex view of human rights, compare Arnd Pollmann and Georg Lohmann (eds), *Menschenrechte: Ein interdisziplinäres Handbuch*, (Stuttgart-Weimar: J.B. Metzler, 2012).

3 See Andreas Fischer-Lescano and Kolja Möller, Chapter 2 in this volume; see, also, Georg Lohmann, "Die unterschiedlichen Menschenrechte", in: Karl Peter Fritzsche and Georg Lohmann (eds), *Menschenrechte zwischen Anspruch und Wirklichkeit*, (Würzburg: Ergon, 2000), pp. 9–23.

4 Vienna Declaration and Programme of Action, World Conference on Human Rights, 12 July 1993, (UN-Doc. A/CONF.157/23, No.5.

Together they respect, protect and secure or enable the participation of every individual human being in the social, cultural and economic spheres of life. Instead of talking of "social" rights in general, one can, therefore, as in the ICESCR, more precisely talk of "economic, social and cultural" rights; in the following, I will use the more precise abbreviation of "ESC" rights in place of the term "social rights". How ESC-rights relate towards the other groups of rights is a contested question, however, and, below, I will defend a certain conception which sees them in equal unity with the other substantive groups.

B. NORMATIVE CONSIDERATIONS FROM A DUTY-BASED OR A RIGHT-BASED PERSPECTIVE

By the term a "normative perspective" on ESC-rights, I mean the discussion of the allegations and normative assets which go along with them, *i.e.*, their conceptual clarification and justification. Especially relevant here are, on the one hand, the assertions and justifications of *who* is the actual bearer of *what* specific human right(s) and, on the other hand, *who* is obligated by these ESC-rights to *what*, *i.e.*, which mandatory addressees are constituted by them and to what they are obliged. We therefore have – by definition – at least two normative perspectives: starting from the *bearers of rights* or from the *addressees of the obligations*. In the following, I will defend the thesis that we will arrive at considerably different results depending upon which perspective we actually follow. From a moral point of view, a duty-oriented perspective seems to be a comprehensive one, but I will argue that the rights-based perspective is the one which deals with human rights adequately, and that a duty-oriented perspective can, so to speak, be considered in the light of it.

In order to clarify the differing normative perspectives, I start very generally by looking at what the consequences are if someone is in need. By the term "need", we can distinguish between a situation in which someone is in "absolute need", which means that his or her life is in danger, or in which he or she is in "relative need", which means that his or her welfare is in danger.[5] Not all ESC-rights are aimed at protecting against or providing remedies for extreme emergencies and absolute poverty (absolute need), some are simply means of empowerment or of enabling people to lead a life with a guaranteed minimum welfare (relative need). However, in both cases, what a person in need has need of is help, support, and the absence of injuries and harm.

If we start with the situation in which other people (people A) are in need, for example, in existential emergencies such as disease, hunger, poverty, high mortality, *etc.*, traditionally they were the moral objects of voluntary help or Christian charity. In cases of voluntarily doing something good, one received

5 For the start, I ignore whether the need is self-inflicted or not.

praise when one helped, but was not blamed if one did not. Of these forms of aid which go beyond strict moral obligations (supererogative actions), the duties of the virtue of charity and helpfulness must be distinguished, to which a person B is prompted to act due to his or her good character and the prevailing customs and moral duties. Here, one receives praise for what one does voluntarily out of virtuousness, and one is blamed if one does not.

Ethics based upon emotions such as the ethics of compassion explain emergency aid as the result of a weak anthropological pre-disposition to feelings of pity or empathy, and they make it appear to be both wise and sensible not to harm others and to help those in need as best as one can.

Here, we have negative duties (the obligation to refrain) and positive duties (the obligation to act), but they depend on having certain feelings (e.g., sympathy) and are generally only conditioned and weak obligations. "Conditioned": if someone feels sympathy, *then* he or she should either do this or that or refrain from it. "Weak": if someone does not act in the manner in which he or she should according to this view, then he or she acts unwisely and one can accuse him or her of lacking compassion.

Only Immanuel Kant and comparable ethics justify unconditioned, universal moral obligations to help others in emergencies. Kant, however, makes a distinction between negative obligations of omission and positive obligations to act. Contrary to what is often assumed, Kant sees positive obligations, I believe, as equally stringently and generally justified as negative obligations; however, they are different in the way that they are "incomplete", for they do not specify what one precisely has to do in a situation in which one is supposed to help. The morally (by the categorical imperative) strictly-established duty to help leaves open what precise or specific action is adequate and reasonable in order to fulfil this duty. In this way, positive duties are "incomplete", *i.e.*, they have to be complemented by more than purely moral considerations and require wise judgement and the ability to act in a way which is appropriate to the situation. Therefore, Kant is treating them, in the *Metaphysik der Sitten*, as duties of virtue. Such moral duties depend on the inner belief and the conscientiousness of the individual helping. From the outside, they can, therefore, not be enforced by any outside means. Although, as we have learned from Adam Smith, the non-fulfilment of such a moral obligation produces affective responses such as a sense of guilt and accusations of guilt, and moral outrage and moral shame for those who are convinced of their duty. But these morally-affective reactions for non-compliance only have social-appellative pressure *if* the individual has a moral sense. This was also the reason why Kant did not want to base moral obligations on moral feelings.

So far, we have looked at the interpretations of "help in need" always from the view of the person (potentially) granting that help (person B), *i.e.*, from the perspective of the obligor. These interpretations change if we turn to look at "help in need" from the perspective of the one who is in need (person A). Here, we can distinguish three kinds of expressions of the person in need (A) towards the helping person (B):

1. A needy person A can *ask* for help; in these cases, the answering assistance by person B is a voluntary benefaction of mercy, charity or general humanity. Where assistance is granted, gratitude towards B is the appropriate response. Considering the gravity of emergencies, scandalous poverty and overlapping exclusions, a plea for help often appears to be inappropriate. If the emergency is too great and *forces* a request for help, it is no longer *asking* in the normal sense, but a pleading, or beseeching for help.
2. In these cases, a person in need can look for stronger affinities that he or she shares with the helping person, which he or she can invoke and which can be a motivation to help. He or she does not *ask*, but *appeals to a third party*: to a commonly-shared value conviction, a common ethical practice (e.g., of a mutual, virtuous helpfulness) or to rationally-justifiable moral beliefs that can *establish* moral obligations to help. The moral justification of auxiliary claims can strengthen the plea; it can be seen as a morally-justified claim, albeit not yet as a right.
3. Only in cases of the third type does the distressed person go beyond merely appellative claims of moral duties and *assert a "right" to assistance by others.* Person B is obliged *because* person A has a right.
4. "Duties" and "rights" are, philosophically speaking, not on the same systematic level: if B has a duty towards A, it does not mean that A has a right and *therefore* that B has a duty. This is especially obvious for moral philosophies in the Kantian tradition. If one talks of "rights", then one pre-supposes a new and different language game, and a new and different institution of the members of a "rights" community. To have a right means to be a recognised member in a community. Here, we need to distinguish entitlements that claim a merely *moral* right, from entitlements in which person A claims a *legal* right. Legal communities differ institutionally from merely moral communities. Unlike mere moral entitlements, in order to claim a right means: a) that the corresponding duties of others can be enforced in one way or another; and b) that there exists a form of legal remedy that can be called upon by the right-holder and that ensures the enforcement and compliance of a right.

Because these two notional implications of "right" can only be realised imperfectly for moral rights, they are – if we want to call them *rights* at all – *weak* rights. They are weak in the sense that the only means of enforcement are affective sanctions, as with moral obligations, and that the authority for complaints is the moral public that is being asked for a moral judgement. This weakness of moral rights does not, however, render them meaningless. In particular, its political significance lies in the fact that a person who claims a morally-justified right sees himself or herself as a generally recognised, and especially respectable and respected person. He or she claims a right for his or her own sake and is, therefore, able to fight for *his or her* right. And, of course, he or she can fight for his or her – so far only morally-granted – right to be converted into a legal regulatory right.

Even if one understands the normative claim to the transformation of weak moral rights into strong legal rights in the sense of natural law, legal human rights have to be a result of a political law-making process by a legitimate legislator. Thus, the above-mentioned substantive group of political human rights becomes important. Although there is not an explicit single human-right of or to democracy, taking all political rights together leads to the claim of democratic law-making. This is also the republican meaning of the post-1945 concept of human dignity, in which the bearer of the right should also become the author of his or her right.[6] It is this anti-paternalistic, democratic nature of human rights that ensures that the transformation process from purely moral rights into politically-set legal law is not a simple change of form, but a complicated historical process of law-making that reflects the intrinsic logic of law and politics.

II. WHAT OBLIGATIONS TO WHAT ADDRESSEES CORRESPOND TO THE ESC RIGHTS?

For the time being, from a rights-based perspective, the obligations corresponding with *human rights* are only legal obligations in the Kantian sense, which are limited to the externally enforceable forms of behaviour and action of others. They constitute *neither obligations towards oneself nor inner obligations* that concern inner attitudes or beliefs. This restriction and abstraction should also be noted when human rights are seen as only moral rights, which are not yet fully institutionalised.

Out of a liberalistic understanding of human rights that pre-dominated until the 1980s, it was believed that human rights only constitute negative injunctive obligations. Thus, social rights, which obviously were connected to positive obligations, were not even seen as proper human rights. This, for sure, was one of the reasons (others included the reservations of the colonial powers and the east-west conflict) why the only programmatic UDHR was juridified not in one, but in two international covenants, with considerable differences in

6 See Georg Lohmann, "Menschenwürde als 'Basis' von Menschenrechten", in: Jan C. Joerden, Eric Hilgendorf and Felix Thiele (eds), *Menschenwürde und Medizin: Ein interdisziplinäres Handbuch*, (Berlin: Duncker & Humblot, 2013), pp. 179–194.

design. From a liberal perspective (still strong in the US today) only the rights of the *International Covenant of Civil and Political Rights* (ICCPR) were seen as legally-binding rights, while the rights of the ICESCR were only seen as "manifesto" rights, that is, as declarations of intent. This liberalistic position has, by now, experienced profound critique and has been rejected by many experts of international law. I will not go into this interesting discussion here, but merely limit myself to mentioning the result. Human rights in general, but ESC rights in particular, correspond both to negative *and* to positive duties. The state of the debate can be found in the talk of a duty trias: the duty to respect, to protect, and to help or fulfil.[7]

Judging from the human rights set in the international human rights covenants (ICESCR), we have three groups of addressees of the corresponding obligations: first of all, the respective state in which a person lives. Second, if the state does not fulfil its duty or does not do so adequately, secondarily and subsidiarily, all the states of the treaty (and, in cases of customary international law, also those states that are not an explicit contracting party of the respective state) will become addressees of the corresponding obligations. Furthermore, all states are required to ensure that the people on their territories comply with human rights when interacting with each other. Thirdly, mediated through a duty of the state to protect, in a mode of "horizontal effect", *all people are indirectly obliged* to respect human rights in their civil interactions with one another.[8]

It remains, furthermore, contested as to whether all the obligations of the duty trias commit all the addressees in the same way; it is often said that they all have negative duties (duty to respect) but that only some – or all, but only in a staggered manner – have positive duties (the duty to protect and to help or fulfil). These and other questions become more tangible if we now consider the legal bailment and the political and legal institutions for the enforcement and realisation of these rights.

III. WHAT RIGHTS SHOULD BE INCLUDED IN THE LIST OF ESC RIGHTS?

The dispute between the two normative perspectives – duty-based or rights-based – shows its relevance, on the one hand, when it comes to the question of what rights should be included in the list of ESC rights, and, on the other hand, when we ask how the duties relating to them can and/or should be

7 See Henry Shue, *Basic Rights: Subsistence, Affluence and US Foreign Policy*, 2nd ed., (Princeton NJ: Princeton University Press, 1996).

8 The question of whether transnational corporations are also obliged by human rights is discussed below.

justified, enforced and imposed. However, I have to limit myself to more general considerations.

Dealing with questions of the justification of ESC rights, we have to distinguish, rather formal questions concerning social human rights in general, from specific, rather substantive questions that concern the justification of a specific ESC right. Since the list of individual social rights is historically open, it seems quite likely that we are dealing with a variety of perspectives of content here. The justification of one ESC right cannot simply be transferred to another; for example, we must establish the important cultural right to education (Article 13, ICESCR) with regard to content in a different way than the social right to an adequate standard of living (Article 11, ICESCR), or the economic right to union formation (Article 8 ICESCR). Nevertheless, and despite the differences in content, it makes sense to look for a unifying principle of ESC rights.

A solely duty-based perspective has to justify and construct ESC rights out of moral considerations. Here, we find quite different approaches, depending on the respective philosophical position. However, they often constitute only *some* of the ESC rights, or speak only of abstract, and very vaguely of, social rights. Moreover, they often understand ESC rights only as a means of securing other rights, and, therefore, seen systematically, determine them as secondary. If, for example, one assumes that everyone has a moral duty to protect the freedom or capacity of human beings to act through rights, then ESC rights emerge as the necessary forms of protection of this freedom or capacity to act. Starting from certain anthropological basic needs, interests and abilities, ESC rights will result from moral justifications regarding the obligations of the recognition and protection of these needs, interests and abilities. If one argues for a justice-based approach, ESC rights result from the obligation to ensure equal distribution of opportunities. In the first case, ESC rights are seen as a means of securing certain normative goals, in the second approach, they appear as an anthropological reportable list of substantive ways of consideration, and, in the third case, they are derived from the super-ordinated principle of obeying the norms of justice and are constructed via single cases. All of these exemplary, listed approaches contain quite acceptable considerations, and each of them is worthy of debate. But, as I would like to argue, they construct human rights from the wrong side and are too one-sided. They ultimately represent a form of moral paternalism and idealism, for, in the end, they determine human rights merely from a moral perspective and ignore their political and legal dimensions.

The fact that a human right is sufficiently justified morally does not automatically make it a legal right. For that, it needs both a political legislative process and a legal setting, either within the framework of a constitution as a fundamental right or as a recognised right of international law. Only by these legal and political settings and events, which are both based, in contrast to moral justification, upon decisions, are human rights adequately institutionalised. Only now can we ask about the contexts of justification and the setting, of legally enforcing and realising, and of complaining, which characterise the realisation and compliancy of human rights.

According to the right-based perspective which I am defending, I start methodically and heuristically from the legal constitution of the human rights. The question of which rights generally belong to the canon of ESC rights has, therefore, in a way, already been decided, and does not have to be lengthily constructed in a duty-based approach. This does not mean, however, that the ESC rights actually listed in the ICESCR are already the final answer to the question of which social rights should actually exist.[9] I do not defend a legal positivist position here. Therefore, considerations of the legal dimension of human rights are to be set, in each case, in relation to arguments from the other dimensions, *i.e.*, to the political setting and institutionalisation, and to moral justifiability (see below). In the actual struggle for human rights, all three dimensions are involved, and they interact in a systematic way, although they can, nevertheless, be distinguished at a theoretical-analytical level. In the following, I would like to discuss (or, at least, thematically present) some exemplary problems of a normative perspective, while, in each case, focusing on one dimension.

IV. A NORMATIVE PERSPECTIVE ON THE LEGAL DIMENSION OF ESC RIGHTS

A. LEGAL-IMMANENT NORMATIVE PROBLEMS: "HUMAN DIGNITY" AND THE "UNIFICATION OR SEPARATION MODEL" OF THE INTERNATIONAL COVENANTS OF 1966

ESC rights are legally established in different regional and international covenants and national constitutions.[10] I will discuss some aspects of this.

Initially, we can observe that the international law documents themselves refer to normative issues. In Article 1 of the UDHR, we find that "all human beings are born free and equal in dignity and rights", and that they "*should*

[9] See, for example, the struggle for water as a human right: Barbara Bleisch, "The Human Right to Water – Normative Foundations and Ethical Implications", (2006) 4 *Ethics and Economy*, pp. 1–23; Asit K. Biswas, Eglal Rached and Cecilia Tortajada (eds), *Water as a Human Right for the Middle East and North Africa*, (Oxford-New York: Routledge, 2008).

[10] See the corresponding articles in Pollmann and Lohmann (eds), note 2 above; Eibe Riedel, Gilles Giacca and Christophe Golay (eds), *Economic, Social, and Cultural Rights in International Law: Contemporary Issues and Challenges*, (Oxford: Oxford University Press, 2014).

act towards one another in a spirit of brotherhood". (my italics) The "spirit of brotherhood" has, since the French Revolution, evoked the moral demands for solidarity, justice and "a dignified life" by which *social* human-rights can be justified.[11] In the preamble of the ICESCR, it explicitly states that "these rights derive from the inherent dignity of the human person".

This notion of human dignity was re-designed in the international human rights documents after the Second World War. It has become a new normative foundation of human rights and has gradually established itself globally in this function. This notion of dignity differs from others (general and special dignity terms) which, before 1945, were always associated with obligations towards both oneself and towards others, but not with the possession of rights. This is (see above), however, what the concept of human dignity has claimed since 1945. At the same time, according to a republican understanding, human dignity demands that all people are not only the bearers of human rights but also that they are the selfsame authors of the laws in which these rights are constituted.[12] Thus, the normative basis of the human rights referred to in the human rights documents has a strong democratic and anti-paternalistic substance. Accordingly, they demand that social rights *not* be separated from other substantive human rights classes (liberal and political rights), as some state socialist interpretations have suggested. They must, I believe, be understood in a way (in accordance with the "model of unification") that calls for the interaction and inter-relationship of the two International Covenants of 1966, the ICPCR and the ICESCR.[13] What this means for the determination of social rights is that they are to be determined by the political participation of relevant stakeholders. This is especially true for the determination of what specific services can be reasonably expected from the state as the addressee of social rights. This will necessarily be a process of political negotiation, and will have to take the economic and other available resources of the state into account.

---

11 Georg Lohmann, "Human dignity and socialism", in: Marcus Düwell, Jens Braarvig, Roger Brownsword and Dietmar Mieth (eds), *The Cambridge Handbook of Human Dignity: Interdisciplinary Perspectives*, (Cambridge: Cambridge University Press, 2014), pp. 126–134.

12 I have explained this in more detail in Georg Lohmann, "Die rechtsverbürgende Kraft der Menschenwürde. Zum menschenrechtlichen Würdeverständnis nach 1945", (2010) *Zeitschrift für Menschenrechte*, pp. 46–63; idem, "Menschenwürde als 'Basis' von Menschenrechten", note 6 above.

13 This is also pointed out by Chisanga Puta-Chekwe and Nora Flood, "From Division to Integration: Economic, Social, and Cultural Rights as Human Rights", in: Isfahan Merali and Valerie Oosterveld (eds), *Giving Meaning to Economic, Social, and Cultural Rights*, (Philadelphia PA: University of Pennsylvania Press, 2001), p. 39 *et seq.*

B. THE NORMATIVE OF THE "GENERAL COMMENTS"

The complex, uneven and slow progress of the enforcement of ESC rights within international law again cannot be treated in detail here. However, I wish to emphasise the "Concluding Observations" and the "General Comments" that the ESC Committee have published since 1989,[14] which have outlined the right-internal, normative perspective on ESC rights in a very challenging way, precisely because they reject excessive interpretations and only make recommendations. If the international and national institutionalisations followed these recommendations, this would be a great gain in the fight for the realisation of social rights.

C. LEVELS OF GLOBAL OBLIGATIONS

Do ESC rights legally have a global radiation? In the ICESCR, each contracting state is to undertake:

> "steps, individually and through international assistance and co-operation, especially economic and technical, to the maximum of its available resources, with a view to achieving progressively the full realization of the rights recognized in the present Covenant by all appropriate means, including particularly the adoption of legislative measures." (Article 2.1)

This may sound like the maximum of pretentious commitment to opportuneness and randomness. But it is the case that, as is often the case with human rights, rhetorical confessions in a written form are transformed into normative standards that then have (or may have) an unexpected political effect. It seems crucial to me that, for a start, the states are willing to see themselves as the first recipients of the obligations corresponding to the ESC rights. This is not only important in normative terms, but also in a factual sense: many ESC rights require the long-term institutionalisation of complex organisations, for example, for the right to education, the establishing of a complex school system, which, in each case, must first be done at national level. And, at the same time, the states must undertake to report internationally on their progress in implementing human rights; and this, it seems to me, is the key step that enables the global range of ESC rights legally. For example, an attempt could be made to create an International Social Court, just as one should have a national social jurisdiction, in order to make individual complaint possible, as contained in the concept of

---

14 See the reports of the Committee on Economic, Social and Cultural Rights available at: www.ohchr.org/en/hrbodies/cescr/pages/cescrindex.aspx. See, also, Riedel, Giacca and Golay (eds), note 10 above.

human rights. The fact that this seems utopian, and politically perhaps neither necessary nor desirable, is another question.

What is crucial here is that, even in the legal dimension of ESC rights, we have an albeit staggered and subsidiary, yet global range of obligations. But it does not commit all the people directly; *i.e.*, the right to education of a person in India does not oblige me to enable him or her to attend school or to ensure that girls have the same opportunities to attend school, *etc.*

However, every person is obliged, mediated through the actions of his or her government, to ensure that his or her state fulfils his or her human rights obligations. Furthermore, he or she further has to make sure that his or her own state participates in an appropriate manner in the international control of its duties, and, where necessary, that it also fulfils its subsidiary duties.

V. SOME REMARKS ON A NORMATIVE PERSPECTIVE ON THE POLITICAL DIMENSION OF ESC RIGHTS

A. POLITICAL STRUGGLES FOR ESC RIGHTS

In general, ESC rights need the political participation of the holder of the rights. Thus, they call for a better, democratic structure of the given policy structures. Of course, ESC rights, like all human rights, are tools in the political struggle for power. And, very often, they are merely an instrument to particular political interests. Thus, the socialist countries tried to favour social human rights at the expense of freedom and political rights. Actually, they institutionalised no real human rights, but only limited basic state supplies with massive restrictions to freedom.

But even after the collapse of the Communist regimes, they have been both the target of, and subject to, political social struggles in general. The classic socially-oriented parties are fighting for an improvement of ESC rights, and because ESC-rights are forced to depend on the political participation and co-decision of the stakeholder (see above), internationally-oriented NGOs support local and international efforts both to improve and to realise ESC rights. While these political struggles were initially limited to the national sphere, they are increasingly becoming internationally-oriented in important areas (development policy, the balancing of the effects of globalisation, global poverty reduction, international health policy, *etc.*).

B. ON THE NORMATIVITY OF POLITICAL LEGAL SETTLEMENTS: DEMOCRATISATION AND ESC RIGHTS

These political struggles manifest themselves in the national and global political public-spheres, where struggles about legal texts and moral justifications take place and where contested subjects are transformed into politically-relevant decisions. "Weak publics" of opinion formation aim at becoming "strong publics" of institutional decision-making procedures. In fact, we have very inadequate structures which reflect the given interests and power structures. From a human rights perspective, the *democratisation and constitutionalisation of international law* are necessary requirements here.[15] With regard to the realisation of ESC rights, democratisation is necessary for yet another reason, too: Amartya Sen has shown that, in the long term, the democratisation of a society is the most effective means of poverty reduction.[16]

C. NEW AND MORE PROBLEMS OF GLOBAL OBLIGATIONS

From the perspective of ESC rights, the diverse ways of globalisation have very different, often ambivalent, consequences. "Politics" is challenged by these processes in quite a new way. The given political structures of global governance are often inadequate, ineffective and, at best, have a slowdown effect (see above.) Although the international community is trying to improve the situation of social rights (see, for instance, the poverty reduction programme in 2000[17]), to date, there is a lack both of the political pressure and of the power that would be needed to achieve the respective decisions.

Now new potential addressees of obligations come into sight. International companies often violate the fundamental conditions for a decent life that have been formulated in ESC rights. In order to do this, they take advantage of the fact that the respective national legal systems of the countries in which they have outsourced their production (and they may re-locate again if it suits their economic interests) are often catastrophically weak, corrupt or ineffective. In my opinion, the attempts by international corporations to escape legal control, for example, by voluntarily undertaking "corporate social responsibility" (CSR)

---

15 I cannot go into this here, but see Georg Lohmann, "Menschenrechte zwischen Verfassung und Völkerrecht", in: Marten Breuer *et al.*, (eds), *Der Staat im Recht*, (Berlin: Dunker & Humblot, 2013), pp. 1175–1188.

16 Amartya Sen, *Development as Freedom*, (New York: A.A. Knopf, Inc., 1999).

17 See The Millennium Development Goals Report 2012, UN Development Report.

within the framework of a Global Compact, are to be viewed as ambivalent.[18] From a right-based perspective, the duties which they are obliged to respect are clear. From a duty-based perspective, however, this seems to be far from clear and is connected with a lot of philosophical problems.[19]

VI. A NORMATIVE PERSPECTIVE ON THE MORAL DIMENSION OF ESC RIGHTS

A. JUSTIFICATIONS IN GENERAL AND THE POLITICAL IMPORTANCE OF PLURALISM OF JUSTIFICATION

From the moral point of view, the justification of social rights has to be established first in general, and then specifically for individual ESC rights. Many moral philosophers displace the problem and search for the justification of moral obligations, which they assume accompanies social rights. Their paradigmatic conceptual model is that one has to ask oneself why one is obliged to help other people in the world who are in need, or why one is, in certain respects, obliged to provide others with housing, food, *etc.*[20] I believe that this model approach is too simplistic, that it suggests misleading questions and false conclusions, and that it often resolves issues (or tries to resolve them) which, from a right-based perspective, have, I believe, already been solved. However, I cannot explore the critique of the duty-based perspective here.

In a rights-based approach, as I said, the mere fact that a right is found in an International Covenant does not establish a moral justification for that right. But what precisely has to be justified? A right, as such, does not become justified, but, first of all, conceptually explicated. What need to be justified are the normative assertions and normative claims that are associated with a right. Take, for example, "the right of everyone to an adequate standard of living …" (Article 11.1 ICESCR). In this article, the normative claims are explicated further, and a *General Comment* explains the associated normative assertions and demands towards the state parties.

---

18 See, for example, Philip Alston (ed), *Non-State Actors and Human Rights*, (Oxford: Oxford University Press, 2006); John Ruggie, "Guiding Principles on Business and Human Rights: Implementing the United Nations 'Protect, Respect and Remedy' Framework", *Report of the Special Representative of the Secretary-General on the Issue of Human Rights and Transnational Corporations and Other Business Enterprises*, 21 March 2011, A/HRC/17/31.

19 For a good discussion, see Christian Neuhäuser, *Unternehmen als moralische Akteure*, (Frankfurt aM: Suhrkamp Verlag, 2011).

20 Peter Singer, in particular, has initiated this model discussion with his paradigmatic case: "Who is Obligated to Rescue a Drowning Child and What is he Obliged to? See Peter Singer, *The Life you can Save*, (New York: Random House, 2009).

What has to be justified in particular are the resulting, staggered obligations of others. But a moral justification claims to be justified not just towards these addressees, but, quite simply, to be justified, that is to say, *objectively* justified. An acceptable justification has to prove itself in the realm of reason. It does not depend on decisions, but on the conviction that there are good reasons for a claim. Philosophically, we have to accept at this point that we have different, competing conceptions and ideas of what a justification actually is. The same is true for the question of whether a problematical assertion is justified or not. This ultimate indeterminacy is, however, not an argument by which to abandon the claim of justifiability as such. Rather, human rights are based upon the assumption that any restriction of freedom needs to be justified to the bearers of rights and any obligation has to be justified to the obligor. They are based upon the culturally-rooted appreciation of the ability to self-determination of each human being; and this is one of the important constitutive features of the concept of human dignity since 1945. The idea that the normative claims of human rights and the duties associated with them must be justified, follows, I believe, from the new normative foundation of the post-1945 human rights: from a new interpretation of human dignity as pre-constitutional principle (GR. *axia*).[21] They have, however, no final normative foundation and are, therefore, like all human inventions, not eternal but finite and historically changeable. Human rights are, therefore, a historical project, even though they claim to hold a non-relative, universal justification for their normative implications.

I would now like to argue that this universal justification claim can be redeemed in various ways. We have a pluralism of approaches of justification, as I have already pointed out above. For sure, the dispute regarding what kind of justification is acceptable for a specific claim, what is true, what is false, is initially a philosophical and a scientific dispute. But a philosophical expert judgement appears in the public dispute over adequate justification only in the form of the public opinion of a citizen. Therefore, it cannot receive recognition as an expert judgement unless it is able to convince other citizens. Now, moral arguments are strong arguments in public debates, just as rights in liberal societies can function as trumps. But they are only "strong arguments" because they can count on an "accommodative" public culture of human rights, which functions, as it were, as the last horizon against which one can argue about human rights in a meaningful way. This is one reason why the human rights declarations and International Covenants contain general claims relating to the cultivation and fostering of such a human rights culture; and this is also why the United Nations Educational, Scientific and Cultural Organization (UNESCO) translates these claims into educational activities.

---

[21] See Lohmann, "Menschenwürde als 'Basis' von Menschenrechten", note 6 above.

B. GLOBAL JUSTICE OR HUMAN DIGNITY AS THE NORMATIVE PRINCIPLES OF THE ESC RIGHTS?

The most demanding moral theories to justify the corresponding normative assertions of ESC rights are theories of justice. We have here, following John Rawls, a number of different theoretical approaches that have come about as particular theories of global justice with remarkable results.[22]

From a duty-based perspective, they can justify far-reaching moral duties which include, especially in terms of social justice, the mutual and universal obligation of all people to a just distribution of goods, a fair equality in exchange relationships and help in emergency situations. From a cosmopolitan view of global justice, for instance, Charles R. Beitz[23] and Thomas Pogge[24] demand a global equitable distribution of goods to enable a minimum standard of living for all people. Beitz and Pogge are using arguments of Rawls, who had expressly limited these arguments exclusively to national circumstances, to the relations of the states. The hypothetical original position is expanded to international relations, and the "veil of ignorance" also hides to which state (rich or poor) the rational actor belongs. Thus, the contractarian justification procedure calls for not only the same individual and political freedoms for all, but also the global validity of the difference principle. Therefore, a re-distribution of goods follows, in order to improve the position of the world's most disadvantaged people.[25] Although Pogge emphasises that he understands human rights in a manner in which the duties corresponding to them are addressed to an international institutional order, the resulting obligations nonetheless only fulfil a purely moral perspective. And although he differs from Peter Singer with this mediating institutional approach, after which people worldwide are directly obliged to aid and re-distribution mutually,[26] the result of his considerations fits a duty-based perspective.[27]

---

22 See, for example, Simon Caney, *Justice Beyond Borders: A Global Political Theory*, (Oxford: Oxford University Press, 2005); David Miller, *National Responsibility and Global Justice*, (Oxford: Oxford University Press, 2007; Christoph Broszies and Henning Hahn (eds), *Globale Gerechtigkeit*, (Frankfurt aM: Suhrkamp Verlag, 2010); my view: Georg Lohmann, "Globale Gerechtigkeit, Menschenrechte und korrespondierende Pflichten. Eine Skizze", in: Hans-Helmuth Gander (ed), *Menschenrechte: Philosophische und juristische Positionen*, (Freiburg-Munich: Alber, 2009), pp. 35–58.

23 Charles R. Beitz, *Political Theory and International Relations*, (Princeton NJ: Princeton University Press, 1979), new edition 1999.

24 Thomas Pogge, *World Poverty and Human Rights*, (Cambridge: Polity Press, 2002).

25 See Thomas Pogge, "Rawls and Global Justice", (1988) 18 *Canadian Journal of Philosophy*, p. 233.

26 See, for example, Peter Singer, *Practical Ethics*, 3rd ed., (Cambridge: Cambridge University Press, 2011).

27 Wolfgang Kersting, "Globale Rechtsordnung oder weltweite Verteilungsgerechtigkeit?", (1995/96) *Politisches Denken Jahrbuch*, p. 226 *et seq.*

Such theories of justice do have their independent and political value. But the idea of justice is wider than the idea of human rights and human rights themselves are only a sub-class of possible moral rights. Thus, theories of justice capture too much on one side, and too little on the other. Compared with the situation resulting from human-rights obligations, they demand too much, because they really need to demand an optimum of justice, whereas a restriction on minimum standards appears contingent. They also demand too little, because, in its purely moral terms, the necessary political participation to decide upon the living standards cannot be taken into account appropriately.[28]

I believe, therefore, that theories of human dignity offer a corrective alternative here. Certainly, they need to understand the concept of human dignity, as indicated in the post-1945 human rights documents. "Human dignity" is determined from the outset in the three dimensions of law, politics and morality. As a legal concept, human dignity allows each person the same self-esteem and self-respect because of his or her equal legal position with all other people. As a political term, it stands for the claim of every human being not only to be a holder of human rights, but also to act with others as the author of his or her rights. As a moral concept, human dignity stands for the universal consideration, feasible in his or her deliberate, self-determined, bodily and spiritual life. "Human dignity" thus functions as a pre-legal or pre-constitutional basis for human rights. It allows the unity of the different groups of the human rights to be defended as a unifying moral principle.[29]

Respect for human dignity includes the criterion of moral justice, as it calls for the impartial treatment of all. But the human dignity approach has, from the outset, added the demand for democratic participation and legal institutionalisation. How this can be done in detail and with reference to the ESC rights in particular has still to be shown. The philosophical perspective can try to emphasise the plurality of normative justifications for transnational social rights and their challenges. It is in social and political struggles that actors choose their respective conceptual framework. The aim of this contribution has been to show how encompassing and well-founded struggles for transnational social rights are, and that their realisation justifies the effort to realise all human rights.

---

28 Both authors have changed their approach now: Charles R. Beitz, *The Idea of Human Rights*, (Oxford: Oxford University Press, 2009); Pogge, note 24 above, second edition, 2008.

29 See Jürgen Habermas, "The Concept of Human Dignity and the Realistic Utopia of Human Rights", (2010) 41 *Metaphilosophy*, pp. 464–480.

CHAPTER 4

CONCEPTUALISING TRANSNATIONAL SOCIAL RIGHTS: DEVELOPMENTS AND FORMS

Alexandra KAASCH

I. INTRODUCTION

As has been elaborated on in the introduction to this volume, there are numerous ways of approaching transnational social rights. This chapter maps and conceptualises transnational social rights from a global social policy perspective. This fulfils two aims: on the one hand, it provides an alternative approach to the study and understanding of transnational social rights; on the other, it contributes to the literature on global social policy by adding to recent attempts at conceptualising and theorising this field of study.[1]

Case studies are one approach used in the literature on global social policy.[2] Theory-testing has also been used as a way to refine and improve existing global social policy concepts.[3] Bob Deacon and Paul Stubbs[4] have applied common concepts from sociological theory (agency, structure, institution, and discourse) to the study of global social policy, and some chapters in a volume on global social governance[5] approach the theorisation of global social policy and

1 See the Special Issue of (2013) 13 *Global Social Policy*, issue 1, available at: http://gsp.sagepub.com/content/13/1.toc.

2 See, for example, Bernhard. Leubolt, "Institutions, Discourse and Welfare: Brazil as a Distributional Regime", (2013) 13 *Global Social Policy*, pp. 66–83.

3 See, for example, Alexandra Kaasch, "Contesting Contestation: Global Social Policy Prescriptions on Pensions and Health Systems", (2013) 13 *Global Social Policy*, pp. 45–65.

4 Bob Deacon and Paul Stubbs, "Global Social Policy Studies: Conceptual and Analytical Reflections", (2013) 13 *Global Social Policy*, pp. 5–23.

5 Alexandra Kaasch and Kerstin Martens (eds), *Actors and Agency in Global Social Governance*, (Oxford: Oxford University Press, 2015).

governance with reference to inter- and intra-actor relationships,[6] and as a meta-theoretical concept.[7]

Nevertheless, it is not only the way, but also the understanding of what exactly makes a theory or a concept, and what the appropriate process of theory-building is, that differs between different scholars and disciplines.[8] At the most general level, theory-building has to do with making sense of something. Often, it is associated with explanations about what is causing a particular, observed outcome (causal models or relationships). A theory, though, also has to do with a generalisation, and, therefore, theory-building can also take the form of establishing typologies and systematising observed phenomena, which then facilitates further, more detailed, and causal theoretical arguments.

This chapter focuses on the systematisation of transnational social rights as one element of global social policies (along with global social re-distribution and regulation). In particular, the meaning of the "social" in global social policy is central here, which contributes to a refined concept of global social policy, and related governance structures, and in this way specifies the meaning and importance of transnational social rights as well.

Despite this explicit and strong connection to the global social policy literature, rather than discussing global social policy as struggles over policy ideas and discourses, this chapter is interested in the processes of the transnational legalisation of international social rights. Although it connects to other global social policy literature in putting a particular emphasis on global social policy actors and the development of a supranational global social policy, the focus is on the legalisation and rights discourses concerning transnational social rights.

II. CONCEPTUALISING GLOBAL SOCIAL POLICY

Global social policy as an academic field has seen a significant increase of studies and publications over the past two decades or so. It has been conceptualised, in particular, in the work of Bob Deacon, Mitchell Orenstein, and Nicola Yeates.[9]

---

6 See Kaasch, note 3 above.

7 Bob Jessop, "Global Social Policy and Its Governance: A Cultural Political Economy Approach", in: Kaasch and Martens (eds), note 5 above.

8 See Karl E. Weick, "Theory Construction as Disciplined Imagination", (1989) 14 *The Academy of Management Review*, pp. 516–517.

9 See Bob Deacon, *Global Social Policy and Governance*, (London-Thousand Oaks CA: SAGE Publications, 2007), and Bob Deacon, Michelle Hulse and Paul Stubbs, *Global Social Policy: International Organizations and the Future of Welfare*, (London: SAGE Publications, 1997), Mitchell A. Orenstein, "The New Pension Reform as Global Policy", (2005) 5 *Global Social Policy*, pp. 175–202, and Nicola Yeates, "Social Politics and Policy in an Era of Globalisation: Critical Reflections", (1999) 33 *Social Policy and Administration*, pp. 372–93, and idem,

Global social policy, in this stream of the literature, is understood as consisting of two forms: prescriptions for national social policy, and emerging supranational social policy.[10] The term "supranational" in this context – in contrast to the discussion about the different connotations with "global" and "transnational" (see below) – refers to the observation that there are forms of a genuine social policy at transnational policy levels. This could be described as having the character of an emerging, though very limited, global welfare state.[11] The term "supranational" is used in this context because it concerns an independent form of social policy, as we find at regional levels (in the EU in particular). Transnational social rights are one element of this "supranational global social policy". Their development and meaning is strongly linked with the other two elements – global social redistribution and regulation. Global social redistribution encompasses the various forms of development aid, global taxes, remittances, and other mechanisms that enable goods, services and financial means to travel and to be (re-) distributed transnationally. Regulation includes international or global labour and social standards, trade matters, voluntary codes of conduct by business, global tax regulation and migration. The social rights component fulfils the function of protecting the individual who is affected by these global processes, or who happens to live in a place with low national social rights protection. Theoretically, transnational social rights also have a negative dimension; for example, when transnational enterprises refrain from particular, hazardous production modes or working conditions. However, in the concept of global social policy presented here, this would form part of the regulation side (which includes voluntary codes of conducts).[12]

The meaning, and usefulness, of *global* in the term "global social policy" is contested, and it is difficult to come to a definite conclusion on whether or not it is suitable. *Global* can be used to refer to a specific dimension of social policy-making, and a particular type of actors and processes involved in social policy, which goes beyond the nation state. The actors concerned are different kinds of organisations that are comprised of regional or global groups of governments and/or various types of civil society organisations (CSOs), business organisations, professional organisations and so on. The processes of policy formulation and/or decision-making are different from those of national policy-making in that they are legitimated in other ways than national

---

"The Idea of Global Social Policy", in: idem (ed), *Understanding Global Social Policy*, 1st ed. (Bristol-Chicago IL: Policy Press, 2008), p. 1.

10 See Deacon, note 9 above, p. 1.

11 For discussion, see Lutz Leisering, "Gibt es einen Weltwohlfahrtsstaat? [Is there a Global Welfare State?], in: Mathias Albert and Rudolf Stichweh (eds), *Weltstaat und Weltstaatlichkeit: Beobachtungen globaler politischer Strukturbildungen*, (Wiesbaden: Verlag für Sozialwissenschaften, 2007), pp. 185–205.

12 For more details on these concepts, see Deacon, note 9 above, and Deacon, Hulse and Stubbs, note 9 above; regular overviews of recent developments are provided by the *Global Social Policy* Digest.

(democratic) procedures (e.g., through mandates by member states and through the specification and interpretation of these mandates by the organisations themselves) and often less, or at least differently, organised (e.g., as networks, policy-learning processes).[13] It needs to be taken into account that there is a disagreement about the usefulness of *global* versus *transnational*. This is due to the connotation of *global* to be applicable in the same way at any place and time (*universal* applicability). The disadvantage of the term *transnational*, however, is that it is – literally – still attached to "the national" while global social policy concepts also include forms of a "truly" (supranational) global social policy, including the development of social rights law. In addition, global social policy studies have also focused on the relationships between global actors (independent of the power of, and their relationships with, their member states). In both cases, the processes are neither exclusively, nor always, shaped by the unit of the nation state. *Transnational*, thus, is rather a useful term when the issue to be explained still connects to national re-distribution, regulation and rights, or in studies that trace the transfer and translation of policies into national contexts.

At the same time, the "*social* (policy)" part of the "global social policy" definition often lacks special discussion. On the one hand, it is frequently observed that ever more policy-fields go global. On the other, there is an increasing tendency to "socialise" globalisation – meaning that ever more aspects of today's globalised world are framed as issues of social policy. While it is certainly true that narrow concepts of clearly distinguishable policy-fields are problematical (as such fields tend to overlap and to depend on each other), looking for appropriate concepts and theories in the study of global social policy, boundaries are a pre-requisite in order to be precise on forms and general mechanisms. This chapter focuses on one particular element within global social policy, namely, transnational social rights, in order to engage with questions of the "social" in global social policy.

Furthermore, Mitchell Orenstein defines global social policies as "those that are developed, diffused, and implemented with the direct involvement of global policy actors and coalitions at or across the international, national or local levels of governance".[14] Global social governance is understood as a multi-actored process of shaping global and national social policies.[15] It involves different types of actors that interact and exert influence over policies by means of collaborative, as well as individual, agency. The mandates and spheres of influence may be overlapping, and specific actors may function in different and multiple roles. The relationships between actors can be characterised by consensual, as well as

---

13 See, for example, Christina Boswell, "The Political Functions of Expert Knowledge: Knowledge and Legitimation in European Union Immigration Policy", (2008) 15 *Journal of European Public Policy*, pp. 471–488.

14 See Orenstein, note 9 above, p. 177.

15 See Deacon, *Global Social Policy and Governance*, note 9 above.

contestational, modes.[16] Struggles over positions drive global social governance, irrespective of whether the content issue is highly or only slightly controversial – global social policy actors are legitimacy-seeking agencies that depend on multiple forms of external and international, long-term as well as short-term, mandates. These mandates are closely related to the governance mechanisms at the disposal of different global actors, and the scope or leeway for developing influence over a social policy issue. Although the transnational social rights concepts developed in this chapter build upon this, it does not engage with their political struggles, but is, instead, interested in the development of social rights as human rights, and the functions of international organisations in putting such rights into international treaties. Nevertheless, this chapter is not about the success of ESCRs in terms of the justiciability, but is an attempt to capture global social policy as a set of social rights emerging and developing at global policy levels.

III. TRANSNATIONAL SOCIAL RIGHTS

While transnational social rights have been considered and conceptualised as an important element of supranational global social policy, they have been little defined as such. There are some contributions, however, usually with regard to particular rights, such as the right to health.[17] This chapter attempts to systematise transnational social rights by distinguishing two forms – those rights that are related to a particular group of (vulnerable) people, and those related to particular social problems.[18] Although this is primarily an exercise of mapping and conceptualisation, some comments will be made about the practical application of the distinction between the two forms of rights (see Section IV).

Most generally, social rights are those rights that are related to the means which enable people to live their lives and take part in societal life.[19] They concern the needs of persons who cannot look after themselves, and social problems or needs that require action by someone other than the person

---

16 See Kaasch, note 3 above.

17 See Wolfgang Hein and Lars Kohlmorgen, "Global Health Governance: Conflicts on Global Social Rights, (2008) 8 *Global Social Policy*, pp. 80–108. See, also, Gunilla Backman *et al.*, "Health Systems and the Right to Health: An Assessment of 194 Countries", (2008) 372 *The Lancet*, pp. 2047–85, available at: www.thelancet.com/journals/lancet/article/PIIS0140-6736(08)61781-X/abstract.

18 In addition, but not addressed in this chapter, there are overarching rights that relate to broader social problems or groups, such as the right not to be poor, the right to development or the right to an adequate standard of living.

19 Hartley Dean, "Social Policy and Human Rights: Re-thinking the Engagement", (2007) 7 *Social Policy & Society*, pp. 1–12.

affected.[20] Accordingly, granting and realising social rights to a significant extent involves resources,[21] and is connected to different forms of re-distribution within societies, as well as to regulation to make sure that particular practices which threaten or harm social rights cannot be sustained.

While the institutionalisation of social rights in national contexts is strongly dependent on the policy and politics of political parties and interest groups, and can be studied as the evolution of welfare states, studying *transnational social rights* needs to be approached by considering global political agencies, structures and institutions.

In this context, though, the definitions introduced above for global social policy more generally, are not fully applicable. The "global" carries different meanings and problems depending on the form, field or issue of global social policy addressed. The processes of defining and adopting "global" social rights are rather *international* ones. The discourses over social rights could be classified as *transnational* or *global*. The application might be a *global* (ideally universal) one, but this is not uncontested as the very concept of social rights is not globally shared, but is, instead, linked to Northern welfare-state conceptions – while some argue that "Southern" social rights, such as those of the *Nuevo* constitutionalism in Latin America – globalise much more easily than Western-rights traditions. At the same time, in combination with global social redistribution and regulation, social rights have been conceptualised, and claimed for – as part of an evolving "supranational global social policy"[22] – an approach that has also grown out of Northern welfare-state traditions and scholarship.

By engaging with social rights as part of (global) human rights, and trying to understand the concept and development of (global) social rights, this chapter is concerned about the "social" element and its meaning. What are social rights? What problems or groups do they connect to? How are they institutionalised at trans- or *supra*-national policy levels?

The meaning of social rights and their degree of realisation have been approached in different ways, for example, from national concepts of social rights to global notions of social rights, or by making distinctions between different forms of universal human rights. Social rights also appear as claims within transformative approaches to what the world should look like from a social policy perspective.

Ramesh Mishra in his contribution "Towards a Global Social Policy" in the *Global Social Policy Reader*,[23] links his discussion of global social rights to the

---

20 Anna Maciejczyk Jaron, "Constitutional Courts as Actors of Fundamental Social Rights", in EUI Social and Labour Law Working Group (ed.): *EUI Working Paper LAW 2009/05*, San Domenico di Fiesole: EUI.

21 For example, Deacon, note 9 above.

22 Ibid.

23 Ramesh Mishra, "Towards a Global Social Policy", in: Nicola Yeates and Chris Holden (eds), *The Global Social Policy Reader*, (Bristol: Policy Press, 2009), pp. 275–280.

development of citizenship in the modern democratic state. Instead of accepting welfare as being bound to stigmatising charity, first social-democratic type welfare states, and subsequently basically all Western countries, connected their welfare states with the institutions of rights or entitlements. This also comes with the idea of universalism – that the right should apply to all citizens of a state. Based upon this concept, Mishra highlights the difficulties of realising social rights, as the conflicts with economic or property rights, which – in a capitalist society – have an important status, and are not easily limited. Mishra adds a discussion about the Westernised idea of individual rights *versus* more community-related rights that might be better understood in other parts of the world, and he questions the tendency of rights to define minimum standards.

Stephen Marks shows how national developments in Mexico and Russia (notably not just the "Western world"), influenced the Constitution of the International Labour Organization (ILO) in 1919, and international labour standards. These developments reflected what he calls a "second generation of human rights, characterized by intervention rather than the abstention of the state. Indeed, the rights to decent working condition, to social security, to education, and to health were inconceivable without an active role by the state. The human rights emerged in the second generation were *claims* rather than freedoms, *positive* rather than negative".[24]

More generally, parallel to the national developments, as a consequence of the experience of the world wars, a process of developing a universal human rights canon took place in the 1940s. The concrete idea of defining human rights has been linked to an initiative of the former US President Franklin D. Roosevelt, who claimed four basic individual rights that should be granted to any individual, which included "freedom from want".[25]

The history of transnational social rights, viewed as part of a UN process on universal human rights, reflects many of the problems and ambiguities of defining and realising transnational social rights. The debates about social rights emerged as part of the development of the universal human rights body. At the most general level, "[i]nternational human rights are those human needs that have received formal recognition as rights through the sources of international law".[26] The institution through which this mainly happens at a global level is the United Nations General Assembly.

Social rights have been defined by the Universal Declaration of Human Rights (UDHR), a key and universal, but non-binding document. They are distinguished from civil and political rights, and have been adopted, together with economic and cultural rights, in the International Covenant on Economic,

24 Stephen P. Marks, "Emerging Human Rights: A New Generation for the 1980s?", (1980–1981) 33 *Rutgers Law Review*, p. 435, at 438.

25 www.fdrlibrary.marist.edu/pdfs/fftext.pdf.

26 Marks, note 24 above, at 436–7.

Social and Cultural Rights (ICESCR) (1966) – a legally-binding document, accessible to joining parties, but without a guarantee regarding the universal application of the norms in the treaty. The fact that these different types of rights became divorced in two covenants shows that "economic, social and cultural rights were essentially subordinated to their civil and political counterparts and became the 'casualties' of Cold War politics".[27]

In 2008, the Optional Protocol to the International Covenant on Economic, Social and Cultural Rights was opened for signing in order to facilitate the possibility for individual complaints in line with other human-rights machinery. These general treaties were followed, and are accompanied, and added to, by a number of conventions and treaties related to particular groups of people, such as the Convention on the Elimination of All Forms of Discrimination against Women (CEDAW), the Convention on the Rights of the Child (CRC), and the Convention on the Rights of Persons with Disabilities, to mention just a few.

The key UN institution responsible for the development, formulation, and realisation of social rights at global level is the UN's Human Rights Council. It is an inter-governmental body comprised of 47 states. The Committee on Economic, Social and Cultural Rights (CESCR) is another important body within the UN system, although it is not an international organisation, but a group of independent experts, which has been tasked with monitoring the implementation of the International Covenant on Economic, Social and Cultural Rights (ICESCR) by its states parties. Importantly, the Committee also publishes interpretations on the provisions of the Covenant ("General Comments"). As a further key actor in terms of formulating social and labour rights, the ILO needs to be taken into consideration here. It developed and adopted a substantial number of social rights, as part of its international labour standards.

IV. TRANSNATIONAL SOCIAL RIGHTS DIMENSIONS

What is the content of (transnational) social rights? We can distinguish between the rights relating to particular groups of people, and the rights on particular social policy-fields or problems. While this is certainly not exhaustive, and might be criticised for not being sufficiently differentiated (which is a more general concern in global social policy studies, as data are scarce and research methods and data collection often explorative), it needs to be taken into account that the "rights *to*" and the "rights *of*", as *transnational social rights* in the sense of this chapter, have to be understood in relation to each other. While they can be distinguished conceptually, the focus on the transnational social rights of a

27 Smita Narula, "The Right to Food: Holding Global Actors Accountable under International Law", (2006) 44 *Columbia Journal of Transnational Law*, p. 691.

particular group, for example, is about the access to the institutions of health care, education, food, and so on (or the obligation of a state or the international community to provide for particular goods and services to be available to needy people). Thus, it concerns the right to participate in the "social infrastructure" as a human being.

A. TRANSNATIONAL SOCIAL RIGHTS *TO* ...

One form of transnational social rights are rights that concern particular social needs or problems, and can be related to "fields" of social policy. These are, for example, the right to health, the right to social security, the right to education, the right to food, and the right to water and sanitation. All of them highlight the importance of a particular set of social standards that – at the very minimum – should be provided upon a universal basis.

These kinds of social rights are characterised by a rather common process of institutionalisation and development. Their promotion or realisation is connected to specific UN bodies, namely, the World Health Organization (WHO), the International Labour Organization (ILO), the UN Educational, Scientific and Cultural Organization (UNESCO), and the Food and Agriculture Organization (FAO). On water issues, the inter-agency mechanism UN-Water interconnects the relevant UN agencies.

These "social rights *to*" are part of the Universal Declaration of Human Rights and specified in the International Covenant of Economic, Social, Cultural Rights. They also feature prominently in the constitutions of the related UN organisations. Since the 1940s, they have all seen frequent mentioning and (re-) affirmation in international declarations, partly specifically-related to a particular social right, partly integrated in declarations on related issues. All of them are specified by so-called "General Comments".

These social rights have also been addressed in both regular and extraordinary major international venues and summits, such as the general assemblies of international organisations, or events such as the regular World Water Summit. Their realisation is further claimed, developed, discussed, and observed by special rapporteurs or independent experts.

Furthermore, these types of rights have, albeit to different extents, been translated into global goals and campaigns, such as the Millennium Development Goals (MDGs), the Education for All (EFA) or Health for All (HfA) campaigns, and, most recently, they form part of the Social Protection Floor initiative.[28]

---

28 See Bob Deacon, Global Social Policy in the Making: The Foundations of the Social Protection Floor, (Bristol: Policy Press, 2013).

The "right to social security" is particularly important from a global *social* policy perspective. It formally originates from Article 22 of the UDHR (1949), but can be traced back further to the Constitution of the ILO (1919). It has, however, so far "remained – almost untouched – on the 'to do list' of the global community of nations".[29] Nevertheless, in 2008, a General Comment (no. 19) on social security specified its meaning. Currently, the ILO led Social Protection Floor initiative is an attempt to bring more life into the right to social security,[30] and the UN's Chief Executive Board adopted the Social Protection Floor as one of its nine initiatives to cope with the effects of the global economic crisis. The implications are less likely to be measurable in terms of the implementation of social protection schemes as a consequence of this UN initiative. Instead, it may make an impact by means of emphasising the importance of strong social protection systems in places where they exist and/or are in danger of being retrenched in attempts to respond to economic crises by cutting public spending.

The right to education, similarly to the right to health, has been supplemented by discourses of "goals and targets".[31] Furthermore, the discourses on these rights are connected to different levels of provision (e.g., primary education, primary health care). The international agreements are clear that at least primary, elementary education and basic health care should be free and accessible to all. Regarding the right to health specifically, this has quite an important and long history, beginning with Article 25 of the UDHR, and is articulated in numerous international treaties and conventions. Since the Alma-Ata Conference and Declaration,[32] the understanding of what it involves has improved. The ICESCR and other international treaties and global goals (such as the MDGs) specify the content and scope of the right to health, although there is not one commonly agreed upon understanding of what exactly must be done to realise the right to health. For example, Wolfgang Hein and Lars Kohlmorgen[33] state that it includes the prevention of epidemic, endemic, occupational and other diseases, and a claim that it creates the conditions that provide for the provision of the appropriate medical services in the event of sickness; however, these documents "are rather inconclusive with respect to the 'standard of health' that is supposed to be 'attainable'". In the year 2000, a General Comment which specifies the right

---

29 Michael Cichon, Christina Behrendt and Veronika Wodsak, "The UN Social Protection Floor Initiative: Moving Forward with the Extension of Social Security", IPG 2/2011:38.

30 See, for example, Magdalena Sepúlveda and Carly Nyst, "The Human Rights Approach to Social Protection", Helsinki: Ministry of Foreign Affairs (Finland). 2012, available at: http://papers.ssrn.com/sol3/papers.cfm?abstract_id=2114384.

31 Pam Christie, "The Complexity of Human Rights in Global Times: The Case of the Right to Education in South Africa", (2010) 30 *International Journal of Educational Development*, pp. 3–11, at 3.

32 The Declaration of Alma-Ata was adopted at the International Conference on Primary Health Care at Almaty (formerly Alma-Ata), Kazakhstan (formerly Kazakh Soviet Socialist Republic), 6–12 September 1978.

33 Hein and Kohlmorgen, note 17 above.

to health was drafted. Although certainly not determining the full and concrete meaning of the right to health, what the document does is to confirm that states parties have particular obligations with regard to the provision of health care. Such documents provide points of reference for state and non-state actors to claim their rights to health and education. By that way, a stronger emphasis on health and education rights might find their way into national legislation.

In terms of their actual realisation, rather depressingly, the related literature states that none of these rights has been developed to any meaningful extent to tackle global social problems.[34] That is despite remarkable advances in ESCR discourses on questions of justiciability,[35] and the development of international indicators.[36]

B. TRANSNATIONAL SOCIAL RIGHTS *OF* ...

Another category of social rights can be identified, relating to particular groups of people. More concretely, we find rights on age-related groups (children and older persons), gender (women's rights), citizenship or migration status (the rights of migrants, refugees, indigenous people and, to some extent, domestic workers), and those rights connected to health rights, which is the case for the rights of persons with disabilities (but also partly concerns women and children's rights).

With the exception of the rights of older persons, which reflect a rather recent development, all of these group-related social rights come with specific UN conventions and declarations. All the related declarations or conventions highlight the particular needs of the respective groups. They do this with explicit reference to the more general human and social rights frameworks and are often, only to some extent, explicit with regard to the concrete social rights involved. Instead, the main emphasis is on the equal treatment of the different groups of societies and non-discrimination, as well as basic protection levels in the case of any form of migration. An interesting case can be found in the rights of indigenous people, which try to catch both – notions of equal treatment, and of being different. The attention to the needs and interests of indigenous people and their participation at all levels of policy-making have, amongst other

34 See, for example, Marks, note 24 above; Cichon, Behrendt and Wodsak, note 29 above, and Christie, note 31 above.

35 See, for example, Michael T. Dennis and David P. Steward, "Justiciability of Economic, Social and Cultural Rights: Should there be an International Complaint Mechanism to Adjudicate the Rights to Food, Water, Housing, and Health?" (2004) 98 *The American Journal of International Law*, pp. 462–515; Salma Yusuf, "The Rise of Judicially Enforced Economic, Social, and Cultural Rights – Refocusing Perspectives", (2012) 10 *Seattle Journal for Social Justice*, pp. 753–791.

36 See, for example, Judith V. Welling, "International Indicators and Economic, Social, and Cultural Rights", (2008) 30 *Human Rights Quarterly*, pp. 933–958.

things, resulted in their being considered more seriously in the context of the definition of the post-2015 development agenda and the drafting of the so-called Sustainable Development Goals (SDGs).[37]

In contrast to the social-policy-field-related rights discussed above, the "rights *of*" have seen a more uneven development, albeit with a rather recent increase in attention, and are much more difficult to systematise. Refugee rights have a long-established tradition with the Convention relating to the Status of Refugees (CRSR) approved in 1951. The Convention on the Elimination of All Forms of Discrimination against Women (CEDAW) originates in the late 1970s/early 1980s. In the early 1990s, the issue was about children's and migrants' rights. The specification of the rights of indigenous people, domestic workers, persons with disabilities and older persons have seen their development since the mid-2000s. However, the historical development of a specific right does not necessarily imply weaker or stronger implications regarding improvements in the situation of the people affected at national and transnational levels. The current issues about large streams of refugees, for example, discussed in the context of dangerous crossings of the Mediterranean Sea, and the question of Europe's responsibilities in protecting these refugees, shed a rather depressing light on the degree to which refugees are granted their rights.

Institutions which specifically relate to the respective target groups of these rights are only partly established. Quite in line with the historical development around the respective rights, in the year 2010, UN Women was established to ensure that women's rights (including their components of social rights) are dealt with by one entity dedicated to the empowerment of women. Children's and migrants' rights have respective committees. The rights of indigenous people are furthered by a "Permanent Forum".

The crucial issue about group-related rights is what makes them *social* rights, or to what extent they can be considered as social rights. The "rights *of*" particular groups always come with reference to the more general human rights, and the economic, social and cultural rights. They are only *social* rights to a particular extent, as they also include political and other rights. The main issues about group-related rights commonly include equal treatment of actually or potentially disadvantaged and vulnerable groups (non-discrimination). However, to some extent, the provision of basic protection levels matters as well. Interestingly, the rights of indigenous people also consider rights to be different. More concretely, group-related rights include elements of the rights to health, education, labour, housing, and the right to social security.[38]

---

37 See, Draft Report, Chapter I: Matters calling for action by the Economic and Social Council or brought to its attention. http://undesadspd.org/Portals/0/UNPFII14_L3.pdf; see, also, https://sustainabledevelopment.un.org/majorgroups/indigenouspeoples.

38 On these specific rights, see, for example, Rosemary Kayess and Phillip French, "Out of Darkness into Light? Introducing the Convention on the Rights of Persons with Disabilities", (2008) 8 *Human Rights Law Review*, pp. 1–34.

One example of such group-related social rights is included in the rights of domestic workers. The general Domestic Workers Convention contains civil, social labour rights – specifically, the rights of domestic workers are connected to work-time issues, health and safety regulations, and food and housing.[39] Mundlak and Shamir have shown that the specific application of such global norms into world-regional norms, such as the ECHR, has enhanced the protection of domestic workers.[40]

Another example can be found in the more recent development of specifying the rights of older persons. Even though the concern about older persons was already on international agendas in the 1980s, the considerations with regard to rights appeared only in the 2000s. The 1982 World Assembly on Ageing adopted the "Vienna International Plan on Ageing" which was then also adopted by the UN General Assembly (GA). This document only referred to the UDHR. The later UN GA "Proclamation on Ageing" did not make a connection between older persons and rights, either. The first signs of changes became visible in the UN Principles of Older Persons (1991). The real change came in 2009 when the Advisory Committee of the Human Rights Council suggested that a study should be conducted on the need to protect the human rights of the older person. Since then, the rights of older persons have increasingly been in focus.

Concerning the practical application of the distinction between the "rights *to*" and the "rights *of*", it is obvious that the "rights *to*" are at the core of the activity of international organisations and are one mechanism which the international community has to develop a basic and common standard of social protection to any "world citizen". It is what passes for a very rudimentary "welfare statism" at global level, in terms of the claims that can be made regarding particular social problems and needs, and what people can expect to be granted irrespective of any particular status or citizenship. Looking beyond the current data regarding nutrition, health, and education, serves to highlight both the immense challenge and the limited progress in realising transnational social rights. This is where the "rights *of*" come in. These represent an advocacy and adjustment tool for claiming and improving the situation for particular groups of people. On the one hand, referring to a particular group is a means of emphasising their status as being particularly vulnerable; on the other, it is a way of engaging with the specific forms of the problems and needs that this particular group have to face. These problems and needs are, naturally, different when it concerns women or children, where the problem is often one that is dependent on the particular structure of national societies, and the claims are often connected to the right to be included in particular institutions. Thus, it is when

---

39 Einat Albin and Virginia Mantouvalou, "The ILO Convention on Domestic Worker: From the Shadows to the Light", (2012) 41 *Industrial Law Journal*, pp. 67–78.

40 Guy Mundlak and Hila Shamir, "The Global Governance of Domestic Work" in: Bridget Anderson and Isabel Shutes (eds), *Migration and Care Labour: Theory, Policy and Politics*, (Basingstoke: Palgrave Macmillan, 2014), pp. 192–213.

we talk about the social rights of refugees, domestic workers or disabled people who are usually characterised by having very specific needs, in addition to the question of whether they are, or can be, included in the existing institutions of social security. For people who fall into several of these categories (for example, female migrant domestic workers), there is a multiplication of vulnerabilities, and the need to give attention to them as a group and to define their "rights *of*", is important in order to improve their protection at different levels.

V. DISCUSSION

The concern, formulation and adoption of transnational social rights have a long history which, to some extent, is integrated into the development of more general universal human rights. Not all of them have developed simultaneously. The above sections have distinguished between global social "rights *to*" (social-policy-field-related) and global social "rights *of*" (group related). While the social "rights *to*" particular standards of social provision have developed rather simultaneously, the "rights *of*" particular groups reveal a rather uneven and recent development.

From a comparative perspective, group-related rights often add up to a rather similar list of essential human rights that need particular consideration when it concerns a potentially or actually vulnerable member of the respective group. The policy-field-related-rights are much more in need of specification and clarification as to the specific meanings or claims around their content. They may also reveal significantly different meanings with regard to their implications in high-income countries and low-income countries, or concerning the question of their implications for national and international policies (for example, aid) respectively.

In contrast to the group-related rights, the social rights that relate to particular policy-fields do not always come with specific declarations, but with goals or guidelines. They are part of the Universal Declaration of Human Rights or are often mentioned and re-inforced by numerous international agreements and declarations.

Each of the policy-field-related-rights is usually connected with the work of a particular UN agency. The social rights of particular groups, in contrast, are, instead, developed by committees and similar units within UN international organisations. Nevertheless, other international organisations may engage in related rights-debates as well. And most significantly, claiming particular rights is an important part of the engagement by various civil society organisations (CSOs).

The international mechanisms serving the realisation of transnational social rights are manifold. At the level of international organisations and institutions, special rapporteurs are particularly important. More concretely, the UN's Human Rights Council uses special procedures to promote transnational social rights. This happens by means of independent experts that are mandated to report and provide advice on various human rights from different perspectives. Apart from taking part in various thematic meetings on the specific rights that they represent, these independent experts – or special rapporteurs – may undertake country visits, communicate with states regarding rights violations, and generate knowledge and expertise on the relevant issues. They frequently report to the Human Rights Council and the UN General Assembly.[41]

This chapter has singled out social rights in order to specify an issue within the study of global social policy. However, with regard to human rights more generally, this is not unproblematical. Andreas Fischer-Lescano and Kolja Möller[42] have argued that the indivisible character of human rights as such makes any classification or "singling out" difficult, as social rights are only to be realised in conjunction with other, *i.e.*, political and legal, rights. Clearly, social and other types of human rights overlap and depend on each other, as do different transnational social rights. Or they are the different sides of the same coin. At the same time, though, the two different types of social rights are identified by somewhat different developments and structures that reveal some trends in current transnational social rights development. While important in terms of improving the conceptualisation of global social policy and transnational social rights, it remains an issue if the tendency to define ever more specific social rights, particularly with regard to different groups, makes the general social rights claims stronger or weaker, and raises questions about the indivisibility of human rights.

At the same time, the question arises as to whether transnational social rights have ever been defined or been considered as concrete standards or levels to be reached. Their conceptualisation as goals, as something in which – at the very least – one should not fall behind, and that should be constantly improved, might be more useful from several perspectives. On the one hand, states will be more willing to sign agreements about goals to be reached than to make any commitment to particular social standards and levels to be realised, particularly if they require resources. On the other hand, cultural differences and concepts might make the definition of concrete, universally applicable contents on social rights very difficult.

Another question would be how desirable (or possible) it is to have absolute standards; for example, is the Global Social Protection Floor a (welcome) step in this direction? Or what comes after the Millennium Development Goals (MDGs)?

---

41 See www.ohchr.org/EN/HRBodies/SP/Pages/Welcomepage.aspx, last accessed 01 June 2015; see, also, Stefan Lorenzmeier, Chapter 5 in this volume.

42 Andreas Fischer-Lescano and Kolja Möller, Chapter 2 in this volume.

In addition, specific transnational social rights debates can be placed within different contexts. Transnational social rights discourses may have an impact on the development of national social rights, and the discourses may transform and inform transnational social rights formulation and its – potential – translation into global goals or targets; and transnational social rights may be contextualised with regard to their transformative power in conjunction with global social re-distribution and regulation. If not at national or local level, transnational social rights can, nevertheless, be utilised to generate transnational obligations or claims as to the mutual support of states in realising transnational social rights (as is happening through the MDG process).

International (social) rights treaties and agreements are usually celebrated as great successes, and developments in the situations of particular groups, or the manifestation of social standards worldwide. At the same time, particularly with regard to the policy-field-related-social rights, it is frequently claimed that they are not specific or powerful enough. In addition, issues concerning the actual change achieved at local levels are frequently raised. Even if the treaties, at least for those countries that ratified them, are binding, sanctioning mechanisms remain weak.

Last, but not least, it needs to be mentioned that – while this chapter has exclusively focused on rights to be furthered by policy-makers at different levels – there are also important issues with regard to the extent to which corporations and other private actors have to be made accountable for respecting social rights.

VI. CASE STUDY: RIGHT TO FOOD

In this final section, we take a look at one particular example, namely, the right to food. How do the findings and considerations presented above apply to the case of the right to food?

The right to food is most clearly a type of social rights in that it is important for people to live their lives and to participate in society. Given that there is food scarcity in major parts of the world, and apart from efforts to generate new resources, there is an important (re-) distributive issue that raises major issues concerning global social (in-) justice and (in-) equality. One way to address these is by responding with individual and collective rights to food. At the same time, it will be necessary to address some of the causes of food shortages, by addressing transnational regulation, and preventing land-grabbing and trading practices which cause damage.

The right to food, apart from being part of the UDHR (Art. 25), is most clearly related to development and humanitarian or aid agendas. It has been defined by the ICESCR as the right to be free from hunger and to have access to sufficient food. It belongs to the group of solidarity rights, leading to state, as well as international, obligations. Special general comment 12 on the right to adequate food of 1999 interprets the article's content and resulting obligations of states. More concretely, this general comment sets out, that states have the obligation to facilitate peoples' access to food in various ways, including the provision of food if needed, and even in times of "severe resource constraints".[43]

Given that there has been a global food crisis for some years now, the discussion about global food policies and rights is importantly linked to this context. And it is precisely due to this process of engaging with a global social problem, namely, food scarcity, that the links between the three elements of global social policy (re-distribution, regulation, and rights) become apparent; the multiple-actor involvement complicates the picture, and the development of transnational social rights becomes significantly inter-linked with other global social policy processes and mechanisms. More concretely, the rights discourse cannot be understood without taking the development of knowledge through global actors into account – it is organisations such as the FAO and the World Bank that define the problem, and these organisations then collect data and monitor the development of this global social problem (e.g., *The Global Monitoring Report 2012*, the World Bank's regular *Food Price Watch*, or the FAO *Food Price Index*), while, in particular, the international financial institutions (IFIs) are also always seen to be part of the problem of the current global economic order.

Supporters of rights-based approaches regret that the focus is not more on the development of a global right to food. Nevertheless, there is a UN Special Rapporteur on the Right to Food, currently Hilal Elver, who acts as an independent expert in order to evaluate the state of the right to food. This includes annual reports to the Human Rights Council and UN General Assembly on the state of the right to food, based upon the monitoring of the food situation worldwide, and reporting of insights from country visits and consultations.

What can also be observed is that the right to food is frequently connected to the rights of particular groups, particularly with regard to women and children. For example, the CEO of "The Hunger Project" emphasised the key role of women in tackling poverty and hunger.[44] This was only one of many recent statements regarding the importance of women in fighting hunger.

Similar to other social rights, the right to food has also been part of the Millennium Development Goals (MDGs), and is in the focus of the post-2015 development agenda. In its report "The Road to Dignity by 2030: Ending Poverty, Transforming all Lives and Protecting the Planet", UN Secretary-

43 Manisuli Ssenyonjo, "Economic, Social and Cultural Rights: An Examination of State Obligations", in: Sarah Joseph and Adam McBeth (eds), *Research Handbook on International Human Rights Law*, (Cheltenham: Edward Elgar Publishing, 2010), pp. 36–70, at 56; for more detail, see, also, Anne Trebilcock, Chapter 8 in this volume.

44 The Hunger Project. Statement by Asa Skogström Feldt, available at: https://sustainabledevelopment.un.org/content/documents/12899hungerproject.pdf.

General Ban Ki-moon gave attention to the aim to end hunger.[45] The right to water and sanitation, and land rights are also partly related. Furthermore, the Ebola outbreak in 2014, significantly deteriorated not only the health situation of the communities affected, but also their status of food security. Furthermore, the process of phrasing and framing a new set of development goals, the so-called Sustainable Development Goals (SDGs), is an important part of the process for strengthening the promotion of the right to food. For example, in his annual report to the UN General Assembly, Special Rapporteur Hilal Elver emphasised the key role of the Global Strategic Framework for Food Security and Nutrition of the Committee on World Food Security[46] for the "implementation of effective models of governance concerning food, agriculture and nutrition for States, intergovernmental actors and the corporate private sector".[47]

Nevertheless, major discourses have concerned the threats to such rights, through privatisation, instead of real progress in people's social rights. Therefore, while we see increasing numbers of social rights on specific issues and on particular groups of people accompanied by numerous initiatives and claims about their realisation, the involvement of multiple actors and the clash of competing interests open ever new spaces for the struggles around transnational social rights.

45 UN General Assembly (2014), "The Road to Dignity by 2030: Ending Poverty, Transforming all Lives and Protecting the Planet", Synthesis Report of the Secretary-General on the Post-2015 Sustainable Development Agenda, available at: http://ow.ly/GTW9B.

46 See www.fao.org/fileadmin/templates/cfs/Docs1213/gsf/GSF_Version_2_EN.pdf, last accessed 1 June 2015.

47 See http://daccess-dds-ny.un.org/doc/UNDOC/GEN/N14/498/25/PDF/N1449825.pdf?OpenElement, last accessed 1 June 2015.

PART II

FOUNDATIONS, INSTITUTIONS AND ENFORCEMENT STRUCTURES

CHAPTER 5

ENFORCEMENT OF TRANSNATIONAL SOCIAL RIGHTS: INTERNATIONAL AND NATIONAL LEGAL ASPECTS

Stefan LORENZMEIER

I. INTRODUCTION

The enforcement of transnational social rights in international and national legal orders is a pivotal issue for the development of and respect for these rights.[1] Individual and collective human rights are a serious matter as they concern the obligations of states to individuals,[2] and the right to food does, moreover, address a fundamental human need.

Social human rights, as second generation human rights,[3] and, as such, situated at the cross-roads between individual and collective rights, are like the classic first generation ones[4] directed vertically at the respective public body, to

---

1 Enforcement is a fundamental part of the "struggle for transnational social rights", as pointed out by Andreas Fischer-Lescano and Kolja Möller, Chapter 2 of this volume.

2 Rolf Künnemann, "The Right to Adequate Food: Violations Related to its Minimum Core Content", in: Audrey Chapman and Sage Russell (eds), *Core Obligations: Building a Framework for Economic, Social and Cultural Rights*, (Antwerp: Intersentia, 2002), pp. 161–163.

3 Asbjørn Eide and Allan Rosas (eds), "Economic, Social and Cultural Rights: A Universal Challenge", in: Asbjørn Eide, Catarina Krause and Allan Rosas, *Economic, Social and Cultural Rights: A Textbook*, 2nd ed., (Leiden: Martinus Nijhoff, 2001), pp. 3–4; Erika Szyszak, "Social Rights in the European Union", in: ibid., pp. 493–4. Mashood A. Baderin and Robert McCorquodale perceive this category to be very unhelpful ("International Covenant on Economic, Social and Cultural Rights: Forty Years of Development", in: Mashood A. Baderin and Robert McCorquodale (eds), *Economic, Social and Economic Rights in Action*, (Oxford-New York: Oxford University Press, 2007), pp. 3–10). In 1987, K.J. Partsch voiced "grave doubts whether the concept of generation of rights is well-founded"; see K.J. Partsch, "The Enforcement of Human Rights and Peoples' Rights: Observations on their Reciprocal Relations", in: Rudolf Bernhardt and John Anthony Jolowicz (eds), *International Enforcement of Human Rights*, (Berlin-Heidelberg-New York: Springer Verlag, 1987), p. 25.

4 See, for example, the individual rights enshrined in Part III of the ICCPR.

wit, the state. Thus, it is the task of states to give these rights the proper effect within their national jurisdictions. Moreover, the distinction between several generations of human rights should not lead to their division. All human rights are, in the words of the 1993 Vienna Declaration on Human Rights, "universal, indivisible, interdependent and interrelated",[5] and the drafting of two different, yet interrelated, Covenants on the subject-matter should not lead to a different conclusion. The original proposal of the Human Rights Commission was a single document entailing civil and political as well as economic, social and cultural rights,[6] which were subsequently split up in separate documents due to political pressure. Even after the split, the United Nations General Assembly, in its decision on the two Covenants, the International Convention of Civil and Political Rights (ICCPR) and the International Covenant on Economic, Social and Cultural Rights (ICESCR), stressed that the two sets of rights are "interconnected and interdependent",[7] and the respective preambles of the Covenants pay regard to both sets of rules as well.[8] The division between the two sets of rules seems to be artificial and should not be pursued further than absolutely required by law. Tribute should also be paid to the aspect that individual civil and political human rights are not limited to the sphere of the ICCPR, but have, due to their interconnectedness, a collective dimension as well. Even the European Court of Human Rights stressed that "no water-tight division" is possible between the individual rights enshrined in the European Convention on Human Rights and the collective ones of the European Social Charter.[9]

---

5 Vienna Declaration and Programme of Action, A/CONF.157/23, no. I.5. It states further that "the international community must treat human rights globally in a fair and equal manner, on the same footing and with the same emphasis. While the significance of national and regional particularities and various historical, cultural and religious backgrounds must be borne in mind, it is the duty of States, regardless of their political, economic and cultural systems, to promote all human rights and fundamental freedoms".

6 HR Commission, UN ESCOR, sup 9 (E/1992), 4 May 1951, pp. 20 *et seq.*

7 GA res 543 (VI), 5 February 1952, preamble.

8 See, for example, the preamble of the ICESCR: "[...] in accordance with the Universal Declaration of Human Rights, the ideal of free human beings enjoying civil and political freedom from fear and want can only be achieved if conditions are created whereby everyone may enjoy his economic, social and cultural rights, as well as his civil and political rights" and the almost identical wording in the ICCPR: "[...] in accordance with the Universal Declaration of Human Rights, the ideal of free human beings enjoying civil and political freedom and freedom from fear and want can only be achieved if conditions are created whereby everyone may enjoy his civil and political rights, as well as his economic, social and cultural rights."

9 ECtHR, 6289/73, *Airey* v *Ireland*, judgment of 9 October 1979, para. 26. For an in-depth analysis of the jurisprudence of the ECtHR in this regard, see Arno Frohwerk, *Soziale Not in der Rechtsprechung des EGMR*, (Tübingen: Mohr Siebeck Verlag, 2012).

II. INTERNATIONAL LEGAL RULES

The international legal embodiment of social human rights can be found in the International Covenant on Economic, Social and Cultural Rights[10] and rules of customary law and/or general principles of law in the meaning of Article 38 para. lit. b) and c) of the Statute of the International Court of Justice.[11]

A. SOURCES OF LAW

The topic of the analysis, the right to food, constitutes a part of the category of "transnational social human rights", and is first and foremost enshrined in Article 11 ICESCR,[12] as part of treaty law,[13] and Article 25 Universal Declaration of Human Rights (UDHR) as part of customary law.[14] Although, at the time of drafting, the UDHR was generally not seen as a binding agreement,[15] which can be inferred from its name ("Declaration", instead of "Convention"),[16] over the due course of time most principles of the UDHR developed into international

10 Of 19 December 1966, entered into force on 3 January 1976. UNTS vol. 993, p. 3. For the drafting history, see Matthew C.R. Craven, *The International Covenant on Economic, Social and Cultural Rights*, (Oxford: Oxford University Press, 1995), reprinted 2002, p. 16 *et seq.*, and Marco Odello and Francesco Seatzu, *The UN Committee on Economic, Social and Cultural Rights: The Law, Process and Practice*, (Oxford: Routledge, 2011), p. 4 *et seq.* See, also, Anne Trebilcock, "Transnational Socio-Economic Rights: Inter-linkages in the Context of the Right to Food", Chapter 8 in this volume, Section IV.1. A history of the provision is provided by Ben Saul, David Kinley and Jacqueline Mowbray, *The International Covenant on Economic, Social and Cultural Rights: Commentary, Cases, and Materials*, (Oxford: Oxford University Press, 2014), "The Right to an Adequate Standard of Living", p. 867 *et seq.*

11 Of 26 June 1945.

12 Kerstin Mechlem, "Food, Right to, International Protection", in: Rüdiger Wolfrum (ed), *Max Planck Encyclopedia of Public International Law*, para. 14, regards the right to food not just as an aspirational goal but as a full-scale right. See, also, Asbjørn Eide, "The Right to an Adequate Standard of Living Including the Right to Food", in: Eide, Krause and Rosas (eds), note 3 above, p. 133 *et seq.* Another noteworthy provision is Art. 54 of Additional Protocol I (protection of victims of international armed conflicts) to the Geneva Conventions, which prohibits *inter alia* the starvation of civilians as a means of warfare.

13 ESC rights have to be perceived, at least in the 21st century, as being full rights and not just aspirational goals or non-justiciable. See Baderin and McCorquodale, note 3 above, pp. 3–10 with further references.

14 Mechlem, note 12 above, para. 13. Critically, see Hans Morten Haugen, The Right to Food and the TRIPS Agreement: With a Particular Emphasis on Developing Countries' Measures for Food Production and Distribution, (Leiden: Martinus Nijhoff, 2007), p. 151 et seq. Moreover, the UDHR can be seen as the initial foundation of SECR. In this regard, see Eide and Rosas, note 3 above, pp. 9–17.

15 GA resolutions are as such not binding on the UN's Member States, see Art. 10 UN Charter.

16 Louis Henkin, "The International Bill of Rights: The Universal Declaration and the Covenants", in: Bernhardt and Jolowicz (eds), note 3 above, pp. 1–5.

norms.[17] Even the United Nations General Assembly intended the UDHR to establish " a common standard of achievement for all peoples and all nations [...]".[18]

Some academic discussion is still continuing with regard to the legal status of the social and economic rights of the UDHR, such as its Article 25 on the right to food.[19] The most extreme view is that all the principles embodied in the UDHR became part of customary law.[20] The majority of legal scholars is fostering a more differentiated approach. They are stressing the historically rather minor status of second generation human rights to first generation rights, and that the former have not acquired the same legal status as the latter.[21] According to this reasoning, the customary status of the right to food cannot be determined exclusively from Article 25 UDHR, but from a plethora of international documents,[22] including Article 55 lit. a) UN Charter[23] and Article 11 ICESCR, in which it is explicitly enshrined.[24] As a result, both views grant the right to food the additional status of a customary right in the meaning of Article 38 para. 1 lit. b) ICJ Statute.

Furthermore, a third possibility is sometimes argued. It is stated that social and economic human rights are not generally part of customary law, because the existence of a customary norm is sometimes very difficult to prove,[25] but these rights are instead part of the general principles of law as laid down in Article 38 para. 1 lit. c) ICJ Statute.[26]

For the scrutiny at bar, it is not necessary to decide comprehensively between the two approaches (customary law or general principle of law) due to their

---

17 Hilary Charlesworth, "Universal Declaration of Human Rights", in: Wolfrum (ed), note 12 above, para. 16.

18 Resolution 217 (III). International Bill of Human Rights.

19 Art. 25 has a very similar wording to Art. 11 ICESCR. It reads in paragraph 1: "Everyone has the right to a standard of living adequate for the health and well-being of himself and of his family, including food, clothing, housing and medical care and necessary social services, and the right to security in the event of unemployment, sickness, disability, widowhood, old age or other lack of livelihood in circumstances beyond his control."

20 Bruno Simma and Philip Alston, "The Sources of Human Rights Law: Custom, *Jus Cogens* and General Principles", (1988) 12 *Australian Year Book of International Law*, pp. 82–84.

21 Smita Narula, "The Right to Food: Holding Global Actors Accountable under International Law", CHRGJ Working Paper no. 7, 2006, p. 70.

22 For example, FAO, Voluntary Guidelines to Support the Progressive Realization of the Right to Adequate Food in the Context of National Food Security, 24 November 2004, available at: www.fao.org/righttofood/en or the resolution 22/9 of the Human Rights Council on the right to food of 9 April 2013, A/HRC/RES/22/9.

23 Alfred Verdross and Bruno Simma, *Universelles Völkerrecht: Theorie und Praxis*, 3rd ed., (Berlin: Duncker & Humblot, 1984), §1247 considers this provision as the foundation for social human rights.

24 See the convincing analysis of Narula, note 21 above, p. 70 *et seq.*, and the conclusion on p. 84. Verdross and Simma, note 23 above, at §1247 in 1984 did not confer the status of a right to the ICESCR, but only as a "programmatic approach".

25 Charlesworth, note 17 above, para. 16.

26 Simma and Alston, note 20 above, p. 82.

independent legal effect, the status of an international non-treaty right. To the author, the status as a customary law is slightly more convincing due to the vast amount of international documents and the rather different legal basis of general principles stemming from the national legal systems. Whether the right to food is substantially enshrined in all domestic legal orders is difficult to prove and, moreover, the *lacunae*-filling function of the general principles speaks against such a reading.

B. IMPLEMENTATION AND SUPERVISION

The rights of the ICESCR have to be implemented. An important aspect in this regard is the supervision of the implementation of the international right to food, which is supervised by various international bodies, especially the Committee on Economic, Social and Cultural Rights (CESCR).[27] In 1999, the CESCR issued General Comment (GC) no. 12[28] on the right to adequate food within the meaning of Article 11 ICESCR,[29] which covers the availability and access to food resources for the member states of the said Covenant.[30] Besides the work of the CESCR, the work of the "Special Procedures of the Human Rights Council", namely, independent experts with mandates to report and advise, has to be mentioned. These special procedures are performed either by an individual or a group of experts, the former being called a "special rapporteur" or "independent expert". They are appointed by the Human Rights Council, serve in their personal capacities, and are to be independent and impartial. Their task is *inter alia* to undertake country visits, sending communications to states, to conduct thematic studies and to raise public awareness on a given human rights issue. This system is a rather new, but central element of the UN human rights monitoring systems.[31] The mandate of the Special Rapporteur on the Right to Food is a good example of this in the context in question. Resolution 6/2 of the Human Rights Council[32] aimed at the then Special Rapporteur Jean Ziegler, for example, states at point 1. (a) that it is his task to "promote the full realization of the right to food and the adoption of measures at the national, regional and international levels for the right of everyone to adequate food [...]". For this, he is to examine ways of overcoming both existing and emerging obstacles (1.

27 The CESCR is the principal UN body; in this respect, see Henry J. Steiner, Philip Alston and Ryan Goodman, *International Human Rights in Context*, 3rd ed., (Oxford-New York: Oxford University Press, 2007), p. 277.

28 Subsequently abbreviated as "GC 12".

29 UN Doc.: E/C.12/1999/5 of 5 May 1999. For an overview of its content, see Odello and Seatzu, note 10 above, p. 219 *et seq.*

30 Haugen, note 14 above, p. 18.

31 Further information can be obtained here: www.ohchr.org/EN/HRBodies/SP/Pages/Introduction.aspx.

32 See http://ap.ohchr.org/documents/E/HRC/resolutions/A_HRC_RES_6_2.pdf.

(b)) and is to present recommendations on possible steps for achieving this aim (1. (e)). The Special Rapporteur is also at the interface *inter alia* of the Human Rights Council, the states and non-governmental organisations (1. (f)). With the introduction of the Special Rapporteur on the Right to Food, a very effective means for the supervision of the implementation of the right to food had been created.

The Food and Agriculture Organization (FAO) is also active in providing guidance on the Right to Food, but has, to date, been unsuccessful in making the work on the right to food one of its priorities.[33] Public awareness is also raised by non-governmental organisations supervising the implementation of human rights.[34] They are active in nearly every aspect of international human rights practice,[35] and frequently report on the human rights situation publicly and, in so doing, put pressure on states and various United Nations bodies,[36] and heavily influence their decisions. It also avails of the use of open letters.

The importance of GC no. 12 for the clarification of the Covenant's right to food and its implementation can hardly be overstated. The comment states convincingly that the right to food is inseparable from social justice, and requires appropriate action at both national and international level.[37] Such action has been instrumental for promoting the right to food.[38] Moreover, GC no. 12 also explicitly states that "the right to adequate food is indivisibly linked to the inherent dignity of the human person" and, as such, it is indispensable for the fulfilment of other human rights.[39]

As conclusively opined by scholars, it is, as a consequence of the above, inseparable from social justice and requires the adoption of respective laws at national and international level.[40] In addition, the ICESCR provision is not only

---

33 See the FAO web site for further information: www.fao.org/righttofood/right-to-food-home/en. The FAO adopted its "right to food guidelines in 2005, see www.fao.org/3/a-y7937e.pdf. The "Voluntary Guidelines have been accepted by the Human Rights Council as "a practical tool to promote the realization of the right to food for all" (Human Rights Council, Resolution 6/2, no. 6; adopted at its 20th meeting, 27 September 2007).

34 See, for example, the work of Amnesty International and Human Rights Watch, described by Aryeh Neier, *The International Human Rights Movement: A History*, (Princeton NJ: Princeton University Press, 2012), p. 186 *et seq.*, "Amnesty International", p. 204 *et seq.*, "Human Rights Watch", and p. 233 *et seq.*

35 David Weissbrodt, "Roles and Responsibilities of Non-State Actors", in: Dinah Shelton (ed), *The Oxford Handbook of International Human Rights Law*, (Oxford: Oxford University Press, 2013), p. 721.

36 Ibid., p. 725.

37 CESCR, GC 12, para. 4.

38 Mechlem, note 12 above, para. 33.

39 CESCR, GC 12, para. 4.

40 See Per Pinstrup-Andersen and Marc Cohen, "Agricultural Biotechnology Risks and Opportunities for Developing Country Food Security", (2000) 2 *International Journal of Biotechnology*, pp. 145–160. See, also, Odello and Seatzu, note 10 above, p. 21 *et seq.*

addressed to states and individuals, but also to the people in accordance with Article 1 ICESCR.[41]

III. INTERNATIONAL ENFORCEMENT OF SOCIAL HUMAN RIGHTS

Internationally, the issue of the enforcement of human rights is usually focused on civil and political rights as traditional first generation individual rights. For the present analysis, a short comparison between the ICCPR and the ICESCR may be used for the discussion of the international enforcement of social human rights.

The enforcement of social human rights at international level, as they are laid down in the ICESCR, is, from the outset, quite distinct from those enshrined in the ICCPR,[42] because Article 2.1. ICESCR speaks only of the "progressive realization of these rights" and that the member states are "to take steps" to achieve the rights recognised in the Covenant. Moreover, in the ICESCR, individual provisions are "couched" as state obligations to recognise such a right and not as a statement of the individual's entitlement to the right.[43] A further important difference between the two covenants is that the ICESCR, in Article 4, entails in only a very general provision for the derogation from its guarantees.

Thus, it was frequently argued formerly that the rights enshrined in the Covenant were not a matter of rights and were only of a political nature.[44] This view is, especially because of 40 years of legal practice, rarely voiced today.[45] Due to permanent societal change, human rights law is among the most living instruments in international law, and, as such, has a growing legal corpus.[46] The difficulty in defining "an adequate standard of living"[47] is still at issue, but a wide, rather open term cannot be held against the possible enforcement of social human rights. This will now be elaborated in depth.

41 The "own means of subsistence" are a part of the principle of self-determination of people. See Haugen, note 14 above, p. 16.
42 Eide and Rosas, note 3 above, pp. 9–10. In the ICCPR, states undertake to respect and ensure civil and political rights.
43 Henkin, note 16 above, pp. 1–15.
44 Eide and Rosas, note 3 above, pp. 9–10.
45 Eibe Riedel, "International Covenant on Economic, Social and Cultural Rights", in: Wolfrum (ed), note 12 above, para. 52.
46 Gerald Staberock, "Human Rights, Domestic Implementation", in: Wolfrum (ed), note 12 above, para. 5.
47 Henkin, note 16 above, pp. 1–16.

A. THE JUSTICIABILITY OF ECONOMIC AND SOCIAL RIGHTS

A common criticism against the implementation of social human rights is that they are not justiciable.[48] The justiciability of economic and social human rights is, from the outset, usually very weak with regard to the said rights due to the wording of the international treaty provisions and their international monitoring mechanism.[49] This led, after the entry into force of the ICESCR in 1976, to its widespread treatment as a second class set of human rights, which is lower in the hierarchy than the rights of the ICCPR and to the widely purported assumption that the rights of the ICESCR are non-justiciable.

This negative assumption has drastically changed over the course of time due to the continuing codification of these rights and the ongoing jurisprudence upon them,[50] and cannot be upheld in a modern human rights system. The *Ogoni* case before the African Commission on Human and Peoples' Rights deserves special mention. In this case, the Commission held that Nigeria had violated *inter alia* its obligation to protect the right to food by destroying the food resources of the *Ogoni* people through the Nigerian security forces and its national oil company.[51]

In the light of this development, the non-justiciability view has lost a lot of argumentative ground and is rarely argued in the scholarly debate today. Furthermore, the modern discussion convincingly considers the non-justiciability view as being arbitrary,[52] and, in the words of the CESCR, it "would drastically curtail the capacity of the courts to protect the rights of the most vulnerable and disadvantaged groups in society".[53]

This view is supported by some additional arguments. According to the CESCR's GC no. 12, Article 11 ICESCR entails three different types of legal obligations for the member states of the Covenant: the obligation to respect, to protect, and to fulfil.[54] In more detail, the obligations require that third parties do not interfere with the enjoyment of the right to food (the obligation to respect), that third parties are prevented from a possible interference (the

48 For a general study, see Fons Coomans (ed), Justiciability of Economic and Social Rights: Experiences from Domestic Systems, (Antwerp-Oxford: Intersentia-Hart Publishing, 2006); Malcolm Langford (ed), Social Rights Jurisprudence: Emerging Trends in International and Comparative Law, (Cambridge: Cambridge University Press, 2009).

49 Martin Scheinin, "Economic and Social Rights as Legal Rights", in: Eide, Krause and Rosas (eds), note 3 above, pp. 29–30 and *infra*.

50 Mechlem, note 12 above, para. 14, where the "deepening understanding" of ESC rights is stressed as well.

51 ACHPR/COMM/A044/1, decision of 27 May 2002.

52 Baderin and McCorquodale, note 3 above, pp. 3–11.

53 CESCR, GC 9, para. 10.

54 CESCR, GC 11, para. 15. Anne Trebilcock, "Transnational Socio-Economic Rights: Interlinkages in the Context of the Right to Food", Chapter 8 in this volume, Section IV.1.

obligation to protect), and finally that the member states adopt the proper measures necessary for the full enjoyment of the right to food (the obligation to fulfil).[55] This understanding of the ICESCR rights, and, namely, the right to food, grants full legal effect to Article 11 ICESCR[56] and is in accordance with the general interpretative principle that international treaties should be interpreted to their full effect.[57]

This line of reasoning is also fostered by GC no. 3 of the ICESCR. Even as early as 1990, the Committee conclusively established the rule that the Covenant entails a minimum core of rights which are incumbent on any state party.[58] It expressly stated that the right to food *might* be violated if a state was not providing a significant number of individuals with essential foodstuffs.

A different reading of the Covenant, to wit, that it does not entail such a core obligation, would largely deprive it of its *raison d'être*.[59] Such a reading would be incompatible with the object and purpose of the ICESCR and would constitute a violation of Article 31 VCLT (Vienna Convention on the Law of Treaties). Yet, it has to be seen in this context that the obligation is limited. Article 2 para. 1 ICESCR refers to a state's available resources, and account has to be taken of the resource constraints in the state concerned.[60] A state relying on this defence for not fulfilling its core obligation has to demonstrate that every effort has been made to use all the resources that are at its disposition in an effort to satisfy the obligation.[61] Hence, every ICESCR member state has to ensure at least the minimal core content of the ICESCR rights, since they are not just soft law.[62]

Furthermore, it is argued against justiciability that economic, social and cultural (ESC) rights are much more resource-oriented than first generation rights. As such, it is not possible to fulfil them at once, but only progressively.[63] This distinction between first- and second-generation human rights would water down the obligations of states under the ICESCR and, generally, cannot be accepted. The CESCR stated conclusively that although this principle is

---

55 The responsibilities are elaborated by Künnemann, note 2 above, p. 161 & 171 *et seq.*

56 Olivier De Schutter, *International Human Rights Law*, 2nd ed., (Cambridge: Cambridge University Press, 2014), p. 285. For the history of the tripartite typology, see ibid., p. 280 *et seq.*

57 "Effet utile", the principle is now embodied in Art. 31 para. 1 VCLT as part of the "good faith" and the object and purpose"; see Richard Gardiner, *Treaty Interpretation*, (Oxford: Oxford University Press, 2008), p. 160.

58 CESCR, GC 3, para.10.

59 Ibid.

60 Ibid.

61 Ibid. A part of the effective application of the right to food is its domestic application, CESCR, GC 9, para. 2 and *infra*.

62 CESCR, GC 3, para. 10.

63 See the analysis by Philip Alston and Gerard Quinn, "The Nature and Scope of State Parties' Obligations under the International Covenant on Economic, Social and Cultural Rights", (1987) 9 *Human Rights Quarterly*, p. 156 *et seq.* Art. 2 para. 1 ICESCR is also leading in this direction.

laid down in Article 2 para. 1 ICESCR, the Covenant also imposes obligations of immediate effect.[64] The obligations of the ICESCR are a combination of obligations of conduct and obligations of result.[65] As a result, ESC rights are not only aspirations, but also full rights which, as a general rule, enjoy greater discretion on the part of the states that implement them. The progressive realisation has also to be seen in accordance with the time of ratification and the entering into force of the ICESCR in 1976,[66] which means that some states have had these obligations for almost forty years, and the argument of "progressive realisation" in connection with the state's resources can hardly be accepted for developed and developing states. The proposed view is supported by the wording of Article 11 para. 1 ICESCR. The provision expressly states that the states have to "ensure the realization of this right" (the right to an adequate standard of living including the right to food). The ordinary meaning of the term "ensure" is almost comparable to a "guarantee", and it must be considered as being a very strong obligation[67] and not just a political aspiration. Lastly, the International Court of Justice in its "Construction of a Wall"- advisory opinion expressly accepted certain provisions of the CESCR as *rights*, namely, Articles 6, 11, 12 and 13 ICESCR.[68] Also the number of national judgments adjudicating on economic, social and cultural is a convincing indicator that these rights are fully justiciable.[69]

Moreover, in 2008, the UN General Assembly adopted Resolution A/RES/63/117 concerning an "Optional Protocol to the International Covenant on Economic, Social and Cultural Rights", which has been ratified by ten states and has recently entered into force.[70] Despite its ratification status, the existence of the Optional Protocol is a strong indicator for the stated change of perception of social human rights,[71] and of the fact that they are conceived as full rights nowadays.

---

64 CESCR GC 3, para. 1.

65 ILC Report, Yearbook of the International Law Commission 1977, para. 8.

66 Eibe Riedel, "New Bearings in Social Rights? – The Communications Procedure under the ICESCR", in: Ulrich Fastenrath, Rudolf Geiger, Daniel-Erasmus Khan and Andreas Paulus (eds), *From Bilateralism to Community Interest: Essays in Honour of Judge Bruno Simma*, (Oxford: Oxford University Press, 2011), pp. 574–575.

67 Haugen, note 14 above, p. 123. On page 124, Haugen concludes that the term "ensure" was included with the understanding of the state parties that it would imply relatively stronger obligations on them.

68 "The wall violates the rights to work, to an adequate standard of living, health and education." See ICJ, "Legal Consequences of the Construction of a Wall in the Occupied Palestinian Territory", ICJ Rep. 2004, para. 130.

69 See, for example, the cases stated by Olivier De Schutter, note 56 above, p. 829 *et seq.*, and the author's contributions on the application of Art. 13 para. 2 lit. c) in Germany.

70 The scope of the Optional Protocol is a complaint procedure whereby *inter alia* individuals are entitled to send a communication to the CESCR in case of a violation of one of the ICESCR rights by a member state, see Art. 2, 3 Optional Protocol.

71 Available at: www2.ohchr.org/english/bodies/cescr/docs/A-RES-63-117.pdf.

Thus, in line with the above-mentioned arguments, it has to be accepted that economic and social human rights are, at least nowadays, fully justiciable and that the opposite view can no longer be sustained. Yet, the interpreters of the law must take the margin of appreciation granted to the states for their implementation into account.

B. INTERNATIONAL MONITORING MECHANISM

In general, international monitoring mechanisms are important for the implementation of human rights because, on the one hand, they fill a gap if national implementation fails to be sufficient, and, on the other, they have an impact on national jurisdictions.[72] *Vice versa*, national jurisprudence influences the interpretation of international human rights as well.[73] Thus, international monitoring is of special relevance because it is a means of supervision and enforcement.[74]

The primary responsibility for monitoring the ICESCR is assigned to the CESCR.[75] Formally, the CESCR is a sub-organ of the ECOSOC (the Economic and Social Council of the United Nations) and an organ, not a treaty body.[76] It should only assist ECOSOC in the consideration of ICESCR member states' reports under Article 16 ICESCR. In addition, the FAO has been entrusted with the task of dealing with "right to food" matters. In 2004, the FAO Council adopted the "Voluntary Guidelines to Support the Progressive Realization of the Right to Adequate Food in the Context of Food Security", which are the most recent pronouncement of the stated right.[77] In the year 2000, another actor joined the international food protection scene: the Special Rapporteur on the Right to Food. The position was established by the UN Commission on Human Rights and is expected to present thematic reports on issues concerning the right to food.[78] According to Article 16 ICESCR, the states are required to submit reports about the measures adopted in order to implement their treaty obligations. The reports are to indicate the factors and difficulties affecting the implementation of the ICESCR.[79] The expert commission prepares "concluding observations" upon the basis of these reports which identify positive and negative aspects.[80]

72 Staberock, note 46 above, para. 3.
73 Ibid., para. 5.
74 Verdross and Simma, note 23 above, §1249.
75 ECOSOC Resolution 1985/17, UN Doc E/1985/85 (1985). Scheinin, note 49 above, pp. 29–45. The development can be seen by Craven, note 10 above, p. 39 *et seq.*
76 Craven, note 10 above, p. 50.
77 Mechlem, note 12 above, para. 34.
78 See the overview by Mechlem, note 12 above, para. 35.
79 Manual on Human Rights Reporting, Office of the High Commissioner for Human Rights, Geneva, 1997, Olivier De Schutter, note 56 above, p. 871.
80 Ibid., p. 871.

The reporting process is supported by non-governmental organisations. They support the first-hand information of the Committee members in the form of the so-called "shadow reports", which are often better documented than the official state reports.[81] The consultative status of non-governmental organisations is even acknowledged in Rule 69 of the Rules of Procedure of the Committee on Economic, Social and Cultural Rights.[82]

The CESCR is made up of independent and impartial experts[83] with a quasi-judicial role due to their independent evaluation of the submitted reports.[84] Beyond this, upon the basis of the evaluation of the reports submitted, the CESCR has to make suggestions on the improvement of a state's performance.[85]

In Resolution 1987/5, the ECOSOC addressed an invitation to the CESCR to issue General Comments. The CESCR followed the invitation, and the GCs are intended to assist the member states in the task of fulfilling their reporting obligations.[86] Despite its questionable legal basis, the competence for the adoption of General Comments stems from the authority to assist the ECOSOC, the practice has not been objected to by the member states,[87] and it can be regarded as a subsequent interpretive practice in the meaning of Article 31 para. 3 lit. b) VCLT.

The role of the General Comments is descriptive and not innovative; they are intended to summarise the view of the ECSCR on a particular issue.[88] They are neither academic works nor administrative acts.[89] Yet, their practical importance has surpassed their pure legal status. It has to be observed that they have, over time, developed into a highly relevant form of commentary on the interpretations of the rights contained in the ICESCR,[90] similar to a re-statement of the law[91] as it is known from the US legal system.

---

81 Ibid., p. 876.

82 Committee on Economic, Social and Cultural Rights, Rules of the Procedure of the Committee, E/C.12/1990/4/Rev.1.

83 See the "Decision of the Committee on Economic, Social and Cultural Rights on the proposed guidelines on the independence and impartiality of members of the human rights treaty bodies", adopted at the CESCR's 49th meeting in November 2012; available at: www2.ohchr.org/english/bodies/cescr.

84 Craven, note 10 above, p. 56.

85 Nisuke Ando, "General Comments/Recommendations", in: Wolfrum (ed), note 12 above, para. 2.

86 UN Doc. E/1988/14, p. 63, para. 367. The GC has to be distinguished from the "concluding observations", which are only addressed at a particular state party, see Ando, note 85 above, para. 2.

87 Craven, note 10 above, p. 90.

88 UN Doc. E/1993/22, p. 19, para.49.

89 Natan Lerner, Religion, Secular Beliefs and Human Rights: 25 Years after the 1981 Declaration, (Leiden: Brill Publishers, 2006), p. 26, note 29.

90 Saul, Kinley and Mowbray, note 10 above, "Introduction", p. 5.

91 Staberock, note 46 above, para. 11. See, also, Odello and Seatzu, note 10 above, p. 195, and the FAO Information Paper, FAO Doc: IGWG RTFG INF/1, Feb. 2004, para. 5 *et seq.*

Thus, the General Comments of the CESCR do not acquire the same legal status as a complaint or petition procedure, but they entail some considerable weight for the interpretation of an ICESCR provision.[92] In a strict sense, they are not legally-binding, but the GCs are, at the very least, a source for assessing and interpreting the ICESCR in a persuasive way.[93] In this context, it is of special note that the GCs, by bringing together the knowledge of a wide range of experts, are the most important interpretative guides for the Covenant.[94] Hence, over time, they have developed into a highly relevant form of commentary on the interpretation of the rights,[95] and are a strong force for the development of social human rights from a purely aspirational character to enforceable human rights. Although the International Court of Justice (ICJ) has not yet paid tribute to the CESCR GCs, it seems very likely that the Court would apply a similar system to that used for the ICCPR, using them as guidance for its own interpretation. Following the stated line of reasoning and by interpreting the provision extensively, they can be considered as a subsequent means of interpretation in the meaning of Article 38 para. 1 lit. d) ICJ Statute, as part of the notion of "judicial decisions", although the GCs are not "judicial" in a strict formal sense.[96]

C. CUSTOMARY LAW/GENERAL PRINCIPLES OF LAW

A different international enforceability of the right to food is ensured by the other sources of Public International Law. In this respect, it does not matter whether it is enshrined in customary law or whether it is a general principle of law. Both set of rules are an independent legal source and establish, in themselves, the independent status of rights that have to be respected by the international actors.[97] These subjects of international law can, unlike the membership in the ICESCR, encompass all international legal entities and have a much wider impact. For instance, while the Covenant is directed exclusively at states, the rules of customary law are also applicable for international organisations and are the traditional subjects of international law, like the Holy See. The European Union is, in line with the well-established case-law of the Court of Justice of the

---

92 Scheinin, note 49 above, pp. 29–45. Craven, note 10 above, p. 91.

93 Riedel, note 45 above, para. 39; Saul, Kinley and Mowbray, note 10 above, "Introduction", p. 5.

94 Ibid., para. 39.

95 Staberock, note 46 above, para. 11 (explicitly so for the ICCPR).

96 The jurisprudence of the ICJ supports this view; see, for example, ICJ, *Wall Advisory Opinion*, ICJ Rep. 2004, p. 136, para. 109 and ICJ, *Diallo*, ICJ Rep. 2010, para. 66 *et seq*. See, also, Alain Pellet, in: Andreas Zimmermann, Karin Oellers-Frahm, Christian Tomuschat and Christian J. Tams (eds), *The Statute of the International Court of Justice: A Commentary*, 2nd ed., (Oxford: Oxford University Press, 2012), Art. 38, para. 318.

97 Pellet, note 96 above, para. 271 *et seq*.

European Union, also bound by customary rules.[98] Thus, the scope of the right to food gains almost universal effect.

IV. NATIONAL LEGAL ORDER

The status and the enforcement of social human rights in national jurisdictions depend upon the respective national legal order. The issue of enforcement arises foremost with regard to legally-binding obligations,[99] and secondly with regard to the directness of the enforcement (*i.e.*, whether the rights can be enforced by natural or legal subjects before national courts). For instance, the right to food is explicitly protected in 24 national constitutions,[100] and 46 constitutions guarantee an adequate standard of living.[101]

A. LACK OF ENFORCEMENT – GENERAL CONSIDERATIONS

In this context, it is argued that social human rights have a lack of enforcement, because they do not create individual rights and cannot, as a consequence, be challenged or brought to life in a domestic court proceeding. In domestic legal systems, an individual is usually only entitled to bring a claim if he or she is the holder of an enforceable right. If this is not the case, a national court would not hear the case based upon this argument. Thus, the aforementioned statement would indeed hamper the legal value of social human rights. Yet, it does not seem to be totally convincing.

The legal binding of social human rights can derive from one of the aforementioned three sources of Public International Law laid down in Article 38 para. 1 lit. a)-c) ICJ Statute. Most important, for the scrutiny at hand, are the sources provided by treaty law and the rules of customary international law. The legal status of the right to food, and hence its enforcement, differs due to its international legal source. Regarding treaty law, the CESCR has stated that any human-rights treaty imposes three different levels of obligations for its member states; namely, the obligations to respect,

98 ECJ, C-162/96, Racke, ECR 1998, I-3688.

99 Staberock, note 46 above, para. 7.

100 Saul, Kinley and Mowbray, note 10 above, "The Right to an Adequate Standard of Living", p. 887 *et seq.*

101 See the overview given by Mechlem, note 12 above, para. 25. The numbers vary, the FAO calculates that 33 states have constitutions which include the right to food in a broader context, see Lidija Knuth and Margret Vidar, *Food and Agriculture Organization of the United Nations, Constitutional and Legal Protection of the Right to Food around the World*, (Rome: FAO, 2011), p. 21.

to protect, and to fulfil, including an obligation to facilitate and an obligation to provide.[102]

In addition, the term "progressive realisation" entailed in Article 2 para. 1 ICESCR is the crucial notion for the national enforcement of the Covenant. Some authors conclude from this that domestic legal implementation is limited to civil and political rights.[103] This view fails to pay sufficient regard to the fact that even the ICESCR secures minimum rights which can be enforced immediately.[104] This is the view of the CESCR as well, which stated even in GC 3, one of its first General Comments, that the obligation to ensure rights without discrimination, the obligation to take steps to ensure these rights, and the respect for a minimum core of rights, all carry immediate obligations.[105] Hence, a violation of the ICESCR exists if a state is not guaranteeing the minimum level of being "free from hunger".[106] In addition, it is disputed as to whether Article 11 can only be realised in a progressive manner in accordance with Article 2 para. 1 ICESCR.

B. TREATY LAW

The member states of the ICESCR have to incorporate the treaty into their domestic law, either by using a monistic or a dualistic system.[107] In a monistic system, an international treaty will become automatically part of the national legal order, while, in dualist countries, a state act of incorporation is necessary.[108] Independently from the dogmatic question of incorporation, the international legal order requires a state to provide the respective treaty with an appropriate status in its legal order.[109] This can be qualified as an international duty of co-operation.[110]

---

102 CESCR, GC 12, para. 15. According to GC 12 the obligation to *respect* ensures that anyone has access to adequate food resources. The obligation to protect means that the states guarantee that no other actor deprives individuals of their access to adequate food. The obligation to facilitate means that a state must pro-actively engage in measures guaranteeing the availability of food resources. Finally, the (legal) access to the right to food must be secured by the Member States. See, also, Eide and Rosas, note 3 above, pp. 9–23 *et seq.*

103 Christian Tomuschat, *Human Rights: Between Idealism and Realism*, 2nd ed., (Oxford: Oxford University Press, 2008), p. 110 *et seq.*, states: "where there is no right there can be no remedy."

104 Staberock, note 46 above, para. 13.

105 CESCR, GC 3, para.1; Staberock, note 46 above, para. 13.

106 CESCR, GC 12, para. 17. As the GC clearly and correctly points out, it has to be distinguished between unable and unwilling states.

107 Scheinin, note 49 above, pp. 29–49.

108 Sandra Liebenberg, "The Protection of Economic and Social Rights in Domestic Legal Systems", in: Eide, Krause and Rosas (eds), note 3 above, pp. 55–77.

109 Staberock, note 46 above, para. 18.

110 Anja Seibert-Fohr, "Neue internationale Anforderungen an die Überführung von Menschenrechtsabkommen in nationales Recht: Das Verhältnis des internationals Pakts

The legal situation led the CESCR in 1990 to issue the statement that, for the implementation of the ICESCR, "legislation is highly desirable".[111] Applying the above-mentioned principles to the right to food entailed in Article 11 ICESCR, the member states have a general duty to incorporate the treaty text directly into their domestic law.[112] This would *inter alia* avoid the translation of treaty provisions and the problems connected with it.[113]

The concept of effective implementation is a central element for the implementation of treaty law, *i.e.*, the means used should produce results which are consistent with the full discharge of the state's obligations.[114] This is rather complicated for social human rights due to their discretionary legal nature. In GC 9, the CESCR addressed this issue and stated that it was obligatory for the states to use all the means at their disposal.[115] Moreover, Article 27 VCLT requires the modification of national legal orders to give full effect to the provisions of a treaty.[116] Special attention should be given to justiciability, which is often the best way to grant an effective domestic legal effect to the Covenant's rights.[117]

Justiciability does not mean that ICESCR rights should be granted the status of self-executing rights. These two legal concepts are independent from each other. It is frequently questioned as to whether a Covenant establishing social human rights can be self-executing. Such an understanding of the ICESCR is not necessarily cogent. The Covenant does not entail a provision excluding such a possibility. Moreover, in its drafting history, such a norm had been discussed but was not accepted.[118] This supports the opinion that the drafters did not want to exclude the possibility of self-execution of the ICESCR rights. As a "living instrument",[119] the states are certainly not bound by the intention of the drafters, but Article 32 VCLT considers the *travaux préparatoires* as supplementary means of interpretation,[120] which can be considered for the understanding of the Covenant. Moreover, social human rights are only becoming more trenchant in the due course of time, and the living instrument-interpretation today is more in favour of accepting the status of self-executing rights than before. Thus, in general, it is possible for states to grant the ICESCR rights self-executing status as part of their implementation procedure.

über bürgerliche und politische Rechte zu nationalem Recht", (2002) 62 *Zeitschrift für ausländisches öffentliches Recht und Völkerrecht*, p. 391 *et seq.*

111 CESCR, GC 3, para. 3.

112 CESCR, GC 9, para. 8.

113 Ibid.

114 CESCR, GC 9, para. 5.

115 UN Doc. E/C.12/1998/24, para.2.

116 CESCR, GC 9, para. 3.

117 Ibid., para. 7.

118 Ibid., para. 11.

119 ICJ, Advisory Opinion, Namibia (Legal Consequences), ICJ Rep. 1071, p. 16, para. 53.

120 See Gardiner, note 57 above, p. 303 *et seq.*

A further distinction has to be drawn between the direct and indirect protection of these rights in the domestic legal orders. Direct protection means that international social human rights can be enforced by the legal action of natural and legal subjects, while indirect protection is a much weaker way of protection through other rules of law, usually by means of interpretation or the application of sets of rules. The direct protection method should be the preferred mechanism for the implementation because it ensures much more diligently the protection of these rights for those in need: to wit, human beings without adequate access to food resources.

C. LIMITATIONS

The right to food is not guaranteed without limits. In this regard, Article 4 ICESCR deserves special attention. This provision regulates the general rule that the rights enshrined in the Covenant can be limited by national laws if these laws are in compliance with the nature of the ICESCR rights and do serve to promote general welfare in a democratic society. This condition is, compared to the one entailed in the ICCPR, far-reaching due to the somewhat undefined limits of the state's right, considered to be "shield and sword" for the member states.[121] This becomes more important in the light of the often open-wording of the ICESCR rights, which have to be implemented and executed by the member states.

As a limitation to the Covenant's rights, the norm has to be interpreted strictly.[122] Article 4 ICESCR is not particularly vague and its requirements can be clearly determined by way of interpretation. The "promotion of the general welfare in a democratic society" is an undefined legal term that leaves much room for interpretation. It grants the member states a very wide margin of discretion that is hardly justiciable. Yet, if a measure is clearly out of bounds and unsuitable for the promotion of the general welfare, it would be incompatible with this requirement. The term "democratic" should not be over-interpreted, and covers a number of democratic theories.

More important for the acceptance of a limitation is the first requirement that the laws have to be in compliance with the nature of the ICESCR rights. Hence, if the right to food constitutes a core obligation that is a fundamental part of the nature of the Covenant, any restriction of the core part of the right would be illegal. This conclusion has to be drawn for the minimum rights entailed in the ICESCR because any limitation would necessarily constitute an infringement of the nature of the Convention.

---

121 Alston and Quinn, note 63 above, pp. 156–193.

122 ICJ, Wall Advisory Opinion, ICJ Rep. 2004, para. 136 *et seq.*

D. CUSTOMARY LAW/GENERAL PRINCIPLES OF LAW

The rules of customary law and the general principles of law can also become part of domestic law; in Germany, this is laid down in Article 25 Basic Law.[123] The provision covers, despite a formerly narrow reading of it, both sources of international law.[124] In general international law, how a rule of customary international law or a general principle of international law is applied in a domestic legal order is an issue of the underlying legal system, a monistic or a dualistic one, as well. The aforementioned ideas apply in this regard, too.

E. INTERPRETATION IN THE LIGHT OF THE ICESCR

An indirect way of enforcing social human rights can be found in the interpretation of national law in the light of the applicable international social norms. Such a procedure is followed by several courts in a number of countries[125] and is a very discretionary approach.[126] The CESCR states that the interpretation in favour of the Covenant is an international obligation of a state.[127]

The weakness of this approach lies in the absolute limit of interpretation, which may constitute a hindrance to provide full effect to social human rights. If the wording or the *telos* of a national norm cannot be interpreted in a favourable way for social human rights, the respective national norm cannot be interpreted in the light of social rights, and these rights, as such, cannot be enforced by using the tool of interpretation. Due to the constraints stated, this approach can rightly be considered as being the weakest one among the various possibilities for norm enforcement.

F. RETROGRESSIVE MEASURES

It is also disputed whether retrogressive measures constitute a violation of the Covenant and can be directly enforced. Strictly argued, the limits of Article 2

---

123 The provision reads: "The general rules of international law shall be an integral part of federal law. They shall take precedence over the laws and directly create rights and duties for the inhabitants of the federal territory."

124 Ondolf Rojahn, in: Ingo von Münch and Philip Kunig, *Grundgesetz-Kommentar*, 6th ed., (Munich: C.H. Beck, 2012), Art. 25 Basic Law, para. 6.

125 See the overview given by Liebenberg, note 108 above, pp. 55–76 *et seq*. In Germany, the ICESCR become prominent in the discussion about the introduction of tuition fees at its universities and had been applied by a number of national courts including the Federal Administrative Court; see Stefan Lorenzmeier, Case note on the ruling of the Federal Administrative Court, ZIS 2009, 438.

126 Riedel, note 66 above, pp. 574–575.

127 CESC, GC 9, para. 15.

para. 1 ICESCR are not applicable in such a situation, because the social human right has been fully realised by a member state and the full realisation is the ultimate obligation of result in Art. 2 para. 1.[128] A possible example is the express codification of access to food resources and the realisation of such a right by national civil and political human rights which also establish social rights.

One school of thought relies on the wording of Article 2.1 ICESCR, and states that the "full realisation" is not covered by the agreement and that such a situation would not deprive a member state, due to the inherent issue of resource availability, of its mandate to ensure only a minimum core standard and start the "progressive realisation" anew. A further argument in this respect is that the ICESCR does not have a clear provision on the limits of the guaranteed rights.[129]

These arguments do not seem to be fully conclusive. A retrogressive measure after full harmonisation has to be considered an *aliud* to the progressive realisation of Article 2 para. 1 ICESCR, but it is, in itself, a violation of the Covenant because the obligation to take steps with a view to achieving the full realisation of the ICESCR-rights could not be fulfilled. As such, the prohibition of regressive measures has to be qualified as an accessory right to the primary obligation of the social human right.[130] Otherwise, every member state would be entitled to circumvent its obligations by using a retrogressive measure, and social human rights could never be realised.

The Committee seems to prefer a third way. It considers retrogressive measures as a justifiable violation of the Covenant.[131] Thus, GC 3 states that retrogressive measures must be "fully justified".[132] Without providing possible grounds for justification, such as the principle of proportionality, the CSCR clarified its position in its 2007 Statement regarding the Optional Protocol to the Covenant by adding that the "burden of proof rests with the state party" to show that it has abided by these conditions of justification for any retrogressive measure.[133] It is argued that the CESCR envisaged two forms of justification, first, an economic crisis in a member state, and, second, the use of a retrogressive measure as a means for the improvement of the totality of the rights of the

128 See, for example, CESCR, GC 3, para. 9.

129 See, for example, the legal discussion in Germany on the re-introduction of tuition fees, especially OVG NRW, 15 A 1596/07, judgment of 9 October 2007.

130 Matthias Kradolfer, "Verpflichtungsgrad sozialer Menschenrechte", (2012) 50 *Archiv des Völkerrechts*, pp. 255–269.

131 Craven, note 10 above, p. 131 *et seq.*

132 CESCR, GC 3, para. 9.

133 CESCR, Statement: An evaluation of the obligation to take steps to the maximum available resources under an Optional Protocol to the Covenant, E/.12/2007/1, 10 May 2007, para. 9. See, also, Saul, Kinley and Mowbray, note 10 above, "Progressive Realization of ICESCR Rights", p. 150.

Covenant.[134] This clearly shows the very practical approach of the Committee.[135] As a result, such measures have to be justified in the light of the full use of the available resources.[136]

Dogmatically, the Committee's view is also not fully conclusive due to the inherent violation of Article 2 (1) ICESCR, which considers the full realisation as the ultimate goal. In this light and even if some do not follow the proposed opinion that retrogressive measures always constitute a breach of the ICESCR, any justification for such a measure can hardly meet the requirements of the proportionality-test, and the vast majority of cases will, in practice, constitute a violation of the Covenant. This is especially true if the retrogressive measure is part of a deliberate policy of the respective state.[137] Hence, retrogressive measures constitute at least a *prima facie* violation of Article 2 para. 1 ICESCR that can only be justified in extreme circumstances such as severe economic crises. A "trade-off" between human rights cannot be accepted as a ground for justification because the Covenant does not accept a hierarchy between the enshrined rights.

G. FURTHER ISSUES

The full implementation of the right to food is not limited to legislative measures. It also requires an adequate institutional framework, political programmes and administrative measures within a state.[138] These types of general measures would lead to a holistic application of social human rights and could foster the general well-being of a society.

The elaborated monitoring system of the CESCR is a tool for the Committee to engage in a dialogue with the member states on their domestic implementation of ICESCR rights.[139] A state with difficulties in providing the required adequate protection of human rights should be given the opportunity to improve its record. The General Comments, as a part of the monitoring system, are designed to provide authoritative guidance to states discharging their reporting obligations.[140] Moreover, they serve to create a harmonious application of social human rights among the member states of the Covenant.

---

134 Craven, note 10 above, p. 132.

135 Saul, Kinley and Mowbray, note 10 above, "Progressive Realization of ICESCR Rights", p. 150.

136 CESCR, GC 3, para. 9.

137 Craven, note 10 above, p. 132.

138 Mechlem, note 12 above, para. 26.

139 Staberock, note 46 above, para. 11.

140 Ibid., para. 11.

V. CONCLUSION

Transnational social human rights such as the right to food are full and enforceable human rights at both international and national level.[141] Their original weakness, the vague, very resource-oriented wording of the obligations, has, over time, developed into a fully enforceable legal right, whose core minimum content is, at the very least, fully justiciable and enforceable at international, and, even more importantly, at national level. Furthermore, the enforcement of social human rights cannot only be achieved by direct measures granting a subjective right, but can also be achieved by indirect measures such as the interpretation of national law in the light of the ICESCR, and should be accompanied by structural as well as political measures. Monitoring mechanisms carried out by treaty and non-treaty bodies as well as the "shadow reports" of non-governmental organisations are an effective tool for the realisation of transnational social human rights at the international and the national level.

In this regard, it seems necessary, for the enforcement of social human rights, that the member states of the ICESCR not only apply the law, but also foster their realisation of social human rights by other means, such as the information on the existence of transnational social human rights and the ratification of other legal documents like the above-mentioned Optional Protocol to the ICESCR. The proposed measures would support the full realisation of transnational social human rights to a great degree.

141 See, also, Andreas Fischer-Lescano and Kolja Möller, "The Struggle for Transnational Social Rights", Chapter 2 in the volume, Section IV.

CHAPTER 6
HORIZONTAL EFFECTS OF HUMAN RIGHTS: THE EU PROPOSAL FOR A NON-FINANCIAL REPORTING FRAMEWORK

Ibrahim KANALAN and Sebastian EICKENJÄGER

I. INTRODUCTION

The accountability of private actors, especially the accountability of multinational corporations (MNCs), for human rights violations is one of the most disputed issues, not only in the academic world, but also in international, regional and national politics.[1] The question of whether private actors should be bound by human rights, and, if so, through which means and to what extent they can be held accountable, is more controversial than ever. This question is one of the major challenges in the twenty-first century.[2] Consequently, a large number of approaches and concepts have been developed in the last decades, which aspire to solve this very question.

Regarding this issue, currently the most contested approach is the struggle to create an international binding business and human rights treaty. The debate on a binding treaty has arisen again in the course of a draft Resolution[3] that

---

1 See Andreas Georg Scherer and Guido Palazzo, "The New Political Role of Business in a Globalized World: A Review of a New Perspective on CSR and its Implications for the Firm, Governance, and Democracy", (2011) 48 *Journal of Management Studies*, p. 899, at 903 *et seq.*

2 See The Panel of Eminent Persons, "*Protecting Dignity: An Agenda for Human Rights*", (2008), available at: www.udhr60.ch/documentation.html.

3 UN Human Rights Council, "Draft Resolution drafted by Ecuador and South Africa: Elaboration of an International Legally Binding Instrument on Transnational Corporations and other Business Enterprises with Respect to Human Rights" (2014), UN Doc A/HRC/26/L.22/Rev.1. See, also, the Resolution drafted by Norway requesting the working group to "launch an inclusive and transparent consultative process (…) to explore and facilitate the sharing of legal and practical measures to improve access to remedy, judicial and non-judicial, for victims of business-related abuses, including the benefits and limitations of a legally binding instrument, and to prepare a report thereon". (UN Human Rights Council

has been submitted to the UN Human Rights Council by Ecuador and South Africa, and which was finally passed in June 2014. The Resolution stipulates the setting up of an open-ended intergovernmental working group with a mandate to elaborate an "international legally binding instrument on transnational corporations and other business enterprises with respect to human rights". In contrast to other initiatives to hold corporations accountable for human rights violations, this approach would be a binding inter-governmental instrument that would be part of international law without any restrictions.[4] While the realisation, possible outcome and content is highly contested and will have to be negotioated in the process set in motion by the UN Human Rights Council,[5] the intergovernmental working group already focused, in its first session, on major topics and issues, namely, the question of the legal nature of MNCs in international law, the human rights to be covered by the instrument, the obligations of states to guarantee that human rights are respected by MNCs, including extraterritorial obligations, enhancing the responsibility (and liability) of MNCs, and the building of national, international and corporation-based mechanisms for access to remedy.[6]

Acknowledging the major importance of a binding treaty on the issue of business and human rights, this chapter aims to address the question of the accountability of private actors, that is, the horizontal effect of human rights, from a different perspective, and to propose an unconventional approach to ascertaining the accountability of private actors for human rights violations.

After sketching the direct legal human rights obligations of multinational business corporations *de lege lata*, in the first part of this chapter we will claim that, by endeavouring to hold private actors accountable for human rights violations and thus binding them to fundamental human rights, it is necessary to go beyond classical concepts and patterns of human rights and international law. Thus, it is essential for a new approach to detach itself from the traditional understanding of human rights, and to consider the origins of human rights as a starting-point for the justification of the validity of human rights in the private sphere. In so doing, first, the justification of the validity of human rights for private actors has to be derived from the normative power of the human rights

(2014), "Draft Resolution drafted by Norway: Human Rights and Transnational Corporations and other Business Enterprises", UN Doc A/HRC/26/L.1).

4 See Bread for the World, FIAN International et al, "Right to Food and Nutrition Watch – The Treaty on TNCs and the Struggle to Stop Corporate Impunity: An Interview with Civil Society", (October 2015), p 39, 40.

5 Recent information on the proposed binding treaty and current statements, initiatives and commentaries are available at: www.business-humanrights.org/en/binding-treaty.

6 UN Human Rights Council, "Draft Report of the Open-ended intergovernmental working group on transnational corporations and other business enterprises with respect to human rights – Report of the Chairperson-Rapporteur: Amb. María Fernanda Espinosa Garcés" (2015).

itself, and, second, the abstract idea of human rights has to be transferred to private actors.

In the second part of the chapter, we will try to bridge the gap between theory and practice. Thus, we want to explore how such a concept can be realised in a progressive manner within the framework of the struggle for transnational social rights.[7] In this respect, we will analyse new approaches on non-financial reporting;[8] to be precise: the actual legislation of the EU on non-financial reporting. In so doing, we will first present a brief introduction on non-financial reporting and the EU legislation in this field. After that, we will review the EU's approach and assess the potential of this initiative for realising the horizontal effect of human rights and thus its potential for the struggle of marginalised persons and groups.

II. ACCOUNTABILITY OF PRIVATE ACTORS

A. ACCOUNTABILITY OF MULTINATIONAL CORPORATIONS *DE LEGE LATA*

Although the violation of human rights by private actors is not a new occurrence, a satisfactory solution to this problem has not been found yet. Mostly in line with the traditional concept of international law, the human rights obligations of private actors and thus the obligations of multinational corporations is rejected since they are not recognised as subjects of international law.[9] Although it is no doubt possible to impose human rights obligations on private actors within the framework of international law by means of international treaties,[10] there is no international treaty which codifies the general accountability of private actors for human rights violations.[11] Customary international law hardly provides any general human rights obligations for private actors.[12] In the national legal order,

7 See Andreas Fischer-Lescano and Kolja Möller, "The Struggle for Transnational Social Rights", Chapter 2 in this volume.

8 Also known as social accounting, social and environmental accounting, corporate social reporting, corporate social responsibility reporting, non-financial accounting.

9 However, the legal personality of multinational corporations is highly disputed. See, for example, Andrew Clapham, *Human Rights Obligations of Non-State Actors*, (Oxford: Oxford University Press, 2006), Chapter 1 and Chapter 6, especially p. 266 *et seq*; Adam McBeth, *International Economic Actors and Human Rights*, (New York: Routledge Publishing, 2010), p. 56 *et seq.*

10 See Steven R. Ratner, "Corporations and Human Rights: A Theory of Legal Responsibility", (2001) 111 *The Yale Law Journal*, p. 443, at 538–539.

11 Occasionally, international treaties exist which regulate the responsibility of private actors for human rights violations, for instance, the Rome Statute of International Criminal Court. See Andrew Clapham, *Human Rights in the Private Sphere*, (Oxford: Clarendon Press, 1993), p. 94 *et seq*; Ratner, note 10 above, p. 467.

12 See John Ruggie, "Business and Human Rights: Mapping International Standards of Responsibility and Accountability for Corporate Acts", Report of the Special Representative

there are some regulations which bind private actors to human rights and hold them accountable for human rights violations.[13] The most prominent provision is the Alien Tort Claims Act (ATCA) in the USA.[14] There are similar provisions in the UK and Australia, and they are also being discussed for the EU.[15] However, these provisions are, on the one hand, solely occasional regulations, while, on the other, they face various difficulties in preventing human rights violations,[16] and can barely provide sufficient protection of human rights.[17] These difficulties include, for instance, the lack of interest on the part of the home states of the business corporations in question to pass comprehensive binding regulations. Host states, on the other hand, are either not interested in regulating, or, due to asymmetrical power relations, not able to regulate the human rights violations of private actors.[18]

Another option in order to hold private actors accountable for human rights violations can be considered by means of public and private codes of conduct (the self-regulation of private actors). In the last decades, such provisions have been of prominence and have led to the creation of a large number of initiatives.[19] Some

---

of the Secretary-General (SRSG) on the Issue of Human Rights and Transnational Corporations and other Business Enterprises (2007) UN Doc A/HRC/4/035 para. 34. But see, also, William S. Dodge, "Corporate Liability Under Customary International Law", (2012) 43 *Georgetown Journal of International Law*, p. 1045.

13 For detailed analysis, see, for example, Sarah Joseph, *Corporations and Transnational Human Rights Litigation*, (Oxford: Hart Publishing, 2004); Jennifer A. Zerk, *Multinationals and Corporate Social Responsibility*, (Cambridge: Cambridge University Press, 2009). See, also, Ratner, note 10 above, pp. 533–536.

14 See, generally, Beth Stephens, "Corporate Accountability: International Human Rights Litigation Against Corporations in US Courts", in: Menno T. Kamminga and Saman Zia-Zarifi (eds), *Liability of Multinational Corporations under International Law*, (The Hague *et al*: Kluwer Law International, 2000), p. 209; Joseph, note 13 above, p. 21 *et seq*.

15 Joseph, note 13 above, p. 113 *et seq*; Olivier De Schutter, "The Accountability of Multinationals for Human Rights Violations in European Law", (2004) CHRGJ Working Paper No 1, available at: www.chrgj.org/publications/docs/wp/s04deschutter.pdf.

16 See, for example, the discussion around the ATCA: Jochen von Bernstorff, Marc Jacob and John Dingfelder Stone, "The Alien Tort Statute before the US Supreme Court in the Kiobel case", (2012) 72 *Zeitschrift für ausländisches Recht und Völkerrecht*, p. 579; Jennifer L. Karnes, Comment: "Pirates Incorporated?: Kiobel v. Royal Dutch Petroleum Co. and the Uncertain State of Corporate Liability for Human Rights Violations Under the Alien Tort Statute", (2012) 60 *Buffalo Law Review*, p. 823.

17 See Alice de Jonge, *Transnational Corporations and International Law: Accountability in the Global Business Environment*, (Cheltenham: Edward Elgar Publishing, 2011), p. 91 *et seq*, & 117; Joseph, note 13 above, p. 153 *et seq*.

18 John Ruggie, "Protect, Respect and Remedy: a Framework for Business and Human Rights", Report of the Special Representative of the Secretary-General on the Issue of Human Rights and Transnational Corporations and other Business Enterprises (2008) UN Doc A/HRC/8/5 paras. 14 *et seq*; Oxfam, *Land and Power – The Growing Scandal surrounding the New Wave of Investments in Land*, (September 2011) Oxfam Briefing Paper, p. 23 *et seq*.

19 See, for example, John Ruggie, Interim Report of the Special Representative of the Secretary-General on the Issue of Human Rights and Transnational Corporations and Other Business Enterprises (2006) UN Doc E/CN.4/2006/97; *idem*, note 12 above, (2007) UN Doc A/HRC/4/035; Clapham, note 9 above, p. 195 *et seq*; S.D. Murphy, "Taking Multinational Corporate Codes of Conduct to the Next Level", (2005) 43 *Columbia Journal of Transnational*

of the most prominent instruments can be found, for instance, in the Guidelines of the Organisation for Economic Co-operation and Development (OECD) regarding the duty of multinational corporations (Guidelines for Multinational Enterprises),[20] or the Tripartite Declaration of the International Labour Organization (ILO) concerning multinational enterprises and social policy.[21] Ultimately, the approach of the business actors to regulate their accountability for human rights violations by themselves can be discussed as an alternative approach to bind private actors to human rights obligations. According to the concept of "Corporate Social Responsibility" (CSR), business actors endeavour to regulate their human rights responsibilities in order to prevent human rights violations.[22] This concept includes the "voluntary" self-binding provisions of business actors to take "social responsibility" for human rights violations.[23]

What all these instruments have in common is that they operate, from the perspective of state law, upon a "voluntary basis" and contain "recommendations" for states or business enterprises. They utilise a vague language with regard to obligations and hardly have any legally-binding nature according to the concept of the state law.[24] In this manner, the OECD Guidelines, for instance, state that the Guidelines are recommendations of the member states to business enterprises. Their observance is voluntary and not legally enforceable.[25] Another weakness of the Guidelines is the insufficient and non-coercive monitoring system.[26]

Law, p. 389; Olivier De Schutter, *Transnational Corporations and Human Rights*, (Oxford-Portland OR: Hart Publishing, 2006); de Jonge, note 17 above, p. 21 *et seq*.

20 OECD, Guidelines for Multinational Enterprises – 2011 updated version. (Paris: OECD Publishing, 2011).

21 The Declaration was adopted at the 204th Session (1977) and amended at its 279th Session (2000) and lastly at its 295th Session (2006).

22 Ruggie, note 12 above, (2007) UN Doc A/HRC/4/035 paras. 63 *et seq*; European Commission, "Green Paper" (2001) (COM (2001) 366) paras. 20 *et seq*; European Commission, "A Renewed EU Strategy 2011–14 for Corporate Social Responsibility", (2011) (COM (2011) 681), p. 6; Murphy, note 19 above.

23 See, for example, the European Commission, "Green Paper", paras. 8 *et seq*, para. 52. See, for a comprehensive concept, the European Commission, "A Renewed EU Strategy", note 22 above, p. 6 *et seq*.

24 See, for example, Justine Nolan, "With Power comes Responsibility: Human Rights and Corporate Responsibilities", (2005) 28 *University of New South Wales Law Journal*, p. 581, 587 *et seq*, & 593 *et seq*; David Kinley and Junko Tadiki, "From Talk to Walk: The Emergence of Human Rights Responsibilities for Corporations at International Law", (2004) 44 *Virginia Journal of International Law*, p. 931 & 950 *et seq*.

25 OECD Guidelines, Concepts and Principles para. 1 (p. 17).

26 The Guidelines provide so-called National Contact Points (NCP) but the object and tasks of this monitoring mechanism are very general, *ibid*., Part II, Implementation Procedure, p. 65 *et seq*. See, also, *Germanwatch*, "Überarbeitung der OECD-Leitsätzefür multinationaleUnternehmen", (May 2011) available at: www.germanwatch.org/en/download/2215.pdf; *Amnesty International*, "The 2010–11 Update of the OECD Guidelines for Multinational Enterprises has come to an end: the OECD must now turn into effective implementation", (23 May 2011), available at: www.amnesty.org/es/library/asset/IOR30/001/2011/es/6bcc9b85-9a89-4511-9712-a965ee267564/ior300012011en.html.

Recently, the former Special Representative of the UN Secretary-General for Human Rights and Transnational Corporations and other Business Enterprises, John Ruggie, proposed a new framework for the accountability of private actors for human rights violations. He elaborated the duties of corporations within the "'Protect, Respect and Remedy' Framework",[27] and, provided the so-called Guiding Principles,[28] with recommendations to implement this concept. According to this concept, business corporations have the obligation to respect human rights, just as states have obligations to protect human rights against the violations which are caused by private actors. As far as the normative foundation of the horizontal effect of human rights is concerned, Ruggie refers to the "social expectation of the society" to impose obligations on private actors. The obligations of business actors to respect human rights are, according to Ruggie, the "the baseline norm for all companies in all situations" which have acquired "near-universal recognition".[29] He bases his concept upon voluntary obligations.[30]

Even though these approaches are important steps to hold corporations accountable for human rights violations, they are, both for the aforementioned reasons and for the fact that they are considered from the state-centric perspective of law as voluntary provisions, not sufficient to protect human rights comprehensively. Ultimately, the theoretical and doctrinal approaches do not provide a persuasive and satisfactory solution to the horizontal effect of human rights, and thus do not hold private actors accountable for human rights violations because they adhere to the orthodox concept of international law[31] and the liberal construction of human rights.[32] In sum, convincing solutions to the *problématique* of the accountability of business corporations for human rights violations have not been found.

---

27 Ruggie, note 18 above, (2008) UNDoc A/HRC/8/5.

28 John Ruggie, "Guiding Principles on Business and Human Rights: Implementing the United Nations 'Protect, Respect and Remedy' Framework", Report of the Special Representative of the Secretary- General on the issue of human rights and transnational corporations and other business enterprises (2011) UN Doc A/HRC/17/31.

29 John Ruggie, "Report of the Special Representative of the Secretary-General on the Issue of Human Rights and Transnational Corporations and Other Business Enterprises", (2009) UN Doc A/HRC/11/13paras. 46–48; idem, note 18 above, (2008) UN Doc A/HRC/8/5 paras. 54–55.

30 Ruggie, note 28 above, (2011) UN Doc A/HRC/17/31 para. 6; idem, note 18 above, (2008) UN Doc A/HRC/8/5 para. 9, 54. See, also, Wouter Vandenhole, "Emerging Normative Frameworks on Transnational Human Rights Obligations", (2012) EUI Working Papers, RSCAS 2012/17, p. 11 *et seq.*

31 Critical to the role of international law for the accountability gap, see Penelope Simons, "International Law's Invisible Hand and the Future of Corporate Accountability for Violations of Human Rights", (2012) 3 *Journal of Human Rights and Environment*, p. 5.

32 See, for a detailed critique, Ibrahim Kanalan, "Horizontal Effect of Human Rights in the Era of Transnational Constellations: On the Accountability of Private Actors for Human Rights Violations", (2014), available at SSRN: http://ssrn.com/abstract=2539110, p. 24 *et seq.*

B. HORIZONTAL EFFECT OF HUMAN RIGHTS *DE LEGE FERENDA*: GOING BEYOND CLASSICAL CONCEPTS AND APPROACHES

Against this background, we would like to offer a new concept for the horizontal effect of human rights and the accountability of private actors, which we will present in two steps. First, we would like to generalise the normative idea of human rights and highlight the reason for the horizontal validity of human rights. And secondly, we will explain why private actors should be bound by human rights. We argue that, for a comprehensive and appropriate concept of horizontal validity, it is essential to go beyond classical patterns. First, it is necessary to base the validity of human rights in the private sphere on the normative idea of human rights itself. Secondly, the horizontal validity requires a new understanding of human rights, that is, to conceive of human rights as a means by which to the regulate communicative processes of all functional systems with individuals. Consequently, the communication of functional systems has to be taken as the starting-point for the accountability of private actors.

1. *Abstraction of the Idea of Human Rights – Addressing the Roots of Human Rights*

The main questions for the foundation of the effect of human rights in the private sphere are as follows: What is the normative idea of human rights, for what do human rights stand? The origin and idea of human rights is one of the most contested and disputed issues within a rights discourse. Nevertheless, there is no universal valid foundation for human rights,[33] and it would exceed the scope of this chapter to re-open this discussion. Consequently, in the following, we will solely outline the main points in order to be able to proceed properly.

Beyond most disputes, a historical consideration displays the formation of human rights as the result of societal struggles, even though it cannot be neglected that functional reasons are probably more decisive than the

33 See, for example, Charles R. Beitz, *The Idea of Human Rights*, (Oxford *et al*: Oxford University Press, 2009); Jerome J. Shestack, "The Philosophic Foundation of Human Rights", (1998) 20 *Human Rights Quarterly*, p. 201; Upendra Baxi, *The Future of Human Rights*, (Oxford: Oxford University Press, 2006); Makua W. Mutua, *Human Rights: A Political and Cultural Critique*, (Philadelphia PA: University of Pennsylvania Press, 2002); Michael Freeman, "The Philosophical Foundations of Human Rights", (1994) 16 *Human Rights Quarterly*, p. 491; David Kennedy, "The International Human Rights Movement: Part of the Problem?", (2002) 15 *Harvard Human Rights Journal*, p. 101; James W. Nickel, "Rethinking Indivisibility: Towards a Theory of Supporting Relations between Human Rights", (2008) 30 *Human Rights Quarterly*, p. 984. See, also, William Twining, *General Jurisprudence: Understanding Law from a Global Perspective*, (Cambridge: Cambridge University Press, 2009).

normative reasons for the formation of rights in general.[34] In its normative conception, human rights are the outcome of diverse struggles, protests, and resistance against injustice generally, and particularly against the absence of freedom, equality, and independence, as well as against imperialism, colonialism, oppression and humiliation, to name but a few.[35] Briefly, it can be said that, in their modern formation, human rights are responses to structural experiences of injustice.[36] Consequently, they do not – in contrast to the claim of liberal theory – operate solely as defensive rights against the interference of the state, that is, the obligation to respect. Instead, they have to be conceived comprehensively, serving as pro-active or positive rights which enable the inclusion of individuals in diverse functional systems, that is, the obligation to protect and fulfil (the inclusionary function).[37] Thus, the accomplishment of human rights is not exclusively normative, but is also functional.[38] Due to the inter-dependence of the structural experiences of injustice and societal expectations (normative reasons), on the one hand, and the formation and shape of human rights according to power formation (functional reasons), on the other, the positivisation of demands and interests is primarily caused by historical-sociological circumstances. Thus, the demands and interests were initially focused on negative rights, and successively on positive rights, with both the elements of protection and fulfilment. The codification and evolution of rights in its progressive and emancipatory manner reflects the needs and interests of the society in question.[39] This process operates in a dialectical manner, and it

---

34 Chris Thornhill, *A Sociology of Constitutions*, (Cambridge: Cambridge University Press, 2011).

35 See, for example, the preamble of the Universal Declaration of Human Rights. See, also, José-Manuel Barreto, "Imperialism and Decolonization as Scenarios of Human Rights History", in: idem (ed), *Human Rights from a Third World Perspective*, (Newcastle: Cambridge Scholars Publishing, 2013), p. 140.

36 Winfried Brugger, "Menschenrechte im modernen Staat", (1989) 114 *Archiv des öffentlichen Rechts*, p. 537; Barreto, note 35 above.

37 Gunther Teubner, *Verfassungsfragmente*, (Frankfurt aM: Suhrkamp Verlag, 2012), p. 207 *et seq*; idem, "Transnational Fundamental Rights: Horizontal Effect?", (2011) 40 *Rechtspilosophie & Rechtstheorie*, p. 191, p. 200 *et seq*, & 203 *et seq*; Gert Verschraegen, "Systems Theory and the Paradox of Human Rights", in: Michael King and Chris Thornhill (eds), *Luhmann on Law and Politics*, (Oxford-Portland OR: Hart Publishing, 2006), p. 101; Niklas Luhmann, *Grundrechte als Institution*, (Berlin: Duncker & Humblot, 1965), p. 138. See, for the inclusionary function of (human) rights especially for the political system, Chris Thornhill, "The Future of the State", in: Poul F. Kjaer, Gunther Teubner and Alberto Febbrajo (eds), *The Financial Crisis in Constitutional Perspective: The Dark Side of Functional Differentiation*, (Oxford-Portland OR: Hart Publishing, 2011), p. 377, at 381; Chris Thornhill, "Re-conceiving Rights Revolutions: The Persistence of a Sociological Deficit in Theories of Rights", (2010) 31 *Zeitschrift für Rechtssoziologie*, p. 109.

38 Accordingly, Thornhill emphasises the inclusionary function of (human) rights as well. He even argues that the formation of (human) rights are primarily functionally conditioned; see Thornhill, note 34 above.

39 In general, in respect to human rights, see Thomas H. Marshall, "Citizenship and Social Class", in: Thomas H. Marshall and Tom Bottomore, *Citizenship and Social Class*,

has to be stressed – in contrast to the common notion of liberal theory – that there is no lucid distinction between the exclusionary and inclusionary function of human rights, and that there is no linear process of the formation and shaping of human rights as the traditional concept asserts. One of the first human rights documents of modernity, namely, the French constitution of 1789 and the subsequent constitution of 1848 after the revolution that year, already codified human rights in "negative" and "positive" forms. Human rights as a whole had exclusionary and inclusionary functions. The fact that the endangerment of human rights was originally caused essentially by the state is due to the fact that the political system with the state at its centre was the most differentiated system of society at the time.[40] On the other hand, this is a very narrow liberal European narrative of human rights. From the perspective of the Third World, there has hardly been a clear distinction between the state and private actors. States *and* corporations were both the actors of colonisation and oppression together.[41] Thus, human rights have not only been a means against the violence of the state, especially the home state, but also a means for indigenous groups, social movements and the struggles of peoples in the Global South to take action against (imperial) host states as well as against the policies of international institutions and transnational corporations.[42] These struggles were not confined to a mere historical moment in the past, but continue to take place as struggles for transnational social rights against national states, international institutions and transnational corporations to this very day.[43]

Thus, the idea of human rights is comprehensive as asserted and cannot be limited to the endangerment exclusively caused by one particular system. The normative idea behind the purpose of human rights was the prevention and elimination of injustice in all its forms, independently of the source of danger, which threatens individuals in their integrity, *vis-à-vis* their lives, their freedom, their interests, *etc.* This is the reason why human rights do not operate as "pre-legal absolute" rights, but rather as "pre-political" and "pre-legal latent rights" which both arise out of *and* are shaped by conflicts both within and between diverse systems, such as politics, morals, religion(s), law, the economy, science, *etc.*[44] The normative basis of human rights lies in its universal demand for social justice; justice within each different functional system and between both

(London: Pluto Press, 1992). See, also, Chris Thornhill, "Towards a Historical Sociology of Constitutional Legitimacy", (2008) 37 *Theory and Society*, p. 161.

40 Gunther Teubner, "The Anonymous Matrix: Human Rights Violations by 'Private' Transnational Actors", (2006) 69 *Modern Law Review*, p. 327 & 336 *et seq*; Christoph Beat Graber and Gunther Teubner, "Art and Money: Constitutional Rights in the Private Sphere", (1998) 18 *Oxford Journal of Legal Studies*, p. 61, at 64 *et seq*.

41 Janet McLean, "The Transnational Corporation in History: Lessons for Today?", (2004) 79 *Indiana Law Journal*, p. 363.

42 Barreto, note 35 above, p. 140–141 & p. 159 *et seq*.

43 See Fischer-Lescano and Möller, note 7 above.

44 See Teubner, note 40 above, p. 336 *et seq*.

the systems and their environment. Thus, it is not only within the jurisdiction of states and thus at national level, but also within world society and thus at transnational level. Human rights are also intended to prevent all conditions and circumstances that threaten and endanger human beings in their vital interests and fundamental rights globally. It is thus not the *source* of danger that is crucial, but rather the existence of danger itself. Thus, the *prevention* of danger has to be considered as a central point. Hence, all actors who could possess the potential to cause threats and danger for human rights have to be addressed. The link (connectivity point) for binding any actor to human rights has to be the potential that these actors possess and the possibility that they will endanger or threaten human rights.[45] Since the important fact is the violation of human rights, the challenge is hence to identify the actors that cause the violations and to hold them accountable.

2. *The Foundation of Human Rights Obligations for Private Actors*

With this premise in mind, that the reason for binding all actors to human rights stems from the normative power of human rights, we now turn to analyse whether, and, if so, why private actors should be bound by human rights.

At the beginning of the codification of human rights in the eighteenth century, it was the state that was powerful and it was the state that constituted the most important actor which caused the most danger or posed the greatest threat to human rights. However, the evolution of society has involved and seen significant changes. The differentiation and fragmentation of society creates new functional systems and thus new diverse actors.[46] Having previously been under the dominance of political power (the state), the diverse functional systems began to become independent and autonomous systems, even though they still remained within the shadow of the political system.[47] Accordingly, the systems-theory approach for the horizontal effect of human rights is based upon this diagnosis, and enters a new terrain in the discourse of the binding of private actors to human rights.[48]

Niklas Luhmann had already diagnosed that the maximisation of the intrinsic rationality of diverse function systems, which is caused by functional differentiation, brings an enormous potential of danger both to society and

---

45 See, also, Ratner, note 10 above, p. 512 *et seq.*, 524 *et seq.*, & 540.

46 See Fischer-Lescano and Möller, Chapter I in this volume. In detail, Andreas Fischer-Lescano and Gunther Teubner, "Regime-Collisions: The Vain Search for Legal Unity in the Fragmentation of Global Law", (2004) 25 *Michigan Journal of International Law*, pp. 999–1045.

47 See Teubner, *Verfassungsfragmente*, note 37 above, p. 179 *et seq.*

48 In general, see Teubner, *Fundamental Rights*, note 37 above; idem, *Verfassungsfragmente*, note 37 above, p. 189 *et seq*; idem, note 40 above. For the first approaches, see, also, Graber and Teubner, note 40 above.

to human beings.[49] In line with this diagnosis, Gunther Teubner claims that "it is the fragmentation of society that is today central to the human rights question".[50] In relation to this, the large number of expansionist systems with their sub-systems, organisations and institutions, on the one hand, and the diverse interactions, on the other, entails large numbers or quantities of communications. Simultaneously, these communications have enormous potential to endanger human rights. Teubner articulates this concisely:

> "There is not just a single boundary concerning political communication and the individual, guarded by human rights. Instead, the same problems arise in numerous social institutions, each forming their own boundaries with their human environments: not only politics/individual, but also economy/individual, law/individual, science/individual, medicine/individual (never as a whole/part relation, but understood as difference between communication and mind/body)."[51]

These communications not only bring advantages, they are also able to threaten the integrity of individuals or even to terminate their existence.

The traditional concepts, based upon the supremacy or primacy of the state, were able to offer a solution only as long as the political system was able to be identified with the society in which it ruled, and was perceived as an essential actor in that society. But the collapse of this concept occurs as result of the fragmentation of society, causing a multiplication of the boundary zones of the autonomous communication-matrices for individuals.[52] The consequence of these events is that the danger does not exclusively result from the communications of the political system and thus does not concern the relation between the state and individuals, but rather concerns the relation between individuals and *all* functional systems with their diverse sub-systems, which, in turn, can be characterised through expansionist tendencies.[53] Hence, the new constellation with regard to the accomplishment (function) of human rights is: functional system X *versus* the individual. The danger and thus the subsequent violation do not result from a single process with a single source and actor (for example, the state), but rather from a large number of anonymous and autonomous globalised communication processes of diverse functional systems.[54] Therefore, and due to the multiplicative systems and the new constellation with its diverse actors, both institutions and communications

---

49 Niklas Luhmann, *Gesellschaft der Gesellschaft*, Vol 2, (Frankfurt aM: Suhrkamp Verlag, 1997), p. 1088 *et seq*. See, also, Fischer-Lescano and Teubner, note 46 above, p. 25 *et seq*.

50 Teubner, note 40 above, p. 339.

51 Ibid., p. 339.

52 Ibid., note 40 above, p. 338 *et seq*; see, also, idem, "Fundamental Rights", note 37 above, pp. 209–212.

53 Idem, *Verfassungsfragmente*, note 37 above, p. 213; idem, "Fundamental Rights", note 37 above, p. 211.

54 Idem, *Verfassungsfragmente*, note 37 above, p. 215 *et seq*; idem, note 40 above, pp. 339–341.

require new solutions, "new types of guarantees", which "limit the destructive potential of communication".[55] What is necessary is a concept that is sensitive and responsive to modifications of this kind, and one which considers this diagnosis as a starting-point.

The ecological concept of fundamental rights observes precisely this diversification and attempts to offer an adequate solution.[56] According to this concept, the question of human rights should not be understood as the tradition assumes, as a balance between society both as a whole and its various parts, but, instead, as a question of the expansive functional systems to their social, human, and natural ecologies.[57] Simultaneously, human rights are conceptualised as a "response to problems that transcend society" and "demand an ecological sensitivity of communication".[58] Human rights, as "intrinsic rights" have the function of constraining communications;[59] that is, to safeguard the "boundary relations" between the functional systems and their environment.[60] However, the function of human rights does not exist exclusively in its negative dimension to prevent exclusion, but also exists in its positive dimension in order to enable inclusion (rights to access).[61] Even if this function is gradually neglected,[62] human rights serve as means to acquire access to diverse functional systems, their institutions and their goods in order to enable them *de facto* to exercise human rights. Ultimately, under these circumstances, the question no longer concerns the access to political systems, but instead concerns the access to *all* functional systems.[63]

Consequently, human rights have to be conceived as a concept which includes all societal institutions and actors that are able to communicate and thus possess the potential to violate human rights. Provided that the problem of human rights always occurs consequentially in relation to communicative processes, that is, whenever a communication is performed, boundaries are transcended and rights are violated.[64] In other words, the matter concerns the re-formulation of

---

55 Idem, note 40 above, p. 339.

56 Ibid., note 40 above, p. 333 *et seq*; idem, *Verfassungsfragmente*, note 37 above, p. 189 *et seq*; idem, "Fundamental Rights", note 37 above, p. 199 *et seq*.

57 See idem, note 40 above, p. 330 *et seq*.

58 Ibid., note 40 above, p. 333.

59 Ibid., p. 334; Graber and Teubner, note 40 above, p. 68 *et seq*.

60 Similar, with regard to the function of the constitution, see Gunther Teubner, "Globale Zivilverfassung: Alternativen zur staatszentrierten Verfassungstheorie", (2003) 63 *Zeitschrift für ausländisches Recht und Völkerrecht*, p. 1, at 10 *et seq*.

61 See Teubner, "Fundamental Rights", note 37 above, pp. 202–206; idem, *Verfassungsfragmente*, note 37 above, p. 202 *et seq*; Niklas Luhmann, note 38 above, p. 42. See, also, Verschraegen, note 37 above.

62 See Teubner, "Fundamental Rights", note 37 above, p. 202 *et seq*; idem, *Verfassungsfragmente*, note 37 above, p. 207 *et seq*.

63 Idem,"Fundamental Rights", note 37 above, pp. 204–205; idem, *Verfassungsfragmente*, note 37 above, p. 208 *et seq*; Verschraegen, note 37 above, p. 107 *et seq*, & 120 *et seq*.

64 Teubner, note 40 above, p. 336 *et seq*.

human rights from conflicts of individuals within society to "conflicts between society and its ecologies", or, respectively, a transformation "from the paradigm of interpersonal conflicts between individual bearers of fundamental rights to that of ecological conflicts between anonymous communicative processes, on the one hand, and concrete people on the other".[65] Examples of this constellation would include human rights violations by business corporations, or by private associations, for instance, religious or sports associations, hospitals, universities, schools, NGOs, *etc.*[66] Translated into legal language, the result is individual lawsuits against private actors concerning the structural violence and exclusion from the systems and their institutions through diverse actors, on the one hand, and the claim to obtain access to diverse systems, institutions and goods, on the other.[67]

The ensuing question is what does this concretely entail for the question of binding private actors to human rights. Considering this from the viewpoint of the new concept of human rights, we are able to draw the following conclusion concerning the accountability of private actors. The necessity to bind private actors to human rights results from the differentiation of the societal systems. According to the new concept of human rights, private actors are bound by human rights because they participate as *subjects* of rights[68] in the communicative processes, which are of relevance for human rights. Being able to participate in communicative processes admits the potential for violating human rights and causing danger. Therefore, it is not crucial whether these actors possess enormous power – even though power is important for all functional systems as well[69] – what is central is their *participation* in communications, and thereby the *possibility* of violations of human rights.

As far as the content and extent of the obligations of the new actors is concerned, it is important to avoid the categorical error of other approaches and not to attempt to transform, even with a modification, "state human rights and obligations" to the other functional systems. Instead, it is suggested that the details be determined according to the specifics of the concrete functional system-regime (regime-specific determination).[70] In other words,

65 *Ibid.*, p. 342. See, also, Teubner, "Fundamental Rights", note 37 above, p. 210 *et seq.*

66 See, also, Teubner, note 40 above, p. 344.

67 See Teubner, note 40 above, pp. 343–344; Teubner, "Fundamental Rights", note 37 above, p. 212 *et seq.*

68 See, generally, for the term "subject of rights", Teubner, "Globale Zivilverfassung", note 60 above, p. 4 *et seq*; Andreas Fischer-Lescano, "Globalverfassung: Verfassung der Weltgesellschaft", (2002) 88 *Archiv für Rechts- und Sozialphilosophie*, p. 349. Similarly, Ruggie does not operate with the traditional concept of subjects of international law. He argues, instead, with the concept of "participants"; see Ruggie, note 12 above, (2007) UN Doc A/HRC/4/035 para. 20; John Ruggie, "Business and Human Rights: The Evolving International Agenda", (2007) 101 *American Journal of International Law*, p. 819 & 824.

69 Teubner, *Verfassungsfragmente*, note 37 above, p. 175 *et seq.*

70 Idem, "Fundamental Rights", note 37 above, p. 195 *et seq.*, 201 *et seq.*

this is a re-formulation of the concept of human rights for the relationship of individuals with other societal institutions.[71] With this premise in mind, the content and extent of the obligations can be determined and defined more precisely in accordance with the following principles. First of all, it is important to conceptualise human rights as provisions with obligations to respect, protect and fulfil. Subsequently, it is necessary to determine the system-specific details and, not repeating the reductionism of the liberal theory, to focus and consider only the preventive function of human rights (the obligation to respect),[72] on which the representatives of this theory constantly insist.[73] Contrary to the reductionist approach, human rights can impose comprehensive obligations on private actors. As the UN Norms stated, human rights encompass the obligation "to promote, secure the fulfilment of, respect, ensure respect of and protect human rights recognized international as well as national law".[74] To sum up, it is not only the obligation to respect, which is valid for private actors, but also the obligations to protect and fulfil. This is not limited to particular circumstances, but has, instead, to be seen as rule.[75] As Teubner states, beyond the obligation to respect, the principle of inclusion has to be generalised in such a manner that "access to the communicative media in all function systems is not only permitted, but is actually guaranteed by means of fundamental rights".[76] Thus, this also applies to business corporations since "the functional differentiation of the societal system, the regulation of the relationship of inclusion and exclusion is transferred to function systems and there is no longer any central authority [...] to supervise the subsystems in this regard".[77]

---

71 Ibid., p. 195–198; see, also, Gunther Teubner, "Das Projekt der Verfassungssoziologie", (2011) 32 *Zeitschrift für Rechtssoziologie*, p. 189 in the context of a new concept of the constitution.

72 Critically, see, also, Teubner, "Fundamental Rights", note 37 above, p. 201.

73 Recently, the concept of the Special Represantative John Ruggie was generally focused primarily on the obligation to respect even though he alludes the obligation of corporations to protect; Ruggie, note 29 above, (2009) UN Doc A/HRC/11/13 paras. 56 *et seq.*

74 Economic and Social Council, Sub-Commission on the Promotion and Protection of Human Rights, "*Norms on the Responsibilities of Transnational Corporations and other Business Enterprises with regard to Human Rights*"(UN Norms) (2003) UN Doc E/CN.4/Sub.2/2003/12/Rev.2, para. 1; see, also, the preamble.

75 Paul Hunt appears to tend to this opine as well, see Paul Hunt, "Special Rapporteur on the Right of Everyone to the Enjoyment of the Highest Attainable Standard of Health – Mission to GlaxoSmithKline", (2009) UN Doc A/HRC/11/12/Add.2, especially para. 17.

76 Teubner, "Fundamental Rights", note 37 above, p. 204 (footnote omitted).

77 Niklas Luhmann, *Die Politik der Gesellschaft*, (Frankfurt aM: Suhrkamp Verlag, 2000), p. 427, quoted in Teubner, "Fundamental Rights", note 37 above, p. 205.

III. THE PRACTICE TEST: TRANSFERRING THE CONCEPT INTO EFFECT?

To exemplify our theoretical approach, we now wish to analyse the recently adopted EU legislation on non-financial reporting,[78] which has attracted widespread attention.

For the purpose of this chapter, we define non-financial reporting as a process of communicating information on both the social and environmental impact and the effects of business conduct. Non-financial reporting in general has its origin in the concept of Corporate Social Responsibility and traditional financial reporting.[79] There are many global initiatives that deal with non-financial reporting,[80] and some of them offer reporting schemes[81] which can be used by companies or groups to report on non-financial matters.[82] While these initiatives are strictly "voluntary",[83] there are many countries that have passed more or less mandatory non-financial reporting-legislation.[84]

---

78 Also known as social accounting, social and environmental accounting, corporate social reporting, corporate social responsibility reporting, non-financial accounting.

79 For further information on origin, main actors and used terminology, see Katelijne von Wensen, Wijnand Broer, Johanna Klein and Jutta Knopf, "The State of Play in Sustainability Reporting in the EU", 2011, available at: www.ec.europa.eu/social/BlobServlet?docId=6727&langId=en, p. 14 *et seq.*

80 At global level, there are initiatives, offered by International Organisations (IOs) and Non-governmental Organisations (NGOs), which are completely voluntary like the OECD Guidelines for Multinational Enterprises, the ISO 26000, ILO Tri-partite Declaration of Principles concerning Multinational Enterprises and Social Policies, the UN "Protect, Respect and Remedy" Framework on Business and Human Rights proposed by the UN-Special-Representative John Ruggie, the Global Reporting Initiative (GRI) and the UN Guiding Principles Reporting Framework offered by the Human Rights Reporting and Assurance Frameworks Initiative (RAFI).

81 Also called reporting standards, guidelines or reporting frameworks.

82 The most used reporting schemes are the Guidelines of the GRI and the United Nations Global Compact Communication on Progress (UNGC COP). Beside that, there are many other standards which partially only refer to special business sectors like the Carbon Disclosure Project (CDP) and the Connected Reporting Framework (CRF) (for further Initiatives see von Wensen, Broer, Klein and Knopf, note 79 above, Appendix C, p. 135 *et seq.*).

83 At international level, there are voices that, on the one hand, demand universal initiatives and, on the other hand, strive for legally binding approaches and standards. At UN level, the outcome document of the UN Conference on Sustainable Development (Rio+20) calls for a universal framework on non-financial reporting (General Assembly (2012) UN Doc A/RES/66/288, para. 47.), and the latest report of the United Nations Secretary-General's High-level Panel on Global Sustainability argues for a mandatory reporting framework (General Assembly, (2012) UN Doc A/RES/66/700, para. 166.). The International Integrated Reporting Committee (IIRC), *i.e.*, is a global initiative of all kinds of actors (*i.e.*, the Global Reporting Initiative (GRI) or UN representatives), which aims to create a universally accepted reporting framework (see www.theiirc.org).

84 For example, the Netherlands, Belgium, Denmark, the United Kingdom, Finland, Spain, France and Sweden. For a brief summary on the recent developments in some of these Member States, see European Commission, Impact Assessment – Accompanying the

The reason why we chose non-financial reporting to exemplify our theoretical approach is that it has certain characteristics that make this approach different from others, which aim to hold multinational corporations liable for human rights violations. In addition, the EU's legislation is of exceptional relevance, because this non-financial reporting-legislation implies obligations for a high number of the world's biggest and most influential MNCs.

The corresponding supranational or national level[85] regulation of MNCs implies legal obligations with regard to their activities abroad, without creating immediate accountability for human-rights-related actions. In this respect, non-financial reporting does not principally refer to compensation for human rights violations, but instead aims to establish human rights protection as a core business concern.[86] Upon this basis, we want to propose the following question: Does the EU's non-financial reporting framework have the potential to promote the accountability of MNCs effectively and significantly strengthen the spaces of societal autonomy towards the economic system?

We begin the following section with an introduction to the topic of non-financial reporting and the legislation within the EU in general. After this, we wish to review the EU's non-financial reporting framework, ask about the European Union's and Member State's international human rights obligations in the field of non-financial reporting and put our findings in the context of our theoretical framework.

A. THE EUROPEAN UNION'S DIRECTIVE ON NON-FINANCIAL REPORTING

Within the EU, the idea of non-financial reporting is rooted in the EU's activities concerning CSR and in the legislative practice of some Member States. The European Parliament recently adopted two resolutions[87] in which

---

document Proposal for a Directive of the European Parliament and of the Council amending Council Directives 78/660/EEC and 83/349/EEC as regards disclosure of non-financial and diversity information by certain large companies and groups, SWD (2013) 127 final, 16 April 2013, Annex III, p. 49 *et seq*; For references to the corresponding legislation see European Coalition for Corporate Justice (ECCJ), "Principles & Pathways: Legal opportunities to improve Europe's corporative accountability framework", November 2010, available at: www.corporatejustice.org/IMG/pdf/eccj_principles_pathways_webuseblack.pdf, p. 11, fn 5.

85 While there a several states that already passed non-financial reporting legislation (see notes 84 above and 106 below), a EU legislation with regard to a mandatory reporting system expands corresponding obligations to a wider scope. In so far, the research on the EU legislation is exemplary for the concept of non-financial reporting in general.

86 Daniel Augenstein, "Study of the Legal Framework on Human Rights and the Environment Applicable to European Enterprises Operating Outside the European Union", 2010, p. 75, para. 232.

87 European Parliament Resolution, Report on Corporate Social Responsibility: Accountable, Transparent and Responsible Business Behaviour and Sustainable Growth, A7-0017/2013,

it acknowledged the importance of transparency. Furthermore, the European Commission announced regulation regarding non-financial reporting in the Single Market Act[88] with the communication entitled "A Renewed Strategy 2011–2014 for Corporate Social Responsibility".[89] The Accounting Directives[90] already dealt with reporting on environmental- and employee-related matters.

On 11 November 2014, the European Union finally adopted Directive 2014/95/EU[91] that explicitly concerns non-financial reporting. Directive 2014/95/EU amends Directive 2013/34/EU on financial reporting (Accounting Directive).[92] The purpose of Directive 2014/95/EU is to harmonise the existing national non-financial information legislation and to establish it where Member States have not enacted regulation in this field.[93] It aims to increase the number of reporting companies and the relevance, consistency and comparability of the information disclosed by large companies.[94] With regard to the EU's strategy on CSR, the Recital states:

> "disclosure of non-financial information is vital for managing change towards a sustainable global economy by combining long-term profitability with social justice and environmental protection."[95]

---

28 January 2013 and European Parliament Resolution, Report on Corporate Social Responsibility: Promoting Society's Interests and a Route to Sustainable and Inclusive Recovery, A7–0023/2013, 29 January 2013.

88 European Commission Communication, Single Market Act – Twelve levers to boost growth and strengthen confidence, COM (2011) 206 final, 13 April 2011; see, also, European Commission Communication, Single Market Act II – Together for new growth, COM (2012) 573 final, 3 October 2012, pp 15 *et seq.*

89 European Commission Communication, A renewed EU strategy 2011–14 for Corporate Social Responsibility, COM (2011) 681 final, 25 October 2011.

90 Company reporting under the legislation of the EU is covered by the Directive 2013/34/EU of the European Parliament and the Council on the annual financial statements, consolidated financial statements and related reports of certain types of undertakings of 26 June 2013, OJ L 182, 29.6.2013, pp. 19–76, which amends the Directive 2006/43/EC of the European Parliament and the Council on statutory audits of annual accounts and consolidated accounts of 17 May 2006, OJ L 157, 17.06.2006, pp. 87–107, and repeals the 4th and 7th Company Law Directives (Fourth Council Directive 78/660/EEC of 25 July 1978, OJ L 222, 14.8.1978, pp. 11–31 and Seventh Council Directive 83/349/EEC of 13 June 1983, OJ L 193, 18.07.1983, pp. 1–17).

91 European Parliament and the Council, Directive 2014/95/EU amending Directive 2013/34/EU as regards disclosure of non-financial and diversity information by certain large undertakings and groups, 2014 O.J. L 330/1, 11 November 2014.

92 See note 90 above.

93 Recital 4 and 5 Directive 2014/95/EU; European Commission, Impact Assessment, note 84 above, p. 23.

94 Recital 21 Directive 2014/95/EU.

95 Recital 3 Directive 2014/95/EU.

It is therefore an important tool to measure, monitor and manage the performance of companies and their impact on society.[96] Regarding the objectives of non-financial reporting, besides the demand for transparency of all affected individuals, communities and NGOs, the interests of the investors, consumers and the companies themselves all play an important role. The European Commission argues that better integration and assessment of non-financial risks in business strategies would enhance the overall perfomance of companies; increased transparancy is expected to enhance consumer and investor trust.[97] Disclosure of non-financial information therefore allows companies to allocate more capital, and helps investors to integrate non-financial matters into their investment decisions.[98] To sum up, besides accountability and transparency, the efficiency of capital markets and the performance of companies are the main concerns of the EU's non-financial reporting legislation.

In the following section of this chapter, we wish to take a closer look at the European Union's Directive on non-financial reporting. For every relevant aspect, we initially want to highlight the possible features of non-financial reporting in general before describing and critically reviewing the arrangement of the Directive.

1. *Obligated Actors*

Firstly, which companies or groups are affected by the non-financial reporting legislation? Most "non-binding" concepts or standards simply refer to "companies".[99] Consequently, it often remains unclear which private actors are covered by the specific terms. While it is not necessary for a "voluntary" framework to specify clearly to whom it applies, for a legally-binding duty at national or European legislative level, it is essential to define the bearers of a statutory duty.

Concerning the size of legally-obliged entities, the main concern raised on this issue is that the duty constitutes an undue administrative and financial burden on small companies.[100] As a result, the Directive covers only "large"

96 Ibid.

97 European Commission, Impact Assessment, note 84 above, p. 23 *et seq*, p. 37 *et seq*.

98 Ibid.

99 Some reporting initiatives do not even restrict the participation on companies or business actors. The GRI for example enables all organisations to report.

100 See Positionspapier der Bundesregierung zur Mitteilung der Europäischen Kommission, "Eine neue EU-Strategie (2011–14) für die soziale Verantwortung der Unternehmen (CSR)", (KOM 2011) (681endg.), 18 November 2011.

undertakings and groups of "public interest"[101] (Art. 19a (1) and 29a (1) Directive 2013/34/EU). To define the term "large undertakings and groups", the Directive refers to the total number of employees and likewise to the total assets and/or annual turnover. According to this, the Directive provides that only undertakings or groups with more than 500 employees, a balance sheet total of 20 million euros or a net turnover of 40 million euros should be subject to new requirements.[102] On the whole, this would approximately cover about 6,000 out of 42,000 "large" companies operating in the EU.[103]

Since the European Union expects non-financial reporting to enhance the overall performance of a company, the criticism can be made that the Directive only covers large companies. Besides this, it has to be emphasised that the Directive only determines a minimum requirement regarding the scope of the application. Recital 14 Directive 2014/95/EU states that Member States are free to expand the reporting obligation to a wider scope of companies. But, at the same time, Recital 14 Directive 2014/95/EU stresses the importance of exempting small- and medium-sized companies from the reporting requirement in order to save them from an undue administrative and financial burden. Member States should still consider whether it would be adequate to diverge from the minimum requirements regarding the net turnover, balance sheet and amount of employees. They also should consider implementing mechanisms and policies that aim to encourage small- and medium-sized companies to report on non-financial matters, for example, by explicitly leaving it up to these companies themselves to decide whether to comply with the reporting requirement while making it mandatory for large companies. This could be an option to stimulate and raise the awareness of small- and medium-sized companies regarding human rights and CSR matters.

2. *Design and Content*

Another important point is the legal design of a reporting framework and the content of the reports. There are different ways of shaping a non-financial reporting-framework and each has different effects on the quantity and quality of the reports.

---

101 The term"public interest" is defined in Art. 2 (1) Directive 2013/34/EU (note 90 above). The definition covers, *i.e.*, companies that are both governed by the law of a Member State and listed on a regulated market, all credit institutions in the EU, all insurance undertakings in the EU and companies that are of significant public relevance because of the nature of their business, their size, or number of employees.

102 See Art. 19a, 29a in conjunction with Art. 3 and 4 Directive 2013/34/EU. Undertakings which are subsidiary undertakings shall be exempted from the obligation to report if these undertakings and their subsidiary undertakings are included in the report of another undertaking (Art. 19a (3) and Art. 29a (3) Directive 2013/34/EU).

103 Daniel P. Kinderman, "The Struggle Over the UN Non-Financial Disclosure Directive", *WSI-Mitteilungen* 8/2015, pp. 613–621, at 616, available at SSRN: www.ssrn.com/abstracht=2614983.

Regarding the legal design, there are two relevant questions: the first concerns the form of the disclosure and the second concerns its legal nature.

a. The Form of the Report

With regard to the first question, the reports could be designed in the form of a statement as a part of the annual report,[104] or as a stand-alone non-financial report which could be annexed to the annual report or published separately.

The Directive leaves reporting companies a wide margin of appreciation on how to present the required information. It is left to the companies to decide as to whether they integrate the non-financial information in the annual report or whether they prepare a stand-alone report, as long as the stand-alone report is published together with the annual report or is made publicly available on the parent undertaking's website, and is referred to in the annual report, Article 19a (4) and Article 29a (4) Directive 2013/34/EU.[105]

b. Legal Nature

Concerning the legal nature of the disclosure, there are three possible variations: initially, the disclosure could be upon a "voluntary" basis or strictly mandatory. Many non-financial reporting frameworks have established a third, allegedly more flexible, approach, namely, the "report or explain" (also "comply or explain") framework.[106] This framework requires companies to report. Failing that, a clear and reasoned explanation of why this is the case must be given.

---

104 An annual report is a report on a company's activities and financial performance throughout the preceding year. The Accounting Directive uses the term "management report", or, with regard to groups, "consolidated management reports" (see Articles 19 and 29 Directive 2013/34/EU).

105 The European Commission opted for the integration of a statement into the annual report and therefore argued that the involvement of the non-financial reporting in the established reporting system, on the one hand, minimises the administrative burden on the affected companies and, on the other, is of advantage compared to the stand-alone-report model, because it ties in with already established proceedings. (European Commission, Impact Assessment, note 84 above, p. 25 *et seq*). The Commission also refers to the estimated costs of compliance in terms of administrative burden, and points out that a disclosure included in the annual reports would cost 600 to 4,300 euro while detailed reporting in the form of a separate document or as an annex to the annual report would require approximately 33,000 to 604,000 euro (European Commission, Impact Assessment, note 84 above, p. 10 & 35).

106 The GRI (see GRI, G4 Sustainability Reporting Guidelines, www.globalreporting.org/resourcelibrary/GRIG4-Part1-Reporting-Principles-and-Standard-Disclosures.pdf, p. 13) as a non-state initiative eg uses the report or explain approach. Furthermore, many states refer to this approach in their non-financial reporting legislation: While for example in Sweden state-owned companies are obliged to report, the Swedish legislation refers to the GRI Guidelines which again use a report or explain approach (see the Swedish Ministry of Finance, *Guidelines for External Reporting by State-owned Companies*, 11 December 2007, available at: www.government.se/content/1/c6/09/41/25/56b7ebd4.pdf, with references to the relevant Swedish legislation). For the Danish experiences with a report or explain

The Directive uses the "report or explain" model. Choosing the option to "explain" is only permitted if the company has no policy on or activity in the required matter. This means that, as long as the company practises a policy or activity relevant under the reporting requirement, it is obliged to report on these matters. Article 19a (1) Directive 2013/34/EU[107] formulates the requirements as follows:

> "Where the undertaking does not pursue policies in relation to one or more of those matters [the companies are ordered to report on[108]], the non-financial statement shall provide a clear and reasoned explanation for not doing so."

The European Commission considered a mandatory option to be more effective, but, at the same time, argued that the "report or explain" option "has the potential to create peer pressure and provide an effective incentive for companies".[109] Furthermore, the European Commission points out that this model would offer "appropriate flexibility to those companies that do not have a specific policy in place in one or more of the above-mentioned areas".[110]

Closely linked to the "report or explain" approach is the exception for the disclosure of information under Article 19a (1) and Article 29a (1) Directive 2013/34/EU that prescribes that:

> "Member States may allow information relating to impending developments or matters in the course of negotiation to be omitted in exceptional cases where, in the duly justified opinion of the members of the administrative, management and supervisory bodies (…) the disclosure of such information would be seriously prejudicial to the commercial position of the group, provided that such omission does not prevent a fair and balanced understanding of the group's development, performance, position and impact of its activity."

The purpose of this exception is to protect the commercial interests of a company in cases where there is the justified assumption that a disclosure of certain information would impede actual negotiations or weaken the bargaining positions of the reporting company.

The problem with the "report or explain" approach and the exceptions under Articles 19a (1) and 29a (1) Directive 2013/34/EU is that these features give companies the opportunity to exclude information that may be of special interest

approach, see the Danish Commerce and Companies Agency, *Corporate Social Responsibility and Reporting in Denmark: Impact of the Third Year Subject to the Legal Requirements for Reporting on CSR in the Danish Financial Statements Act*, 2013, available at: csrgov.dk/file/358879/csr_rapport_2013_eng.pdf; see, also, European Commission, Impact Assessment, note 84 above, p 25, Annex VI, p. 67 *et seq.*

107 See, also, Art. 29a (1) Directive 2013/34/EU.

108 For the required content of the reports, see Section II.1.b.iii.

109 European Commission, Impact Assessment, note 84 above, p. 29.

110 European Commission, Impact Assessment, note 84 above, Annex VI, p. 61.

for "an understanding of the (companies) development, performance, position and impact of its activity" from the reports. With regard to the objectives, spirit and purpose of the Directive, it is necessary that the legislation in the Member States specify the precise requirements regarding the explanation or justification for not reporting on specific matters. This would include requiring companies to point out explicitly the omitted disclosure in the report and describe as precisely as possible the content and the context of the omitted disclosure. This includes a formal duly-justified explanation of why and for what reason the information had not been disclosed and should, in particular, apply to the requirement in the context of the exceptions of Articles 19a (1) and 29a (1) Directive 2013/34/EU.

c. Content

Besides the legal design, the content of the disclosure is of significant relevance. At first, there is no universal definition of the term "non-financial information". While the Accounting Directive, before its amendment by Directive 2014/95/EU, referred to environmental and employee-related concerns,[111] most voluntary frameworks refer to human rights, social and environmental impact, anti-corruption, governance, diversity, and conditions of employment.[112]

The Directive now names environmental, social and employee matters, respect for human rights, anti-corruption and bribery matters, as the minimum of the themes to be covered by the reports (Art. 19a (1) and 29a (1) Directive 2013/34/EU). Relating to these matters, the report is to provide sufficient information to furnish an understanding of a companies development, performance, position and the impact of its various activities, as per Articles 19a (1) and 29a (1) Directive 2013/34/EU. In this regard, the reports shall include:

> "(a) a brief description of the undertaking's business model;
> (b) a description of the policies pursued by the undertaking in relation to those matters, including due diligence processes implemented;
> (c) the outcome of those policies;
> (d) the principal risks related to those matters linked to the undertaking's operations including, where relevant and proportionate, its business relationships, products or services which are likely to cause adverse impacts in those areas, and how the undertaking manages those risks;
> (e) non-financial key performance indicators relevant to the particular business."

---

111 See Art. 19 Abs. 1 Directive 2013/34/EU.

112 The UNGC's Ten Principles, for example, cover Human Rights (Principle 1 and 2), conditions of employment (Principles 3–6), environment (Principles 7–9) and anti-corruption (Principle 10) and the G4 reporting scheme of the GRI contains to the categories economic, environment and social, with sub-categories like human rights, labour practices, society and product responsibility.

Thus, the Directive instructs companies to provide information on their specific characteristics, their general governance, and typical risks regarding their activities. Moreover, the relevant information has to cover a description of a company's policies and risk-management strategies regarding the non-financial aspects of the company's activities as well as the methodology used to assess the relevant information and implement its findings in its further strategies and decisions.[113] It is in this context in particular that the "report or explain approach" reveals its purpose because it offers companies the possibility of reporting on relevant areas, whereas it does not oblige them to report on areas that they do not wish to pursue.

Even though the requirements give brief instructions on which matters and which fields of a company's activities and structures to report on, compared to the currently available reporting guidelines, the instructions and requirements of the Directive remain very vague. In praxis, for reporting companies, it poses a major challenge to identify the relevant and required information and to present it in a manner which is consistent with the provisions of the Directive. For these reasons, companies often rely on reporting guidelines offered by IOs or NGOs such as the UN Global Compact (UNGC) or the Global Reporting Initiative (GRI) in order to prepare their reports. Options on the methodology of the disclosure regarding these guidelines vary from narrative-based concepts (in which each company has a lot of freedom) to models with more or less strictly-framed indicators (*i.e.*, in the form of a questionaire) to which companies have to comply.[114]

The Directive itself contains no such indicators or guidelines on which companies can orientate themselves. However, it recognises that an EU-standard would maximise the comparability of the gained information.[115] But, since the creation of reporting guidelines takes time and it is necessary to consult the relevant stakeholders, the Directive refers to the existing reporting standards while at the same time advising the European Commission to prepare non-binding guidelines on the methodology for reporting non-financial information.[116] Until then, Articles 19a (1) and 29a (1) Directive 2013/34/

113 See European Commission, Impact Assessment, note 84 above, p. 25.

114 The minimum requirements to the UNGC COP (see UNGC, "Basic Guide to the Communication on Progress, 2012", available at: www.unglobalcompact.org/docs/communication_on_progress/Tools_and_Publications/COP_Basic_Guide.pdf) leave companies a wide latitude on the way they report on the UNGC Ten Principles while the G4 reporting scheme of the GRI uses indicators (for example, human rights or environment) and specifications to guide companies' reports (see GRI, "G4 Sustainability Reporting Guidelines", www.globalreporting.org/resourcelibrary/GRIG4-Part1-Reporting-Principles-and-Standard-Disclosures.pdf, p. 47 *et seq.*).

115 See, also, European Commission, Impact Assessment, note 84 above, p. 29. Concurrently, the European Commission argued that this option would afford "the completion of a long and uncertain process of development and implementation of such standards". Furthermore, it would be a considerable administrative burden for companies and would lack the sufficient flexibility as it would oblige companies to report on this regionally-defined standard.

116 See Art. 2 Directive 2014/95/EU.

EU instruct Member States to provide that reporting companies may rely on national, Union-based or international reporting guidelines,[117] and, if they do so, they are to specify upon which guidelines they have relied.

Financial Reporting in practice demonstrates that a smart mixture of governmental and private control in the form of an interlegal approach that leaves it up to the supranational and national level to implement reporting obligations and monitoring mechanism, and up to the "transnational" level to create the reporting standards can be the key to a proper reporting framework. However, in support of an EU-based reporting guidelines, it can be argued that common schemes (such as those of the GRI or the UNGC) leave companies too much room for "green washing" and their own estimation of to what extent they report.[118] Accordingly, reports are often very short and cursory and/or include information on "green" programmes and technologies instead of information on high-risk activities or incidents with impact on the environment or on human rights. NGOs *inter alia* legitimately demand information on all the actual impact of the company's operations.[119] Besides this, the requirements often do not consider the impact of third-country subsidiaries and the suppliers of the European companies that are covered by the proposal, even though these

117 The Directive specifically names the United Nations (UN) Global Compact, the Guiding Principles on Business and Human Rights implementing the UN "Protect, Respect and Remedy" Framework, the Organisation for Economic Co-operation and Development (OECD) Guidelines for Multinational Enterprises, the International Organization for Standardization's ISO 26000, the International Labour Organization's Tripartite Declaration of principles concerning multinational enterprises and social policy and the Global Reporting Initiative (see Recital 9 of the Directive).

118 William S. Laufer, "Social Accountability and Corporate Greenwashing", (2003) 43 *Journal of Business Ethic*, pp. 253–261; Craig Deegan and Michaela Rankin, "Do Australian companies report environmental news objectively? An analysis of environmental disclosures by firms prosecuted successfully by the Environmental Protection Authority", (1996) 9 *Accounting, Auditing & Accountability Journal*, pp. 50–67 *et seq*; O. Boiral, for example, argues that sustainability reports (in this case under the A and A+ GRI standard which generally is said to be the strictest scheme in the field of reporting standards) "can be viewed as simulacra that camouflage real sustainable-development problems, presenting an idealized version of company situations" (Olivier Boiral, "Sustainability Reports as Simulacra? A Counter-Account of A and A+ GRI reports", (2013) 26 *Accounting, Auditing & Accountability Journal*, p. 1036-1071). For deficiencies in the UNGC COP-framework, see, also, Surya Deva, *Regulating Corporate Human Rights Violations: Humanizing Business*, (London-New York: Routledge, 2012), p. 96 *et seq.*

119 See *Amnesty International*, "Corporate non-financial reporting: Amnesty International position paper", April 2013, available at: www.amnesty.org/en/library/asset/POL30/001/2013/en/f3dae509-bd55–46ae-aad7–2c909ef97771/pol300012013en.html: "Reports on all actual (major/severe) impacts of the business operations (…) should include both the incidents of negative impact that the company accepts occurred and issues consistently raised by local communities and civil society groups, even if the company disputes the allegation. (…) Impact reports should state: location of event, what happened, who was affected, what was affected (specifically land, food, water, etc.). Where the incident involves disputed allegations, the company should set out the position of the affected people, as well as the reasons why the company disputes the allegations made."

parts of their business activities provide a high-risk-potential for human rights violations.[120] Thus, it is now up to the European Commission to create reporting guidelines that take the above-mentioned shortcomings of the actual reporting guidelines into due consideration. Regarding the convergence with human rights standards in the field of business and human rights, initiatives such as the Human Rights Reporting and Assurance Frameworks Initiative (RAFI), which tries to create a reporting standard that aims to put the Guiding Principles into practice and thereby directly refers to actual human rights standards, can serve as a role model.

d. Provisional Conclusion

For a provisional conclusion, one could state that the form and the content of the disclosure need to be clearly defined to assure that companies both know and are able to inform in a comprehensive, reliable and homogeneous way.

3. *Monitoring, Evaluation, Enforcement Mechanisms and Sanctions*

Furthermore, questions of implementation and enforcement are of exceptional relevance. There are many ways of shaping the corresponding mechanisms. Conceivable practices vary from models with no enforcement, verification or evaluation, to strict models with "effective, proportionate and dissuasive sanctions",[121] and evaluation and verification by independent bodies.[122]

On matters of implementation and enforcement, the European Commission distinguishes between monitoring and evaluation. During the legislative process, the European Commission suggested that, in the field of monitoring, the Member States be required to gather the reports and information through special agencies or Securities Markets' Regulators.[123] For the purpose of sharing the gained information, the European Commission also proposed that the Accounting Regulatory Committee (ARC),[124] an institution set up by the European Commission with the function of advising in matters of financial reporting, be provided as a forum with the mandate to examine the statements

---

120 See Augenstein, note 86 above, p. 75, para. 232; The ECCJ criticises that the reqirement to report on supply chains is only required "if relevant and proportionate" without further specification (European Coalition for Corporate Justice (ECCJ), Assessment of the EU Directive on the disclosure of non-financial information by certain large companies, May 2014, available at: www.business-humanrights.org/sites/default/files/media/documents/eccj-assessment-eu-non-financial-reporting-may-2104.pdf, p. 3.

121 ECCJ, note 84 above, p. 13.

122 Ibid., p. 12.

123 European Commission, Impact Assessment, note 84 above, p. 43.

124 The Accounting Regulatory Committee (ARC) has been set up by the European Commission, and is composed of representatives from Member States and chaired by the European Commission. It has the regulatory function to provide an opinion on the Commission proposals to adopt an international accounting standard in the area of financial accounting.

and reports in order to ensure compliance, compare the information provided by companies with similar operations, and ensure that affected companies report in a consistent manner.[125] With regard to content, the evaluation suggested by the European Commission would aim to see to what extent the pursued impacts actually materialise.[126] This would cover, on the one hand, matters of quantity (more reports), and, on the other, the quality of the reports, which would at best lead to improved transparency.[127] In sum, the proposals of the European Commission ramain very vague; they do not contain a co-ordinated monitoring or evaluation mechanism that is aimed at responding to the individual reports.

The Directive itself does not contain specific provisions regarding the monitoring and evaluation of the reports. Under Article 3 Directive 2014/95/EU, the European Commission is advised to "submit a report to the European Parliament and to the Council on the implementation of this Directive, including, among other aspects, its scope (...), its effectiveness and the level of guidance and methods provided". Sanctions or other enforcement or monitoring mechanisms are not foreseen in the Directive.

Only the tenth recital refers to monitoring and enforcement, by emphasising that Member States should ensure that adequate and effective means exist to guarantee disclosure of non-financial information.

> "To that end, Member States should ensure that effective national procedures are in place to enforce compliance with the obligations laid down by this Directive, and that those procedures are available to all persons and legal entities having a legitimate interest, in accordance with national law, in ensuring that the provisions of this Directive are respected."

It remains unclear how the "national procedures" should be shaped and when such a procedure should be initiated. Nevertheless, the tenth recital clarifies that, on the one hand, Member States are expected to set up a form of monitoring and enforcement mechanism, while, on the other, they are free to decide on how to shape these mechanisms.

It is quite clear that a reporting obligation without proper monitoring and enforcement mechanism can hardly achieve its objectives. In the context of financial reporting, Hong Phu Dao very rightly pointed out that "a high quality financial reporting requirement [...] requires also a mechanism to oversee the appropriate application" because "in the absence of adequate enforcement, the accounting rules may remain simply requirements on paper".[128]

---

125 European Commission, Impact Assessment, note 84 above, p. 43.

126 Ibid.

127 Ibid.

128 T.H.P. Dao, "Monitoring Compliance with IFRS: Some Insights From the French Regulatory System", (2005) 2 *Accounting in Europe*, p. 107 & 108.

For the objective of implementing human rights matters in the internal structures and everyday decisions of a company, it is necessary set up a monitoring and verification system which can directly respond to the company's reports. There are several reasons for such an approach, which will be highlighted very briefly:

First, a proper monitoring and enforcement mechanism could help to instruct companies to live up to their obligations or commitments regarding human rights. Even though preparing a report leads (at least in some way and to some extent) to a process of evaluation of the activities and the internal structures of a company, without a monitoring there is no guarantee that the implied strategies, policies and risk-assessment mechanisms are efficient and/or satisfy human-rights standards. In this regard, NGOs, for example, revealed that nearly 80 per cent of the surveyed companies that are obliged by US-law to report on their activities regarding minerals, did not fully comply with the legal requirements and that the majority of the reporting companies did not report on the country of origin for their minerals.[129]

Second, the monitoring and enforcement mechanims could serve as a platform for an ongoing dialogue about the implementation of human rights within the internal structures of a company. A monitoring body could help to instruct a company on how to internalise human rights obligations and commitments. At the same time, civil society could actively be included into the monitoring and enforcement procedure by giving them, for example, the right to initiate a procedure or to submit their own reports on a company's activities (so-called shadow-reports). By doing so, reporting companies could be made to face specific incidents, negative business-impacts or business-activity-related issues. In turn, the monitoring body could respond to the information provided by the companies and the NGOs by issuing recommendations or guidelines for the further implementation of the reporting obligations and human rights in general. Regarding the afore-mentioned example, a monitoring mechanism, in this case, could guide and instruct companies to comply with their reporting obligations under US-law and include the NGO's suggestions on how to improve the reporting praxis.[130]

Third, the monitoring mechanism could serve as a platform to put business-related human-rights provisions into practice. The major problem with the implementation of human rights in the context of business is that, while there are many standards, commitments, codes of conduct, policies and strategies regarding human rights, there are only few mechanisms that are able to put them

---

129 Amnesty International and Global Witness, "Digging for Transparency: How U.S. companies are only scratching the surface of conflict minerals reporting", April 2015, available at: www.amnestyusa.org/sites/default/files/digging_for_transparency_hi_res.pdf, p. 15 *et seq*, 27 *et seq*.

130 The report contains a seperate section on how companies can improve future reports (see *Amnesty International* and *Global Witness*, note 129 above, p. 29 *et seq*.

into practice. Therefore, human rights standards often remain "reqirements on paper". The Guiding Principles, for example, contain a lot of specific responsibilities for companies to respect human rights. Of exceptional relevance are procedural responsibilities such as the creation of a policy commitment, a strategy for due dilligence processes, a strategy to assess and address risk (and impact), processes to remediate human rights impacts and reporting requirements.[131] Human rights related procedures, for example, contained in the Guiding Principles 15 *et seq*., are the basis for unfolding and putting substantive human rights standards into practice. To review and follow the way in which companies implement these procedural and substantial responsibilities, it is necessary to install mechanisms that are able to monitor these responsibilities and give general guidance on how to put them into practice.

Fourth (and directly linked to the problem of putting (procedrual) responsibilities into praxis), a monitoring mechanism that responds to the reports of companies would be able to evaluate and consider the ways in which the internal structures of a company can be adjusted to the requirements of the Directive and of the Guiding Principles. Monitoring bodies would not only have to consider shortcomings with regard to a specific case, but would also have to focus on the internal structures, policies and strategies, and the overall performance of a company in the context of human rights. Compared to individual complaint procedures, the monitoring procedure could therefore continuously react and give guidance on structural shortcomings.

In the end, without any mechanism to review the reports and address any specific deficits, there is no guarantee that the reports are exhaustive and there is no possibility of following up and efficiently supporting further actions. In addition, the "report or explain" approach and the exceptions under Article 19a (1) and Article 29a (1) Directive 2013/34/EU allow companies to desist completely from reporting on non-financial matters or to neglect specific topics or fields within their operational operations. Even if a company or group fails to explain why it has not reported or why it has neglected specific aspects covered by the Directive, there are no judicial instruments to sanction such conduct. In particular, the possibility of omitting – deliberately or through oversight – some topics or operational processes from the disclosure leaves the door open to companies simply to avoid or to omit to report on specific themes, incidents or structures. The obligation to explain why no information has been provided is very indefinite and, above all, not enforceable, which makes it an inadequate tool if there are no mechanisms for verifying the explanations furnished.

To compensate for this quality deficit or to extend a proper non-financial reporting framework, the actual practices of, for example, European and German monitoring and enforcement bodies in the field of financial reporting

131 See Guiding Principles 15 *et seq*.

could serve as a role model or even a point of contact.[132] In the case of Germany, there are two bodies that monitor and enforce the reporting obligation. A body of the first instance is set up as a private association, composed of specialised representatives of all the relevant stakeholders in the field of financial reporting who are competent to carry out the actual monitoring and evaluation process. The body of the second instance is governmental and capable of imposing sanctions and other mandatory orders on a reviewed company. A concrete monitoring and enforcement procedure will be launched on two occasions: first, there is an *ad-hoc* procedure that begins when a stakeholder informs the body about a specific instant or form of misconduct. Second, there is a progressive procedure of randomly evaluating reports of the obligated companies.

B. TRANSNATIONAL SOCIAL RIGHTS AND THE EUROPEAN UNION AND MEMBER STATE LEGAL OBLIGATIONS

The non-financial reporting framework presented in the Directive has to be seen as another step to achieve the goals of the European Union's CSR-strategy. It is therefore set to be continuously refined, especially in the light of "best practices" with regard to Member State approaches to the implementation of the provisions in their national legislation. Nevertheless, it is deplorable that the European Commission did not explicitly consider and discuss its own legal human rights obligations and those of the Member States sufficiently to prevent European companies from violating transnational social rights abroad. Neither the Directive itself, nor the published legislative material, in particular the European Commission's Impact Assessment, refer to actual human rights obligations.

The Committee on Economic, Social and Cultural Rights (CESCR) repeatedly stated, that states have an extraterritorial obligation to protect foreign individuals or communities effectively against infringements of their transnational social rights with regard to the activities of companies which have their main seat within the jurisdiction of that state.[133] States are obliged to

---

132 For the organisation of the German financial supervisory system, see R. Bockmann, Internationale Koordinierung nationaler Enforcement-Aktivitäten: Eine kritische Analyse unter besonderer Berücksichtigung der Deutschen Prüfstelle für Rechnungslegung, (Wiesbaden: Gabler Verlag, 2012). For the European financial supervisory system, see E. Wymeersch, "The Reforms of the European Financial Supervisory System: An Overview", (2010) 7 European Company and Financial Law Review, p. 240 et seq.

133 Committee on Economic, Social and Cultural Rights (CESCR), "Statement on the Obligations of States Parties Regarding the Corporate Sector and Economic, Social and Cultural Rights", UN Doc E/C.12/2011/1, 11 May 2011; see, also, CESCR, GC No. 14, UN Doc E/C.12/2000/4, 11 August 2000, para. 39; for the extraterritorial obligations of Germany with respect to investments of german companies abroad see CESCR, UN Doc CO, E/C.12/DEU/CO/5, 12 July 2011, para. 10; The Maastricht Principles on Extraterritorial Obligations

establish appropriate laws and regulations, as well as monitoring, investigation and accountability procedures to set and enforce standards for the performance of companies.[134] As elaborated above, proper non-financial reporting, monitoring and enforcement mechanisms would aim to assess, monitor and improve the human-rights performances of companies.

The Guiding Principles confirm the practice of the Committee (CESCR). The first principle clearly states that states "must protect against human rights abuse within their territory and/or jurisdiction by third parties, including business enterprises. This requires taking appropriate steps to prevent, investigate, punish and redress such abuse through effective policies, legislation, regulations and adjudication". Principle 3 points out that states should "provide effective guidance to business enterprises on how to respect human rights throughout their operations" and "encourage, or where appropriate require, business enterprises to communicate how they address their human rights impacts" to comply with their duty to protect human rights.

In sum, a brief review of international human rights law leads to the assumption that the EU Member States[135] are obliged to take effective legislative steps to regulate the conduct of corporations with regard to the progressive realisation of rights, *i.e.*, as recognised in the CESCR. On the one hand, it can be argued that the EU and its Member States in some respect have a margin of appreciation in the area of extraterritorial jurisdiction over corporate human rights abuses and, therefore, the boundaries between what is legally-binding and what is "politically opportune" are often blurred.[136] On the other hand, there is clearly a lack of regulation in this field. The brief examination of the Directive

in the area of ESC rights (Olivier De Schutter, Asbjørn Eide, *et al.*, "Commentary to the Maastricht Principles on Extraterritorial Obligations of States in the Area of Economic, Social and Cultural Rights", (2012) 34 *Human Rights Quarterly*, pp. 1084–1169) refer to the practice of the Committee and other human rights bodies when stating a state obligation to regulate private conduct (Principle 24) and states must adopt and enforce measures to protect economic, social and cultural rights "as regards business enterprises, where the corporation, or its parent or controlling company, has its centre of activity, is registered or domiciled, or has its main place of business or substantial business activities, in the State concerned" (Principle 25).

134 CESCR, "Statement on the Obligations of States Parties Regarding the Corporate Sector and Economic, Social and Cultural Rights", note 133 above.

135 For the question of whether EU is obliged by international human rights codifications, see Andreas Fischer-Lescano, *Human Rights in Times of Austerity Policy: The EU Institutions and the Conclusion of Memoranda of Understanding*, (Baden-Baden: Nomos Verlag, 2014), p. 22 *et seq.* On the relationship between the EU and Member States international human rights obligations, see Tawhida Ahmed and Israel de Jesús Butler, "The European Union and Human Rights: An International Law Perspective", (2006) 17 *European Journal of International Law*, pp. 771–801; The Regional Office for Europe of the UN High Commissioner for Human Rights, "The EU and International Human Rights Law", 2008, available at: www.europe.ohchr.org/Documents/Publications/EU_and_International_Law.pdf.

136 Augenstein, note 86 above, p. 77, para. 240; Michael Krennerich, *Soziale Menschenrechte – Zwischen Recht und Politik*, (Schwalbach: Wochenschau Verlag, 2013), p. 106 & 361 *et seq*; CESCR, "Statement on the Obligations of States Parties Regarding the Corporate Sector and

demonstrates that there is no doubt that non-financial reporting can be rated as an effective tool to improve the behaviour of corporations with regard to human rights. At the same time, legislative measures in this field tend to have very little intensity as they only burden the companies and groups affected with financial and administrative costs, while completely omitting any regulation of their commercial activities. Regarding financial and administrative costs, it is hard to understand why companies or groups which are considered as "large" and which exceed either a balance sheet total of 20 million euros or a net turnover of 40 million euros should be financially or administratively unburdened in a field which is accentuated not only as a main objective of the EU,[137] but also enhances the companies' overall performance and the efficiency of capital markets.[138] To date, the EU and some Member States in particular, such as Germany,[139] have not taken adequate legal or political steps to prevent their own citizens and national entities from violating economical, social and cultural rights in other countries. Appropriate and effective legislative steps, for example, non-financial reporting equipped with a proper monitoring and enforcement mechanism, are long overdue.

The European Commission has invested a lot of effort in trying to appease companies and opposing groups by focusing on investors' interests and stressing the "business case"[140] of non-financial reporting. The human rights of the affected individuals and communities, and the obligations of both the EU and the Member States with regard to these rights, seem to play only a minor role in the European Union's legislative intentions. In any case, the European Union's and the Member States' extraterritorial obligations were not explicitly reflected during the legislative process. For these reasons, the European Union should explicitly consider international human rights obligations when considering ways for a further development of its non-financial reporting framework, and the Member States should consider their human rights obligations with regard to the implementation of the Directive by creating both reporting obligations that narrow the possibilities of "green washing", and monitoring and enforcement

---

Economic, Social and Cultural Rights", note 133 above; CESCR, GC No. 14, note 133 above, para. 54.

137 Art. 2 EUV.

138 European Commission, Impact Assessment, note 84 above, p. 23.

139 *Germanwatch* and *Miseror*, for example, demand the German Government to comply with the EC's request (Communication "A renewed EU strategy 2011–14 for Corporate Social Responsibility", COM (2011) 681 final, 25 October 2011) to establish a plan for the implementation of the UN-Guiding Principles on Business and Human Rights (*Germanwatch* and *Miseror*, "Nationaler Aktionsplan zur Umsetzung der UN-Leitprinzipien für Wirtschaft und Menschenrechte – Anforderungen an den Umsetzungsprozess in Deutschland", July 2012, available at: www.germanwatch.org/de/download/6648.pdf).

140 It is often argued that CSR pays off in general (see Jeffrey Unerman and Brendan O'Dwyer, "The Business Case for Regulation of Corporate Social Responsibility and Accountability", (2007) 31 *Accounting Forum*, pp. 332–353; Phillip Schreck, *The Business Case for Corporate Social Responsibility*, (Heidelberg: Physica-Verlag, 2009).

obligations that are effectively able to enforce compliance with the obligations laid down by the Directive.

IV. CONCLUSION

To return to the further elaborated approach to corporate accountability and to switch the focus to the potential effects of a sustainable non-financial reporting framework, we now wish to put our findings on the EU's non-financial reporting framework into the context of our theoretical approach by referring to the question established above: Does the EU's non-financial reporting framework have the potential to promote the accountability of MNCs effectively and significantly strengthen spaces of societal autonomy towards the economic system?

Non-financial reporting has the potential to preserve the autonomy of social systems or regimes against the expansive drive of the economic system in different ways. Besides the fact that it could serve as a source of information for the victims of human rights violations by MNCs and therefore could prepare the ground for countering economic forces that restrain or block the fulfilment of transnational social rights,[141] there could be effects of a more general character that would significantly strengthen spaces of societal autonomy towards the economic system and contribute to the enforcement of human rights against economic actors.

It can be argued that only the economic system and the business actors can decide whether to adjust their communications in favour of their social environment. Because the system remains autopoietic,[142] and, therefore, internal communications only refer to previous internal communications, the difficult task of reciprocally harmonising the function of a social system with its output can only be accomplished by a system-intern reflexion, which can be initiated from the outside of a system, but cannot be replaced.[143] Gunther Teubner states that these initiations can only be successful if they orientate themselves on the system's ways or modes of self-change and aim to give impulses that can be translated into inner growth processes.[144] The task would be to combine massive external pressure and irritation with intrinsic changes.[145]

Based upon our theoretical approach, under which human rights regulate communicative processes of all functional systems and, therefore, also have to

141 See Michael Freeman, "Conclusion: Reflections on the Theory and Practice of Economic and Social Rights", in: Lanse Minkler (ed), *The State of Economic and Social Human Rights: A Global Overview*, (New York: Cambridge University Press, 2013), p. 386.

142 Luhmann, note 49 above, p. 757.

143 Teubner, note 37 above, p. 134.

144 Ibid., p. 134 *et seq.*

145 Ibid., p 135.

regulate the communicative processes of the economic system with regard to its social environment, the starting-point for strengthening the enforcement of human rights against economic actors has to be located within the economic system itself. To determine the further embodiment of human rights and to make human rights protection a core business concern regarding the every day decision-making, *i.e.*, to adjust internal communications in favour of human rights, it is necessary to evaluate how human rights matters are currently implemented in the internal structures of the economic system and by the economic actors. In this regard, proper non-financial reporting, is a vital tool that can institutionalise a mandatory framework not only to initiate, but also to enhance and guide, the process of self-evaluation in terms of system internal self-reflexion.[146] By establishing proper non-financial reporting, monitoring and enforcement mechanisms that directly respond to the reports, internal learning effects could be combined with external pressure, guidance and assistance. Companies could be faced with internal structural shortcomings, and monitoring bodies could point out ways to abolish these shortcomings. In order to increase the extent or reach of external pressure, it is important to include civil society in the reporting, monitoring and follow-up process. To avoid a replication of factual positions of power in negotiating positions – which can be observed in the actual non-financial reporting frameworks ("greenwashing") – it is essential to empower the under-privileged positions by mandatory legal mechanisms.[147] Spaces of autonomy have to be legally-assured by legally-framed negotiating positions.[148] In this sense, the participation of civil society in the monitoring of non-financial reporting has to be seen as the implementation of the function of human rights to enable inclusion.

146 See David Hess, "Social Reporting: A Reflexive Law Approach to Corporate Social Responsiveness", (1999) 25 *Journal of Corporation Law*, pp. 41–84; Gunther Teubner, "Substantive and Reflexive Elements in Modern Law", (1983) 17 *Law and Society Review*, pp. 239–286.

147 See Ingeborg Maus, "Perspektiven 'reflexiven Rechts' im Kontext gegenwärtiger Deregulierungstendenzen", (1986) 19 *Kritische Justiz*, pp. 390–405.

148 Ibid., p. 404.

CHAPTER 7

LABOUR RIGHTS AND THE ILO: THE CHALLENGE OF TRANSFORMING INFORMAL ECONOMIC ACTIVITIES TO PROMOTE TRANSNATIONAL SOCIAL RIGHTS

Domestic and Care Work as Core Issues

Eva SENGHAAS-KNOBLOCH

INTRODUCTION

At its one hundredth session in June 2011, the International Labour Conference – the tripartite plenary (comprising government, employers' and workers' delegates) of the International Labour Organization (ILO) – adopted Convention 189 on *Decent Work for Domestic Workers*, together with the non-binding Recommendation 201 on the same subject.[1] Juan Somavía, the then General Director of the International Labour Office, noted with satisfaction on this occasion that:

> "We are moving the standards system of the ILO into the informal economy for the first time, and this is a breakthrough of great significance. History is being made."[2]

Surprisingly, the Convention had already come into force in 2013 after ratification by Bolivia, Guyana, Nicaragua, Paraguay, Uruguay, Mauritius,

---

1 For the legal characterisation of the different ILO instruments, the obligations of the members states and the system of supervision, see Anne Trebilcock, Chapter 8, Section IV.2 in this volume. For the procedures of the ILO, see, also, ILO, *Rules of the Game, A Brief Introduction to International Labour Standards*, (Geneva: ILO 2009 rev'd ed., Chapters 3 and 4).

2 ILO, *The Informal Economy and Decent Work. A Policy Resource Guide Supporting Transitions to Formality*, (Geneva: UN and ILO, 2013), Chapter 4, "The Regulatory Framework and the Informal Economy", p. 8. All documents are available at: www.ilo.org.

South Africa, the Philippines, Italy and Germany – far more than the two states required for its enforcement.

It was, indeed, Juan Somavía, who came into office in 1999 as the first Non-Westerner, who had alerted the constituents of the ILO (governments', employers' and workers' representatives) to the highly-vulnerable circumstances of the majority of people in the contemporary world of work. It was he who promoted the new *Decent Work Agenda*, an integrated programme to improve internal co-ordination between the organisation's diverse activities in standard-setting and capacity-building, and to strengthen the voice of the ILO in global governance institutions, particularly *vis-à-vis* the dominant international financial agencies, the World Bank and the International Monetary Fund, and the World Trade Organization (WTO). With this new emphasis, he sought to revitalise the spirit of the ILO Declaration of Philadelphia of 1944 (which today is part of the ILO Constitution) with its primacy on freedom and the principles of social justice for all;[3] and he was able to rely on the activities and the experiences within the organisation[4] that went back to the 1960s, when, in the wake of de-colonisation, new states were founded and became ILO Member States with socio-economic and socio-political structures that were very different from those of the early industrialised countries. The universal promotion of gainful work under free and equal conditions for all became a central topic at that time, and slowly helped the new states to overcome the colonial vestiges of forced labour which had prevailed within the former colonies of the Member States of the organisation since its foundation in 1919 as part of the Peace Treaty of Versailles.[5]

After the period of de-colonisation in the1960s, the challenge of transforming former Communist state economies into market-oriented states in the 1990s once again underlined the necessity to understand the structural relationship between the formal and the informal economy, and to reach out to those working people who are not recognised, registered or counted in national statistics, who

---

3 In the Declaration of Philadelphia, which was adopted during the 26th Session of the International Labour Conference, it is stated: "The Conference reaffirms the fundamental principles on which the Organization is based and, in particular, that labour is not a commodity; freedom of expression and of association are essential to sustained progress; poverty anywhere constitutes a danger to prosperity everywhere; the war against want requires to be carried on with unrelenting vigor within each nation, and by continuous and concerted international effort in which the representatives of workers and employers, enjoying equal status with those of governments, join with them in free discussion and democratic decision with a view to the promotion of the common welfare."

4 See Gerry Rodgers, Eddy Lee, Lee Swepston and Jasmien van Daele, *The ILO and the Quest for Social Justice, 1919–2009*, (Geneva: ILO, 2009), p. 222 *et seq*. See, also, Alain Supiot, *The Spirit of Philadelphia: Social Justice vs. the Total Market*, (London-New York: Verso Books, 2012).

5 See Daniel Maul, Human Rights, Development and Decolonization: The International Labour Organization, 1940–70, (Basingstoke: Palgrave McMillan, 2012); Eva Senghaas-Knobloch, Reproduktion von Arbeitskraft in der Weltgesellschaft. Zur Programmatik der Internationalen Arbeitsorganisation, (Frankfurt aM: Campus Verlag, 1979).

lack social protection, protection by labour legislation and protective measures at the workplace. In 2002, not least because of the vast increase in insufficiently-protected working people even in the core industrialised countries, the ILO constituents adopted the broader concept of the *informal economy*, which also takes into account the grey areas between formal and informal economic activities, and includes what had hitherto been understood as the "informal sector" in developing countries. The ILO *Resolution on Decent work and the Informal Economy* of 2002 states:

> "The term 'informal economy' is preferable to 'informal sector' because the workers and enterprises in question do not fall within any one sector of economic activity, but cut across many sectors. ...The term 'informal economy' refers to all economic activities by workers and economic units that are – in law or in practice – not covered or insufficiently covered by formal arrangements. Their activities are not included in the law, which means that they are operating outside the formal reach of the law; or they are not covered in practice, which means that – although they are operating within the formal reach of law, the law is not applied or not enforced; or the law discourages compliance because it is inappropriate, burdensome, or imposes excessive costs."[6]

With its impetus to include all working people, the Decent Work Agenda fostered a fresh look into the Conventions and Recommendations of the ILO; evidence shows that it may not be deduced from the lack of concrete protection at work in many states that the scope of ILO standards is limited to formal employment only. Contrary to a widespread misconception, as a recent publication by the International Labour Office (the administrative staff of the ILO) on the application of international labour standards (ILS) emphasises,

> "the ILO's mandate is not limited to workers in the traditional meaning of the word; it extends to all human beings. There is a common misconception that ILS are not applicable to the informal economy when in fact, most ILS are applicable to all workers, dependent and independent, and are as relevant to the informal economy as to the formal economy."[7]

---

6 ILO 2002 Resolution and Conclusions Concerning Decent Work and the Informal Economy, International Labour Conference, 90th session, 2002 Geneva, para 3, available at: www.ilo.org/public/english/standards/relm/ilc/ilc90/pdf/pr-25res.pdf. It is also emphasised that activities for legal goods and services that are not in conformity with registration requirements or immigration formalities should be distinguished from criminal and illegal activities which it would not be appropriate to protect. See the assessment of the then Deputy Director, Policy Integration Department of the International Labour Office: Anne Trebilcock, "Decent Work and the Informal Economy", Discussion Paper Nr. 2005/04, United Nations University, World Institute for Development Economic Research.

7 ILO, *The Informal Economy and Decent Work. A Policy Resource Guide*, Geneva 2013, Section 4.2, p. 7. This guide draws from Anne Trebilcock, "International Labour Standards and the Informal Economy", in: Jean-Claude Javillier and Bernard Gernigon (eds), *Les normes*

This statement alludes to a relatively new approach to understanding international labour standards in the light of the indivisible human rights within which, as Andreas Fischer-Lescano and Kolja Möller are arguing, one can identify distinct kinds of social rights;[8] at the same time, it addresses the potential tension between national and international law and transnational social rights.

The following deliberations intend to shed light on the long-standing issues related to the intricacies and dynamics of the informal economy as well as to the challenges that have to be faced in the endeavour to make international and transnational social rights a reality for all working people. The chapter focuses on the new ILO *Convention 189 on Decent Work for Domestic Workers* in order to exemplify the related issues. Domestic work encompasses a range of noumerous informal activities; the Convention covers activities that are of vital necessity to people and societies, but are traditionally considered to be outside the scope of labour law and not contributing to societal development or public welfare. In the following, the first two sections address the diverse phenomena of informal work, the problems of measurement and the different analytical approaches to explaining the persistence of the informal economy. The third section outlines the framework of the ILO *Agenda of Decent Work* and its relevance for tackling informality, whereas the fourth section discusses the policy issues of domestic and care work in relation to the ILO Convention 189 on *Decent Work for Domestic Workers*. This is followed by a brief look at a political initiative for the *Recommendations on Care* of the Social Platform (an NGO network in the European Union) and some concluding remarks.

I. THE MEANING AND MEASUREMENT OF THE "INFORMAL SECTOR" AND THE "INFORMAL ECONOMY"

The phenomenon of informal work was first recognised in the 1960s. In the context of the ILO *World Employment Programme* under the leadership of Louis Emmerij,[9] the International Labour Organization initiated the so-called Employment Strategy Missions to Brazil, Sudan and Kenya, with the participation of other special UN organisations and the World Bank. The reports of these missions demonstrated that it would not be possible to absorb all labour

internationales du travail: un patrimoine pour l'avenir: Mélanges en l'honneur de Nicolas Valticos, (Geneva: ILO, 2004), pp. 585–613.

8 See Chapter 2, Section IV.1 in this volume.

9 Louis Emmerij, "A New Look at Some Strategies for Increasing Productive Employment in Africa", (1974) 110 *International Labour Review*, pp. 199–218. See, also, David A. Morse, "The World Employment Programme", (1968) 97 *International Labour Review*, pp. 517–524.

power into the modern urban capitalist economy in the foreseeable future. At the same time, it was evident that there was no unemployment in the European sense of the word, but that migrants from rural to urban areas with no social protection needed to carry out diverse activities in order to survive. Contrary to the then prevailing theory of a dualist character of the economy in these countries, such activities could not be categorised as traditional. Repair work and other small handicraft work, petty trade with industrial goods, vending home-made food on the street, *etc.*, are all activities related to the modern formal sector and to urban living, albeit without being part of the modern sector.[10] The authors of the Kenya report recommended "new policies for promoting the informal sector and linking it with the formal sector".[11]

The term *informal sector* was first used in the Kenya report to describe such economic survival activities. The informal sector there was characterised by self-employment as the specific form of production and operation, the use of very simple means of production and an unregulated market; the *working poor* were emphasised as an attendant social fact. Interestingly, at the time, there were endeavours in the World Bank to define the informal sector by the social vulnerability of those working in that sector;[12] however, in the 1980s, the conceptional hegemony of neo-liberalism gained the upper hand. The lending practices of the two Washington-based international financial institutions were determined by the de-regulation of international trade, loans that were conditional on privatisation and the removal of state regulations such as minimum wages or even the elimination of trade unions, which were deemed to impede investments (this was the so-called Washington Consensus). The ILO became increasingly marginalised within this transnational constellation.[13]

In 1991, the ILO put informal employment as a major item on the agenda of its annual International Labour Conference for the first time. In his report, the then General Director Michel Hansenne described it as a "dilemma of the informal sector", in as much as it provided employment and income, but, at the same

10 ILO, Employment, Incomes and Equality: A Strategy for Increasing Productive Employment in Kenya, (Geneva: ILO, 1972), p. 503 et seq.

11 Hans Singer and Richard Jolly, "Unemployment in an African Setting. Lessons of the Employment Strategy Mission to Kenya", (1973) 107 *International Labour Review*, p. 107 as cited in Rodgers, Lee, Swepston and van Daele, note 4 above, p. 190. See, also, ILO, *Employment, Incomes and Equality. A Strategy for Increasing Productive Employment in Kenya*, (Geneva: ILO, 1972).

12 These early insights were not further pursued for the time being, however. The ILO's World Employment Programme fostered the strategy of supporting small-scale self-employed producers and people working on their own account primarily through qualification and appropriate loan conditions and co-operatives, without a strong emphasis on social protection and rights. In the subsequent decades, the World Bank and the IMF, which had meanwhile adopted a neo-liberal agenda, forestalled any endeavours to implement minimum social standards.

13 The features of this transnational constellation are outspelled by Andreas Fischer-Lescano and Kolja Möller, Chapter 2 in this volume.

time, lacked labour and social standards as well as protection from harassment and arbitrary actions of state representatives.[14] In 1993, the International Conference of Labour Statisticians (ICLS) adopted a definition of the *informal sector* that was subsequently integrated into the revised international System of National Accounts (SNA). From the very beginning, however, the definition agreed upon, which referred to *economic units*, was deemed inadequate to cover the true diversity of economic activities carried out. It was feared – and correctly so – that many self-employed or own-account workers, of whom a very large number are women, did not define themselves as businesses or economic units or that some forms of employment, for example contract work, would fall into a grey area between self-employment and wage labour. The failed attempts in 1997 and 1998 to set up a new ILO Convention on Contract Labour (referring to workers dependent on one employer but not declared as employees) highlights the difficulties of defining criteria which establish whether an employment relationship exists or not. In 2006, the Employment Relationship Recommendation (Recommendation 198) was adopted to provide clarification and promote national protection standards.

Against the background of these issues, the statisticians of the so-called Delhi Group (the Indian government had the presidency), together with the global network WIEGO (Women in Informal Employment: Globalizing and Organizing) and the ILO Department of Statistics, formed a working group that, in 2002, drew up a definition of *informal employment* that was also accepted by the 17th International Conference of Labour Statisticians (ICLS) the following year.[15] According to this definition, *informal employment* can exist both in the *informal* and in the *formal* sector. While the term *informal sector* refers to business units, the term *informal employment* is concerned with forms of employment. Both concepts imply an understanding of the *informal economy* in times of globalisation. The issue of *informal employment* and *informal economy* was placed in the context of the new ILO agenda for *worldwidedecent work*, which emphasises that the "commitment to decent work is anchored in the Declaration of Philadelphia's affirmation of the right of everyone to 'conditions of freedom and dignity, of economic security and equal opportunity'".[16] The term *informal economy* was therefore central to the 90th session of the International Labour Conference in 2002. According to this new consensus, the term *informal economy* encompasses "all economic activities that are, in law or in practice, not

14 ILO, *The Dilemma of the Informal Sector*, Report of the Director General, International Labour Conference, 78th Session, Geneva 1991; Paul Bangasser, "The ILO and the Informal Sector. An Institutional History", Geneva, ILO Employment Paper 2000/9.

15 For details, see Ralf Hussmanns, "Measuring the Informal Economy. From Employment in the Informal Sector to Informal Employment", ILO Policy Integration Department, Bureau of Statistics, International Labour Office, Working Paper 53, Geneva, 2004.

16 ILO 2002 Resolution and Conclusions Concerning Decent Work and the Informal Economy, para. 1, note 4 above.

covered or insufficiently covered by formal arrangements"; it "includes wage workers and own-account workers, contributing family members and those moving from one situation to another, it also includes some of those who are engaged in new flexible work arrangements who find themselves at the periphery of the core enterprise or at the lowest end of the production chain; there may be grey areas where the economic activity involves characteristics of both formal and informal economy".[17]

The broad spectrum of heterogeneous situations of workers with very varying social and legal standards, are described in the *ILO Policy Resource Guide on the Informal Economy* of 2013, which highlights governance deficits:

- "*unregistered workers* (those in a genuine employment relationship but who do not enjoy any rights – the situation is worse if they are irregular migrants or if their employer is unregistered);
- *under-registered workers* (those who receive part of their earnings informally – they are registered as part-time workers but in fact work full-time – which means that less taxes are paid on their behalf);
- *disguised workers* (those who perform the same tasks as "regular" employees but often do not have the same rights because they are employed under different contracts such as civil or commercial contracts);
- *ambiguous workers* (those about whom doubts are raised concerning whether they are employees or not);
- *vulnerable own-account workers* (those who are genuinely self-employed but vulnerable and exploited);
- *employees in precarious situations* (fixed-term, part-time or temporary workers who may not enjoy the same rights as "regular" workers, or do not enjoy the same rights in practice);
- *special cases* (domestic workers, home workers, and other types of workers who are not always covered by employment laws); and
- *workers in triangular relationships* (often, one does not know who the employer is because of the involvement of one or more third parties in the relationship; this includes situations where one resorts to an employment agency, or in which there is franchising)."[18]

In qualitative studies and narratives, the workers living in these different situations are given a face:

---

17 International Labour Organization, "The Informal Economy. Enabling Transition to Formalization". Tripartite Interregional Symposium on the Informal Economy. Geneva, 27–29 November 2007, p. 3.

18 ILO, *The Informal Economy and Decent Work: A Policy Resource Guide*, (Geneva: ILO, 2013), Chapter 4, pp. 4–5.

"Anuja sells fish in the street. Often police officers demand payments from her, because she has no licence and does not know how to get one."[19]

Anuja is thus a *vulnerable own-account worker*, at the mercy of the goodwill of potentially corrupt representatives of the state.

Maria, 48 years old, living in the North of Lima is a *disguised worker*:

"I knot bracelets, sew beads onto jumpers and bags, do whatever comes my way. The enterprises don't give women like us permanent employment because they say we are too old. That's why we work at home on our own account. This means that the businesses don't have to insure us. We have no employment contract and get no pension. We have no form of social protection… if we have an accident or fall ill, nobody feels in the least responsible for us."[20]

A much less visible, but recently publicly-debated field of informal work is that of the domestic work of undocumented workers. Domestic work is a domain for irregular female workers, frequently undocumented migrant workers or recently-immigrated citizens. In Germany, they often come from East Europe or from Latin American countries. Paula represents a case of an *unregistered irregular* migrant worker:

"Paula bore eight children, two died and four live in Ecuador. After her separation from her husband, Paula came to Hamburg with her youngest daughter, where another of her daughters was already living illegally with her husband and their three-year-old child. …In order to pay the fares she took out a loan at an interest rate of 12 per cent per month, which she is still paying off. In Hamburg, Paula is struggling to survive, as she now only has two cleaning jobs after two of her employers moved away."[21]

The rise in informal work in Europe came mainly in the wake of the end of the East-West conflict, the shock strategies of marketisation in the former Communist countries and the general policies of privatisation, liberalisation, de-regulation and the flexibilisation of the labour market by the international financial agencies and national governments. Informal work is therefore often linked with labour migration from South to North and East to West. In Germany, this can be observed on construction sites, in agriculture, the catering

19 Ingeborg Wick, *Frauenarbeit im Schatten. Informelle Wirtschaft und Freie Exportzonen*, (Siegburg-Munich: Südwindinstitut für Ökonomie und Ökumene, 2009), p. 18, (translation from German).

20 Ibid.

21 Maria S. Rerrich, *Die ganze Welt zu Hause. Cosmobile Putzfrauen in privaten Haushalten*, (Hamburg: Hamburger Edition, 2006), p. 87 *et seq.*, (translated from German).

trade, abattoirs,[22] and in the case of the so-called 24-hour care-workers. Workers from Poland, Bulgaria and Rumania work as posted workers, sometimes without contracts at all; or with labour contracts but without compulsory social security contributions; or as self-employed/own-account workers upon the basis of services and work contracts. For many years, workers from East European countries have been given placements under the *EU Posting of Workers Directive*. These workers are hired in various forms of the so-called *triangular employment relationships*.

These portrayals and descriptions illustrate how workers in the informal economy are ensnared in very unequal power relations and thus become highly vulnerable in social terms and with regard to their fundamental rights at work. Since the adoption of the *Resolution on Decent Work and the Informal Economy* at the International Labour Conference in 2002, the insight has gained ground that the issues pertaining to the informal economy are governance issues and that it is necessary to address the wide range of vulnerabilities under which working people may suffer.[23] The Resolution refers in paragraph 14 to "inappropriate, ineffective, misguided or badly implemented macroeconomic and social policies", including structural adjustment programmes, privatisation and re-structuring without an explicit employment-creation policy. It is also noted that "women and youth make up the bulk of workers in the informal economy" (para. 17), whereby women "generally have to balance the triple responsibilities of breadwinning, domestic chores, and elder care and childcare" (para. 20).

Despite "predictions to the contrary, employment in the informal economy has risen rapidly in all regions of the developing world, and various forms of non-standard employment have emerged in most regions of the developed world".[24] This statement by Marilyn Carr and Martha Alter Chen at the beginning of this century is even more valid 10 year later. The informal economy has continued to

---

22 See the weekly *Der Freitag*, 8 April 2011, p. 15. Not until September 2013 did employers in the meat industry (*Schlachtindustrie*) in Northern Germany finally, under substantial political and public pressure, declare their willingness to bargain collectively with the food union (NGG *Nahrung Genussmittel Gaststätten)* on minimum labour conditions and wages.

23 See the two background documents for the Conference: ILO, *Decent Work and the Informal Economy*, (Geneva: ILO, 2002) and ILO, "Women and Men in the Informal Economy. Statistical Picture", Geneva, International Labour Office, Employment Sector, 2002.

24 Marilyn Carr and Martha Alter Chen, "Globalization and the Informal Economy. How Global Trade and Investment Impact on the Working Poor", International Labour Office, Employment Sector, Working Paper on the Informal Economy Nr 1, 2002, 1. Statisticians at the 17th International Conference of Labour Statisticians (ICLS) corroborated that informal employment comprises the total number of informal jobs, whether carried out in formal sector enterprises, informal sector enterprises, or households; including employees holding informal jobs; employers and own-account workers employed in their own informal sector enterprises; members of informal producers' co-operatives; contributing family workers in formal or informal sector enterprises; and own-account workers engaged in the production of goods for their own end use by their household. See ILO, *The Informal Economy and Decent Work: A Policy Resource Guide*, (Geneva: ILO, 2013), Chapter 2, p. 5.

grow. It is meanwhile obvious that the majority of all working women and men earn their living under very vulnerable, insecure conditions in both rural and urban areas. The share of informal employment can only be estimated, mainly upon the basis of household surveys: "The informal economy around the world today represents 52.2 per cent of total employment in Latin America, 78.2 per cent in Asia and 55.7 per cent in Africa",[25] with substantial differences between North Africa and Sub-Saharan Africa. In the developed regions, informal work is estimated at less than 10 per cent but increasing.[26]The grand promise of global prosperity and welfare under the prevailing conditions of economic globalisation has not come true.

II. ANALYTICAL APPROACHES TO EXPLAINING THE PHENOMENON OF INFORMAL EMPLOYMENT

With the acknowledgement, first, of the phenomenon of the working poor in the *informal sector*, then of *informal employment* and its gradual expansion, there was an increased interest in analytical explanations and policy options. Both within and outside the ILO, various analytical and political approaches were initiated.[27]

The traditional economic theory of *dualism* that was conceived in the 1950s referred to developing countries only; this theory assumed the co-existence of a modern economy alongside a traditional sector with a surplus rural labour force that could be regulated through measures to encourage rural-urban migration.[28] The relationship structure between the metropoles of the global economy and their peripheries was not taken into account.

The steady growth of zones of working poor in the urban regions of the Third World gave rise to a definition of the term *informal sector* by the ILO Employment Strategy Missions (of which the mission to Kenya was already mentioned) that constituted a kind of neo-dualist perspective. It acknowledged that the informal economic activities in the small-scale production of goods

25 See *Globalization and Informal Jobs in Developing Countries*, a joint study of the International Labour Office and the Secretariat of the World Trade Organization, Geneva, 2009, p. 27.

26 Alejandro Portes and William Haller, "The Informal Economy", in: Neil J. Smelser and Richard Swedberg (eds), *Handbook of Economic Sociology*, (Princeton NJ: Princeton University Press, 2005), pp. 403–422, at 404 *et seq.*

27 Dharam P. Ghai (ed), *Decent Work: Objectives and Strategies*, (Geneva: ILO, 2006). See, also, Caroline E.N. Moser, "Informal Sector or Petty Commodity Production: Dualism or Dependence in Urban Development?", (1978) 6 *World Development*, pp. 1041–1064.

28 Arthur W. Lewis, "Economic Development with Unlimited Supplies of Labour" (1954, reprinted) in: A.N. Argawala and S.P. Singh (eds), *The Economics of Underdevelopment*, (New Delhi-Oxford: Oxford University Press, 1971), pp. 400–449.

and in petty trade in urban regions could be described as neither traditional nor modern work activities, but constituted a distinct economic form. Low productivity in this area is brought about by difficulties in gaining access to the necessary material and immaterial resources. The prevailing growth strategies for the formal sector alone were considered inadequate to promote national development.[29]

Once it had been acknowledged that, even with high growth, the *informal* sector of the economy in developing countries does not inevitably shrink but can even expand, there arose a need for further explanation. One explanation, taking a *judicial* perspective, focused on regulatory frameworks. Particular significance was attached here to obstacles which prevent small and micro-businesses from registering with the various pertinent state authorities and to a lack of property rights.[30]

In a pointedly *neo-liberal, micro-economic* approach, the existence of informal self-employed workers in all regions of the world (but especially in highly developed countries) is regarded as a deliberate, often justified decision made by women and men working on a tight budget to circumvent legal regulations because of the high costs and low returns involved, because they prefer self-employment to dependent work, and because they know that they have the social support that they can fall back on if needs be, without formalised measures such as contribution-based minimum social protection.[31]

The *structural-systemic* approach, by contrast, points to asymmetric global economic interdependencies and power relations. As early as 1971, Aníbal Quíjano from Peru formulated a path-breaking theory focusing on political and economic dependency structures between and within countries. According to this theory, the modern economic sector in peripheral capitalist (developing) countries is dominated by external economic forces and is, at the same time, externally oriented, which inhibits the growth of coherent internal macro-economic cycles, and gives rise to structural heterogeneities and the hierarchical stratification of different modes of production: local small-producers of consumer goods are increasingly driven out of the market by cheap imports from capitalist mass production, thereby creating a marginalised economic pole and marginalised labourers with extremely low incomes at subsistence levels and no prospect of upward social mobility.[32] This theory of structural heterogeneity,

---

29 Salem V. Sethuranam, "The Urban Informal Sector. Concept, Measurement and Policy", (1976) 114 *International Labour Review*, pp. 69–81.

30 Hernando de Soto, *The Mystery of Capital: Why Capitalism Triumphs in the West and Fails Everywhere Else*, (New York: Basic Books, 2000). Victor E. Tokman, "Modernizing the Informal Sector", in: José Antonio Ocampo and Jomo K.S. (eds), *Towards Full and Decent Employment*, (Hyderabad: United Nations, 2007), pp. 255–276.

31 William F. Maloney, "Informality Revisited", (2004) 32 *World Development*, pp. 1159–1178.

32 Aníbal Quijano, "Marginalisierter Pol der Wirtschaft und marginalisierte Arbeitskraft", in: Dieter Senghaas, (ed), *Peripherer Kapitalismus. Analysen über Abhängigkeit und Unterentwicklung*, (Frankfurt aM: Suhrkamp Verlag, 1974), pp. 298–341. See, also, Anibal

which focuses on predatory and exploitative relations between different modes of production both within and between countries, has been taken up again in a new endeavour to explain the continued expansion of informal economic activities in all regions of the world (for example, by Marilyn Carr and Martha Alter Chen),[33] with special emphasis on power imbalances in gender relations.

Already since the 1970s, more and more multinational and transnational corporations with headquarters in the industrialised countries (and more recently also in Asian threshold countries) have invested in Southern countries not only in the extraction of raw materials and the production of agricultural goods for export, but have also built plants all over the world for the production of industrial goods or industrially-manufactured foodstuffs. Their aim is not only to open up new local markets, but also to reduce costs for the supply of goods in their own domestic markets. These cost-cutting strategies are particularly rife in the numerous "Export Production Zones" (EPZs). EPZs are intended to attract foreign capital with special labour legislation and tax incentives (with tax rates below the respective national standard rates), and the recruitment of primarily young women at very low wage-rates. A more recent trend can be seen in the outsourcing strategy and the consequent expansion of transnational production and trade chains for clothing, electronic components, and traditional (for example, shea butter) and non-traditional (for example, roses and other flowers) agricultural produce under sub-standard labour conditions, which also draw particularly on the labour force of young women.[34] These trade chains are controlled by a handful of trade groups. Large corporations also invest substantial amounts of their profits in speculative businesses that have no real economic relevance, but nevertheless have an impact on the material circumstances of working people.

As a consequence of this structural asymmetry of globalisation, and contrary to the promises of prosperity that trade liberalisation and the de-regulation of capital transfer would bring, between 1960–62 and 2000–02, the income gap between the richest and the poorest countries increased significantly, and inequality has also widened within countries.[35] Wage differentials worldwide

---

Quijano, "Coloniality of Power, Eurocentrism, and Latin America", (2000), manuscript available at: www.unc.edu/~aescobar/wan/wanquijano.pdf, last accessed 18 June 2014.

33 See note 24 above.

34 See, for instance, Leonhard Plank, Cornelia Staritz and Karin Lukas, *Labour Rights in Global Production Networks: An Analysis of the Apparel and Electronics Sector in Romania*, (Vienna: Kammer für Arbeiter und Angestellte für Wien, 2009). The denial of even the most rudimentary work protection standards was made public to a broad audience in connection with the large number of deaths through fires and suicide in Bangladesh and China.

35 World Commission on the Social Dimension of Globalization, *A Fair Globalization: Creating Opportunities for All*, (Geneva: ILO, 2004), p. 36. Hamish Jenkins, Eddy Lee and Gerry Rodgers, *The Quest for a Fair Globalization Three Years on: Assessing the Impact of the World Commission on the Social Dimension of Globalization*, (Geneva: International Institute for Labour Studies, 2007), p. 17.

have increased dramatically, albeit with regional variations. In the wake of tax reductions, especially relating to capital income, state expenditure on education, health and other public goods and services plummeted in many countries as tax revenues shrank.[36] Since the beginning of the still ongoing bank and debt crisis in 2008, this situation has deteriorated further in many places. This has particularly affected women.

In developing countries, women suffer, for example, from the elimination of smallholder livelihoods through imports of subsidised agricultural products from industrialised countries (*i.e.*, the USA and the EU). At the same time, they experience constraints on the labour market, not least because the provision of domestic-care activities is traditionally deemed to be the responsibility of women. There is a strong correlation between disregard and contempt for domestic-care work arising from hierarchical gender relations and the rise in informal employment.[37]

This attitude towards care work applies also to Europe, albeit with different features. For competitive reasons EU employment policy endeavours to ensure as high an employment ratio of women as possible. The new target of the European Commission for 2020 is a 75 per cent employment rate for men and women.[38] However, the new, individualistically oriented "adult worker model"[39] has no place for vital care activities, and a growth in atypical, informal employment is the result. In this way, EU policy has appropriated the aspirations of women to attain economic independence without implementing the necessary socio-political measures to satisfy their emancipatory demands: the adult worker model of the EU does not take into account that a complete commodification of all vital necessary physical and mental care activities is impossible, and it ignores the structural contradictions between the flexibility demands of care in the domestic area and the flexibility demands in paid work.

The increased employment of women in the Global North means that they have less time to devote to unpaid family tasks, while men's time budgets have hardly changed at all. This has given rise to a growing demand for affordable care work. The decisive element here is the socio-structural basis upon which this demand for domestic services arises and is responded to. Put simply, there

---

36 In Bangladesh, for example, primary school education for informally working children is largely dependent on intermittent project funding through which civil society workers are paid. See Andrea Schapper, *From the Global to the Local: How International Rights Reach Bangladesh's Children*, (London-New York: Routledge, 2014).

37 Maria Floro and Mieke Meurs, "Global Trends in Women's Access to 'Decent Work'", in: ILO-FES Dialogues on Globalization, Occasional Papers, Geneva, 2009.

38 European Commission, Communication from the Commission, "A Strategy for Smart, Sustainable and Inclusive Growth", Brussels, 3 March 2010.

39 On the definitions, see Susy Giullari and Jane Lewis, "The Adult Worker Model Family: Gender, Equality and Care", in: UNRISD, Social Policy and Development Programme Paper Nr. 19, April 2005; for a general outline, see Nancy Fraser, *Justice Interruptus: Critical Reflections on the "Postsocialist" Condition*, (New York-London: Routledge, 1997).

are two opposing political strategies: Scandinavian countries tend to take the socio-politically more ambitious "high road", while Great Britain (like the USA) has chosen a development path that is criticised as the "low road".[40]

The "low road" develops in a socio-political context in which a high degree of social inequality tends to be tolerated, and well-off families or women in paid employment are able to afford to pay domestic workers or informal domestic help to provide the necessary care. The underlying policy is to try and keep public social expenditure as low as possible. This is the main reason for the recent growth of international or transnational "care chains"[41] as a type of "international division of reproductive labour",[42] in which female migrants are paid to carry out the necessary domestic-care activities in high-income households. This current trend has been mainly observed in the USA and in many European countries. In the wake of the state debt crisis, the provision of public social services has been further reduced. The more ambitious "high road", by contrast, implies a relatively low degree of social inequality, which is primarily achieved by means of a well-funded public sector, in which decent work in the social services – mostly provided by women here too – is possible.[43]

Women's participation in the labour market has grown worldwide. Between 1980 and 2008, it grew from 50.2 to 51.7 per cent, while that of men sank from 82.0 to 77.7 per cent; these aggregate figures contain large regional disparities, however.[44] The increase in female employment under precarious conditions is

40 As termed by Steffen Lehndorff, Das Politische in der Arbeitspolitik: Ansatzpunkte für eine nachhaltige Arbeits- und Arbeitszeitgestaltung, (Berlin: Edition Sigma, 2006).

41 For this concept, see Arlie R. Hochschild, "Global Care Chains and Emotional Surplus Value", in: Will Hutton and Anthony Giddens (eds), *On The Edge: Living with Global Capitalism*, (London: Jonathan Cape, 2000); and Helma Lutz (ed), *Gender Mobil? Geschlecht und Migration in transnationalen Räumen*, (Münster: Westfälisches Dampfboot, 2009).

42 The original insight behind the concept of "care chains" was developed by Rhacel Parrenas, "Migrant Filipina Domestic Workers and the International Division of Reproductive Labor", (2000) 14 *Gender and Society*, pp. 560–580. See, also, Fiona Williams, "Towards a Transnational Analysis of the Political Economy of Care", in: Rianne Mahon and Fiona Robinson (eds), *Feminist Ethics and Social Policy: Towards a Political Economy of Care*, (Vancouver-Toronto: University of British Colombia Press, 2011), pp. 21–38. Empirical analyses of the situation of irregular female labour migrants in Europe (Belgium, France, Germany, Greece, Italy and Spain) can be found in Anna Triandafyllidou (ed), *Irregular Migrant Domestic Workers in Europe. Who Cares?*, (Farnham-Burlington VT: Ashgate Publishing, 2013).

43 See, for example, Hildegard Theobald, "Care-Politiken, Care-Arbeitsmarkt und Ungleichheit: Schweden, Deutschland und Italien im Vergleich", (2008) 18 *Berliner Journal für Soziologie*, pp. 257–281. See, also, Cornelia Heintze, "Auf der Highroad – der skandinavische Weg zu einem zeitgemäßen Pflegesystem. Ein Vergleich zwischen fünf nordischen Ländern und Deutschland", Expertise im Auftrag der Abteilung Wirtschafts- und Sozialpolitik der Friedrich-Ebert-Stiftung, Bonn, 2012. available at: http://library.fes.de/pdf-files/wiso/09243-20120730.pdf, last accessed 6 June 2013.

44 Shara Razavi, Cammilla Arza, Elissa Braunstein et al., "Gendered Impacts of Globalization. Employment and Social Protection", United Nations Research Institute for Social Development (UNRISD), Geneva 2012, p.3, available at: www.unrisd.org/80256B3C005BCCF9/search/6E16D1DC33F5D82BC12579D000478859?OpenDo

particularly high both in the European Union and in Latin America. The gap between regions and countries has triggered the widescale migration of an unprecedented proportion of women, particularly domestic and care workers. In 2013, the number of domestic workers on a global scale was estimated at 50 to 100 million; "one in every 13 female wage workers is a domestic worker (or 7.5 per cent), and the ratio is as high as one in four in Latin America and the Caribbean (26.6 per cent) and almost one in three in the Middle East (31.8 per cent)."[45] Domestic work is thus a prominent example of informal work.

III. THE ILO AGENDA OF DECENT WORK AND THE ISSUE OF DOMESTIC AND CARE WORK

To counter the trends towards unprotected labour, the Decent Work Agenda is built on four interdependent pillars. These are: rights at work, promotion of employment, social protection, and social dialogue. "The essence of the decent work approach is to maximize the synergies among its different elements and find policy and institutional options to overcome conflicting relationships and constraints."[46] These strategic aims were consolidated at the International Labour Conference in 2008 by adoption of the *Declaration on Social Justice for a Fair Globalization*.[47]

For a long time, discourses in the fields of labour law and human rights were disconnected, although as early as 1944 the constitutionally-enshrined ILO *Declaration of Philadelphia* used a rights-based language which was later largely adopted for the formulation of social rights in the *Universal Declaration of Human Rights* of 1949 and the *International Covenant on Social, Economic and Cultural Rights*[48] of 1966. In response to the shortcomings of member states in adhering to and implementing its standards (of which 76 Conventions were (still) considered up-to-date in 2013), the International Labour Conference adopted the *ILO Declaration on Fundamental Principles and Rights at Work* in 1998. The ground for this was prepared by the International Social Summit in Copenhagen in 1995. This Declaration consolidated four internationally recognised norms, the principles of which are binding for the Member States of the ILO under their

cument, last accessed 10 August 2012. See, also, Fiona Robinson, "Care Ethics and the Transnationalization of Care", in: Mahon and Robinson (eds), note 42 above, pp. 127–144.

45 ILO, Domestic Workers across the World: Global and Regional Statistics and the Extent of Legal Protection, Geneva 2013, p. 19 *et seq.*

46 Ghai, note 27 above, p. 22.

47 Available at: www.ilo.org/global/meetings-and-events/campaigns/voices-on-social-justice/WCMS_099766/lang--en/index.htm, last accessed 16 June 2014. This is also the basis for ongoing ILO initiatives to formalise the informal economy.

48 Rodgers, Lee, Swepston and van Daele, note 4 above, p. 44. See Eddy Lee, "The Declaration of Philadelphia. Retrospect and Prospect", (1994) 133 *International Labour Review*, pp. 467–484.

constitutional obligations. These are: (a) freedom of association and the effective recognition of the right to collective bargaining; (b) the elimination of all forms of forced or compulsory labour; (c) the abolition of child labour; and (d) the elimination of discrimination in respect of employment and occupation. The Declaration underscores that "it is urgent, in a situation of growing economic interdependence, to reaffirm the immutable nature of the fundamental principles and rights embodied in the Constitution of the Organization and to promote their universal application".[49]

The rationale behind the promotion of fundamental principles and rights lies in the underlying conviction of the ILO, formulated at the beginning of the Declaration, that:

> "the ILO should, now more than ever, draw upon all its standard-setting, technical cooperation and research resources in all its areas of competence, in particular employment, vocational training and working conditions, to ensure that, in the context of a global strategy for economic and social development, economic and social policies are mutually reinforcing components in order to create broad-based sustainable development."

The complementarity of economic and social development must be considered a principal axiom of the ILO.[50] It includes the necessity of continuous critical assesssments of those economic and financial policies which reinforce socially destructive trends. The reports for the follow-up processes of the Declaration of 1998 and the Declaration of 2008 are standing topics on the agenda of the yearly International Labour Conference with a view to monitoring trends and progress. Besides dealing with compliance issues, these reports also testify to the ILO's activities in capacity-building and in technical co-operation for the promotion of compliance. It is clear from this approach that human rights and workers' rights are indivisible. Human rights cannot be considered as "primarily oriented toward limiting the power of state", while "labor rights are primarily oriented toward limiting the power of private actors in the market" as Kevin Kolben suggests.[51] Rather, states have to provide laws and institutional means to protect workers' rights as human rights.

The fundamental rights of the 1998 Declaration alone do not guarantee substantial protection in terms of either a sufficient livelihood, healthy working-conditions, or social security; they are insufficient to improve the living conditions of workers. Yet, to promote human dignity at work they are

49 See the text available at: www.ilo.org/declaration/thedeclaration/textdeclaration/lang--en/index.htm, last accessed 25 October 2013.

50 Markus Demele, *Entwicklungspolitik als Arbeitspolitik*, (Marburg: Metropolis, 2013), p. 92 *et seq*.

51 See the arguments of Kevin Kolben, "Labor Rights as Human Rights?", (2010) 50 *Virginia Journal of International Law*, pp. 450–484.

incontestable. The rights correspond to eight fundamental ILO Conventions, which are today understood as the core labour norms (these are: C 87 and C 98 on freedom of association and the protection of the right to organise, and the right to organise and collective bargaining respectively; C 29 and C 105 on forced labour and its elimination; C 138 and C 182 on the elimination of child labour and particularly its worst forms; and C 100 and C 111 on the abolition of discrimination in employment). The most important gaps in adherence and implementation still prevail with respect to C 87 und 98, regrettably in the large economies of China, India and the USA. Despite the broad international consensus on fundamental rights, the international financial institutions only reluctantly changed their declared policy. The World Bank eventually changed its Standard Bidding Documents in 2007, and, besides the conditions relating to child labour and forced labour, also included conditions with respect to workers' associations and discrimination. However, these changes have still not been incorporated into the "harmonised" SBDW framework (Standard Bidding Documents for the Procurement of Works).[52]

The applicability of international labour standards in the informal economy is not restricted to fundamental rights. A close scrutiny of the wording of the recommendations and conventions and the reports of the independent supervising mechanisms of the Committee of Experts for the Application of Conventions and Recommendations (CEARC) demonstrates the relevance of the international labour standards also for the informal economy. Anne Trebilcock[53] provides detailed evidence that many Conventions either *include* workers in the informal economy or *explicitly* address them. The first group of Conventions is exemplified by the Employment Policy Convention 122 of 1964, which requires ratifying states to "declare and pursue, as a major goal, an active policy to promote full, productive and freely chosen employment" (Art. 1.1), taking into account national conditions and practices and consulting the "persons affected by the measures taken" (Art. 3). Workers in the informal economy are affected, and therefore included. In its review of the application of this Convention, the supervising Committee of Experts on the Application of Conventions and Recommendations referred to these workers as the most vulnerable and worst protected, and underscored the high concentration of child labourers and and women workers in the informal economy.[54] Convention 150 on Labour Administration of 1978, as an example of the second group of Conventions,

52 International Labour Conference, Report VI: *Fundamental Principles and Rights at Work. From Commitment to Action*, (Geneva: ILO, 2012), available at: www.ilo.org/washington/resources/selected-ilo-publications/WCMS_176149/lang--en/index.htm, p. 94, footnote 23.

53 See, for this section, particularly, Anne Trebilcock, "International Labour Standards and the Informal Economy", in: Javillier and Gernigon (eds), note 7 above, pp. 425–613; see, also, Werner Sengenberger, *Globalization and Social Progress: The Role and Impact of International Labour Standards*, (Bonn: Friedrich Ebert Stiftung, 2002).

54 See Trebilcock, note 53 above, p. 593.

directly refers to informal workers. It calls for the gradual expansion of labour administration functions to cover "workers who are not, in law, employed persons, such as ... self-employed workers...occupied in the informal sector" (Art. 7).

The *Convention on Employment Policy* of 1964 is of direct relevance for the second pillar of the Decent Work Agenda: the promotion of *employment* and gainful work. When, in 1969, the ILO entered the arena of development policy with its World Employment Programme, it represented a dissident voice against the – still dominant – notion of simply equalising development with economic growth. It was the legacy of this notion, which is blind to the lessons of history,[55] that employment and decent work were not incorporated as sub-goals of Goal 1 (poverty reduction) into the Millennium Development Goals of the United Nations until 2005.

The third pillar, *social protection*, is of particular urgency for the majority of people working in the informal economy.[56] Upon the basis of field studies in several countries, Michael Cichon and Krzysztof Hegemejer were able to make calculations which demonstrated that these countries could improve social protection for a large number of working people considerably by investing only a small share of their GNP.[57] The ILO promotes a re-evaluation of social protection in terms of investment in the future for social coherence and development rather than a cost factor.[58] In this respect, the significance of co-operatives, self-help organisations for micro-insurance and similar instruments cannot be overstated.

Social Dialogue, the fourth pillar of the Decent Work Agenda, underscores the ILO's unique tripartite policy process aimed at consensus upon the basis of collective self-organisation and dialogue as strategic objectives. A collective voice for workers (as for employers) is a creed of the ILO. It pre-supposes the right to free association and a representative voice in all decisions affecting working and living conditions. It encompasses deliberations at international level as in the ILO, nation-state level and regional and local levels, and also within specific industries.[59] After years of reluctance and decline in membership, unions and international union federations now promote and support union-

55 Dieter Senghaas, The European Experience: A Historical Critique of Development Theory, (Oxford: Berg Publishers, 1985) original: Von Europa lernen: Entwicklungsgeschichtliche Betrachtungen, (Frankfurt aM: Suhrkamp Verlag, 1982).

56 Ashwani Saith, "Social Protection, Decent Work and Development", in: Ghai (ed), note 27 above, pp. 127–173.

57 Michael Cichon and Krzysztof Hegemejer, "Changing the Development Policy Paradigm. Investing in a Social Security Floor for All", (2007) 60 *International Social Security Review*, pp. 169–196.

58 Dev Nathan and V. Kapalna, "Issues in the Analysis of Global Value Chains and their Impact on Employment and Incomes in India", (Geneva: ILO, 2007), available at: www.ilo.org/wcmsp5/groups/public/---dgreports/---inst/documents/publication/wcms_193512.pdf.

59 See Konstaninos Papadakis (ed), *Cross-Border Social Dialogue and Agreements: An Emerging Global Industrial Relations Framework?* (Geneva: International Institute for Labour Studies, 2008).

building among the informally employed or their integration into their own organisations. The largest organisation of indigent, self-employed women workers is the Self-Employed Women's Association (SEWA)[60] in India, registered in 1972, on the initiative and under the leadership of lawyer and parliamentarian Ela Bhatt. In recent years, powerful associations and unions of domestic workers have also been set up in Latin America and have played a crucial role in the adoption of C 189.

With Convention 189, together with Recommendation 201,[61] the ILO responded to the increasing number of vulnerable domestic workers, who are mostly informal workers and often also migrants. Over a number of years, reports of violence and abuse, human trafficking and forced prostitution, especially among minors, have generated widespread publicity on the critical situation of women and girls providing domestic services abroad or in the cities of their own countries. In 2008, in the light of this situation, the Governing Body of the ILO put the issue of "decent work for domestic workers" on the agenda for the International Labour Conference in 2010 und 2011. This set the ILO's standard political debating and voting procedure in motion for the adoption of new internationally-binding labour norms.[62] Upon the basis of two reports submitted by the International Labour Office on the situation of domestic workers in law and in practice,[63] along with a survey of the member countries, the first plenary debate took place in June 2010,[64] and a preliminary draft for an instrument under international law was dispatched to all member states with a request for comments. As required in the ILO with its tripartite membership, comments were submitted by governments, employers' associations and trade unions.[65] In addition, replies were received from the International Trade Union Confederation (ITUC), the International Organisation of Employers (IOE) and the International Confederation of Private Employment Agencies. Observations on the proposed text were sent by several UN institutions such as the Committee

---

60 Nalini Nayak, "Organizing the Unorganized Workers: Lessons from SEWA Experiences", (2013) 48 *The Indian Journal of Industrial Relations*, pp. 402–414.

61 Retrievable on the ILO webpage at: www.ilo.org/global/standards/lang--en/index.htm. On background and procedures, see Eva Senghaas-Knobloch, "Beispiellos und herausfordernd - ein neuer internationaler Arbeitsstandard für menschenwürdige Arbeit von Hausangestellten", (2012) 29 *Feministische Studien*, pp. 119–127, which includes valuable information by Hildegard Hagemann from Justitia et Pax and Karin Pape from IUF.

62 See the materials on the ILO homepage at: www.ilo.org, under the heading International Labour Conference.

63 ILO, Decent Work for Domestic Workers, Report IV (1) and Report IV (2), International Labour Conference, 99th Session, Geneva 2010; ILO. See, also, ILO, *Expanding the Scope of Application of Labour Laws to the Informal Economy. Digest of Comments of the ILO's Supervisory Bodies Related to the Informal Economy*, (Geneva: ILO, 2010).

64 The documentation of the debate of the pertinent committee can be found under: www.ilo.org/wcmsp5/groups/public/@ed_norm/@relconf/documents/meetingdocument/wcms_145507.pdf, last accessed 27 December 2013.

65 ILO, Decent Work for Domestic Workers. Report IV (2A), International Labour Conference, 100th Session 2011.

on the Rights of the Child, and also civil society stakeholders such as Anti-Slavery International, Human Rights Watch, RESPECT Network,[66] the Migrant Forum in Asia, and a number of domestic workers' associations. These comments were taken into consideration in the second drafts for the Convention and the Recommendation, which, after revision during the Conference, were adopted on the 16 July 2011.

For the three constituent groups of the ILO, the whole process was a challenge. The government representatives were required to comment on two international legal instruments (a convention which, after ratification, would be binding under international law, and a recommendation on specific measures) for a group of workers predominantly employed in the *informal economy*, and consequently outside of regular employment. The employers' associations at this point had hardly any associations for domestic work or similar organisations within their ranks because they did not consider themselves responsible for the so-called domestic sphere. As for the trade unions and international trade union federations, these had only begun 10 or 15 years previously to open up generally to informal employees, and particularly employees in private households.

IV. DOMESTIC WORK AND THE RENEWAL OF SOCIAL DIALOGUE

For the first time in its history, the ILO opened up its tripartite deliberations in the Conference to representatives of workers who did not meet the usual credentials for delegates. This was made possible by workers' representatives at the International Conference including representatives of domestic workers in their delegations as technical staff, holding briefings with them and giving them a voice at special group meetings. The author of the International Labour Office's Law and Practice Report for the issue of domestic labour, Adelle Blackett,[67] regards this procedure as an expression of a "renewal of tripartism".[68] Using a concept of Markus Demele[69] it can be understood as "tripartism plus social dialogue", by which he means the inclusion of representatives of social movements for hitherto unrepresented workers at all levels: this concept highlights the importance of institutionalised, inclusive social dialogue.

---

66 The European *Respect* Network was established in 1997 and comprises female domestic workers', migrant and support organizations from eight EU states (Britain, Belgium, France, Holland, Italy, Spain, Greece and Germany). The name is an acronym of Rights, Equality, Solidarity, Power, Europe Corporation Today.

67 This section draws heavily on Adelle Blackett, "The Decent Work for Domestic Workers Convention and Recommendation", (2011) 106 *The American Journal of International Law*, pp. 778–794.

68 Ibid., pp. 790.

69 Demele, note 50 above, p. 426.

Taken as a whole, the various commentaries submitted clearly demonstrated the extreme heterogeneity of the legal and factual circumstances of domestic work. The governments of industrial countries (for example, France) pointed out that, for certain occupational groups such as childminders and professional outpatient nurses, there already existed specific national regulations. Article 2.3 of the Convention stipulates:

> "Each Member which avails itself of the possibility afforded in the preceding paragraph shall, in its first report on the application of the Convention under Article 22 of the Constitution of the International Labour Organisation [sic], indicate any particular category of workers thus excluded and the reasons for such exclusion and, in subsequent reports, specify any measures that may have been taken with a view to extending the application of the Convention to the workers concerned."

The fact that Convention 189 on Decent Work for Domestic Workers was adopted by far more than the necessary two-thirds majority of all delegates of the International Labour Conference (the employers' and employees' delegates are not bound to the votes of the government representatives of their countries) was, in no small part, thanks to a broad alliance of organisations working to this end. In particular, the Latin American domestic workers' associations and their regional network (CONLACTRAHO)[70] as well as strong domestic workers' unions in South Africa, India and Hong Kong, in combination with European national trade unions[71] such as UNITE in the UK and FNV-Bondgenoten in the Netherlands as well as the International Union of Food and Allied Workers (IUF), joined forces with broad women's support networks such as the IDWN[72] and WIEGO,[73] civil society and church organisations, with the backing of the International Labour Office-staff as well as the group of workers' representatives[74] at the annual International Labour Conference. This was a lesson that can be drawn from the history of the Convention's adoption by the International Labour Conference: It is precisely the co-operation between collective organisations working in the interest of their members, on the one hand, and the advocacy activities of associations and groups in social

70 "La Confederación Latinoamericana y del Caribe de Trabajadoras del Hogar" includes 14 countries in that region. I am grateful to Karin Pape for her draft text, ILO Convention C 189 – A Good Start for the Protection of Domestic Workers, which will shortly appear in the *International Labour Review*, for this and other information on the organisation.

71 The ILC had been preceded by conferences of the European Trade Union Confederation in Brussels in 2005 and Amsterdam in 2006.

72 IDWN (International Domestic Workers Network) is a support network for domestic workers that was established by lobbyists campaigning for Convention 189 and became an official organisation in October 2013 at its founding congress in October 2013.

73 WIEGO (Women in Informal Employment: Globalizing and Organizing) is a global network combining trade unions, co-operatives and development organisations. See its homepage at: http://wiego.org/wiego/about-wiego.

74 The three constituent groups of the ILO have their own forms of organisation.

movements forging alliances, on the other, which give recognition and voice to the hitherto unrecognised, vulnerable and individualised workers.[75] The experience underscores the necessary struggle for transnational social rights in adequate *fora*.[76]

The aim of Convention 189 is the protection of *all domestic workers* (Art. 2.1). Domestic workers are any persons "engaged in domestic work within an employment relationship" (Art. 1b), whereby the term *domestic work* is defined as "work performed in or for a household or households" (Art. 1a). "A person who performs domestic work only occasionally or sporadically and not on an occupational basis is not a domestic worker" (Art. 1c). By this definition, an employment relationship can exist between a worker and the representative of a private household or between a service agency and a domestic worker. The definition of domestic work deliberately lacks an enumeration of specific activities. The defining characteristic is the work location; whereas traditionally the household was separated as a private sphere from the public sphere (to which employment belonged), this definition emphasises that activities carried out upon an occupational basis within a household are of the same character as when carried out outside the household, *i.e.*, in institutions. This definition might help to expose *disguised* employment relationships.

The main philosophy behind this definition is the conviction that there "is no fundamental distinction between work in the home and work beyond it, and no simple definition of public-private, home-workplace and employer-employee. Caring for children and the disabled or elderly persons in the home or in a public institution is all part of the same regulatory spectrum, wherein a range of migration and other policies shape both the supply of and the demand for care services," as Blackett states.[77] Equal treatment of domestic workers implies that also those who work upon a part-time basis for more than one household fall within the scope of the Convention, as are those employed in an agency which places or posts them. Such workers are in typical *triangular* employment relationships.

Article 2 provides exemptions from the scope of the Convention. After consultation with the competent organisations, ILO Member States which ratify it may wholly or partly exclude a) "*categories of workers who are otherwise provided with at least equivalent protection*" (*i.e.*, nurses), and b) "*limited categories of workers in respect of which special problems of a substantial nature arise*". In subsequent reports, these ILO Member States are held to "*specify any measures that may have been taken with a view to extending the application of the Convention to the workers concerned*". Since self-employed domestic workers

75 Kolben, by contrast to this assessment, (see note 51 above) emphasises the differences in organisational culture between unions and social movement groups.

76 See Andreas Fischer-Lescano and Kolja Möller, Chapter 2 in this volume.

77 Law and Practice Report, para. 38, Blackett, note 67 above, p. 783.

are by definition not "in an employment relationship", they are not covered, and the challenge will be to find ways and means also to protect those in *pseudo* self-employment.

With the formulation in Article 3, "to respect, promote and realize the fundamental principles and rights at work", the Convention adopts the language of the ILO's Declaration on the fundamental principles and rights at work of 1998, in which, of all international standards in paid labour, four groups were particularly emphasised as so-called core labour standards. The special emphasis of these fundamental rights at work and the reference to a number of related UN conventions in the preamble of the new ILO Convention makes it quite clear that any form of domestic employment of girls and boys, women and men that is reminiscent of feudal and/or colonial relations or forced labour has no legitimation whatsoever and constitutes a violation of human rights. This eliminates the legal and moral basis for the denomination and practice of servants in (quasi-) feudal relationships and provides for the abolition of any type of forced labour and bonded labour or similar forms comprising traditional and modern forms of unfree labour in the domestic realm.[78]

With regard to child labour, the Convention responded to figures collected by the ILO's Statistical Information and Monitoring Programme on Child Labour, according to which at least 15.5 million children aged 5–17 years old were engaged in domestic work worldwide in 2008. The number of child domestic workers aged 5–14 years old is estimated at 7.4 million, with girls by far outnumbering boys.[79] Accordingly, Article 4 of the Convention is very explicit. The ILO-Members have to set a minimum age for domestic workers which should not be less than 18 years old and, in any case, not below statutory school-leaving age.[80] Article 6.2 of Recommendation 201 further stipulates that:

> "Members should give special attention to the needs of domestic workers who are under the age of 18 and above the minimum age of employment as defined by national laws and regulations, and take measures to protect them, including: (a) strictly limiting their hours of work to ensure adequate time for rest, education and training, leisure activities and family contacts; (b) prohibiting night work; (c) placing restrictions on work that is excessively demanding, whether physically or psychologically; and (d) establishing or strengthening mechanisms to monitor their working and living conditions."

---

78 A biographical book of a Nepalese girl gives evidence of deep-rooted ethnic discrimination: Urmila Chaudhary, *Sklavenkind. Verkauft, verschleppt, vergessen. Mein Kampf für Nepals Töchter*, (Munich: Knaur, 2011).

79 ILO, *Domestic Works across the World*, (Geneva: ILO, 2010), pp. 23–24.

80 The International Labour Office estimates that there are at least 15.5 million child domestic workers. See www.ilo.org. See, also, Giuseppe Nesi, Luca Nogler and Marco Pertile (eds), *Child Labour in a Globalized World: A Legal Analysis of ILO Action*, (Geneva-Aldershot: Ashgate Publishing, 2008).

Article 5 of the Convention addresses the widespread mistreatment of domestic workers. It requires measures by the member states to protect domestic workers "*against all forms of abuse, harassment and violence*". Equal treatment of domestic workers with all other workers according to national law is the main philosophy of the Convention. Yet, there are situations that differ from those of other workers, namely, when domestic workers live in the households in which they work – a widespread phenomenon in countries with feudal or neo-feudal state orders, but also in industrialised democratic countries. Article 6 therefore requires that:

> "each Member shall take measures to ensure that domestic workers, like workers generally, enjoy fair terms of employment as well as decent working conditions and, if they reside in the household, decent living conditions that respect their privacy."

Article 7 provides for "information in an appropriate, verifiable and easily understandable manner and preferably, where possible, through written contracts in accordance with national laws, regulations or collective agreements", in particular: the name and address of the employer and of the worker; the address of the usual workplace or workplaces; the starting date; the type of work to be performed; the remuneration, the method of calculation and the periodicity of payments; the normal hours of work; paid annual leave, and daily and weekly rest periods; the provision of food and accommodation (if applicable); the period of probation or trial period (if applicable); the terms of repatriation (if applicable), and terms and conditions relating to the termination of employment.

Article 10 refers specifically to the regulation of working hours and requires ILO Member States to take measures:

> "towards ensuring equal treatment between domestic workers and workers generally in relation to normal hours of work, overtime compensation, periods of daily and weekly rest and paid annual leave in accordance with national laws, regulations or collective agreements, taking into account the special characteristics of domestic work."(Art. 10.1)

> "Weekly rest shall be at least 24 consecutive hours." (Art. 10.2)

Of critical importance is the provision that:

> "periods during which domestic workers are not free to dispose of their time as they please and remain at the disposal of the household in order to respond to possible calls, shall be regarded as hours of work to the extent determined by national laws, regulations or collective agreements, or any other means consistent with national practice." (Art. 10.3).

The ongoing struggle within the European Union over the issues of working time and time on call – *i.e.*, among medical doctors – conveys an idea of the conflicts that are foreseeable.

Articles 11 and 12 provide for decent wages, Article 13 for a secure and healthy working environment, Article 14.1 for social security, and Article 14.2 for maternity protection. While Article 8 requires emigration states to ensure by law that domestic workers emigrating to other countries are informed about working conditions, labour contracts and the right to be repatriated, Article 15 requires the inspection of private employment agencies also in receiving countries.

Articles 16 and 17 stipulate the establishment of effective, accessible complaint mechanisms as well as a type of labour inspection – which is sensitive to the character of private homes – to ensure that all domestic workers, either by themselves or through a representative, have effective access to courts, tribunals or other dispute-resolution mechanisms under conditions that are not less favourable than those available to workers generally. Labour inspection (regulated in the socalled governance ILO Convention No. 81 from 1947 and the Protocol to this Convention from 1995) is certainly a very important issue.

The Convention lays the foundation, based upon human rights, for the right to decent work for all domestic workers under international labour law. The implementation and enforcement of the Convention has yet to take place. It is the task of the alliances to accomplish this through women's human rights, labour law, and development networks in each country contacting trade unions that are open to their concerns, government administrations and also, where possible, the relevant employers' associations first to overcome the worst forms of indecent working conditions (forced labour and child labour) for domestic workers, and then, in a second step to promote the respective national and local economic, cultural and legal frameworks for the effective implementation of the Convention.

The spectrum of work activities covered by the Convention is broad and involves different regulations and established routines in different countries. In Germany, the "*Tagesmütter*" or "*Tagesväter*" model (a child-minder who works in his or her own home) often entails self-employment under precarious conditions. Verbal or irregular agreements concerning domestic cleaning are very widespread, particularly where the work is carried out on an hour-by-hour basis in different households. Here, it is essential to establish forms of work organisation which, on the one hand, fulfil the obligation to adequate social and work protection, and, on the other, are easily accessible, do not push the cost of employment above that of possible demand, and leave room for the trust and confidentiality required for employment in private households.[81]

---

81 Manuela Tomei, "Decent Work for Domestic Workers. Reflections on Recent Approaches to Tackle Informality", (2011) 23 *Canadian Journal of Women and the Law*, pp. 185–211.

The Convention recognises that those who are engaged in paid domestic work often have commitments in their own family networks, and often must provide unpaid care for their own relatives. Working time, its limitation, and consideration of the needs of those dependent on vital care are, therefore, all core issues of any form of domestic work, particularly care work. Migrant care workers who are mostly women often leave their own families to earn money for them by caring for members of other families. The lack of income on their side and the lack of time to provide care on the part of their employers both serve to produce the migrant care-work constellation that only superficially seems to benefit both sides. Yet, the migrant care workers do have their own care obligations. They often leave a care deficit in their home country since men rather seldom take over the respective tasks when women go abroad to earn a living. Apparently, the culturally-based gender division of labour is not easily changed even if it is under stress.

The transnational care worker constellation is based upon a vast income gap and vast economic discrepancies at global level, and is in danger of exacerbating the disparities between the sending and receiving countries. The transnational division of reproductive or care labour is clearly not a sustainable path towards overcoming these disparities or care deficits. To address the care crisis in the EU, the receiving countries of care workers in Europe need to reverse their dominant policy priorities and regulate the working time in a "care-sensitive" ("*pflegesensibel*") way in order to provide adequate time for unpaid care activities.[82] As significant as the Convention 189 is for improving the living and working conditions of domestic and care workers, it is not sufficient to overcome the worldwide care deficits.

Despite the strong demand for care workers, economic disparities both between and within states, and the material needs of immigrant women, in combination with hierarchical gender relations, give rise to low-paid, irregular employment and adverse working conditions,[83] thereby exposing the shallowness of the market rhetoric. The provisions of Convention 189 reflect

---

82 See the studies in Germany: Stefan Reuyß, Svenja Pfahl, Jürgen Rinderspacher and Katrin Menke, *Pflegesensible Arbeitszeiten. Perspektiven der Vereinbarkeit von Beruf und Pflege*, (Berlin: Sigma, 2012); and Jürgen Rinderspacher, Irmgard Hermann-Stojanov,Svenja Pfahl and Stefan Reuyß, *Zeiten der Pflege. Eine explorative Studie über individuelles Zeitverhalten und gesellschaftliche Zeitstrukturen in der häuslichen Pflege*, (Berlin: Sigma, 2009); since a care-sensitive working time also applies to the working conditions of professional care worker in institutions, some contradictions regarding priorities between paid care work and unpaid care activities will probably remain unresolved. For the lack of recognition and appreciation, see, also, the results of an empirical study in Germany hospitals and institutions for long-term care in: Christel Kumbruck, Mechthild Rumpf and Eva Senghaas-Knobloch (with a contribution by Ute Gerhard), *Unsichtbare Pflegearbeit. Fürsorgliche Praxis auf der Suche nach Anerkennung*, (Berlin: Lit Verlag, 2010).

83 Agnieszka Satola, "Ausbeutungsverhältnisse und Aushandlungsprozesse in der Pflege- und Haushaltsarbeit von polnischen Frauen in deutschen Haushalten", in: Ursula Apitzsch and Marianne Schmidbaur (eds), *Care und Migration. Die Ent-Sorgung menschlicher*

these underlying global macro-economic imbalances. Its enforcement thus faces daunting challenges. Its effective implementation requires a renunciation of deep-seated convictions, routines and policies relating to governance and the legal system, macroeconomic policies, representation and voice, and skill formation. The report of the outgoing Director General in 2011 to the 100th Session of the International Labour Conference, entitled *A New Era of Social Justice*, underscored the necessity for new macroeconomic policies. To accentuate the need for transition, in 2015, the International Labour Conference adopted Recommendation 124 *Concerning the Transition from the Informal to the Formal Economy*, urging all members to identify the nature and extent of the informal economy in their territory. In so doing, they should make use of the participation of representative collective actors in the informal economy.

V. THE "RECOMMENDATIONS ON CARE" OF THE EU-BASED SOCIAL PLATFORM AND THE PROMOTION OF A "CARING SOCIETY"

The whole set of issues outlined above is the key concern of the European Social Platform too. This is a platform of forty-six European rights and value-based NGOs working in the social sector. While the activities of the Social Platform concentrate on the European Union level, it also supports the promotion of these values at global level. At its annual convention in 2011, the Social Platform adopted the *Recommendations on Care* (hereafter referred to as the *Recommendations*) which aim at a "*caring society*". These address the issue of support both for unpaid care-givers/providers and for skilled professional workers within the whole spectrum of assistance for people in need of care.

As with the Convention and the pertinent Recommendation of the ILO, rights – in particular human rights – are the point of reference of the Social Platform's *Recommendations*. Unlike the ILO, however, which deals exclusively with paid occupation in an employment relationship, the Platform defines its approach as holistic and includes all aspects of occupational, as well as non-occupational,[84] care work. It covers all general and specific situations in which people are reliant on care work in the course of their lives – in childhood, if they have disabilities, are ill or frail, in old age and in special cases of need.

Reproduktionsarbeit entlang von Geschlechter- und Armutsgrenzen, (Opladen-Farmington Hills MI: Verlag Barbara Budrich, 2010), pp. 177–194.

84 Unfortunately, the *Recommendations* adopt a language in which unpaid, non-occupational care work for family and relatives is called "informal care". This leads to misunderstandings in the international discussion.

> "Our starting point is that care is a human right: the right to care and to be cared for is a fundamental part of our lives as everyone is a care giver or care receiver at some point and potentially at multiple stages throughout life."[85]

With its emphasis on human rights on both sides of a care relationship (that of care receivers and of care givers), in private and in occupational care, the Platform's *Recommendations* primarily aim at normative, human rights based policies for a societal development concerned with improving social standards and the quality of life. Its holistic approach includes the consideration of the rights of those in need of care, the quality of care activities, and the rights and working conditions of the carers, regardless of whether they carry out care work in gainful employment or not.

The *Recommendations* cut across four policy areas, and address the challenges posed by contemporary developments in European societies that make political re-orientation essential. These four areas are: social and demographic changes; the increased participation of women in gainful employment; "individualisation processes"; and the general fact that too little public money is invested in the provision of high-quality care and support. The Social Platform points out that, currently throughout the EU, around 20.5 million people – of whom 78 per cent are women, are registered as employed in this sector (not taking unregistered workers into account). The proportion of part-time and fixed-term employment and the disparity between male and female earnings here are both above average.

Parallel to the ILO strategy for social protection, the Social Platform considers a socio-political paradigm shift to be essential. Decent social services should thus no longer be regarded as a cost factor, but as a "social investment" in the future on which social integration and cohesion, anti-discrimination and gender equality all depend. It calls for the development of indicators for the measurement of social returns on such an investment. At the same time, it points to the danger that the investment metaphor might detract attention from the fact that care activities are not just services provided in the general interest, but are also a human right.

The first policy area addressed in the Social Platform's *Recommendations on Care* concerns the fundamental rights of *care users*. These include the guaranteed right to a private and family life, equality in the choice of care provision and universal access to affordable care. The practice of separating parents and children on the grounds of poverty alone, for example, unacceptable living conditions, should be overcome. In this respect, the *Recommendations* refer to Articles 19 and 21 of the Treaty of Lisbon, in which the Charter of Fundamental Rights is made binding; the EU should accede to the Council of Europe and UN

---

85 See the document at: www.socialplatform.org/wp-content/uploads/2013/03/20121217_Social Platform_Recommendations_on_CARE_EN1.pdf, last accessed 8 April 2015.

human-rights treaties and implement the Beijing Platform for Action; and the EU Structural Funds should be used to help finance such measures.

The second policy area discussed in the *Recommendations* is the reconciliation of the care activities, the work and the private lives of non-occupational carers in accordance with the EU Charter of Fundamental Rights, including the right to gender equality (Art. 23), the right to fair and just working conditions (Art. 31), and the right to public service provision (Art. 36). The objective is to ensure that responsibilities[86] for care activities are fairly shared both between men and women and between generations, and to guarantee the fundamental rights of family carers and voluntary care workers. Around 80 per cent of care and support work in the EU is provided by relatives, two thirds of whom are women, whereby the participation of mothers in paid employment is on average around 11.5 per cent lower than that of women without children, while that of fathers is about 8.5 per cent higher than that of men without children. Decision-makers at EU level are reminded, in this connection, of the European Pact for Gender Equality (2011–2020), of the Directive on Maternity Leave, the European Directive on Care Leave, the need to acknowledge the new diversity of family structures, as well as pension entitlements from non-vocational care work and the provision of other kinds of support and assistance.

The third policy area of the *Recommendations* is concerned with the quality, accessibility, affordability and availability of care services for all in need across Europe. This is in response to the demographic ageing processes in Europe and the frequently expressed opinion that long-term care in old age is no longer affordable, especially in the light of the austerity measures particularly in the social services sector. The Social Platform re-iterates the view that the provision of such services should not primarily be for the purpose of generating profits. Decision-makers at EU level are called upon to guarantee that the austerity measures imposed in the wake of the financial and debt crisis are reconcilable with Article 9 of the Treaty of Lisbon. A coherent package of policy measures is called for that will carry weight in the care sector in the EU and in the individual Member States.

The fourth policy area dealt with in the *Recommendations* concerns decent working conditions and quality employment for care workers, including vocational training and equal treatment at work, particularly with respect to the status of migrant care workers. The *Recommendations* point to the still glaring disparity of wages particularly in the care and support sector even though equal pay is one of the oldest contract obligations of the EU. At the same time, the problem of recruitment and migration of qualified care-workers from the new eastern Member States into western EU states is addressed – again, in the area of

86 See Mechthild Rumpf, "Häusliche Pflegearrangements und ihre Zukunftsfähigkeit", in: Kumbruck, Rumpf and Senghaas-Knobloch, note 82 above, pp. 152–163; see, also, Part III of Kumbruck, Rumpf, Senghaas-Knobloch, note 82 above, pp. 346–352.

institutional long-term care and domestic care. The Social Platform recommends that all EU Member States ratify ILO Convention 189.[87] A comprehensive revision of the EU Working Time Directive is considered to be of particular urgency with a view to regulating compensatory rest time and recognising on-call duty. Migrant care-workers from outside the European Union should have the same guaranteed rights as EU citizens, and those with irregular residence status should be legalised. The Recommendations of the Social Platform demonstrate that "the time has come for the creative legal forces of civil society around the world to overcome the impasses of transnationalisation", as Fischer-Lescano and Möller argue.[88]

VI. OUTLOOK

With their orientation towards human and fundamental rights, ILO Convention 189 and the *Recommendations* of the European Social Platform stand in stark opposition to pre-dominant economic thinking. They both reflect the discrepancy between the normative commitments made by the states and the prevailing economic policy, which contradicts people's expectations of public welfare provision, especially within the EU. At the same time, the campaign argues pragmatically, with its utilitarian, social investment approach.

It thus becomes apparent that the policy of the International Labour Organization, geared to the concept of decent work, and the Social Platform's political vision of a "caring society" complement each other. The central objective of both programmes is a radical transformation that generates greater public awareness of the essential everyday care activities that have hitherto remained concealed. The Social Platform is even more radical in as much as it also addresses unpaid essential care activities as public "relational goods".[89] This concept refers to the fundamental human condition of relating to other humans and being existentially dependent on each other's help. Striving for autonomy and reliance on others are not mutually-exclusive opposites, but are both part of people's lives. This perspective ties in with the proposal of growing numbers of initiatives, movements of thought, and innovators of new ways of living and working, that "caring for others" should be seen as a right that must re-define the relationship between labour and social policy.[90]

---

87 While the EU may make recommendations on the ratification, it is not a member of the ILO and therefore not entitled to make ratifications.

88 Andreas Fischer-Lescano and Kolja Möller, Chapter 2 in this volume.

89 Social Platform, Recommendations on Care, note 84 above, p. 12, available at: http://cms.horus.be/files/99907/MediaArchive/Events/111020_SP%20recommendations%20on%20Care_final.pdf.

90 On the term "caring for others", see Ute Gerhard, "Sorgen für andere als Maßstab für eine neue Sozialpolitik", in: Kumbruck, Rumpf and Senghaas-Knobloch, note 82 above, pp. 63–84.

ILO Convention 189 highlights the necessity for care and support provided against remuneration to be also possible without coming into conflict with the applicable labour and social rights. This will require intensified social dialogue at all levels, and, above all, it requires the universal enforcement of the freedom of association. Convention 189 became possible because of an extraordinary alliance of organised domestic workers with unions, NGOs and other advocacy groups. The same or a similar alliance is needed for its practical implementation. In this context, the establishment of complaint mechanisms is crucial. In addition, the regulatory gap in the case of dependent self-employed workers[91] shows that this group of care workers needs new forms of organisation, where possible in co-operative form. ILO Recommendation 193 on Promotion of Cooperatives from 2002 is to be used as a guide to the means for strengthening voluntary democratic associations to pursue common aspirations.[92]

The prevailing world economy is still largely blind to the elementary tasks of social reproduction and social cohesion, because, until now, it has been able to ignore the essential tasks of care and attendance – traditionally carried out, without pay, by women. The backlash of this neglect now manifests itself in the form of worldwide, yet unevenly distributed, care deficits. If a normative consensus could be reached that those providing essential care activities – and this includes women migrants from low-income countries – should be given citizenship rights in the countries in which they do care work,[93] this would be an extraordinary step on the way to more equal gender relations, to solidarity in the world of work, and to the promotion of universal social rights.

91 See Eva Kocher, "Die Grenzen des Arbeitsrechts. Der rechtliche Schutz der Erwerbsarbeit außerhalb von Arbeitsverhältnissen", (2013) 46 *Kritische Justiz*, pp. 145–155.

92 See Anne Trebilcock, Chapter 8, Section IV.2.a in this volume.

93 See, also, Joan Tronto, "Feminists Democratic Ethics of Care and Global Care Workers. Citizenship and Responsibility", in: Mahon and Robinson (eds), note 42 above, pp. 162–177, at 175.

PART III

ENFORCEMENT OF TRANSNATIONAL SOCIAL RIGHTS

CHAPTER 8

TRANSNATIONAL SOCIO-ECONOMIC RIGHTS: INTER-LINKAGES IN THE CONTEXT OF THE RIGHT TO FOOD[1]

Anne Trebilcock

I. INTRODUCTION – WHAT IS MEANT BY THE "RIGHT TO FOOD" AND WHY FOCUS ON IT?

A substantial body of international law, not all of it well known, already exists in relation to the right to food. "International law" is taken here to incorporate both "hard" law, enshrined in treaties that normally create binding obligations on states when they ratify them, and "soft" law, *i.e.*, non-binding instruments that provide guidance and usually reflect expertise and political will. This chapter recalls the classical framework surrounding the right to food, enshrined above all in the International Covenant on Economic, Social and Cultural Rights, while highlighting linkages to lesser known sources, particularly in relation to labour and gender issues. It is situated within a much larger discussion around transnational legal norms, which are "dynamic, multi-layered and complex".[2] The right to food concerns both consumers and all those involved in food production and distribution. While inter-connections exist among various international social rights, these linkages could be much better exploited to strengthen more effective action in relation to the right to food.

Although the focus here is largely positivist, looking at norms generated through primarily inter-governmental processes, non-state actors have obviously played a critical role in shaping and vindicating the right to food. The launch in 2013 of the Global Network for the Right to Food and Nutrition, which brought together numerous NGOs and social movements long active in the field, marked

1 This manuscript was finalised on 20 May 2015.

2 Kyriaki Topidi and Lauren Fielder (eds), *Transnational Legal Processes and Human Rights*, (Farnham: Ashgate Publishing, 2013), p. 4.

a milestone in strengthening joint action.[3] The growing phenomenon of private norm creation is also important and often intersects with public international law standards.[4] How international organisations, states, enterprises, civil society groups and individuals use various legal norms in practice shapes international social law relating to the right to food. Particularly since the nomination by a UN Secretary General of a Special Rapporteur on the Right to Food, both awareness and understanding of the right to food have increased considerably.[5]

As part of transnational law, which recalls the contested character, constituencies and communities of law,[6] the right to food displays elements of both traditional international law and counter-hegemonic challenges[7] to it. As such, "the right to food can be mapped on two levels: on one, as a formal, legal obligation of states under international law; and on another, as a popular demand for access to food as a means of survival".[8] According to Susan Randolph and Shareen Hertel, a purely state-centric approach is problematical because (a) it fails to address the responsibilities of actors such as transnational corporations or international financial institutions, (b) it defines state responsibilities too narrowly, and (c) it does not acknowledge the complicity of those who benefit from an unjust global economic order.[9] And as the new Special Rapporteur on the Right to Food, Hilal Elver, has asserted, "To treat the concept of law as being entirely dependent on the State is to overlook the unique nature of social norms".[10]

Furthermore, pressure is growing on corporations for greater accountability, as reflected in the UN Guiding Principles on Business and Human Rights of

3 The Food First Information and Action Network serves as facilitating secretariat of the network. See www.fian.org, for a copy of the network's Charter.

4 See, for example, the Report of the Special Rapporteur on the Right to Food, Olivier De Schutter: "Agribusiness and the Right to Food", UN Doc. A/HRC/13/33 (22 December 2009).

5 Numerous resolutions of the United Nations (UN) General Assembly, along with resolutions and decisions of the Human Rights Council and of human-rights treaty bodies, have kept the right to food in the eye of policy-makers. A list of these appears on the website of the Special Rapporteur on the Right to Food, available at: www.ohchr/EN/Issues/Food/Pages/FoodIndex.aspx.

6 See Peer Zumbansen, "Transnational Law, Evolving", in: Jan M. Smits (ed), *Elgar Encyclopedia of Comparative Law*, 2nd ed. (Cheltenham: Edward Elgar Publishing, 2012), pp. 898–925, and Andreas Fischer-Lescano and Kolja Müller, "Struggle for Transnational Social Rights", Chapter 2 in this volume. As an example of how such contestation plays out in practice in relation to legal strategies for the vindication of labour rights, see Ashwini Suktankar, "Global Organizing and Domestic Constraints", (Chapter 2), in Adelle Blackett and Anne Trebilcock (eds), *Transnational Labour Law*, (Cheltenham: Edward Elgar Publishing, 2015), pp. 37–50.

7 See, for example, Topidi and Fielder, note 2 above, and the introductory chapter of this volume.

8 Susan Randolph and Shareen Hertel, "The Right to Food: A Global Perspective", in: Lanse Minkler (ed), *The State of Economic and Social Human Rights: A Global Overview*, (Cambridge: Cambridge University Press, 2013), p. 22.

9 *Ibid.*, pp. 26–27.

10 Report of the Special Rapporteur on the right to food, Hilal Elver, "Access to Justice and the Right to Food: The Way Forward", UN Doc. A/HRC/28/65 (12 Jan. 2014), para. 64.

2011.[11] The Guiding Principles, which emerged after extensive multilateral consultation involving civil society and business, include the rights captured in the ESC Covenant, the Universal Declaration of Human Rights and the 1998 ILO Declaration on Fundamental Principles and Rights at Work (described below). The follow-up mechanisms put in place under the Guiding Principles, at both international and national levels, could serve as *fora* for civil society to raise food-rights issues in relationship to enterprise behaviour. More importantly, embedding respect for human rights into business practices will be necessary for lasting change in firms' behaviour.[12] All the same, past experience with purely voluntary unilateral initiatives has left many activist groups deeply suspicious of corporate capture of regulatory and participatory processes in relation to the right to food.[13]

Moreover, structural problems in the international system certainly do persist, undermining the realisation of the right to food. In particular, the rules governing international trade and national agricultural policy, along with economic incentives along the transnational food-production chain, prevent fulfilment of access to adequate food for all. Stronger accountability mechanisms in relation to the right to food are also required in several respects: taking the gender dimension more seriously into account, enhancing monitoring and available remedies for violations, and strengthening systemic policy coherence. Emerging initiatives around the right to food offer some promise for improvement in the situation, but they are no substitute for more far-reaching reforms. These are needed because, among other reasons, "current food systems are deeply dysfunctional".[14] This is a major reason why some 805 million people – one in nine worldwide – are still chronically undernourished.[15]

11 UN Doc. A/HRC/17/31 (21 March 2011), endorsed by the Human Rights Council in Res. 17/4 on 16 June 2011. The Council has also set up a Working Group to examine the feasibility of adopting a legally-binding instrument on the subject; see Doc. HRC/26/L.22/rev.1, adopted 26 June 2014. See, also, Olivier De Schutter, "Corporations and Economic, Social and Cultural Rights", in: Eibe Riedel, Gilles Giacca and Christophe Golay (eds), *Economic, Social and Cultural Rights in International Law*, (Oxford: Oxford University Press, 2014), pp. 192–224. (De Schutter, who succeeded Jean Ziegler, is former Special Rapporteur on the Right to Food.).

12 See, for example, Peter Utting and José Carlos Marques (eds), *Corporate Social Responsibility and Regulatory Government: Towards Inclusive Development?*, (Basingstoke: Palgrave Macmillan, 2013), and Stepan Wood, "The Case for Leverage-based Corporate Human Rights Responsibilities", in: Wesley Cragg (ed), *Business and Human Rights*, (Cheltenham: Edward Elgar Publishing, 2012), pp. 135–77.

13 For some civil society views, see Civil Society Synthesis Paper, "Ten Years of the Right to Food Guidelines – Progress, Obstacles and the Way Ahead", (FIAN, 2014), available at: www.fian.org/library/publications.

14 Report submitted by the Special Rapporteur on the Right to Food, Olivier De Schutter, UN Doc. A/HRC/19/59 (26 December 2011), para. 48.

15 Food and Agricultural Organization, "The State of Food Insecurity in the World: Strengthening the Enabling Environment for Food Security and Nutrition", (Rome: FAO, 2014).

Of these, 70 per cent are women,[16] making it imperative to strengthen the gender dimension in realisation of the right to food. The pernicious effects of undernourishment in infants and children (especially early death or stunting) are especially dramatic, as noted in the 2014 Rome Declaration on Nutrition.[17]

What is meant by the right to food? The Universal Declaration of Human Rights of 1948 enshrined everyone's right to "a standard of living adequate for the health and well-being of himself and his family, including food..." (Art. 25(1)).[18] The International Covenant on Economic, Social and Cultural Rights of 1966, which entered into force in 1976, incorporated it in "the right of everyone to an adequate standard of living for himself and his family, including adequate food..." (Art. 11(1)). The Covenant further recognised "the fundamental right of everyone to be free from hunger", and spelt out measures to improve methods of production, conservation and distribution of food and to ensure an equitable distribution of world food supplies in relation to need (Art. 11(2)).

To this end, the parties to the Covenant are to take steps to ensure the realisation of the right to food, recognising "the essential importance of international co-operation based on free consent". The Covenant referred, in particular, to making use of scientific knowledge, disseminating knowledge about nutrition, and developing or reforming agrarian systems in order to achieve the most efficient development and utilisation of natural resources. (This last element would today need to be read in the context of the principles of sustainable development.) The first paragraph of Article 11 can be seen as establishing an objective which states should strive to achieve, while the second paragraph sets the minimum standard that is immediately applicable, *i.e.*, freedom from hunger and the means to achieve it.[19] While attention has traditionally focused on an insufficient quantity of food, the qualitative nature inherent in the right to "adequate" food also extends to contemporary concerns over obesity linked to calorie-rich, but unbalanced, diets. This is reflected in the Rome Declaration on Nutrition, which reaffirmed "the right of everyone to have access to safe, sufficient, and nutritious food consistent with the right to adequate food".[20] As explored below, other international instruments also address the right to food, and it is important to recognise their inter-linkages.

16 Human Rights Council Advisory Committee, Study on Discrimination in the Context of the Right to Food, UN Doc. A/HRC/AC/6/CRP.1 (2010), para. 38.

17 FAO/WHO, Rome Declaration on Nutrition, 2nd International Conference on Nutrition, (Rome, 19–21 November 2014), ICN2 2014/2, para. 12.

18 This right is generally seen as including the right to clean water. However, since the right to water has its own legal regime, it is not treated here other than incidentally.

19 Christophe Golay, "Droit à l'alimentation et accès à la justice: Exemples au niveau national, regional et international", in: FAO, *Études sur le droit à l'alimentation*, (Rome: FAO, 2009), pp. 10–13. See, also, Philip Alston and Katerina Tomasevski (eds), *The Right to Food: Towards a System for Supervising States' Compliance with the Right to Food*, (Leiden: Martinus Nijhoff, 1984).

20 Rome Declaration, note 17 above, para. 3.

II. WHAT IS THE BACKGROUND OF THE RIGHT TO FOOD?

The roots of the modern concept of rights trace back to the eighteenth century.[21] In the more recent past, the background to the emergence of the right to food included the development of humanitarian law in the context of armed conflict, early concerns of the International Labour Organization (founded in 1919) in relation to the welfare of workers, migrants and their families,[22] the 1941 Atlantic Charter's call for "freedom from want", the experiences of prisoners of war, occupied populations and displaced persons both during and after two world wars,[23] and the adoption of the United Nations Charter in 1945. Moreover, the ILO's Declaration of Philadelphia, adopted in 1944 and soon thereafter incorporated into its Constitution, speaks directly to "the war against want", "the raising of standards of living", "a minimum living wage", and "the provision of adequate nutrition".[24]

With the creation of other UN Specialized Agencies and Funds, the centre of gravity on food and nutrition issues naturally moved to the Food and Agriculture Organization (FAO) of the UN, the International Fund for Agricultural Development, the World Food Programme and the World Health Organization (without taking into account developments in the realm of humanitarian law or environmental law). Today, the Committee on World Food Security (a multi-stakeholder forum hosted by the FAO), the United Nations Human Rights Council and its Advisory Committee, the Committee on ESC Rights (Economic, Social and Cultural), and the Special Rapporteur are the main public international law actors in relation to the normative aspects of the right to food, with WHO active on nutrition issues, UNICEF on child nutrition,

---

21 See, for example, Daphne Barak-Erez and Aeyal M. Gross, "Introduction: Do we Need Social Rights: Questions in the Era of Globalisation, Privatisation, and the Diminished Welfare State", in: Daphne Barak-Erez and Aeyal M. Gross (eds), *Exploring Social Rights: Between Theory and Practice*, (Portland OR: Hart Publishing, 2007), p. 1.

22 A review of the ILO's engagement on legal issues relating to agricultural and rural workers appears in Jennie Desrutins, "Les travailleurs agricoles et ruraux", in: Jean-Marc Thouvenin and Anne Trebilcock (eds), *Droit International Social*, (Brussels: Bruylant, 2013), vol 1, pp. 1110–1128.

23 For a fascinating account of disputes that arose over the type of food being provided to displaced persons and the occupied population in post-WWII Germany (the Europeans did not appreciate peanut butter, for instance), see Atina Grossmann, "Grams, Calories and Food: Languages of Victimization, Entitlement, and Human Rights in Occupied Germany", in: Akira Iriye, Petra Goedde and William I. Hitchcock (eds), *The Human Rights Revolution: An International History*, (Oxford: Oxford University Press, 2012), pp. 113–132.

24 Declaration concerning the aims and purposes of the International Labour Organization (also called the Declaration of Philadelphia), adopted on 10 May 1944, annexed to the ILO Constitution and incorporated into it by Article 1 (Instrument of Amendment of 1945, which entered into force on 26 September 1946). The Preamble to the ILO Constitution, which formed Chapter XIII of the Treaty of Versailles that ended the First World War, states that "universal and lasting peace can be established only if it is based upon social justice".

and the ILO on relevant international labour standards. Multi-institutional and multi-stakeholder initiatives are contributing to the development of the right to food and its application in practice (see Section V. below).

The historical (and artificial) division between socio-economic rights and civil and political rights[25] has implied that,

> "questions of distribution are excluded from the rights discourse twice over: by both the exclusion of social rights [from the mainstream] and the exclusion of distribution concerns from the realm of civil rights."[26]

Fortunately, a unitary approach to human rights has gained ground, in recognition that all of them have some distributive implications.[27] Positive rights and positive duties exist in the context of several socio-economic rights, including the right to food.[28] Although economic and social rights are now accepted as part of the international legal obligation of states, backed up by international supervisory bodies, there is still some resistance to the recognition of established international social rights,[29] particularly when they challenge a liberal economic order.

III. IS IT A SOCIAL OR AN ECONOMIC RIGHT? OR A SOCIO-ECONOMIC RIGHT?

While the Covenant does not identify which rights are considered under it to be economic, social or cultural, it is commonly held that Article 11 on an adequate standard of living is one of the "economic" rights.[30] This is also the case for Article 6 on the right to work, Article 7 on conditions of work and remuneration, Article 8 on organisation in trade unions, Article 9 on social security, and the provisions of Article 10 that address maternity protection for working mothers and protection of children from economic exploitation. Today, the rights reflected in the ESC Covenant have, perhaps aside from its provisions on culture, become agglomerated as "international social rights". However, if

---

25 For a fuller discussion, see Stefan Lorenzmeier, Chapter 5 in this volume.

26 Barak-Erez and Gross (eds), note 21 above, p. 7.

27 Ibid., at 7–9, and Upendra Baxi, "Failed Decolonisation and the Future of Social Rights: Some Preliminary Reflections", in: Barak-Erez and Gross (eds), note 21 above, pp. 41–55.

28 Sandra Fredman, *Human Rights Transformed: Positive Rights and Positive Duties*, (Oxford: Oxford University Press, 2008), pp. 129–132.

29 For a description, see, for example, Manisuli Ssenyonjo, *Economic, Social and Cultural Rights in International Law*, (Oxford-Portland OR: Hart Publishing, 2009), pp. 14–17. For an example of the controversy, see Conor Gearty and Virginia Mantouvalou, *Debating Social Rights*, (Oxford-Portland OR: Hart Publishing, 2011).

30 See, for example, Gerald J. Beyer, "Economic Rights: Past, Present and Future", in: Thomas Cushman (ed), *Handbook of Human Rights*, (Oxford: Routledge, 2012), p. 291.

one looks at what is generally considered "international economic law", none of these elements is included within its scope. Rather, distinct and more robust transnational legal regimes have arisen in relation to trade, investment, finance and commodities.[31] This disjunction lays bare structural problems that remain to be resolved.

The categorisation has several implications. As a social right, the right to food is reflected as importantly in soft law instruments as in treaty provisions. The quest for more effective means of its implementation is constantly being pursued, since the current ones are clearly inadequate.[32] As Manisuli Ssenyonjo notes,

> "Social rights are also artifacts of political struggles, the product of a time- and place-specific consensus about the requirements of social peace and economic progress."[33]

The combination of these characteristics implies the involvement of non-state actors, a topic that continues both to bedevil and to enrich the public international law debate.[34] This is partly for theoretical reasons, since the system is based upon state sovereignty. But practical challenges also play a role, since these actors – ranging from peasant groups to multinational corporations – can have very different interests and capacities to exert power in the development and implementation of transnational norms.

Kerry Rittich has observed that,

> "What most distinguishes social rights is the decision to ... intervene in the structure of social and economic inequality. It is this aspiration from which the policy consensus has most clearly retreated... Social rights and social policy have traditionally been motivated by the desire to mitigate the effects of market forces on both individuals and society at large..."[35]

This makes social rights particularly vulnerable to a paradigm in which self-regulating markets and a reduced role for the state are in vogue. Yet, the social

31 These regimes are usefully summarised in Commission on Human Rights, *Globalization and its Impact on the Full Enjoyment of Human Rights*, UN Doc. E/CN.4/Sub.2/2001/10, (2 August 2001).

32 Anne Trebilcock, "Spécificités quant aux techniques de la mise en oeuvre et de contrôle: à la recherche de nouveaux chemins", in: Thouvenin and Trebilcock (eds), note 22 above, pp. 106–146.

33 Ssenyonjo, note 29 above, p. 112.

34 See, for example, Manisuli Ssenyonjo, "Non-State Actors and Economic, Social, and Cultural Rights", in: Mashood A. Baderin and Robert McCorquodale (eds), *Economic, Social and Cultural Rights in Action*, (Oxford: Oxford University Press, 2009), pp. 109–138.

35 Kerry Rittich, "Social Rights and Social Policy: Transformations on the International Landscape", in: Baderin and McCorquodale (eds), note 34 above, p. 133.

dimension remains, since "distributive justice and social concerns are in play at virtually every level of the economic and regulatory order".[36]

IV. THE "HARD" AND "SOFT" LAW OF THE RIGHT TO FOOD

The right to food is reflected in both the "hard" law of treaties, which create binding obligations, and "soft" law. Soft law can take the form of declarations, resolutions, recommendations, guidelines, codes of practice and the like. It can be derived from hard law, and deepen it, but it should not rewrite it. As explored below for legal instruments concluded primarily under the auspices of the UN and some specialised agencies, a large body of international law already exists on the right to food. What is needed is a greater appreciation of how the various elements fit together, alongside civil society's insistence on more vigorous monitoring mechanisms and remedies for rights violations, as a basis for more effective action.

A. TREATIES CONCLUDED UNDER UN AUSPICES: DEVELOPMENT OF THE NOTION OF THE RIGHT TO FOOD

The Committee on Economic, Social and Cultural Rights (CESCR), established in 1989 as the monitoring body under the Covenant, set out the nature of the obligations of States Parties to the Covenant in its General Comment No. 3. The principal obligation under Article 2 of the Covenant is for a state to take steps to achieve progressively the full realisation of a right set out in the Covenant, both by appropriate means and by utilising "maximum available resources".[37] Employing the now well-established UN human-rights framework of "respect, protect and fulfil", the CESCR, in its General Comment No. 12, has explained this in the context of the right to food as follows:

> "The obligation to respect existing access to adequate food requires States parties not to take any measures that result in preventing such access;
>
> The obligation to protect requires measures by the State to ensure that enterprises or individuals do not deprive individuals of their access to food;

36 Ibid., p. 121.

37 CESCR, General Comment 3, The Nature of States Parties' Obligations (14 December 1990) UN Doc E/1991/23, Annex III, recalled in General Comment No. 12, Right to Adequate Food (12 May 1999), UN Doc E/C.12/1999/5, para. 14.

> The obligation to fulfill (facilitate) means the State must pro-actively engage in activities intended to strengthen people's access to and utilization of resources and means to ensure their livelihood, including food security; ...
>
> Whenever an individual or group is unable, for reasons beyond their control, to enjoy the right to adequate food by the means at their disposal, States have the obligation to fulfill (provide) that right directly."[38]

The General Comment also addressed implementation issues, including monitoring and remedies.[39]

In General Comment No. 12, the Committee stated that the core content of the right implies:

> "the availability of food in a quantity and quality sufficient to satisfy the dietary needs of individuals, free from adverse substances, and acceptable within a given culture; [and] the accessibility of such food in ways that are sustainable and that do not interfere with the enjoyment of other human rights."[40]

The notion thus incorporates food safety. "Sustainability" entails the idea of long-term availability and accessibility, which encompasses both economic and physical aspects.[41] As "core" content, these aspects of the right to food are non-derogable, even in times of disaster, conflict or economic crisis. According to Manisuli Ssenyonjo, this means that:

> "even in times of severe resource constraints the State must protect the most disadvantaged and marginalized members or groups of society by adopting relatively low-cost targeted programmes."[42]

Following the entry into force of the Optional Protocol to the Covenant on 5 May 2013, the Committee may also now have the opportunity to examine the right to food more closely in the context of an individual or a group communication.

In addition, other widely-ratified international treaties also recognise the right to food. The most developed of these is the Convention on the Rights of the Child, which contains a number of provisions relevant to the right to food: Art. 6(2) on survival and development, Art.19(1) on protection from neglect, Art. 24(2)(c) on health, including provision of adequate nutritious foods to combat malnutrition, and Art. 27(3) on parental responsibility, with support

38 General Comment No. 12, para. 15; see, also, www.ohchr.org/EN/Issues/Food/Pages/FoodIndex.aspx.

39 See Stefan Lorenzmeier, Chapter 5 in this volume.

40 CESCR, General Comment No. 12, para. 8.

41 Ibid., para. 13.

42 Manisuli Ssenyonjo, "Economic, Social and Cultural Rights: An Examination of State Obligations", in: Sarah Joseph and Adam McBeth (eds), *Research Handbook on International Human Rights Law*, (Cheltenham: Edward Elgar Publishing, 2010), pp. 36–70, at 56.

to be provided under particular conditions, including with regard to nutrition. Furthermore, the Convention on the Rights of Persons with Disabilities (2006) recognises the right of such persons to an adequate standard of living for themselves and their families, including adequate food (Art. 28). And the Convention on the Elimination of All Forms of Discrimination against Women (CEDAW), which cuts across the range of issues necessary for the empowerment of women, offers an excellent platform for exploring the gender dimension of the right to food. Without being acknowledged as such, thinking around this instrument[43] appears to have informed the former Special Rapporteur's report on women's rights and the right to food.[44]

Expert committees established under various other global treaty regimes have mentioned the right to food in connection with those instruments, although, of course, like the ESC Committee, their views are not binding on the states parties. The Committee on the Rights of the Child (CRC) has explored the importance of adequate nutrition in several of its general comments. General Comment 7 on child rights in early childhood recalled the responsibility of states to ensure access to good nutrition, in order to combat both malnutrition and obesity (Para. 27(a)).[45] It also pointed out the importance of breastfeeding, and cross-referenced the guarantees provided by the ILO's Maternity Protection Convention, 2000 (No. 183).[46] This comment also brought out the importance of the right to non-discrimination guaranteed by Article 2 of the Convention, noting that girls and indigenous children are at special risk of reduced levels of nutrition. In its General Comment on the right to health,[47] the CRC re-iterated the link between maternal and infant health, and provided more detailed guidance on direct nutritional interventions, the promotion of breastfeeding, school feeding, measures against obesity, and education on healthy eating (paras. 35, 43 to 47 and 59). It again urged compliance with the International Code of Marketing of Breast-milk Substitutes and later relevant WHO resolutions (paras. 44 and 81). The CRC also highlighted food security in its General Comment on state obligations regarding the impact of the business sector on children's rights.[48]

---

43 See, for example, Marsha A. Freeman, Christine Chinkin and Beate Rudolf (eds), *The UN Convention on the Elimination of All Forms of Discrimination against Women: A Commentary*, (Oxford: Oxford University Press, 2012).

44 Report submitted by the Special Rapporteur on the Right to Food, Olivier De Schutter: "Women's Rights and the Right to Food", UN Doc. A/HRC/22/50, (24 December 2012).

45 General Comment No. 7 (Rev.) on Implementing Child Rights in Early Childhood, CRC/C/GC/7/Rev.1, (20 September 2006).

46 Earlier ILO instruments contained similar but weaker provisions; they remain in force for many countries that have not ratified the more recent standard.

47 General Comment No. 5 (2013) on the Right of the Child to the Enjoyment of the Highest Attainable Standard of Health (Art. 24), CRC/C/GC/15, (17 April 2013).

48 General Comment No. 16, CRC/C/GC/16, (17 April 2013).

The CEDAW Committee is considering a general comment on the rights of rural women under Article 14 of CEDAW, which refers to equal treatment in land and agrarian reform, and access to agricultural credit, important factors for food production (see Art. 14(2(g)). Article 13 also refers to forms of credit, access to which is critical in agricultural production. In comments to states parties, the Committee, citing various Articles, has addressed the equal access of women to food in emergency situations, the right of rural women to food, adequate nutrition during pregnancy, and lactation and malnutrition as aspects of women's health.[49]

All of the UN Conventions mentioned have optional protocols under which individuals and groups can file communications; these can reinforce future action in national courts. This is important, since "the ability of the international normative frameworks, policies and mechanisms to protect victims from violations of economic, social and cultural rights depends ultimately on how they are implemented at national level as well as on the degree to which they reach individuals in their context".[50]

B. RELEVANT ILO CONVENTIONS AND RECOMMENDATIONS

While other UN specialised agencies such as the FAO and the WHO primarily rely on soft law instruments, such as those highlighted in Section V. below, the ILO's mandate to set international labour standards has been primarily, but not exclusively, expressed through the adoption by the International Labour Conference of Conventions (treaties) and Recommendations (non-binding instruments). A number of them either directly address the production or provision of food, or tackle issues that have an important bearing on the enjoyment of the right to food by workers and their families. In some cases, this has included rights relating to land. The problems of poverty, low income, inequality and disempowerment form the sad nexus between these instruments and people's right to food. Aside from the fundamental Conventions (see below), most of the relevant ILO instruments are relatively unknown. To his credit, the Special Rapporteur has referenced the protection of workers in the agricultural sector in his reports,[51] but there are other pertinent standards as well. The ILO's Maternity Protection Convention, 2000 (No. 183), for instance, which

49 See Beate Rudolf, "Article 13", in: Freeman, Chinkin and Rudolf, note 43 above, pp. 342–343.

50 Christophe Golay, Irene Biglino and Ivona Truscan, "Economic, Social and Cultural Rights", (2013) 2 *European Journal of Human Rights*, p. 296.

51 See note 4 above, paras. 10–20. Ganesh has also argued in favour of linking food producers' welfare to their right to food. Aravind R. Ganesh, "The Right to Food and Buyer Power", (2010) 11 *German Law Journal*, pp. 1190–1244.

encourages breastfeeding, was mentioned in the Framework for Action adopted alongside the Rome Declaration on Nutrition.[52]

A unitary system of supervision of obligations under the ILO Constitution applies to all ratified Conventions. Only the International Court of Justice can give an authoritative interpretation of ILO Conventions, but a supervisory system has been established in the ILO to provide for a non-binding review. The independent, high-level Committee of Experts on the Application of Conventions and Recommendations (CEACR) examines government reports, along with possible observations from workers' and employers' organisations, on the effect given to a ratified Convention by a ratifying member state. The CEACR traditionally meets each year with the CESCR, thus reducing the risk of divergence on issues of mutual concern. The Applications Committee of the annual Conference, at which the representatives of employers and workers sit alongside governments, permits a more political discussion of selected cases. The ILO Governing Body can also request reports on non-ratified Conventions and Recommendations which are then synthesised by the CEACR; this so-called general survey by the CEACR is also discussed by the Applications Committee. Constitutionally provided procedures for filing representations and complaints are also available, although less often used.[53]

Not long after the ESC Covenant was adopted, an analysis compared its provisions with ILO instruments then in existence, identifying only a handful of them in relation to Article 11.[54] Today, a more integrated analysis would highlight more Conventions and Recommendations, some adopted later, that are of particular relevance to the realisation of the right to food. In addition, follow-up under ILO Declarations adopted in 1998 and 2008 provide an additional lens for looking at this question. The relevant instruments can be grouped under fundamental principles and rights at work, social protection and governance, and instruments relating directly to food: its production, its provision, or earning wages sufficient to purchase it, including by specific categories of persons such as agricultural workers or indigenous peoples.

---

52 FAO/WHO, Framework for Action, Second International Conference on Nutrition, (Rome, 19–21 November 2014), ICN2 2014/3 Corr. 1, p. 5, n 8.

53 For an overview of the system, see ILO, *Rules of the Game: A Brief Introduction to International Labour Standards*, 2nd rev'd. ed., (Geneva: ILO, 2014).

54 Comparative analysis of the international human rights Covenants and international labour Conventions, ILO, LXIX *Official Bulletin* (1969) 151, paras. 84–86. It highlighted only the Social Policy Convention (Non-Metropolitan Territories) Convention, 1947 (No. 82), the Social Policy (Minimum Standards) Convention, 1962 (No. 117), the Plantations Convention, 1958 (No. 110), and the Indigenous and Tribal Populations Convention, 1957 (No. 107), along with several Recommendations. Of these, only Convention No. 110 and its accompanying Recommendation (No. 110), along with the Workers' Housing Recommendation, 1961 (No. 115; see its paras. 7(e), 8(f), 15(c)), and the Tenants and Sharecroppers Recommendation, 1968 (No. 132), are still considered by the ILO to be up-to-date. The Indigenous and Tribal Peoples Convention, 1989 (No. 169) replaced C. 107, which nevertheless remains in force for some States. ILO instruments are available at www.ilo.org in the NORMLEX database.

1. *Fundamental Principles and Rights at Work*

As one outcome of the so-called "social clause" debate in trade negotiations in the 1990s, the International Labour Conference adopted the ILO Declaration on Fundamental Principles and Rights at Work in 1998.[55] Under it, ILO members are obligated, by virtue of ILO membership, to respect, promote and realise four principles relating to freedom of association and collective bargaining, and to the elimination of child labour, forced labour and discrimination in employment/occupation. The ILO has identified eight fundamental Conventions relating to these principles, all of which are now almost universally ratified.[56] Each has relevance to the realisation of the right to food.

The ILO reported in 2010 that 69 per cent of all child labour occurs in agriculture, often under hazardous conditions.[57] While progress has been made in reducing it, the young age of the children involved, ingrained attitudes and perceptions about the roles of girls and boys, denial of education, a lack of regulation and its enforcement, along with inadequate income-earning options for their parents, all serve to make tackling rural child labour especially challenging.[58] As one response, the ILO instituted a new multi-stakeholder initiative to target the elimination of child labour in the context of support for small farmers, as part of efforts to break the cycle of poverty.

Children and adults alike may be subject to forced labour, especially in the form of bonded labour, as a means to avert acute poverty or starvation.[59] In addition, excessive charges imposed for food and drink, among other items, also form part of the pattern of debt bondage involving rural forced labour,[60] labour trafficking, and exploitation by some labour migration recruitment agencies.

55 A legal analysis of the Declaration is provided by Claire La Hovary, *Les droits fondamentaux au travail: Origines, statut et impact en droit international*, (Paris: Presses universitaires de France, 2009). A brief description appears in Anne Trebilcock, "The ILO Declaration on Fundamental Principles and Rights at Work: A New Tool", in: Roger Blanpain and Chris Engels (eds), *The ILO and the Social Challenges of the 21st Century: The Geneva Lectures*, (The Hague: Kluwer, 2001), pp. 105–116.

56 These are the Forced Labour Convention, 1930 (No. 29), the Abolition of Forced Labour Convention, 1957 (No. 105), the Freedom of Association and Right to Organise Convention, 1948 (No. 87) and the Right to Organise and Collective Bargaining Convention, 1949 (No. 98), the Equal Remuneration Convention, 1951 (No. 100), the Discrimination (Employment and Occupation) Convention, 1958 (No. 111), the Minimum Age Convention, 1973 (No. 138) and the Worst Forms of Child Labour Convention, 1999 (No. 182). Almost all states have ratified the vast majority of these instruments. Ratification information is available in the NORMLEX database on the ILO website, www.ilo.org, under labour standards.

57 ILO, *Accelerating Action against Child Labour*, Global Report under the follow-up to the ILO Declaration on Fundamental Principles and Rights at Work, (Geneva: ILO, 2010), p. 56.

58 ILO, *Promotion of Rural Employment for Poverty Reduction*, International Labour Conference, 97th Session, Report IV (Geneva: ILO, 2008), pp. 89–90.

59 ILO, *A Global Alliance against Forced Labour*, Global Report under the follow-up to the ILO Declaration on Fundamental Principles and Rights at Work, (Geneva: ILO, 2005), p. 31.

60 Ibid., p. 41.

The right to food, like other ESC rights, is accompanied by a general prohibition on discrimination on grounds of race, colour, sex, language, age, religion, political or other opinions, national or social origin, property, birth or other status.[61] Inequality – whether due to sex, race, social origin, migrant status or other situation – is closely associated with poverty and limitation of the right to food. Ethnicity-based discrimination plays a very detrimental role in some countries. The former Special Rapporteur's Report on Women's Rights and Food casts light on the many facets of gender-based discrimination that are involved, from the home, to education, to the labour market. An FAO/IFAD/ILO report focused on the serious gender-based discrimination which permeates agricultural work.[62] Disadvantages relating to denial of access to land, other property and credit, as well as to discrimination in job opportunities, remuneration, education and training, combine in a vicious circle of disempowerment, with consequences in relation to food.[63] In some countries, women need their husband's permission to join a co-operative or trade union, or to sign a contract to buy land. These are all practices condemned by international law, under both CEDAW and ILO Conventions[64] as well as the Covenants.

Freedom of association and collective bargaining play a key role in ensuring respect for the right to food. The chief ILO Conventions on this topic are the Freedom of Association and Protection of the Right to Organise Convention, 1948 (No. 87), which is mentioned in Article 8(3) of the ESC Covenant, and the Right to Organise and Collective Bargaining Convention, 1949 (No. 98). They provide the essential guarantees for workers and employers to form and join associations of their own choice and for these organisations to engage in their activities without previous government authorisation or interference.

An early ILO instrument, the Right of Association (Agriculture) Convention, 1921 (No. 11), had already affirmed that all those engaged in agriculture have the same rights of association and combination as industrial workers (Art. 1). The Rural Workers' Organisations Convention, 1975 (No. 141) spelt out in more detail how persons engaged in agriculture, handicrafts or a related occupation in a rural area can be guaranteed the right of association free from all interference, coercion or repression (Art. 3). The contribution that such organisations make to improving employment opportunities, general conditions of work and life in

---

61 ESC Covenant, Art. 2; see, also, General Comment No. 12, para.18, and General Comment No. 20 concerning non-discrimination in economic, social, and cultural rights, E/C.12/GC/20 (2 July 2009).

62 FAO/IFAD/ILO, Gender Dimensions of Agricultural and Rural Employment: Differentiated Pathways out of Poverty – Status, Trends and Gaps, (Rome: FAO, 2010).

63 Special Rapporteur on the Right to Food, Women's Rights and Food, para.5; ILO, "Gender at the Heart of Decent Work", (Geneva: ILO, 2011).

64 See, especially, Convention on the Elimination of All Forms of Discrimination Against Women (Arts. 2, 5, 11, 13 and 14), ILO Conventions No. 100 and 111, the Discrimination (Employment and Occupation) Recommendation No. 111, and the Workers with Family Responsibilities Convention, 1975 (No. 156) and Recommendation (No. 165).

rural areas, as well as increasing the national income and achieving its better distribution, is recognised in Article 6. The accompanying Recommendation (No. 149) highlights the role such independent, non-discriminatory organisations can play in programmes of agricultural development and agrarian reform (para. 5).

Unfortunately, even with these legal protections, freedom of association and collective bargaining are still too often denied to workers in the agricultural sector. As the ILO Committee of Experts has pointed out, rural workers, especially those in agriculture, face both legal impediments and practical challenges to exercising these rights.[65] The same is true for workers in many export-processing zones, in which food is often transformed before marketing.

Collective bargaining, through which representative organisations of workers reach collective agreements with employers or their associations, also plays a role in the realisation of the right to food. In addition to their important function of agreeing on wage levels that permit the purchase of adequate food for families, such accords may also provide for standards for food and catering made available at the workplace.

In addition, the Cooperatives Recommendation, 2002 (No. 193) is relevant to both food producers and consumers. Under it, a co-operative is defined as "an autonomous association of persons united voluntarily to meet their common economic, social and cultural needs and aspirations through jointly owned and democratically controlled enterprise". (para. 2). The Recommendation sets out several means of strengthening co-operatives and some measures that governments can take to provide a supportive policy and legal framework for them.

Strengthening organisations such as farmers' unions, rural women's associations, co-operatives and trade unions along the food-supply chain could create a more level playing-field for the realisation of the right to food. Hard law instruments and soft law initiatives support the creation of effective, free, democratic institutions that are accountable to their members, and their implementation should be encouraged. They provide the legal protection for effective participation – a factor stressed as critical in numerous reports of the Special Rapporteur.[66]

2. *Social Protection*

The Universal Declaration of Human Rights affirms the right to social security in the context of the realisation of rights indispensable for a person's dignity

65 See ILO, 2008, note 58 above, pp. 87–88.
66 See, for instance, UN Doc. A/HRC/22/50, para. 38.

(Art. 22).[67] In his analysis of Article 11 of the Covenant, Asbørn Eide has pointed out that an adequate standard of living is to be realised as a right or claim in the context of human dignity, not as an act of charity.[68] It is thus not surprising to see that light has been cast on social security and social protection measures as critical means for ensuring enjoyment of the right to food. Social protection can be seen as the other side of the coin of food security, since it guards against shocks caused by famine or natural disasters. According to the High Level Panel of Experts on Food Security and Nutrition, social protection (which they take to mean agricultural input subsidies, public-works programmes, food price stabilisation and subsidies and social transfers) plays a key role in ensuring food security.[69] The Rome Declaration on Nutrition called for women's full and equal access to social protection.[70]

The ILO's approach to social protection grows out of experience under the Social Security (Minimum Standards) Convention, 1951 (No. 102), which, among other things, covers family benefits as well as maternity allowances. Family benefits can be in the form of payment, provision of necessities such as food, or a combination of these (Art. 42). In part because this Convention is geared mainly to the formal economy, the ILO decided to adopt the ILO Social Protection Floors Recommendation, 2012 (No. 202). It sees social protection as "an important tool to prevent and reduce poverty, inequality, social exclusion and social insecurity".[71] The instrument calls for minimum national guarantees of access to essential health care and to basic income security which together secure effective access to goods and services defined as necessary at national level (para. 4). It specifically highlights maternity protection and "basic income security for children, at least at a nationally defined level, providing access to nutrition…" (para. 5(b)). The Recommendation also contains provisions on governance aspects and strategies to support such guarantees. It serves as a platform for multi-stakeholder initiatives,[72] and has received support from the Human Rights Council upon the basis of a report by the Special Rapporteur on Extreme Poverty and Human Rights.[73] The instrument foresees attention

67 Janelle M. Diller, *Securing Dignity and Freedom through Human Rights: Article 22 of the Universal Declaration of Human Rights*, (Leiden: Martinus Nijhoff, 2012), pp. 85–89 and 140–144.

68 Asbjørn Eide, "Human Rights-Based Development in the Age of Economic Globalization: Background and Prospects", in: Bard A. Andreassen and Stephen P. Marks (eds), *Development as a Human Right: Legal, Political and Economic Dimensions*, (Cambridge MA: Harvard University Press, 2006), Chapter 11.

69 High Level Panel on Food Security and Nutrition, *Social Protection for Food Security*, (Rome: CFS/HLPE, 2012).

70 Rome Declaration, note 17 above, para. 13(j)).

71 The preamble refers to Article 11 of the ESC Covenant.

72 A wide range of international institutions are involved; at national level, initiatives are country-led. See www.socialprotectionfloor.org.

73 Final draft of the guiding principles on extreme poverty and human rights, submitted by the Special Rapporteur on Extreme Poverty and Human Rights, Magdalena Sepúlveda Carmona, UN Doc. A/HRC/21/39, (18 July 2012), para. 20.

to gender equality, which is critical in the design and implementation of social-protection measures in the context of the right to food.[74]

3. *Governance (including Terms of Employment and Conditions of Work)*

In its approach to international labour standards today, the ILO Governing Body has identified what were referred to in the 2008 Declaration on Social Justice for a Fair Globalization as "governance" Conventions: those dealing with employment policy, labour inspection, and tripartite consultation. In the context of the right to food, the Labour Inspection (Agriculture) Convention, 1969 (No. 129) and the Recommendation that complements it (No. 133), deserve particular mention. They set out the functions of labour inspection in this area and provide for organisational and other measures to ensure its expertise, independence and efficacy in enforcing the law, providing advice and reporting.

The notion of governance can be interpreted more broadly, to extend, for instance, to arrangements for ensuring that wages are sufficient to cover the cost of food. Aside from Convention No. 98 on collective-bargaining, the leading instrument on this is the Minimum Wage Fixing Convention, 1970 (No. 131), which calls for establishing a consultative system to set the level of legal minimum wages in a way that takes into account the needs of workers and their families, in particular the cost of living, as well as other economic factors (Art. 3). The Minimum Wage Fixing Machinery (Agriculture) Convention, 1951 (No. 99) takes a similar approach for workers employed in agricultural undertakings and related occupations. Here, partial payment of minimum wages in the form of allowances in kind may be permitted, if the allowances are appropriate for the use and benefit of the worker and his or her family, and if the attributed value is fair and reasonable (Art. 2).

The link between earnings and the prices of goods and services was reflected in the ILO's earlier statistical database, LABORSTA, which has now been replaced by ILOSTAT. Among the topics covered were consumer-price indices, including retail prices of selected food items, and household income and expenditure in relation to wages. In 2003, the International Conference of Labour Statisticians adopted resolutions on the technical aspects of both. The Labour Statistics Convention, 1985 (No. 160) sets out minimum standards, supplemented by guidelines in a Recommendation (No. 170). The Convention foresees progressive expansion of the statistics that member states are to collect, compile and publish, including statistics on consumer-price indices and household expenditures (Art. 1(f) and (g)). The Recommendation refers specifically to food in relation to consumer prices (para. 7(2)). Convention No. 160 provides for the collection, compilation and publication of data by ratifying states on not only a range of labour issues, but also consumer-price indices

[74] Women's Rights and the Right to Food, note 63 above, paras. 22–28.

(Art. 1(f)) and household or family expenditures (Art. 1(g)). For countries accepting the obligation in relation to consumer price indices, they are to be computed in order to measure variations over time in the prices of items representative of the consumption patterns of significant population groups or of the total population. In the accompanying Recommendation (No. 170), food is, of course, included among important consumption items to be covered by consumer-price indices (para. 7(2)). Such data can be read alongside the FAO's Food Price Indices. These track changes in international prices of major food commodities and prices of a basket of food commodities.

In a broad sense of governance, rules on working time – which, together with hourly or daily wages, will determine a worker's gross earnings – can also be relevant to his or her enjoyment of the right to food. "Time poverty" affects poor working-women in particular, with hours spent in obtaining and preparing food for the family not captured by economic data. In formal employment, breaks that are too short to permit the consumption of nutritious meals can also play a role in undermining the right to food. The Welfare Facilities Recommendation, 1956 (No. 102) provides that "special consideration should be given to providing shift workers with facilities for obtaining adequate meals and beverages at appropriate times" (para. 13). This Recommendation makes a number of other detailed suggestions about workplace canteens (paras. 4 to 15). It encourages the provision of advice on types of meals, nutrition and hygiene standards, and the accommodation aspects of canteens. It notes that trolleys offering packed-meals and beverages for sale should not be used in workplaces "in which dangerous or harmful processes make it undesirable that workers should partake of food or drink there" (para. 10(2)). In a more limited sense, the Working Conditions (Hotels and Restaurants) Recommendation, 1991 (No. 179), which supplements Convention No. 172 of the same name, calls for the number and length of meal breaks to be determined in the light of the country's customs and traditions (para. 9).

Finally, the comparative analysis of ILO instruments carried out shortly after the ESC Covenant was adopted identified the comprehensive Social Policy (Basic Aims and Standards) Convention, 1962 (No. 117) as most relevant. While this Convention is no longer promoted for ratification, perhaps because it rests on a model of planned development, it remains in force for 32 states and could, therefore, be the object of procedures under the ILO Constitution. Article 4 of the Convention highlights measures for the promotion of productive capacity and the improvement of the standards of living of agricultural producers. These include eliminating the causes of chronic indebtedness and "the control, by the enforcement of adequate laws and regulations, of the ownership and use of land resources to ensure that they are used, with due regard to customary rights, in the best interests of the inhabitants of the country". Further measures include the supervision of tenancy arrangements and the encouragement of the formation of co-operatives. Moreover, measures are to be taken "to secure for independent producers and wage earners conditions which will give them scope to improve living standards by their own efforts and will ensure the maintenance of minimum standards of living..." (Art. 5(1)). Here, account is to be taken of "such essential family needs of the workers as food and its nutritive value..." (Art. 5(2)). Convention No. 117 also addresses remuneration, as well as non-discrimination and migrant workers.

4. *Categories of Workers and the Right to Food*

Other ILO Conventions and Recommendations address the right to food directly in relation to particular categories: agricultural and rural workers in various situations, seafarers and fishers aboard vessels, some other categories in which the place of work may also impose special constraints (domestic workers, construction workers, miners), and indigenous peoples.

a. Agricultural and Rural and Other Workers

As noted by the UN Human Rights Council, "70 per cent of hungry people live in rural areas and 50 per cent are small-scale farm-holders" who are highly vulnerable to food insecurity.[75] Agriculture provides a livelihood for more people, as producers or wage labour, than any other sector, but features a productivity level that is ten times lower than for services and industry.[76] Not surprisingly, then, agricultural wage-labourers are found at the extreme lower end of income distribution,[77] and face special challenges in relation to the right to food.[78] Several ILO instruments provide elements for improving their conditions, to be accompanied by deeper reforms. These will be necessary if the contribution of agricultural workers to sustainable agriculture is to be enhanced.[79]

The Plantations Convention, 1958 (No. 110), whose definition of plantation was amended by a Protocol, addresses the engagement and recruitment of migrant workers for plantation operations, contracts of employment, the abolition of penal sanctions, the protection of wages and fixing their minimum, weekly rest, annual holidays with pay, maternity protection, compensation to workers' in case of occupational injury, freedom of association, the right to

---

75 Resolution on the right to food, UNDoc. A/HRC/RES/28/10 (2 April 2015), para. 19.

76 David Cheong, Marion Jansen and Ralf Peters (eds), *Shared Harvests: Agriculture, Trade and Employment*, (Geneva: ILO/UNCTAD, 2013), p. 13.

77 Ibid., p. 9.

78 Report of the Special Rapporteur on the Right to Food, Agribusiness and the Right to Food, UN Doc.A/HRC/13/33, paras.10–27.

79 Peter Hurst *et al.*, Agricultural Workers and their Contribution to Sustainable Agriculture and Rural Development, (Geneva: FAO/ILO/IUF, 2007).

organise and collective bargaining, labour inspection, housing (including the provision of cooking facilities) and medical care. Aside from the provisions aimed at the payment of wages sufficient to obtain food, Article 27(3) stipulates, "Where food… or other essential supplies and services form part of remuneration, all practicable steps shall be taken to ensure that they are adequate and their cash value properly assessed". A similar provision appears in Article 4 of the Protection of Wages Convention, 1949 (No. 95), which is much more widely ratified than Convention No. 110.[80] The provision of food and the monetary value that may be attributed to it is an issue also addressed by the Domestic Workers Convention, 2011 (No. 189) (see its Arts. 7(h) and 12(2)). This Convention, incidentally, forms an important part of the puzzle of the care economy that is a key aspect of gendered labour, also in relation to the right to food.[81]

In addition, the generally applicable Occupational Safety and Health Convention, 1981 (No. 155) has been supplemented by a more specific instrument, the Safety and Health in Agriculture Convention, 2001 (No. 184). It aims at avoiding on-the-job accidents and occupational diseases which can severely curtail a worker's ability to work and access adequate food. The newer instrument is complemented by Recommendation No. 192, which calls on employers to provide workers in agriculture with an adequate supply of safe drinking-water and facilities for eating meals (para. 10).

Finally, the Tenants and Sharecroppers' Recommendation, 1968 (No. 132) encourages the progressive increase in their well-being, facilitating their access to land and the voluntary establishment of representative organisations, and the efficient use of natural and economic resources, ideally as part of a comprehensive national agrarian reform plan (paras. 4 to 9). The Recommendation addresses both the production and consumption perspective. Thus, rents should be set at a level that permits a standard of living for the occupant "which is compatible with human dignity", and "promotes progressive husbandry" (para. 10(a)(i) and (iii)). Rent payments should be postponed or reduced in the event of crop failure or other unforeseeable disasters (para. 11). Contracts should "encourage good agricultural practices" (para. 14(1)(c)). Furthermore, "[w]here appropriate … tenants, sharecroppers and similar categories of agricultural workers should be authorized to use some land for producing food for themselves and their families" (para. 19). These groups should also be protected against the risks of loss of income resulting from drought, floods, animal and plant diseases and the like (para. 20(1)). Co-operative institutions among these workers are also encouraged (para. 21).

80 Convention No 95 has been ratified by 98 countries, whereas Convention No 110 is in force for only 12 States.

81 Women's Rights and the Right to Food, note 63 above, paras. 3–5.

ILO Conventions on the rights and working conditions of seafarers and fishers also contain provisions relating to these workers' right to food. The Maritime Labour Convention 2006, which entered into force in 2013 for the majority of the world's shipping, includes food and catering among the necessary decent working and living conditions on board vessels (Art. IV and Regulation 3.2). As under earlier ILO standards in this field, seafarers are to be provided with food free of charge during their engagement, and the food must be of "appropriate quality, nutritional value and quantity that adequately covers the requirements of the ship and takes into account the differing cultural and religious backgrounds" of the crew (Regulation 3.2, detailed further in Standards A3.2 and B3.2). Similarly, the Fishing Convention, 2007 (No. 188), which will revise earlier instruments once it enters into force, calls for national legislation requiring that the food on board ship be of sufficient nutritional value, quality and quantity and provided at no cost to the fisher unless permitted by a collective agreement (Art. 27; see, also, Annex III, paras. 78–79). Guidelines recently adopted under the auspices of the FAO, in relation to the entire fish production chain, do not mention this instrument, but they do contain a general reference to "relevant ILO Conventions".[82]

Other occupations are also targeted by ILO instruments. Depending on the duration of the work and its location, and the number of construction workers, adequate facilities for obtaining or preparing food and drink nearby should be provided for them if not otherwise available (Safety and Health in Construction Recommendation, 1988 (No. 175), Para. 51(1)). A similar provision appears in the Safety and Health in Mines Recommendation, 1995 (No. 183). The Domestic Workers Recommendation, 2011 (No. 201) also stipulates that when food is provided, it should include "meals of good quality and sufficient quantity, adapted to the extent reasonable to the cultural and religious requirements, if any, of the domestic worker concerned" (para. 17(d)).

b. Indigenous Peoples

The Human Rights Council recently called upon states to take special action to combat the root causes of the disproportionately high level of hunger and malnutrition among indigenous peoples.[83] While the non-binding Declaration on the Rights of Indigenous Peoples adopted by the UN General Assembly in 2007 and the World Conference on Indigenous People, held in 2014, may be more widely known, the only binding treaties in this area are the Indigenous and Tribal Peoples Convention, 1989 (No. 169), and the instrument it

[82] FAO, "Voluntary Guidelines for Securing Sustainable Small-Scale Fisheries in the Context of Food Security and Poverty Eradication", (Rome: FAO, 2015), para. 6.12.

[83] Human Rights Council, Resolution on the Right to Food, UN Doc. A/HRC/22/L.16 (15 March 2013), adopted on 21 March 2013.

revised, the Indigenous and Tribal Populations Convention, 1957 (No. 107).[84] Convention No. 169 promotes the full realisation of indigenous peoples' social, economic and cultural rights, and provides for consultation, participation and, in some cases, decision-making in areas which concern (see especially Art. 6). In particular, governments are to take measures in co-operation with these peoples "to protect and preserve the environment of the territories they inhabit" (Art. 7(4)).

Part II (Arts. 13 to 19) of the instrument, on land, contains a number of guarantees. In direct protection against land-grabbing, Article. 14(1) provides in part,

> "The rights of ownership and possession of the peoples concerned over the lands which they traditionally occupy shall be recognized."

As necessary, Governments are to take steps to identify these lands and to "guarantee effective protection of their rights of ownership and possession" (Art. 14(2)), including adequate procedures to resolve land claims (Art. 14(3)). The Convention also contains protection against removal from the lands that indigenous peoples occupy (Art. 16) and against unauthorised intrusion or use (Art. 18). Consultation is required "whenever consideration is being given to their capacity to alienate their lands or otherwise transmit their rights outside their own community" (Art. 17(2)). National agrarian programmes are to secure these peoples equivalent treatment to other sectors of the population with regard to the provision of land "for providing the essentials of a normal existence" (Art. 19(a)). The ILO Committee of Experts has, on a number of occasions, called on governments to give effect to such provisions. Its detailed comments are, in some cases, informed by observations submitted by workers' or employers' organisations about specific conflicts. Recently, the Committee has raised issues about land demarcation and titling under Article 14 with the governments of Argentina, Brazil, Chile, Paraguay and Peru.[85] Among its most frequent comments are those reproaching inadequate consultation by many governments, often in connection with development projects or mining concessions.

---

84 Convention No 169 has been ratified by 22 states, while Convention No 107, which is closed to further ratification, remains in force for 17 states.

85 Report of the Committee of Experts on the Application of Conventions and Recommendations, International Labour Conference, 102nd session, 2013, Report III (Part IA), p. 819 *et seq.*

V. MULTI-INSTITUTIONAL ENGAGEMENT FROM VARYING PERSPECTIVES

Explicitly or implicitly, the international law of the right to food underpins many of the institutional initiatives, some involving multiple stakeholders, taken in relation to hunger, nutrition and other aspects of the right to food. Over the past several decades, the international community's reliance on global summits and their follow-up has been relevant to the development of soft law in relation to the right to food. In 1995, the World Social Summit and its follow-up highlighted the need for complementarity between social and economic goals. The World Food Summits, the most recent one convened in 2009, have produced declarations addressing it, especially relating to food security. The World Food Summit of 1996 stated that food security existed "when all people, at all times, have physical and economic access to sufficient, safe and nutritious food to meet their dietary needs and food preferences for an active and healthy life".[86]

In June 2012, the United Nations Conference on Sustainable Development agreed on a framework for development that includes three interconnected objectives: economic development, social inclusion, and environmental sustainability.[87] This Conference saw the launching of the Zero Hunger Challenge; it called for universal access to adequate food year-round, the prevention of child stunting, the sustainable transformation of food systems, increasing both the productivity and the incomes of smallholder farmers, and reduction in food loss and waste. More broadly, the United Nations Millennium Declaration (2000) and the Millennium Development Goals (MDGs) have focused attention on the right to food, by setting, as the first goal, "[the] eradicat[ion of] extreme poverty and hunger". Target 1C for this goal was halving, between 1990 and 2015, the proportion of the population who suffer from hunger. Under the same goal, Target 1B was to "achieve full and productive employment and decent work for all, including women and young persons". The MDGs have catalysed agencies across the UN system to think about how their missions relate to them and stimulated public-private partnerships on several issues. It is now anticipated that the UN General Assembly will adopt a set of Sustainable Development Goals and targets in 2015. Proposed Goal 2 is to end hunger, achieve food security and improved nutrition and promote sustainable agriculture. A separate Goal 8 would associate sustained, inclusive and sustainable economic growth with full and productive employment and decent

---

86 World Food Summit Plan of Action, World Food Summit, Rome, 13–17 November 1996, para. 1.

87 As characterised in Report of the Secretary-General, "A Life of Dignity for All: Accelerating Progress towards the Millennium Development Goals and Advancing the United Nations Development Agenda beyond 2015", UN Doc. A/68/202 (26 July 2013), para. 74.

work.[88] Such a reshuffling of goals would not remove the link between work and the right to food, but it would circumscribe it more narrowly to those active in food production as part of "sustainable agriculture". As urged by UN Women (the lead UN unit on gender issues), a stand-alone goal on gender equality and empowerment of women is also proposed.

In relation to the right to food, the restructured Committee on World Food Security (CFS) serves as a key global forum for debate aimed at policy convergence on food security issues, agriculture and nutrition (the FAO, the IFAD and the WFP serve as the CFS Secretariat). The CFS brings together governments, civil society organisations, private sector entities and foundations. In 2012, the CFS approved the Voluntary Guidelines on the Responsible Governance of Tenure of Land, Fisheries and Forests in the Context of National Food Security. It now intends to build on the Principles for Responsible Agricultural Investment that Respects Rights, Livelihoods and Resources, developed earlier by the FAO, the IFAD, the UNCTAD and the World Bank.[89] The "Scaling up Nutrition" movement, a public-private partnership, aims to reduce malnutrition and child stunting. Another example is the IFAD's Value Chain Development Programme, which focuses on cassava and rice, and involves producers, processors and their organisations, public and private institutions, service providers, road builders, policy developers and regulators.[90] In addition, the member organisations of the UN High-Level Task Force on the Global Food Security Crisis are collaborating with the G20 on agricultural productivity growth, and in the context of the Agricultural Market Information System (AMIS). The AMIS is intended to enhance transparency in global markets for wheat, corn, rice and soya beans.

These multi-institutional efforts can complement important steps taken in individual organizations, such as the FAO. In 2004, the FAO adopted the Voluntary Guidelines to support the progressive realisation of the right to adequate food in the context of national food security, known as the RtAF Guidelines.[91] Inspired by the ESC Committee's General Comment No. 12, they have been described as "a landmark commitment" and "a clear roadmap for human rights-based development".[92] The guidelines take a holistic approach, covering, among many topics, good governance, market systems, labour, food safety, nutrition and the international dimension. On the tenth anniversary of the RtAF Guidelines, civil society groups called for them to be reaffirmed, while

88 See https://sustainabledevelopment.un.org/sdgsproposal.

89 IFAD, Annual Report, Doc. AR/2012/e/5, p. 35. See, also, Human Rights Council, UN Doc. A/HRC/RES/28/10, (2 April 2015).

90 Ibid., pp. 37–38.

91 See www.fao.org/docrep/meeting/009/y9825e/y9825e00.HTM. The guidelines were mentioned as a practical tool in the resolution on the right to food adopted on 19 December 2011 by the UN General Assembly; A/RES/66/158, (27 March 2012).

92 Eide, note 68 above, p. 247.

insisting on improved accountability and monitoring, democratisation of the food system and creation of space for real participation.[93] They, along with other guidelines, were included in recommendations contained in the Framework for Action under the Rome Declaration on Nutrition.

Some initiatives related to the right to food are not new. The path-breaking WHO International Code of Marketing Breast-milk Substitutes, developed together with UNICEF, was adopted in 1981 and highlighted by the Special Rapporteur.[94] An even older arrangement is the Codex Alimentarius, consisting of standards based upon scientific evidence provided through independent expert meetings convened by the FAO and the WHO. Since its creation in 1963, the Codex Alimentarius Commission has adopted several hundred standards on the quality and nutritional value of foods, as well as on safe food production.[95] The series of WHO guidelines on food safety and nutrition, some developed with the FAO, should also be mentioned.

Whether captured in "hard law" treaties or "soft law" tools such as guidelines, greater accountability for realizing the right to food is needed. One important trend has been the development of a series of indicators against which various attributes of a right can be measured. The CESCR has suggested means of interpretation in order to overcome the difficulty posed by the relative vagueness of the "right to an adequate standard of living". In particular, it has emphasised the use of indicators and benchmarks as a means of measuring progress over time.[96] As Asbjørn Eide (who has taken a leading role on this issue) has pointed out, the Committee has often asked for detailed information, with particular attention to especially vulnerable or disadvantaged groups.[97] In several conclusions and recommendations addressed to member States in relation to their reports, the CESCR has looked at the indicators that they use, such as the cost of the monthly "food basket".[98]

While the use of indicators has been justifiably criticised and faces practical obstacles, such measurement can be helpful in certain instances in relation to the right to food.[99] The Office of the High Commissioner for Human Rights

93 See 10 Years of the Right to Food Guidelines, note 13 above.

94 Report submitted by the Special Rapporteur on the Right to Food, Olivier De Schutter, Doc. A/HRC/19/59, (26 Dec. 2011), paras. 50–51.

95 Christopher Wanjek, "Food at Work: Workplace Solutions for Malnutrition, Obesity and Chronic Diseases", (Geneva: ILO, 2005), pp. 384–387.

96 Yuval Shany, "Stuck in a Moment in Time: The International Justiciability of Economic, Social and Cultural Rights", in: Barak-Erez and Gross (eds), note 21 above, p. 77, at 81.

97 Asbjørn Eide, "Economic and Social Rights", in: Janusz Symonides (ed), *Human Rights: Concepts and Standards*, (Aldershot: Ashgate Publishing and UNESCO, 2000), p. 131.

98 Ibid., p. 86.

99 Randolph and Hertel, note 8 above, Eide, note 68 above, pp. 211–215, and Maarten Immink and Margret Vidar, "Monitoring the Human Right to Adequate Food at Country Level", in: Gudmundur Alfredsson, Jonas Grimheden, Bertrand G. Ramcharan and Alfred de Zayas, *International Human Rights Monitoring Mechanisms*, (Leiden: Martinus Nijhoff, 2009), pp. 313–323, at 319–320.

led consultations in 2006–2007 that produced illustrative indicators, including on the right to adequate food. They contain structural, process and outcome elements.[100] Structural indicators reflect ratification or adoption of legal instruments and establishment of essential mechanisms. Process indicators link state policy instruments with development milestones, such as on land tenure, land reform or percentage of the population covered by food subsidies.[101] Outcome indicators reflect attainment at the individual and collective level, such as caloric intake. The identification of indicators and their priority of application must involve participation of those affected as well as of experts. The Framework for Action under the Rome Declaration calls on national governments to establish nutrition targets and immediate milestones, using agreed international indicators for nutrition outcomes.[102]

Each agency, of course, approaches the issues using the lens of its own mandate. Through its "Decent Work Agenda",[103] the ILO looks at the right to food across the value chain, from production to consumption. Poor diet in the forms of malnutrition in some countries and obesity in others has been linked to lost productivity. An ILO study on food at work concluded that:

> "Too often, food at work is seen as an afterthought or a hindrance by employers and is often a 'missed opportunity' to increase productivity and morale. Canteens, if they exist, routinely offer an unhealthy and unvaried selection. Vending machines are regularly stocked with unhealthy snacks. ... Street foods can be bacteria-laden. Workers sometimes have no time or place to eat or no money to purchase food."[104]

The study showcased practical initiatives that can improve the situation in relation to the right to food in a work setting.

In 2011, the ILO Governing Body endorsed a strategy for the Decent Work for Food Security Programme.[105] It aims to promote sustainable livelihoods and food security of small-scale producers and agricultural workers and their families through decent work in agro-food value chains with high employment, income generation and productivity potential. The links in the chain are agriculture, fishing and aquaculture production, food manufacturing and packaging, transport and storage, trade and retail distribution, food services and

100 Report on Indicators for Promoting and Monitoring the Implementation of Human Rights, HRI/MC/2008/3, 6 June 2008, p. 24.

101 Eide, note 68 above, pp. 213–214.

102 Framework for Action, note 52 above, p. 7.

103 The Decent Work Agenda, pursued by the ILO since 1999, focuses on fundamental rights at work, decent employment, social protection and social dialogue. Its aim is to promote opportunities for all women and men to obtain decent and productive work, in conditions of freedom, equity, security and human dignity.

104 See Wanjek, note 95 above (press summary).

105 ILO, GB.312/POL/7 and Record of Decisions (November 2011).

consumption. Key decent work deficits are identified for each, with low pay or income a common thread.

Initiatives of this type, often involving multiple stakeholders, are a clear trend in food-related transnational work. In a positive sense, they open up engagement to a wider range of actors, and push different parts of the UN system and beyond to comprehend issues better and act in greater synergy. Common frameworks permit re-focusing each agency's particular lens from another angle, such as the right to food. On the other hand, there are many of such frameworks and agendas, each competing for resources and media attention. And, regrettably, few sufficiently embed gender in their design, implementation or monitoring. In light of the stronger emphasis on gender in more recent soft law tools such as the Rome Declaration and Plan of Action, it is hoped that this situation will improve.

VI. SYSTEMIC ISSUES REMAIN TO BE TACKLED

The proposed Sustainable Development Goals currently under discussion could play a useful role in moving the right to food forward. In his recent report, the UN Secretary-General identified four building-blocks: a vision for the future "firmly anchored in human rights and universally accepted values and principles, including those encapsulated in the Charter, the Universal Declaration on Human Rights and the Millennium Declaration"; a new set of goals and targets; a global partnership for development; and a participatory monitoring framework "for tracking progress and mutual accountability mechanisms for all stakeholders".[106] Among the related actions identified are the empowerment of girls and women, the addressing of climate change and environmental challenges, the promotion of inclusive and sustainable growth and decent employment, the fostering of a renewed global international development co-operation framework, and the end of hunger and malnutrition. The latter will require "a combination of stable and adequate incomes for all, improvements in agricultural productivity and partnership, strengthen sustainability, child and maternal care and strengthened social protection for vulnerable populations".[107] Each of these is relevant to an integrated appreciation of the right to food and its legal underpinnings.

Taking gender seriously implies creating accountability for gender outcomes. For this reason, UN Women, the UN Entity for Gender Equality and the Empowerment of Women, has backed the stand-alone gender goal for the post-MDG framework. A fair amount is already known about the dynamics of gender,

[106] UN Doc A/68/202 (26 July 2013), para. 75.
[107] Ibid., para. 91.

land reform, and access to financial empowerment for women.[108] The same is true of the inter-generational gender/malnutrition nexus.[109] The former Special Rapporteur thus suggested that,

> "the outcomes to be achieved should be defined through indicators based on the normative components of the right to food, and disaggregated by ethnicity, age and gender… [so that] a gender-sensitive approach will be adopted in all sectors… [and] tracked and addressed effectively."[110]

The current Special Rapporteur is continuing to stress the key role of women's empowerment in relation to realisation of the right to adequate food.[111] This analysis needs to take macroeconomic factors on board as well.[112]

In short, a more integrated approach is needed. In the human rights area, both the CRC and the CESCR have generally done a good job in picking up the elements of hard and soft law from the Specialized Agencies, and pushing the international financial institutions to respect ESC rights. In its General Comment No. 12, the CESCR noted that the right to adequate food requires the adoption of an appropriate economic, environmental and social policy.[113] In the Secretary-General's proposed framework for Sustainable Development Goals, the right to food is covered by virtue of the mention of the Universal Declaration. The risk of fragmentation of international law here relates not to collision, but to omission and failure to capitalise on all existing standards.

This process will necessarily entail going beyond the scope of what is normally considered international social law. Today, "new factors are contributing to a rapidly changing and globalizing political economy of agriculture. These include an increasing role of trade in agriculture, population growth, high unemployment rates, expansion of biofuel production, market speculation, changing nutrition in emerging markets, food insecurity, land-grabbing and climate change".[114] A multi-sector approach is needed. Climate change will

---

108 See, for example, lessons set out in Commission on Legal Empowerment of the Poor, *Making the Law Work for Everyone*, vol. II (Working Group Reports) (New York: UNDP, 2008) 7, 83, 91–92; L. Cotula, *Gender and Law: Women's Rights in Agriculture*, (Rome: FAO, 2006); FAO/IFAD/ILO, *Gender Dimensions of Agricultural and Rural Employment: Differentiated Pathways out of Poverty: Status, Trends and Gaps* (Rome: FAO, 2010); and Mayra Buvinic, Rebecca Furst-Nichols and Emily Courey Pryor, *A Roadmap for Promoting Women's Economic Empowerment*, (New York: UN Foundation/Exxon Mobil, 2013).

109 See, for example, Women's Rights and the Right to Food, note 44 above, para. 4.

110 Ibid., para. 48. See, also, the illustrative indicators on the right to adequate food, which called for disaggregation by prohibited grounds of discrimination, including sex. See note 99 above.

111 See, for example, her recommendations in A/HRC/28/65, note 10 above, para. 72(e).

112 See, for example, UNRISD, *Gender Equality: Striving for Justice in an Unequal World*, (Geneva: United Nations Research Institute for Social Development, 2005), Chapters 2 to 4.

113 CESCR, General Comment No. 12, para. 4.

114 Cheong *et al.*, note 76 above, p. 1.

inevitably play a role in the realisation (or not) of the right to food, since it threatens to harm the natural resource base of agriculture. Transformation of agriculture away from "conventional, industrial, monoculture-based production highly dependent on external inputs" could turn it from being part of the problem to contributing to a solution.[115] Treaties such as the Convention on Biological Diversity and the International Treaty on Plant Genetic Resources for Food and Agriculture are therefore also of direct relevance to realisation of the right to food.

Addressing the issues within the UN system alone, without structural changes in international economic law, will not be sufficient. As long ago as 1944, this was recognised in the ILO's Declaration of Philadelphia, which provides that international economic and financial policies should be accepted only in so far as they promote – and do not hinder – the goals of social justice (which includes the right to food).[116] Its principles were recalled in the 2008 Declaration on Social Justice for a Fair Globalization, which also echoed the call for greater policy coherence made by the World Commission on the Social Dimension of Globalization.[117] The International Finance Corporation's Sustainability Framework and Performance Standards are a noteworthy development in this direction.[118] In a similar spirit, the CESCR and the HRC have urged the International Monetary Fund and the World Bank to pay greater attention to the protection of the right to food in their lending policies, credit agreements and other measures, and to avoid any action that could have a negative impact on the realization of the right to food.[119] In 2011, the former Special Rapporteur submitted guiding principles to the Human Rights Council on human-rights impact assessments of investment and trade agreements.[120] Principles for Responsible Investment in Agriculture and Food Systems were then sent to the FAO for consideration.[121]

115 Ibid., p. 8.

116 Declaration of Philadelphia, note 24 above, para. II.

117 World Commission on the Social Dimension of Globalisation, *Fair Globalization: Creating Opportunities for All*, (Geneva: ILO, 2004) 133–135. Various outcome documents of the G20 have also called for greater policy coherence.

118 International Finance Corporation, The International Bill of Rights and IFC Sustainability Framework (1 January 2012), 21, available at: www.ifc.org. Various performance standards cross-reference Article 11 of the ESC Covenant and Article 25 of the Universal Declaration.

119 General Comment 12, para. 41. See, also, Fons Coomans, "Application of the International Covenant on Economic, Social and Cultural Rights in the Framework of International Organisations", (2007) 11 *Max Planck Yearbook of United Nations Law*, pp. 367–375.

120 Report of the Special Rapporteur on the Right to Food, addendum: *Guiding Principles on Human Rights Impact Assessments of Trade and Investment Agreements*, UN Doc. A/HRC/19/59/Add.5, (19 December 2011).

121 See Doc. A/HRC/RES/28/10, p. 3.

The role that trade can play in all of this remains complex,[122] and it, too, has a gender dimension.[123] On several occasions, the Human Rights Council has called for a successful, development-oriented outcome of the Doha Round of trade negotiations as a condition for permitting full realisation of the right to food. It has also urged states to ensure that their international political and economic policies, including trade agreements, do not have a negative impact on the right to food.[124] Choices made in relation to trade policy should better reflect the possible impacts on the realisation of the right to food and on the people involved in its production, processing and distribution. Linkages between the trade law regime, although trapped within a traditional paradigm, and elements of the right to food also offer an avenue to explore. An example is the Codex Alimentarius in relation to international trade law. As the WHO notes,

> "While Codex standards are non-mandatory, they gained the status of international benchmarks for food safety under the World Trade Organization (WTO) Agreement on the Application of Sanitary and Phytosanitary Measures in 1995. This has resulted in a marked increase in the global relevance of the standards, which have been used on several occasions by WTO to find a solution for trade conflicts."[125]

As the former Special Rapporteur on the Right to Food urged,

> "combating the different faces of malnutrition requires ... reforming agricultural and food policies, including taxation, in order to reshape food systems for the promotion of sustainable diets. Strong political will, a sustained effort over a number of years, and collaboration across different sectors, including agriculture, finance, health, education and trade, are necessary for such a transition."[126]

---

122 See Cheong *et al.*, note 76 above, pp. 13–26. See, also, Matias E. Margulis, "The World Trade Organization and Food Security after the Global Food Crises", in Daniel Drache and Lesley A. Jacobs (eds), *Linking Global Trade and Human Rights*, (Cambridge: Cambridge University Press, 2014), pp. 236–255, and Holger P. Hestermeyer, "Economic, Social, and Cultural Rights in the World Trade Organization", in: Riedel *et al.*, (eds), note 11 above, pp. 260–285, esp. pp. 278–279 and 294, in relation to invocation of the right to food in the context of the General Agreement on Tariffs and Trade (GATT) and the Trade-Related Aspects of Intellectual Property Rights Agreement (TRIPS).

123 See Gunselierik, "Gender Aspects of Trade", in: Marion Jansen, *Trade and Employment: From Myths to Facts*, (Geneva: ILO/EC, 2011), pp. 171–211.

124 See, for example, Human Rights Council, Resolution on the Right to Food, UN Doc. A/HRC/RES/22/9, adopted on 21 March 2013, paras. 24–25.

125 See Codex Alimentarius – Protecting Consumers' Health through Safe and Nutritious Food – The First 50 Years, www.who.int/features/2013/codex_alimentarius/en/index.html.

126 Report of the Special Rapporteur on the Right to Food, Olivier De Schutter, on the Right to an Adequate Diet: The Agriculture-food-health Nexus, presented to the UN Human Rights Council (A/HRC/19/59, 26 Dec. 2011), para. 49.

To these could be added labour and the environment,[127] among others, in moving towards a more transformative approach to achieving the right to food. Above all, stricter accountability, including the gender dimension, through monitoring and greater access to effective remedies, is needed across the spectrum of sectors and international actors – public and private.[128] Drawing on a widened range of international law instruments, and spurred on by civil society, the Special Rapporteur and others should continue to raise systemic issues.[129] Without their resolution, it is unlikely that the right to food enshrined in international law will ever be fully realised in practice. The transnationalisation of social rights, with new actors and new tools building on those that exist, offers fresh perspectives for coming closer to its achievement.

---

127 Stéphanie Chuffart and Jorge E. Viñuales, "From the Other Shore: Economic, Social, and Cultural Rights from an International Environmental Law Perspective," in: Riedel *et al.* (eds), note 11 above, pp. 286–307, inviting analysis of how the Aarhus Convention might serve as useful inspiration in relation to, *inter alia*, the right to food (see pp. 289–90 and 305–307).

128 See CESCR, General Comment No 12, para. 20. The new Special Rapporteur has so far put the accent on enhancing access to justice in the context of the right to food.

129 See, for example, Olivier De Schutter, *International Trade in Agriculture and the Right to Food*, Occasional Paper No. 46, (Geneva: Friedrich Ebert Stiftung, 2009).

CHAPTER 9

AGROENERGY AND THE RIGHT TO FOOD: THE EU BIOFUEL MANDATE AND TRANSNATIONAL SOCIAL RIGHTS

Steffen Kommer

INTRODUCTION

This chapter explores the potential and limits of Transnational Social Rights with a view to the adverse effects of global biofuel markets. The increasing use of crops for energy production is blamed for driving up international agricultural prices, replacing food production and causing local "land and water grabs" in developing countries. Until now, only few lawyers have framed the "fuel *versus* food" debate in a human rights discourse. In 2007, Jean Ziegler, the former Rapporteur on the Right to Food, started to call for a general moratorium on agrofuels.[1]

Emphasising the emancipatory potential of Transnational Social Rights, Andreas Fischer-Lescano and Kolja Möllers cite the global food crises as an example of interactions between different transnational crises, such as climate change, financial speculation, and migration.[2] They encourage social movements to draw attention to injustice by intervening in legal processes. However, they leave open the question of Transnational Social Rights could be operationalised in legal proceedings. The global "biofuel boom" illustrates that Economic, Social and Cultural rights (ESC rights), especially the right to food, need to be re-thought in transnational constellations. I will analyse to what extent biofuel projects and the support policies could result in violations of the right to food. As Audrey R. Chapman already pointed out in 1996, a "violation approach" could

1 Jean Ziegler, Report of the Special Rapporteur on the Right to Food, Protecting the Right to Food in Biofuel Production, UN Doc. A/62/289 (22 August 2007), para. 22.

2 Andreas Fischer-Lescano and Kolja Möller, *The Struggle for Transnational Social Rights*, Chapter 2, Section II.

be a useful strategy to enhance the effectiveness of ESC rights.[3] While Chapman especially focused on violations by state actions at national level, this case-study focuses on the extra-territorial responsibility of the European Union (EU).

The first section starts with a definition of agrofuels (Section I.A) and gives a short overview of the economic, social and environmental impact on "food security" at global level (Section I.B). While most studies weigh the risks and benefits of biofuels, transnational peasant movements emphasise the contradiction between large-scale monocultures for energy production and the ideal of "food sovereignty" (Section I.C). The second section describes the EU biofuel policy and highlights its external effects (Section II). To comply with the biofuel target of the Renewable Energy Directive (RED),[4] EU Member States need to import feedstock from third countries. The third section addresses the normative collision between the EU biofuel target and Transnational Social Rights (Section III). It will be asked whether the RED encourages "land and water grabs" in developing countries which result in violations of individual rights (Section III.B). Moreover, the conflict between the RED and the collective dimension of the right to food will be explored (Section III.C).

I. IMPACTS AND CONFLICTS AT GLOBAL LEVEL

More than 60 countries around the world have mandatory blending quotas for biofuels or similar supporting mechanisms in place.[5] As a pioneer, Brazil started to promote biofuels from sugar cane in the 1970s, as a reaction to high oil and low sugar prices on international markets.[6] Besides Brazil, the United States is the main producer of ethanol biofuels made from maize.[7] The EU is the largest global market for biodiesel mostly from rapeseed.

A. AGROFUELS

In the following, I will use the concept of "agrofuels" instead of the commonly-used term of "biofuels" to point out the specific spatial conflict between bioenergy and food production. While the generic term "bioenergy" stands for

---

3 Audrey R. Chapman, "A 'Violation Approach' for Monitoring the International Covenant on Economic, Social and Cultural Rights", (1996) 18 *Human Rights Quarterly*, pp. 22–66.

4 Directive 2009/28/EC of the European Parliament and the Council of 23 April 2009 on the promotion of the use of energy from renewable sources.

5 See HLPE. *Biofuels and Food Security*. A Report of the High Level Panel of Experts on Food Security and Nutrition (June 2013), available at: www.fao.org/fileadmin/user_upload/hlpe/hlpe_documents/HLPE_Reports/HLPE-Report-5_Biofuels_and_food_security.pdf, pp. 32–33.

6 Ibid., pp. 31–32.

7 Ibid., pp. 28–29.

all energy produced from biomass,[8] the sub-topic of "agroenergy" refers only to energy generation from feedstock cultivated on land. While "conventional biofuels" are produced from plants traditionally used for food or feed production (especially oil crops, cereal and sugar crops), "second-generation biofuels" could be generated from biological wastes, agricultural residues or algae.[9] But even "advanced biofuel technologies" could be labelled as agrofuels if they are produced from non-food crops (for example, grasses and miscanthus) which need fertile soils to produce significant yields. However, in 2011, "first-generation biofuels" represented 99.85 per cent of global consumption.[10]

B. IMPACTS ON FOOD SECURITY

In principle, all governments, international bodies and expert groups agree that food security should not be threatened by increasing agrofuel production.[11] This concept was developed at the level of the UN Food and Agriculture Organization (FAO) in the 1970s.[12] According to the Rome Declaration of the World Food Summit in 1996, the paradigm of food security is accomplished:

> "when all people, at all times, have physical and economic access to sufficient, safe and nutritious food to meet their dietary needs and food preferences for an active and healthy life."[13]

Governments expect agrofuels to promote rural development, energy independence and greenhouse gas savings. However, the "biofuel-boom" tends to aggravate the existing global hunger crises with more than 805 million people suffering from under-nourishedment or malnutrition.[14] Several expert bodies, such as the High Level Panel of Experts (HLPE) of the FAO Committee on World Food Security, have recommended the abolition of biofuel targets and all other forms of subvention.[15]

---

8 Compare definition of "biomass" in Art. 2 (c) Directive 2009/28/EC.

9 See, *inter alia*, European Commission, *Biofuels in the European Union: A Vision for 2030 and Beyond*, Final Report of the Biofuels Research Advisory Council (2006).

10 See HLPE *Biofuels 2013*, note 5 above, p. 45.

11 See, *inter alia*, High-Level Conference on World Food Security, *The Challenges of Climate Change and Bioenergy*, (5 June 2008), No. 7 (f).

12 FAO, *Trade Reforms and Food Security: Conceptualizing the Linkages, Food and Agriculture Organization*, (Rome: FAO, 2003), available at: www.fao.org/docrep/005/y4671e/y4671e00.htm, p. 26.

13 World Food Summit, *Rome Declaration on World Food Security*, (Rome, November 1996).

14 FAO, WFP and IFAD, The State of Food Insecurity in the World: Strengthening the enabling environment for food security and nutrition, 2014, (Rome, FAO, 2014), available at: www.fao.org/3/a-i4030e.pdf, p. 8.

15 HLPE, *Price Volatility and Food Security. A Report of the High Level Panel of Experts on Food Security and Nutrition*, (Rome: FAO HLPE, 2011), available at: www.fao.org/fileadmin/user_

1. *Global Food Prices*

The "global food crisis" in 2007/2008, characterised by rapidly soaring international food prices, pushed up the number of chronically hungry people by 75 million.[16] The High Level Panel of Experts (HLPE) estimates that agricultural prices will continue to fluctuate and increase in the near future.[17] An inter-agency report of the leading international bodies, such as the FAO and the World Bank, identifies biofuels as a "significant factor" in price volatility.[18] According to the study, during the 2007–2009 period, biofuels accounted for a significant share of the global use of several crops (20 per cent for sugar cane, 9 per cent for vegetable oil and coarse grains, and 4 per cent for sugar beet). In a recent study on bioenergy, the HLPE asserts that "the steeply rising demand for the production of biofuels was identified as an important factor by many observers and a wide range of organizations".[19]

In terms of food security, rising food prices threaten the economic *access* to adequate food for low-income households. According to the FAO, the majority of rural dwellers in developing countries are net purchasers of food.[20] These persons are landless labourers, pastoralists, fisher-folk, and forest users or smallholders who do not own sufficient land to produce enough food for their families, and represent 80 per cent of the hungry people in the world.[21] Hence, the urban poor represent only 20 per cent of the chronic under-nourished persons who spend more than half of their income on food.

2. *Food Production*

Expanding energy crops compete with food production. In terms of food security, the dimension of *availability* is threatened by agrofuels, to the extent that productive resources are diverted away from food production. While the demand for energy is potentially infinite, natural resources such as land and water are scarce. Today's biofuel production already mobilises around 2–3 per

---

upload/hlpe/hlpe_documents/HLPE-price-volatility-and-food-security-report-July-2011.pdf, recommendations 4a, 13 and 40; Interagency Report, *Price Volatility in Food and Agricultural Markets: Policy Responses*, Policy Report including contributions by FAO, IFAD, IMF,OECD, UNCTAD, WFP, the World Bank, the WTO, IFPRI and the UN HLTF (2 June 2011), Recommendations 6 and 27.

16 FAO, The State of Food Insecurity in the World: High Food Prices and Food Security – Threats and Opportunities, 2008, (Rome: FAO, 2008), available at: www.fao.org/docrep/011/i0291e/i0291e00.htm, p. 6.

17 HLPE, *Price Volatility*, note 15 above, p. 21.

18 Interagency Report, *Price Volatility*, note 15 above, para. 19.

19 HLPE *Biofuels 2013*, note 5 above, p. 13.

20 FAO, *The State of Food and Agriculture, Biofuels: Prospects, Risks and Opportunities, 2008*, (Rome: FAO, 2008),available at: www.fao.org/docrep/011/i0100e/i0100e00.htm, pp. 75–79.

21 See UN Millennium Project 2005, *Halving Hunger: It can be Done*, Task Force on Hunger, pp. 3–4.

cent of arable lands globally.[22] The Organisation of Economic Co-operation and Development (OECD) calculated that the US, Canada and the EU would require between 30 and 70 per cent of their respective current crop areas to cover only 10 per cent of their transport fuel consumption with internal agrofuel production.[23]

On the other hand, by the year 2050, increasing populations and incomes are expected to require 70 per cent more food production globally compared to 2009 levels.[24] Today's population of around 7 billion is expected to increase to about 9 billion by the year 2050.[25] At the same time, in the course of the economic growth in countries undergoing economic transformation such as China and India, a more vegetarian diet is gradually being replaced by a diet containing more meat and dairy products.[26] Hence, the German Advisory Council on Global Change (WBGU) warns that the worldwide bioenergy boom "could become a critical factor for global food and feed production".[27]

3. *Resource Depletion*

The intensive production of agrofuels could have an impact on natural resources, resulting *inter alia* in loss of soil quality, erosion and large requirements of water and chemical inputs.[28] Industrial production depends on high input rates (fertiliser agro-chemicals and irrigation), monocultures and mechanisation. Agriculture is already responsible for 13.5 per cent of global emissions.[29] Agriculture makes use of 70 per cent of all water withdrawn from aquifers, streams and lakes.[30] As the International Assessment of Agricultural Knowledge, Science and Technology states, agriculture has become "a major contributor to natural resource depletion and degradation, acting through habitat loss and fragmentation, invasive alien species, unsustainable use (over

22 HLPE *Biofuels* 2013, note 5 above, p. 82.

23 OECD, *Agricultural Market Impacts of Future Growth in the Production of Biofuels*, Working Party on Agricultural Policies and Markets, (Paris: OECD, 2006), p. 31.

24 FAO, *The State of World's Land and Water Resources for Food and Agriculture: Managing Systems at Risk*, (Rome, FAO, 2011), available at: www.fao.org/docrep/017/i1688e/i1688e.pdf, p. 9.

25 Ibid., p. 4.

26 WBGU, *Future Bioenergy and Sustainable Land Use*, German Advisory Council on Global Change, (Berlin, 2009), No. 5.2.3.

27 Ibid., No. 5.2.1.

28 See D. Diop, M. Blanco, A. Flammini, M. Schlaifer, M.A. Kropiwnicka and M. Mautner Markhof, "Assessing the Impact of Biofuels Production on Developing Countries from the Point of View of Policy Coherence for Development", Final Report for the European Commission, (February 2013), pp. 72–89, available at: http://ec.europa.eu/europeaid.

29 IPCC, *Synthesis Report*, An Assessment of the Intergovernmental Panel on Climate Change, (Valencia 2007), Figure 2.1.

30 FAO, The State of World's Land and Water Resources 2011, note 24 above, p. 9.

harvesting), pollution (especially of aquatic systems) and, increasingly, climate change".[31]

C. AGROFUELS AND FOOD SOVEREIGNTY

While the concept of food *security* represents an "analytic tool" to evaluate the impact of biofuels, the paradigm of *food sovereignty* stands for the ideal of self-determination in local food systems and a general scepticism against agrofuels. In 2007, at a meeting of representatives from different organisations of small-scale farmers, artisanal fisher-folks, indigenous people, landless, rural workers, pastoralists, and forest communities in Nyéléni, the concept of *food sovereignty* was declared as:

> "the right of peoples to healthy and culturally appropriate food produced through ecologically sound and sustainable methods, and their right to define their own food and agriculture systems."[32]

1. *Smallholders and Industrial Agriculture*

The ideal of *food sovereignty* stands for a focus on "the aspirations and needs of those who produce, distribute and consume food at the heart of food systems and policies rather than the demands of markets and corporations".[33] Today, a broad consensus exists that the marginalisation of smallholders is a major reason for the global hunger crises.[34] For instance, the Global Strategic Framework for Food Security recommends increasing "smallholder-sensitive investments" in agriculture.[35] The Framework was developed by the Committee on World Food Security as an overarching framework and a single reference document for food security and nutrition strategies. Nearly 90 per cent of more than 500 million farms are small, defined as having less than two hectares of land.[36] They contribute substantially to global food production and are mainly situated in East and South Asia and Sub-Saharan Africa. Most of the smallholders are predominantly subsistence-oriented and represent half of all the hungry people in the world.

---

31 Beverly D. McIntyre, *inter alia* (ed), *Global report, Agriculture at a Crossroads*, International Assessment of Agricultural Knowledge, Science and Technology for Development (IAASTD), (2009), No. 7.1.1.

32 Declaration of Nyéléni (Nyéléni Village, Sélingué, Mali, February 2007), available at: www.nyeleni.org.

33 Ibid.

34 Interagency Report 2011, note 15 above, Annex B, para. 4.

35 Committee on World Food Security, *Global Strategic Framework for Food Security and Nutrition*, CFS 2012/39/5 Add.1 (Rome October 2012), lit. B, paras. 37–41.

36 IAASTD *Agriculture at a Crossroads* 2009; see note 31 above, pp. 5–8.

The question remains as to whether traditional agriculture should be integrated in value chains or promoted with the aim of sustainable local food systems. According to the "classical model", economic development increases worker productivity, and consequently results in reduced employment rates in the agrarian sector.[37] In other words, smallholders have "either to grow in size or to disappear".[38] The struggle to protect their livelihoods could be perceived as the last resistance of socially "embedded" agriculture against the delayed "Great Transformation" in the Global South, which transforms land, labour and money into "fictitious commodities".[39] But this pathway is increasingly criticised. In contrast to the period of industrialisation in Europe, job opportunities in the cities (or other countries) are not sufficiently available to absorb the rural poor.[40] Moreover, the industrialisation of agriculture is connected to large ecological impacts.[41]

2. *Land Concentration*

Since 2007, the EU biofuel policy has been criticised for promoting the dominant agro-industrial model and resulting in the marginalisation of smallholders.[42] In 2011, a coalition of social movements and non-governmental organisations (NGOs) demanded a general ban on land deals.[43] Asbjørn Eide states that "the long-range consequences of monoculture production for agrofuels in developing countries can be even more serious than the impacts of the soaring food prices".[44] Evidence from Brazil shows that expansion of agrofuel crops tends both to stabilise existing land concentration and to hinder the implementation of agrarian reforms.[45] Because biofuel mandates focus only on quantity objectives,

---

37 HLPE, Investing in Smallholder Agriculture for Food Security. A Report of the High Level Panel of Experts on Food Security and Nutrition, (Rome, FAO HLPE, 2013), available at: www.fao.org/fileadmin/user_upload/hlpe/hlpe_documents/HLPE_Reports/HLPE-Report-6_Investing_in_smallholder_agriculture.pdf, p. 21.

38 Ibid., p. 54.

39 Karl Polanyi, The Great Transformation: The Political and Economic Origins of Our Time, (Boston MA: Beacon Press, 1944).

40 HLPE, Investing in Smallholder Agriculture for Food Security, note 37 above, p. 54.

41 See Section I.B.3 above.

42 See World Rainforest Movement, We want Food Sovereignty, Not Biofuels, Open Letter to the European Parliament (2007); Econexus, Call for an Immediate Moratorium on EU Incentives for Agrofuels, EU imports of Agrofuels and Agroenergy Monocultures (2007).

43 International Land Coalition, Tirana Declaration. Securing Land Access for the Poor in Times of Intensified Natural Resources Competition, (2011) www.landcoalition.org; World Social Forum, Dakar Appeal against the land grab, (March 2012).

44 Asbjørn Eide, *The Right to Food and the Impact of Liquid Biofuels (Agrofuels)*, FAO Right to Food Studies (Rome: FAO, 2008), available at: www.fao.org/docrep/016/ap550e/ap550e.pdf, p. 17.

45 Pastoral Land Commission, Agroenergy: Myths and Impacts in Latin America, (2007), p. 17 *et seq.*

large-scale plantations have a comparative advantage.[46] The HLPE concludes that "the bio-energy market tends to promote large industrial plantations with efficient crop handling and processing".[47]

II. THE EU BIOFUEL MANDATE

While the first section provided an overview of the global scenario, this section describes the effects of the EU biofuel policy.

The Renewable Energy Directive (RED) entails a binding mandate which requires all EU Member States to source 10 per cent of all energy used in the transport sector from renewable sources by the year 2020.[48] Although this target could, theoretically, be fulfilled through the promotion of electric cars (combined with solar and wind energy) or any other alternative energy, it was always predicted that biofuels would account for the major part of all renewable energy consumption in transport by 2020.[49] Thus, the RED establish a *de facto* biofuel mandate of up to 10 per cent in the transport sector.

Although the EU has trade restrictions in place, the Member States have become dependent upon biofuel imports.[50] The EU has a traditional dependence on oil crop imports. In 2010, around 40 per cent of biodiesel and 20 per cent of bioethanol were imported.[51] The EU Commission expects that about half of the biofuels consumed in the EU by the year 2020 will be domestically produced, with rapeseed being the main feedstock.[52]

In addition, biomass plantations on land in the EU previously used for other domestic purposes such as food and feed could worsen agricultural trade deficits.[53] For instance, the increased rapeseed oil diversion into biodiesel

---

46 Ben White and Anirban Dasgupta, "Agrofuels Capitalism: A View from Political Economy", (2010) 37 *Journal of Peasant Studies*, pp. 593–607.

47 HLPE, Land Tenure and International Investments in Agriculture 2011, a Report of the High Level Panel of Experts on Food Security and Nutrition, (Rome, FAO HLPE, 2011), available at: www.fao.org/fileadmin/user_upload/hlpe/hlpe_documents/HLPE-Land-tenure-and-international-investments-in-agriculture-2011.pdf, p. 21.

48 Compare Art. 3 (4) Directive 2009/28/EC.

49 European Commission, *Renewable Energy: A Major Player in the European Energy Market*, communication from the commission to the European Parliament, the Council, the European Economic and Social Committee, and the Committee of the Regions, (June 2012).

50 HLPE, *Biofuels* 2013, note 5 above, No. 1.2.

51 Ecofys, Frauenhofer, BBH, EGG, Winrock International, *Renewable Energy Progress and Biofuels Sustainability*, Report prepared for the European Commission, Tender No.: ENER/C1/463-2011-Lot2 (September 2012), p. 33.

52 European Commission, Commission Staff Working Document, Impact Assessment, COM(2012) 595 final, p. 21.

53 See UK renewable Fuels Agency, The Gallagher Review of the indirect effects of biofuels production, (July 2008), p. 36.

within the EU results in significant "indirect land use changes" (ILUCs) because the demand for vegetable oil must be covered by imports of palm oil from Indonesia.[54] Thus, even the domestic production of agrofuels in the EU could have external effects on the agriculture of third countries. The HLPE asserts that the EU biofuel policy has "triggered the creation of an increasingly globalised biofuels and biofuels feedstock market, involving a key role for developing countries' agriculture".[55]

In 2007, the Commission estimated that the rising biofuel demand in the EU would cause a total land use change of 17.5 Mha by the year 2020.[56] The Commission expects that half of all the raw materials used as biofuels in the EU will be imported.[57]

III. THE CONFLICT WITH THE TRANSNATIONAL SOCIAL RIGHTS

The external effects of the EU biofuel mandate (direct imports and indirect land-use changes) lead to the question of whether the EU could be held responsible for violations of the right to food in third countries. This section addresses a specific normative collision between the EU biofuel target and Transnational Social Rights.

A. THE EXTRA-TERRITORIAL DIMENSION OF THE RIGHT TO FOOD

The right to food is explicitly recognised as a fundamental right in various regional and universal human-rights treaties.[58] The right to food was first mentioned in the Universal Declaration of Human Rights and afterwards codified in the International Covenant on Economic, Social and Cultural Rights (ICESCR) as part of the broader right to an adequate standard of living (Art. 11 (1) ICESCR).[59] While all 28 EU Member States signed and ratified the covenant, the EU is not a party to the ICESCR. However, it seems convincing that, beside

54 See Mark Harvey and Scott Pilgrim, "The New Competition for Land: Food, Energy, and Climate Change", (2011) 36 *Food Policy*, p. 543.

55 HLPE, *Biofuels 2013*, note 5 above, No. 1.2.

56 European Commission, The impact of a minimum 10% obligation for biofuel use in the EU-27 in 2020 on agricultural markets, 30.04.2007, AGRI G-2/WM D(2007), p. 8.

57 European Commission, Impact Assessment 2012, note 52 above, p. 21.

58 See overview of Bart Wernaart, "The Plural Wells of the Right to Food", in: Otto Hospes and Irene Hadiprayitno (eds), *Governing Food Security: Law, Politics and the Right to Food*, (Wageningen: Wageningen Academic Publishers, 2010), pp. 43–79.

59 Art. 25 of Universal Declaration of Human Right, Resolution 217 (III), UN GA, Official Records third Session (part I) Resolutions (Doc. A/810), 71; International Covenant on

the Member States, the EU *as a whole* has a general duty to respect and protect the enjoyment of the right to food. First, the EU is bound by the right to food via international customary law.[60] Second, the EU is bound by its own Charter of Fundamental Rights. Although the Charter does not recognise the right to food explicitly, it could be argued that the right to social security (Art. 34), the right to (land) property (Art. 17), and the right to respect for private and family life (Art. 7) contain at least some dimensions of the right to food.

1. *The Committee on Economic, Social and Cultural Rights*

Already in its General Comment No. 12 (1999) the Committee on Economic, Social and Cultural Rights (CESCR) acknowledged a transnational dimension of the right to food. The CESCR is a quasi-judicial body of 18 international human-rights experts, the main function of which is the periodical supervision of the reports of state parties. Since 1990, the CESCR has published non-binding General Comments, which clarify the normative content of ESC rights. General Comment No. 12 is called "the currently most authoritative interpretation" of the right to food.[61]

In this commentary the Committee first describes some basic elements as structural features which determine the individual enjoyment of the right to food. The term "*availability*" refers to the quantitative dimension of a right, in particular the underlying infrastructure, goods and/or services which are needed for the satisfaction of basic needs protected by an ESC right. In its General Comment No. 12, the Committee asserts that food must be available at any time "in a quantity and quality sufficient to satisfy the dietary needs of individuals, free from adverse substances, and acceptable within a given culture".[62] The term "*accessibility*" contains a physical and an economic aspect. Access must be given for physically vulnerable individuals (for example, infants and elderly people) and disadvantaged groups (including the victims of natural disasters).[63] In addition, adequate food (or other basic goods or services) must be *affordable*. This means that "the financial costs associated with the acquisition of food for an adequate diet should be at a level such that the attainment and satisfaction of other basic needs are not threatened or compromised".[64] In point of fact, these definitions are almost identical to the

---

Economic, Social and Cultural Rights, UN. Doc. A/RES/21/2200A, 16 December 1966, 993 UNTS 3.

60 See Smita Narula, "The Right to Food: Holding Global Actors Accountable under International Law", (2006) 44 *Columbia Journal of Transnational Law*, p. 691.

61 CESCR, General Comment No. 12 (1999): *The Right to Adequate Food* (Art.11), UN Doc. E/C.12/1999/5, see Sven Söllner, "The 'Breakthrough' of the Right to Food", (2007) 11 *Max Planck Yearbook Volume*, p. 396.

62 CESCR, General Comment 12, note 61 above, para. 8.

63 Ibid., para. 13.

64 Ibid.

main dimensions of "food security".[65] Actually, the concepts of *availability* and *accessibility* represent a collective good which could have local, national or even global dimensions.

Moreover, the CESCR points out two different types of state duties. While the focus lies on obligations at national level, the Committee also described basic duties at international level. The Committee affirms that states parties "should take steps to respect the enjoyment of the right to food in other countries, to protect that right, to facilitate access to food and to provide the necessary aid when required".[66] The negative dimension of the extra-territorial obligation to respect requires state parties to refrain at all times from food embargoes or similar measures which endanger conditions for food production and access to food in other countries.[67] In its General Comment on the Right to Water (No. 15), the CESCR clarifies that:

> "international cooperation requires States parties to refrain from actions that interfere, directly or indirectly, with the enjoyment of the right to water in other countries. Any activities undertaken within the State party's jurisdiction should not deprive another country of the ability to realize the right to water for persons in its jurisdiction."[68]

2. *The Maastricht Principles*

In 2011, a group of experts in international law adopted the Maastricht Principles on Extra-territorial Obligations in the area of Economic, Social and Cultural rights (the ETO Principles).[69] According to the ETO Principles, states have to respect, protect and fulfil ESC rights *extra-territorially*. These general standards are to be applied in relation to the conflict between the EU biofuel policy and the right to food.

B. THE INDIVIDUAL DIMENSION

In this section, I will ask whether the EU could be held responsible for individual violations of the right to food in third countries.

65 See Section I.B above.
66 CESCR, General Comment 12, note 61 above, para. 36.
67 Ibid., para. 37.
68 CESCR, General Comment 15 (2002): The right to water, UN Doc. E/C.12/2002/11, para. 31.
69 Maastricht Principles on Extraterritorial Obligations of States in the Area of Economic Social Cultural Rights (September 2011), available at: www.maastrichtuniversity.nl/humanrights.

1. *Land Grabbing*

Large-scale land acquisitions for biomass plantations in developing countries which are encouraged by the EU biofuel demand could displace local smallholders and thereby lead to "land and water grabs". For millions of small-scale producers, it is only access to fertile soil, fresh water, seeds and other resources that can guarantee them a life without hunger. While the phenomenon of high investments in farmland is not entirely new, it has accelerated since the start of the "global food crisis" in 2007/2008.[70] The World Bank estimates that investors expressed interest in more than 50 million hectares of land globally between October 2008 and August 2009,[71] and demand for biofuel feedstocks has become a major factor for land investments.[72] According to the Land Matrix Database of the International Land Coalition there have been more than 1,000 finalised land deals since the year 2000, which represent an area of more than 38 million hectares of land.[73]

The potential impact and benefits of large-scale land deals in developing countries are highly debated. The World Bank points out the potential chances for innovations in the agricultural sector.[74] Land investments could create employment opportunities and smallholders could benefit as integrated contract farmers. For other authors, the central issue in sub-Saharan Africa would be to strengthen access to land and the ability to exploit available unutilised land by the majority of the rural poor.[75] Ironically, with regard to its own case studies, the World Bank concludes that "the expectations of local populations were often frustrated and, instead of generating sustainable benefits, contributed to asset loss and left local people worse off than they would have been without the investment".[76]

2. *Right to Land*

The question remains as to whether single "land and water grabs" could be labelled as human rights violations. National courts around the world have

---

70 Olivier De Schutter, *Large-scale Land Acquisitions and Leases: A Set of Minimum Principles and Measures to Address the Human Rights Challenge*, a Report of the Special Rapporteur on the right to food, UN Doc. A/HRC/13/33/Add.2 (2009), para. 12.

71 Klaus Deininger and Derek Byerlee, "Rising Global Interest in Farmland, Can it Yield Sustainable and Equitable Benefits?", (World Bank Report, 2011), p. 67.

72 Ibid., p. 11 and 51.

73 The Land Matrix Global Observatory, International Land Coalition (ILC), available at: www.landmatrix.org (January 2015).

74 Ibid., p. 34.

75 T.S. Jayne, J. Chamberlin and M. Muyanga, *Emerging land Issues in African Agriculture: Implications for Food Security and Poverty Reduction Strategies*, Stanford Symposium Series on Global Food Policy and Food Security in the 21st Century (2009).

76 Deininger and Byerlee, note 71 above, p. 71.

recognised the right to food as a minimum condition for a dignified existence.[77] But should the existing access to land of smallholders be seen as being protected by human rights? As Denise González Núñez argues, the recognition of a right to land would be necessary to fill the existing gaps in international human rights law.[78] Millions of small-scale farmers, pastoralists and herders are only holders of "traditional land rights", which might not be recognised by national constitutions.[79] In fact, every year millions of people are forcibly evicted due to development projects.[80]

In 2008, the transnational social movement *La Via Campesina* launched a campaign for an International Declaration of Peasants' Rights, which attempts to translate the ideal of food sovereignty into the language of human rights.[81] The text represents only a first draft for a UN Declaration and is still being discussed in the Human Rights Council. It contains a broad list of ambitious peasants' rights, including the freedom to determine the price and the market for agricultural production (Art. 8).[82] However, I will argue that the declared right to land and territory in its negative dimension represents a valuable interpretation of existing human rights. As Article 4.5 of the Draft Declaration stipulates:

> "Peasants have the right to security of tenure and not to be forcibly evicted from their lands and territories. No relocation should take place without free, prior and informed consent of the peasants concerned and after agreement on just and fair compensation and, where possible, with the option of return."

In the view of Poul Wisborg, land rights cannot be human rights because they are "not universally necessary to protect the existence of dignity of human beings".[83] But this perspective ignores the special connection between existing

---

77 See Christophe Golay, *The Right to Food and Access to Justice: Examples at the National, Regional and International Levels*, Right to Food Studies, (Rome, FAO 2009), available at: www.fao.org/docrep/016/k7286e/k7286e.pdf, pp. 29–58.

78 See Denise González Núñez, "Peasants'Right to Land: Addressing the Existing Implementation and Normative Gaps in International Human Rights Law", (2014) 14 *Human Rights Law Review*, p. 602.

79 See Lorenzo Cotula, Moussa Djiré and Ringo W. Tenga, *The Right to Food and Access to Natural Resources*, Right to Food Studies, (Rome, FAO, 2008), available at: www.fao.org/docrep/016/k8093e/k8093e.pdf, p. 21; Olivier De Schutter, "The Emerging Human Right to Land", (2010) 12 *International Community Law Review*, p. 314 *et seq.*

80 See Núñez, note 78 above, p. 591 *et seq.*

81 Declaration of Peasants' Rights – Women and Men, *La Via Campesina*, International Peasant Movement available at: http://viacampesina.net/downloads/PDF/EN-3.pdf.

82 UN Human Rights Council Advisory Committee, eighth session, Final study on the advancement of the rights of peasants and other people working in rural areas, UN Doc. A/HRC/AC/8/6 (18 January 2012), Annex.

83 Poul Wisborg, "Human Rights Against Land Grabbing? A Reflection on Norms, Policies, and Power", (2013) 26 *Journal of Agricultural and Environmental Ethics*, p. 4.

land use and the right to food.[84] As the CESCR proclaims, states have the primary duty to respect and protect the existing access to food, which refers to "any acquisition pattern or entitlement through which people procure their food".[85] One possibility is explicitly mentioned as the opportunity to feed oneself from "productive land or other natural resources".[86] In its landmark decision in the *Ogoni* case, the African Commission on Human and Peoples' Rights held that:

> "the minimum core of the right to food requires that the Nigerian Government should not destroy or contaminate food sources. It should not allow private parties to destroy or contaminate food sources, and prevent peoples' efforts to feed themselves."[87]

In the words of Jean Ziegler, the right to food should, above all, entail "the right to be able to feed oneself in dignity", which includes the right to "ensure and produce one's own subsistence".[88] But should all the production of every type of food be protected by the right to food? Some authors argue that a right to produce should only be recognised if land use represents the only option to achieve adequate food.[89] In other words, land use needs to be connected to local or household food security. Following this point of view, a right to land could be neglected if a realistic alternative to generate sufficient income (formal employment or off-farm business activities) exists,[90] or if people have access to social security schemes. Indeed, 19 out of the 49 low-income countries did not have a single social protection programme in place when the 2007/08 food crisis began.[91]

However, in my opinion, access to land and other productive resources should not be seen as a simple means to achieve food security, but as a possibility or opportunity for individual and collective self-constitution. As the CESCR states, natural resources, including land and water, should not primarily be treated as "economic goods".[92] In its General Comment No. 21 on the Right of Everyone to Take Part in Cultural Life (Art. 15 ICESCR), the Committee stresses that "methods of production or technology" and even "food" should be

---

84 Cotula, Djiré and Tenga, note 79 above, p. 27.

85 CESCR, General Comment 12, note 61 above, para. 13.

86 Ibid., para. 12.

87 ACHPRCom, SERAC, *Center for Economic and Social Rights* v. *Nigeria*, 2001, para. 65.

88 Jean Ziegler, *Report of the Special Rapporteur on the Right to Food*, (January 2008), UN Doc. A/HRC/7/5, para. 18.

89 See Cotula, Djiré and Tenga, note 79 above, p. 23.

90 Ibid., p. 59.

91 HLPE, *Social Protection and Food Security*. A Report by the High Level Panel on Experts and Nutrition of the Committee on World Food Security, (Rome: FAO, 2012), Figure 1 (p. 23).

92 See CESCR General Comment No. 15 (2002), *The Right to Water*, para. 11.

recognised as cultural goods.[93] In addition, everyone should have "the right to learn about forms of expression and [...], to follow a way of life associated with the use of cultural goods and resources such as land, [and] water".[94] In the words of Olivier De Schutter, the former Rapporteur of the Right to Food:

> "For some of the groups that are the most vulnerable today, this means protecting existing access to land, water, grazing or fishing grounds, or forests, all of which may be productive resources essential for a decent livelihood. In such cases [...] the right to food may complement the protection of the right to property or of indigenous peoples' relationship with their lands, territories and resources."[95]

A right to produce food on land for smallholders (*the right to self-supply*) would acknowledge the socio-cultural dimension of land. This connection becomes apparent in the definition of a peasant in the Draft Declaration as:

> "a man or woman of the land, who has *a direct and special relationship with the land and nature through the production of food or other agricultural products.* Peasants work the land themselves and rely above all on family labour and other small-scale forms of organizing labour."[96] (emphasis added)

3. *Guidelines on the Responsible Governance of Tenure*

This interpretation of the right to food is supported by the Voluntary Guidelines on the Responsible Governance of Tenure, endorsed in May 2012 by the Committee on World Food Security.[97] The Guidelines were developed in a broad consultation process over three years with the participation of NGOs and social movements.[98] They recommend all governments to recognise the tenure rights of indigenous peoples and other communities with customary tenure systems, as well as of informal tenure rights.[99] Although, the Guidelines are not binding "hard law", they do not represent just "soft law" with no legal effects. They provide guidance and information on internationally-accepted practices and

---

93 CESCR, General Comment No. 21 (2009): *The Right of Everyone to Take Part in Cultural Life*, (Art. 15), UN Doc. E/C.12/GC/21, para. 13.

94 Ibid., para 15 (b).

95 Olivier De Schutter, *Report on Access to Land and Security of Tenure*, Special Rapporteur on the Right to Food, (August 2010), UN Doc. A/65/281, para. 3.

96 Art. 1 (1) of International Declaration of Peasants' Rights.

97 FAO Voluntary Guidelines on the Responsible Governance of Tenure of Land, Fisheries and Forests in the Context of National Food Security (9 March 2012); Council, Report of the 38th (Special) Session of the Committee on World Food Security (11 May), Hundred and Forty-fourth Session (Rome, June 2012).

98 See Philip Seufert, "The FAO Voluntary Guidelines on the Responsible Governance of Tenure of Land, Fisheries and Forest", (2013) 10 *Globalization*, pp. 182–184.

99 VGGT 2012, note 97 above, Part 3: Legal Recognition and Allocation of Tenure Rights and Duties.

can be used *inter alia* by implementing agencies and judicial authorities.[100] They might even contribute to the creation of customary international law.

The *right to self-supply* implies primarily freedom from "forced evictions". Complementing the right to adequate housing, a clear violation occurs when smallholders are removed from their lands (and homes) against their will, without appropriate forms of legal or other forms of protection.[101] In addition to this negative aspect, the *right to self-supply* could contain a positive dimension when "forced evictions" are committed by private actors. For instance, the Committee urged Paraguay both to prevent the eviction of peasant and indigenous families caused by soya expansion, and to address the claims made by peasant and indigenous families.[102] In this situation, the *right to self-supply* corresponds with the "obligation to protect". With regard to the "transfer of tenure rights", the Guidelines note that "investments should do no harm, safeguard against dispossession of legitimate tenure right holders and environmental damage, and should respect human rights".[103]

4. *Justification*

A second argument against the recognition of a right to land is that such a human right could sanction unjust land-tenure and hinder socially-important projects.[104] However, the same argument could also be used as an objection against the right to property. But neither this civil right nor a social right to land would be absolute.

First, the state or investor could seek the consent of the right holders. The concept of Free, Prior Informed Consent (FPIC) was developed for consultations with indigenous people affected by extractive industry projects.[105] Many states, including countries in sub-Saharan Africa such as Mozambique and Tanzania, recognise the principle of FPIC as a legal requirement for community consultations and hearings when land is transferred to new users.[106] However, in practice, the implementation of FPIC rules is often deficient due to an information gap, incomplete records and vague provisions on benefit sharing.[107]

---

100 Ibid., Part 1, No. 1.2.1 and 2.2.3.

101 See CESCR, General Comment No. 7 (1997): *Right to Adequate Housing* (Art. 11.1): forced evictions, UN Doc. E/1998/22- E/C.12/1997/10, Annex IV, para. 3.

102 CESCR, Concluding Observation, *Paraguay* (January 2008), UN Doc. E/C.12/PRY/CO/3, paras. 17 and 28.

103 VGGT, note 97 above, Part 4, No. 12.4.

104 Wisborg, note 83 above, p. 4.

105 Art. 32 UN Declaration on Rights of Indigenous People. Resolution adopted by the General Assembly, UN Doc. A/RES/61/295 (13 September 2007).

106 Lorenzo Cotula, Sonja Vermeulen, Rebeca Leonard and James Keeley, *Land Grab or Development Opportunity*? Agricultural Investment and International Land Deals in Africa, FAO, IFAD, IIED (Rome: FAO, 2009), available at: www.fao.org/docrep/011/ak241e/ak241e00.HTM, p. 70.

107 Ibid., p. 72.

The CFS Guidelines include the principle of consultation and participation,[108] but this principle demands only formal proceedings, and, in contrast to the concept of FPIC, does not necessarily require the consent of the affected community.[109]

Second, according to general human-rights standards, evictions can be justified for a legitimate purpose, provided that they are not discriminatory, that they respect the requirements of due process, and are accompanied by fair compensation.[110] The *right to self-supply* would require not only compensation based upon market value, but also adequate access to a food alternative, which, in most cases, can only be effectively guaranteed through land which provides equal productive value.[111]

5. *De Facto Violations*

Recent case studies on land acquisitions for agrofuels in sub-Saharan Africa illustrate that, even when the consent of local communities was achieved and all formal requirements of the FPIC process were respected, the implementation of the project could result in a *de facto* violation of the right to food. As the NGO *ActionAid* points out:

> "In 2009, Sun Biofuels Ltd, a UK-registered biofuel company, began clearing land to establish an 8,200 hectare biofuel plantation in Kisarawe, Tanzania. By mid 2011, they had cleared some 2,000 hectares and replanted with jatropha. [...] In August 2011, like many biofuel companies before it, Sun Biofuels went into administration and fired almost all of the 700 local workers. The company was immediately sold [...]. The new owners decided to scale back the operations to a small pilot project [...]. Only a handful of people are now employed, while the damage to the land is largely done already."[112]

As a result, the agrofuel project violated the *right to self-supply* of the affected people because of the resulting less land available for food production.

6. *Accountability*

But even in clear cases of the forced eviction of subsistence farmers for agrofuel export projects, it would be difficult to hold the importing state responsible. While the described duty to respect and protect tenure rights primarily

108 VGGT, note 97 above, Part 3, No. 3B.6; Part 3; 12.8.
109 Ibid., Part 3, No. 9.9.
110 See CESCR General Comment No. 7, note 101 above, para. 3.
111 Cotula, Djiré and Tenga, note 79 above, p. 28.
112 *Action Aid*, Fuel for though: Addressing the social impacts of EU biofuels policies (April 2012), pp. 20–23 available at: www.actionaid.org.

concerns the home state, the responsibility of the importing state requires the demonstration of a specific *nexus*. If the determinable criteria were the "effective control" over a private actor or special aid by a state, it would be impossible to hold the importing state responsible. A single "land grab" would only be attributable to a foreign state if it were directly involved, for instance, through the granting of a direct investment credit for a particular project.

In my opinion, it would be sufficient to demonstrate that a specific agrofuel project in a third country was planned for export to the EU. This would be the case if the agrofuel demand from the EU were a significant investment factor. The EU could be held responsible because the extensive binding biofuel mandate creates an artificial demand for biomass imports. According to the progress study ordered by the European Commission, "possibly 10% of the biofuel production and new projects in regions with concerns on land-use rights could have eyed the EU market".[113] For example, the enterprise *Sun Biofuels* has cited the EU biofuel policy and the prospects of export markets as an important reason for the development of jatropha and biofuels in Tanzania.[114] Therefore, it could be concluded that the EU has the duty to compensate the people affected by the project.

C. THE COLLECTIVE DIMENSION

On the other hand, it could be argued that this *single case approach* is too restricted. The focus on concrete "land grabs" ignores the general impact of agrofuels on "food security" and the conflict with "food sovereignty" as described in the first part of Section I. Moreover, in practice, it would be difficult to prove responsibility on the part of the EU for single violations. In the pilot phase, at the very least, most projects in Africa could be intended to produce for domestic markets. However, even with an initial export orientation, it would be difficult to prove that the EU was foreseen as the main export market.

Instead of claiming compensation for single "land and water grabs", *EuropAfrica*, a campaign that connects African farmers' platforms and European civil society organisations, requests the complete removal of the RED biofuel target.[115] Referring to the right to food and the ETO principles, the network notes that the EU and its Member States have violated their international obligations. According to ETO Principle 13,

113 Ecofys *et al.*, note 51 above, p. 302.

114 *ActionAid*, note 112 above, pp. 20–23.

115 *EuropAfrica*, *(Bio)Fuelling Injustice?* Europe's responsibility to counter climate change without provoking land grabbing and compounding food insecurity in Africa (2011).

> "States must desist from acts and omissions that create a real risk of nullifying or impairing the enjoyment of ESC rights extraterritorially."[116]

Such impacts in third countries must be "a foreseeable result of their conduct".[117]

EuropAfrica argues that the EU and its Member States could have anticipated the negative impact of their biofuel policy on human rights in sub-Sahara Africa. In a broad study, the network identifies the link between the EU biofuel mandate and land grabbing in Africa.[118] Furthermore, the authors list all the impacts of agrofuel production, especially regarding food security and sustainable small-scale agricultural production.[119]

Similarly, De Schutter takes an overall view by criticising the EU biofuel policy for promoting land leases or acquisitions in sub-Saharan Africa, which increase the pressure on the natural resources needed for food production and inject significant additional demand into the commodities markets, and therefore has a significant impact on prices.[120]

This form of reasoning could be labelled as a *holistic approach*. In contrast to the *single case approach*, which has a compensatory character, the *holistic approach* takes a preventive view. Social and environmental impacts are considered as potential human-rights violations. Implicitly, these authors point to the collective dimension of the right to food. This new perspective is convincing, because it focuses not only on single cases but also reflects the conflict between biofuels and the right to food as a transnational conflict between the rising demand for modern bioenergy and food security at local, national and global levels, and thus recognises the special relationship of land for smallholders and their struggle for food sovereignty.

However, the question remains as to whether the assumptions made by *EuropAfrica* and De Schutter could actually be verified by courts, at least with the help of expert evidence. Because the *holistic approach* takes into account all the forms of impact of agrofuels, the factual allegations appear to be too complex for legal proceedings.

1. Food Insecure Countries

The facts might be adequately reduced when viewed in the more focused context of a single country. In the extreme case of a very large "land grab" such as the Daewoo case in Madagascar, where about 1.3 million hectares were leased to

116 ETO-Principles, note 69 above, No. 13 – *Obligation to Avoid Causing Harm.*
117 Ibid.
118 *EuropAfrica*, note 115 above, pp. 49–60.
119 Ibid., pp. 61–75.
120 Olivier De Schutter, Note on the Impacts of the EU Biofuels Policy on the Right to Food, Statement based upon letter sent to EU institutions (16 April 2013), available at: www.srfood.org.

a foreign company,[121] this could even result in a violation of the right to self-determination, codified in Article 1 of the ICESCR and the International Covenant of Civil and Political Rights (ICCPR).[122] Section 2 states that "all peoples may, for their own ends, freely dispose of their natural wealth and resources. In no case may a people be deprived of its own means of subsistence". Thus, the EU could be obliged to avoid imports from countries with gross deficits in food production or distribution. With this in mind, *EuropAfrica* states:

> "Yet, it is striking to note that *agrofuels are produced and/or planned to be produced in some of the most food insecure countries* in Africa. For instance, in Mozambique, where approximately 35% of households are chronically food insecure, a mere 32,000 hectares out of the 433,000 approved for agriculture investment between 2007 and 2009 were for food crops."[123] (emphasis added)

It would be consistent to exclude all 34 countries which currently require external assistance for food.[124] The FAO uses three categories: exceptional shortfalls in food production/supplies, widespread lack of access, and severe localised food insecurity.[125]

In my opinion, it must be proved that the exportation of agrofuels or agrofuel feedstock to the EU at the very least worsen the food security of a country to a significant degree. This proof would require a broad study which considered all economic, social and environmental impacts and benefits of agrofuel production for export, including the creation of employment and tax revenues. In contrast, most studies highlight the gains of bioenergy as a contribution which could serve the country's internal energy demand.[126] From a national food security perspective, it makes no differences whether food is imported or produced domestically, at least until food is available and accessible at all times to satisfy the needs of the population.[127] Only the concept of food sovereignty clearly stands for a priority of local food production.

However, even now it can hardly be proved that the EU biofuel mandate has contributed significantly to national food insecurity in third countries.[128]

---

121 See Olivier De Schutter, *Mission to Madagascar*, Report of the Special Rapporteur on the Right to Food (2011), para. 24.

122 International Covenant of Civil and Political Rights, A/RES/21/2200A, 16.12.1966, 999 UNTS 171.

123 *EuropAfrica*, note 115 above, p. 62.

124 FAO, *Crop Prospects and Food Situation*, No. 3 (October 2013), available at: www.fao.org/docrep/018/aq116e/aq116e00.htm, pp. 2–5.

125 Ibid.

126 See Irini Maltsoglou and Yasmeen Khwaja (eds), "Bioenergy and Food Security, The BEFS Analysis for Tanzania", "The Bioenergy and Food Security Project Food and Agriculture Organization of the United Nations", (Rome: FAO, 2010), available at: www.fao.org/docrep/012/i1544e/i1544e.pdf.

127 Cotula, Djiré and Tenga, note 79 above, p. 20.

128 With regard to Senegal and Tanzania, see Diop, Blanco *et al.*, note 28 above, Annex 4 and 5.

Agrofuels and feedstock were mostly imported into the EU from countries which have highly-competitive agricultural sectors, namely, Argentina, Brazil and the USA (soya), Brazil (sugar cane), USA (maize), and Indonesia and Malaysia (palm oil).[129] Imports from the least developed countries were rather negligible.[130] Actually, *EuropAfrica* assumes that the precautionary principle should be applied in the context of agrofuels. It argues that there is a strong presumption that land expansion for biofuel production, including for EU imports, will largely take place in Africa.[131]

2. *Land-Use Rights*

It seems more precise to argue that the EU biofuel policy already threatens local food security by creating a real risk for legitimate land-use rights in the Global South. As De Schutter rightly points out, the RED encourages land leases or acquisitions in sub-Saharan Africa and other regions, where the rights of the current land users are often inadequately protected and negative risks are particularly high.[132] Actually, the case study on Kenya used by *EuropAfrica* to specify the implications of agrofuels at national level demonstrates only the adverse effects for smallholders, who lose access to land and water.[133] Moreover, the study entails a list of 15 agrofuel projects financed by European investors which had negative impact on local food security or ignored the right to consultation of the affected villages.[134] As a recent study financed by the European Parliament points out that Western companies have played a central role in land acquisition, particularly in biofuel investments, and particularly in Africa, and cites numerous examples.[135]

3. *Social Sustainability Criteria*

It could be argued that the EU has at least a duty to implement binding social sustainability criteria for agrofuel projects.[136] Generally, the EU has a responsibility for the acts of corporations which have their head offices in the Union. As Fons Coomans points out, the failure of the home state to regulate a corporation which is engaged in the forced evictions of small-scale farmers

---

129 Ecofys *et al.*, note 51 above, Table 44 (p. 231) and Table 45 (p. 232).
130 Diop, Blanco *et al.*, note 28 above, p. 26.
131 *EuropAfrica*, note 115 above, p. 55.
132 De Schutter, note 120 above, p. 55.
133 *EuropAfrica*, note 115 above, pp. 45–48.
134 Ibid., Annex V, p. 117.
135 Lorenzo Cotula (2014): Addressing Human Rights Aspects of "Land Grabbing". European Union, EXPO/B/DROI/2014/06, pp. 13–15.
136 See Eide, note 44 above, pp. 46–47 and 49–51.

abroad would result in a violation of the right to food.[137] As Sigrun Skogly states, international corporations which invest in export crops should be regulated in a manner that secures adequate compensation and safeguards for subsistence farmers.[138] The FAO Guidelines emphasise that states (especially the home states of transnational corporations) should provide access to effective remedies for all negative impact on human rights and legitimate tenure rights by business enterprises.[139]

A recent impact study financed by *EuropAid* recommends the implementation of safeguards for foreign direct investment in agricultural land and the inclusion of social criteria.[140] As it stands, the RED entails only "sustainability criteria" which focus on minimum greenhouse gas saving thresholds.[141] While even "land with high biodiversity value"[142] is excluded, the question of which land could be designated with high economic, social or cultural value is left open.

The EU should use existing social standards. The provisions on the large-scale transactions of tenure rights of the FAO Guidelines urge prior independent assessments, including the identification of the rights and livelihoods of the people affected by the investment, such as small-scale producers.[143] In a positive sense, investment should at least "comply with national laws and international core labour standards".[144] In 2009, De Schutter listed eleven "Minimum human rights principles applicable to large-scale acquisitions or leases".[145] Besides the concept of Free Prior Informed Consent (FPIC), some of the most important criteria are benefits for the local population from the revenues generated by the investment agreement,[146] the promotion of farming systems that are sufficiently labour intensive,[147] and a clause which provides that a certain minimum percentage of the crops produced be sold on local markets.[148]

Nevertheless, as the Commission explicitly stated in relation to environmental standards, it would be problematical to monitor adequate implementation in third countries.[149] According to the RED, equivalent norms

137 Fons Coomans, "The Extraterritorial Scope of the International Covenant on Economic, Social and Cultural Rights in the Work of the United Nations Committee on Economic, Social and Cultural Rights", (2011) 11 *Human Rights Law Review*, p. 31.

138 Sigrun Skogly, "The Right to Adequate Food: National Implementation and Extraterritorial Obligations", (2007) 11 *Max Planck Yearbook of United Nations Law*, p. 354.

139 VGGT, note 97 above, Part 2, No. 3.2.

140 Diop, Blanco *et al.*, note 28 above, No. 7.2.1.1 and No. 7.2.8.

141 Art. 17 (2) Directive 2009/28/EC.

142 Art. 17 (3) Directive 2009/28/EC.

143 VGGT, note 97 above, No, 12.10.

144 Ibid., No. 12.4.

145 See Olivier De Schutter, note 70 above, Annex.

146 Ibid., principle 4.

147 Ibid., principle 5.

148 Ibid., principle 8.

149 European Commission, Annex of the Impact Assessment: Document accompanying the Package of Implementation measures for the EU's objectives on climate change and renewable energy for 2020, SEC(2008) 85, VOL. II, 143.

for agrofuel plantations in third countries should be integrated in subsequent bilateral or multilateral agreements with the main producing countries.[150] However, no such agreement has been concluded to date. At the very least, the EU should promote agreements which entail comprehensive binding sustainability criteria for agrofuels at international level.

4. *Food Prices*

Another main concern is the high risk of increased food prices due to biofuel expansion. In its Statement to the World Food Crisis, the CESCR has urged all states:

> "to take urgent action:, including by: ...
> Limiting the rapid rise in food prices by, *inter alia*, encouraging production of local staple food products for local consumption instead of diverting prime arable land suitable for food crops for the production of agrofuels, as well as the use of food crops for the production of fuel."[151]

De Schutter states that biofuel policies aimed at promoting the use of agrofuels from feedstock represent "deliberately *retrogressive measures*".[152] Applying the corresponding CESCR doctrine,[153] he argues that these policies "could only be justified under international law if very strong arguments are offered, showing that the benefits from agrofuels outweigh the negative impacts".[154] He refers to several studies which evaluate the effects of the global demand for agrofuel on international food prices. But these studies consider the cumulative effect of all agrofuel support policies. Focusing on potential human-rights violations, it would be necessary to identify the inflationary impact on staple foods, which could be attributable to certain forms of conduct.

While most studies assess the impact of the US biofuels policy,[155] a recent report by the Institute for European Environmental Policy (IEEP) focuses on the impact of the EU's mandate on food prices by the year 2020.[156] The IEEP reviewed several modelling studies which all suggest that the EU biofuel

---

150 Art. 18 (4) Directive 2009/28/EC.

151 CESCR, Statement to the World Food Crisis, adopted on 19 May 2008 during its fortieth session (25th meeting), para. 11.

152 Olivier De Schutter, *Building Resilience: A Human Rights Framework for World Food and Nutrition Security.* Report of the UN Special Rapporteur on the Right to Food, UN Doc. A/HRC/9/23 (September 2008), Annex II, para. 5.

153 CESCR, General Comment No. 3 (1990): the nature of state parties obligation (Art. 2 (1)), para. 9.

154 Ibid.

155 See HLPE, *Biofuels 2013*, note 5 above, No. 3.3.2.

156 Bettina Kretschmer, Catherin Bowyer and Allan Buckwell, *EU Biofuel Use and Agricultural Commodity Prices: A Review of the Evidence Base*, Institute for European Environmental Policy (June 2012), available at: www.ieep.eu.

mandate would be responsible for basic food commodity price increases. Given the stronger reliance on biodiesel use in the EU, most significant price increases are projected for oilseeds (up to 20 per cent) and vegetable oils (up to 36 per cent).[157] This led the NGO *Oxfam* to conclude that:

> "Given the importance of cooking oil in the preparation of the food eaten by billions of people every day, spikes in its price have a significant impact on poverty and hunger, for people in both importing and exporting countries."[158]

The NGO *ActionAid* (which ordered the study), like *EuropAfrica*, recommends removing the EU biofuel target.[159] At the very least, the EU should demonstrate that the positive effects outweigh the negative impacts of its biofuel policy.

D. HUMAN RIGHTS IMPACT ASSESSMENT

In order to evaluate all the positive and negative aspects of its biofuel policy, the EU should conduct a Human Rights Impact Assessment.[160] In this regard, ETO Principle 14 reads:

> "States must conduct prior assessment, with public participation, of the risks and potential extraterritorial impacts of their laws, policies and practices on the enjoyment of economic, social and cultural rights."[161]

The Committee on Economic, Social and Cultural Rights (CESCR) is of the opinion that rich state parties should evaluate the impact of policies promoting agrofuels for the enjoyment of the ESC rights of other countries. Within the state reporting procedure, the CESCR was concerned about reports that Belgium's new Agrofuels Act is likely to encourage large-scale cultivation of these products in third countries where Belgian firms operate and could lead to negative consequences for local farmers.[162] In reaction to an NGO "shadow report",[163] the Committee recommended:

---

157 Ibid., p. 5.

158 *Oxfam*, "The Hunger Grains – The Fight is on. Time to Scrap EU Biofuel Mandates", (September 2012), p. 14, available at: www.oxfam.org.

159 *ActionAid*, Biofuelling the global food crisis: why the EU must act at the G20, (2012), 13, available at: www.actionaid.org.uk.

160 *EuropAfrica*, note 115 above, p. 89.

161 Maastricht Principles, note 69 above, No. 14 – *Impact Assessment and Prevention.*

162 CESCR, Concluding Observations – *Belgium*, 23 December 2013, E/C.12/BEL/CO/4, para. 22.

163 FIAN (2013): Response to Committee members' questions related to FIAN Belgium's Statement on Belgium's fourth report to the UN Committee on Economic, Social and Cultural Rights (pre-Sessional Working group of the Committee on Economic, Social and Cultural Rights – 21st of May 2013), September.

> "that the state party systematically conduct human rights impact assessments in order to ensure that projects promoting agrofuels do not have a negative impact on the economic, social and cultural rights of local communities in third countries where Belgian firms working in this field operate."[164]

Although the European Union is not a party of the ICESCR, even the EU is obliged to monitor the effects of its biofuel target. Actually, the RED explicitly states that the Commission is to report every two years on the impact of the Community biofuel policy on "the availability of foodstuffs at affordable prices", on "respect of land-use rights", and on "wider development issues" in third countries.[165] Actually, the Commission should take into account the effects of all its agroenergy support policies. The RED entails the general target of at least a 20 per cent share of energy from renewable sources in the Community's gross final consumption of energy by the year 2020.[166] In 2010, 62 per cent of all alternative energy produced in the EU came from bioenergy.[167] While heat from wood and forest products represents the biggest share,[168] food plants are not only used for agrofuel production but also used as a source for "green" gas and electricity.[169]

From a right to food perspective, the effects of agroenergy should not be evaluated only in terms of economics, but also with a focus on the most vulnerable. As Ann Sofie Cloots points out:

> "Many studies reflect somewhat utilitarian cost-benefit analysis, calculating how many people will benefit and how many will be hurt, then simply offsetting the one by the other. A genuine right-to-food analysis, however, should [...] distinguish, for example, between the impact on rural and urban poor; farmers, processing firms and distributors; large scale producers and smallholders; and landowners and landless farmers."[170]

In its first Renewable Energy Progress Report (2013), the Commission highlights the positive effects of the EU biofuel policy.[171] However, as the NGO *ActionAid* pointed out, the Commission limits itself to the analysis of the impact of the EU

164 CESCR, Concluding Observations – *Belgium*, para. 22.

165 Art. 17 (7) Directive 2009/28/EC.

166 Art. 3 (1) Directive 2009/28/EC.

167 European Commission (2014): State of play on the sustainability of solid and gaseous biomass used for electricity, heating and cooling in the EU, Brussels, 28 July 2014, SWD(2014) 259 final, Annex 1 (p. 28).

168 Ibid., p. 29.

169 Ibid., p. 32.

170 Ann Sofie Cloots, "Biofuels and the Right to Food: An Uneasy Partnership", in: Olivier De Schutter and Kaitlin Y. Cordes (eds), *Accounting for Hunger: The Right to Food in the Era of Globalisation*, (Oxford-Portland OR: Hart Publishing, 2011), p. 108.

171 European Commission, Report from to the European Parliament, the Council, the European Economic and Social Committee and the Committee of the Regions. Renewable Energy Progress Report.", SWD(2013) 102 Final.

consumption of biofuels only up to the end of the year 2010.[172] From a human rights perspective, it would be necessary to evaluate the general impact of the EU policy target of 10 per cent renewable energy in transport fuels by the year 2020.

1. *Positive Effects*

In its Progress Report, the Commission states that the EU biofuel policy created more than one million jobs abroad.[173] This calculations seems a bit exaggerated. Actually, this number is based upon an impact study ordered by the bioenergy industry that calculated the employment effect of the global biofuel market.[174]

Moreover, it is highly disputed as to whether agrofuels have a green house gas saving potential.[175] And the question of how indirect land-use changes (ILUCs) should be considered is particularly controversial.[176]

In October 2012, the Commission reacted to various expert reports on the negative effect of ILUCs on climate change, and released a proposal for emending the RED.[177] The amount of food-crop-based biofuels which have a higher ILUC potential is to be limited to the current consumption level of 5 per cent up to the year 2020. However, the proposal is still being debated.

2. *Global Land Availability*

According to the Commission, the worldwide biofuel expansion still seems to be far from reaching its spatial limits. In its impact study in 2012, the Commission refers to the results of a recent Special Report of the Intergovernmental Panel on Climate Change (IPCC), which concluded that 780 million hectares of land are globally available for use for biomass production without impacting on global food security.[178]

But this perspective conflicts with the *telos* of Article 11 (2) of the ICESCR. This provision provides that states parties should take into account:

---

172 See Magdalena A. Kropiwnicka, The European Commission's *Renewable Energy Progress and Biofuels Sustainability Reports 2013*: A Critical Analysis of the Coverage of Land Rights and Socio Economic Impacts, Briefing for *ActionAid International*, 03 May 2013, available at: www.actionaid.org.

173 European Commission, Progress Report, note 171 above, p. 12.

174 See Ecofys *et al.*, note 51 above, p. 302 referring to J.M. Urbanchuk, Contribution of biofuels to the global economy, CardnoEntrix, prepared for Global Renewable Fuels Association, 3 May 2012, Table 4 (p. 17).

175 See HLPE, *Biofuels 2013*, note 5 above, p. 49.

176 Ibid., p. 89.

177 European Commission, Proposal for a Directive of the European Parliament and of the Council amending Directive 98/70/EC and Directive 2009/28/EC, SWD(2012) 343 final.

178 European Commission, Impact Assessment 2012, note 52 above, No. 2.2.3 referring to IPCC, *Renewable Energy Sources and Climate Change Mitigation*, Special Report of the Intergovernmental Panel on Climate Change, (2012), 226, Table 2.3.

"the problems of both food-importing and food-exporting countries, to ensure *an equitable distribution of world food supplies* in relation to need." (emphasis added)

The ideal of an "equitable distribution" could be extended to the idea of fair benefit sharing of global land resources, independent of whether they are used for food, feed, fuel or any other reason. Whereas the CESCR traditionally highlights that states parties are obliged to use all the resources available with a view to progressively achieving the full realisation of ESC rights (Art. 2 (1) ICESCR),[179] the question would reverse from resource scarcity to resource sufficiency. The central question would not be whether the EU is using its resources in an efficient way, but rather whether the EU agrofuel policy could result in the illegitimate over-exploitation of global land and water resources. It could be stressed that the EU should not import more agrofuels or related feedstocks of energy crops than it exports. It should, at the very least, take the existing agricultural trade balance into account. The EU is "virtually" importing land from third countries. According to an NGO study, "already in 2007, 40% of Europe's land footprint – the land used for crop production and livestock farming which was required to satisfy the demand for products in Europe – was located in other regions of the world".[180]

3. *Land-Use Rights*

Moreover the focus on "technical potentials" for biomass production is highly problematical, because it ignores the fact that supposedly "idle land" is often used by invisible users such as smallholders, pastoralists, herders and indigenous communities.[181] The findings about "available land" are based upon satellite and aerial photographs which cannot show the existing land-based social relations.[182] Although the IPCC stated that most potential land for biomass production is in Africa (35%) and Latin America (21%), the Commission ignores the fact that "there is rarely any valuable land that is neither already being used in some way, nor providing an important environmental service".[183]

With regard to land rights, the Commission stated that it is not yet clear whether the EU biofuel demand contributes to any abuse.[184] This conclusion is extremely dubious. First, the Commission ignores the result of the background study, which claims that "land and water grabs", which correspond to up to

179 See CESCR, General Comment 12, note 73 above, para. 21 and 25.
180 Global 2000 & SERI, Hidden Impacts, How Europe's resource over-consumption promotes global land conflicts, February 2013, p. 3 available at: www.reduse.org.
181 See Cloots, note 170 above, p. 103.
182 HLPE, Land Tenure and International Investments in Agriculture, note 47 above, pp. 25–26.
183 Ibid.
184 European Commission, Progress Report, note 171 above, p. 11.

160,000 hectares, can be linked to the rising EU biofuel market.[185] Second, the Commission declined to undertake any field study and did not evaluate any NGO reports about European biofuel companies involved in "land and water grabs".

4. *Food Prices*

The European Commission has never calculated the expected price increases caused by the RED until the year 2020 at global level. In its impact assessment of 2012, the Commission generally stated that:

> "the expected increase in demand for biodiesel and bioethanol to 2020 will increase the pressure on global commodity markets, particularly for vegetable oil as the EU demand for biodiesel represents a more significant share of the total production."[186]

The Progress Report (2013) only calculated the EU contribution to historic price peaks. According to the Commission:

> "grain use for bioethanol production constituted 3% of total cereal use in 2010/2011 and is estimated to have minor (1–2%) price effect on the global cereals market. EU biodiesel consumption is greater, and the estimated price effect on food oil crops (rapeseed, soybean, palm oil) for 2008 and 2010 was 4%."[187]

Already in its impact assessment of 2008, the Commission acknowledged potential negative impact, but very much stressed the fact that the increased prices would benefit food producers and could re-vitalise rural areas globally.[188] In general, high food-prices could be seen as an opportunity for agrarian economies and farmers.[189] At macroeconomic level, net food-exporting countries could benefit from rising commodity prices. On the other hand, the current 66 Low-Income and Food Deficit-Countries were immediately affected by price rises. These countries depend on international markets for the importation of staple foods and have a very low *per capita* gross national income.[190] Moreover, rising food prices are a serious danger for the poorest, which already face a "*de facto* discrimination" caused by social disadvantages.[191]

---

185 Ecofys *et al.*, note 51 above, p. 302.

186 European Commission, note 52 above, No. 5.2.4.

187 European Commission, note 171 above, p. 12.

188 European Commission, Impact Assessment 2008, note 148 above, pp. 130–131.

189 See WBGU, note 26 above, No. 5.2.5.2.

190 FAO, List of LIFDCs (2014), available at: www.fao.org/countryprofiles/lifdc/en.

191 See CESCR, General Comment No. 20 (2009): Non-discrimination in Economic, Social and Cultural Rights (Art. 2 II), para. 8.

Today, approximately 1.21 billion people live below the poverty line (*i.e.*, on an income of less than 1.25 US dollars per day).[192]

CONCLUSION

This case study illustrates the challenge of re-thinking the right to food in transnational constellations. Although the case of biofuels demonstrates the complexities of global agricultural markets, it seems possible to operationalise the right to food to an extent which allows violations, responsibilities and right-holders to be identified.

From an individual perspective the emerging *right to self-supply* protects the existing access of smallholders to land and other productive resources. This right is violated when large-scale land acquisitions for agrofuel production result in forced evictions or local food insecurity. It seems to be arguable that even the EU, as an importing state, is responsible for single "land grabs" under the that the investment was mainly motivated by the possibility of exporting agrofuels or related feedstocks into the EU.

With regard to the collective dimension of the right to food, it could be argued that the EU biofuel target represents a retrogressive measure because it causes higher world prices for oilseed and vegetable oils, incentivises "land and water grabbing" for plantations of energy crops in third countries, and aggravates the existing negative land footprint of the Union. Until today, the EU has not been able to prove that the benefits from its agrofuel policy outweigh the adverse effects. Comprehensive human rights impact assessments of its agroenergy support policies are still missing.

192 UN Economic Commission for Africa, *inter alia*, *Millennium Development Report 2013*, Assessing Progress in Africa towards the Millennium Development Goals (2013), p. 1.

CHAPTER 10

BETWEEN RIGHTS AND POWER ASYMMETRIES: CONTEMPORARY STRUGGLES FOR LAND IN BRAZIL AND COLOMBIA

Maria BACKHOUSE, Jairo BAQUERO MELO and Sérgio COSTA

I. INTRODUCTION

Many factors explain the current increasing visibility of land conflicts in Latin America. To begin with, this intensification involves a re-configuration of conflicts that date back to the European colonisation of Latin America and to the expropriation from the original populations during this period. Over the centuries, these conflicts have taken on new forms, following the variations of capital accumulation dynamics and the changes in legislation and policies that regularise land ownership and use.

The recent re-positioning of Latin America within the global division of labour, marked by the growing importance of a new mix of commodities on the regional export agenda, aggravates these existing conflicts. Lands that previously had little value, and that are far away from the larger settlements, come to be disputed to such a degree that the exploration of their subsoil or surface to cultivate agricultural products has transformed them into a promising source of profit.[1]

Additional reasons for these land conflicts are the search for new energy sources and the expansion of transportation and communication infrastructures. In this regard, the growing production of agro-fuels and the expansion of the areas occupied by hydro-electric dams, in addition to new highways, railroad lines, electrical transmission lines, *etc.*, transform the way in which large extensions of land are used and in many cases lead to the removal of the traditional occupants from these areas. A similar process can be observed

1 Eduardo Gudynas, "Estado compensador y nuevos extractivismos", (2012) 237 *Nueva Sociedad*, pp. 128–146.

in negotiations regarding climate change control or national/local initiatives to compensate for the environmental impact of human activities (through the creation of parks, protected areas, *etc.*). These measures impose limits on land use and restrict opportunities for the survival of the resident populations. In other cases, these populations are transformed into guardians of the areas integrated to the imagined global environmental patrimony, and are financially compensated to do so.[2]

Finally, the growing interest in the speculative use of lands should also be emphasised. It is well known that land is a traditional instrument of value – and not only in Latin America. In the conjunctures of the current economic crisis and the strong volatility of financial applications, the importance of speculative investments in land has grown dramatically, aggravating local conflicts.

The exacerbation of land conflicts in Latin America takes place in a context marked by enormous growth at the international and local levels in the body of international law, as related to transnational social rights (see Andreas Fischer-Lescano and Kolja Möller, Chapter 2 in this volume). A similar dynamic is also observed in case of the production and implementation of environmental law, involving the interplay of actions of governments, local communities, NGOs, environmental activists, and experts) and also in case of rights and guarantees established for cultural minorities. The issue of land titles is at the core of the new minority rights, as defined in a broad and bold way in 1989 by the International Labour Organization Convention 169, as well as the UN Declaration on the Rights of Indigenous Peoples in 2007, and other international agreements. Latin America is the region of the world with the largest number of countries that have not only ratified Convention 169 but also whose local laws have included legal protection for minorities (ILO 2009).

In the Colombian case, the ILO Convention 169 was ratified through Law 21 of 1991 and national regulations, especially Law 70 of 1993, which gave territorial rights to the Afro-descendant communities, as well as the right to prior, free, and informed consent in cases of development projects affecting their territories. In view of this fact, the local communities and NGOs cite the Article 7 of ILO Convention 169 to demand the respect of communities' land rights. In 2001, the Colombian Constitutional Court, bearing into consideration Law 70, claimed that Afro-Colombians are covered by the same international ILO status as the indigenous people (Constitutional Court of Colombia, 2001).

In the Brazilian case, land rights of Afro-descendant communities were recognised in the Constitution of 1988, Article 68. The process of titling is

---

2 Astrid Ulloa, "Producción de conocimientos en torno al clima. Procesos históricos de exclusión/apropiación de saberes y territorios de mujeres y pueblos indígenas", desiguALdades.net Working Paper Series 21/2012 (Berlin, desiguALdades.net Research Network on Interdependent Inequalities in Latin America).

defined by Decree 4.887, which was adopted in 2003. The ILO Convention 169 was ratified through Decree (*Decreto Legislativo*) 143 in 2002. However, it has not been implemented yet.

The importance of granting land titles in order to protect cultural and ethnic minorities rests on the pivotal relationship between these minorities and their physical environment. This relationship is central to the very idea of cultural minority in Latin America. It involves in most cases indigenous populations, such as the *Quilombo* or *Palenque* communities; that is, settlements originally formed by peoples who had escaped slavery, in addition to other groups treated as traditional populations and who, in general, inhabit remote regions far from urban centres. The self-definition of these populations as minorities is fundamentally based upon the demand for recognition of certain distinct forms of land use and environmental resources, supposedly guided by the understanding of the environment transmitted across many generations. In this sense, the land, or more suitably, the territory that carries the key to identity is represented as a central source of material and symbolic reproduction for these populations.[3]

From a geographical standpoint, lands that have won new economic and political meaning in recent years due to the re-positioning of Latin America as a supplier of commodities and as a global environmental reserve overlap with territories occupied by minorities.[4] This causes the local land conflicts in Latin America today to be frequently marked by confrontation between seemingly irreconcilable rationalities, discourses, political strategies, and legal frameworks, such as:

a) The priority given to economic development and the need to use all available land surfaces for productive activities: agribusiness, mining, expansion of transportation infrastructure, diversification of the energy matrix, *etc.*
b) The expansion of transnational legal instruments geared to assure minimal social standards as well as the dissemination in most Latin American countries of social policies designed to protect "vulnerable groups" such as poor peasants and "traditional populations".

3 See José Maurício Arruti, Mocambo: antropologia e história no processo de formação quilombola, (São Paulo-Bauru, ANPOCS/EDUSC, 2006), Jan Hoffman French, *Legalizing Identities: Becoming Black or Indian in Brazil's Northeast*, (Chapel Hill NC: University of North Carolina Press, 2009), and Diana Ojeda, "Green Pretexts: Ecotourism, Neoliberal Conservation and Land Grabbing in Tayrona National Natural Park, Colombia", (2012) 39 *The Journal of Peasant Studies*, pp. 357–375.

4 Andrea Zhouri and Raquel Oliveira, "Development and Environmental Conflicts in Brazil. Challenges for Anthropology and Anthropologists", (2012) 9 *Vibrant*, pp. 183–208, at 187 *et seq.*

c) Appeal for moderate use or even a complete renunciation of the use of natural resources in order to compensate for the global climate and environmental impact of economic activities undertaken in other regions.
d) The need for the (re-) conversion of land into cultural territories to conserve traditional ways of life and the transmission of ancestral knowledge.

In Latin American countries such as Colombia, there are other processes in which communities – and supportive NGOs and activists – appeal to other instruments of international law. In cases of violent violation of human rights, communities can resort to instruments embedded within International Humanitarian Law to protect civil populations from the effects of the wars. And considering the trend of countries to accept the jurisdiction of the Inter-American Court of Human Rights, there is an ongoing trend in which the communities, NGOs and activists appeal to this Court to denounce cases such as collective human rights violations, as in the case of the Colombian Afro-descent population. In this sense, the articulation of several instruments of international law, or the interplay of different elements of the transnational social rights, can be taken as a contemporary form to halt land-grabbing processes occurring in local settings in Latin America. The extent of the success of these processes are to be evaluated in the mid- and long-term; but, at least in the short run, the instruments of international law provided elements to contend and resist land-grabbing. Recent land-grabbing is a transnational social problem (Andreas Fischer-Lescano and Kolja Möller, Chapter 2 in this volume), because it is rooted in the food, financial and energetic crises starting at least from 2008, which saw/led to transnational actors (governments, transnational and national companies, investors, *etc.*) seeking to buy land in countries in Africa, Latin America and Asia.[5] Land grabbing disrupts the food supply in the targeted countries because it is aimed to expand monocultures such as oil palm (see Andreas Fischer-Lescano and Kolja Möller, Chapter 2 in this volume). The World Bank has proposed the regulation of land grabbing by offering the advocacy of good governance, or Code of Conduct on land grabbing. This proposal has been criticised because it does not have "a pro-poor orientation in the sense of proceeding a social-justice driven analysis of the causes of (rural) poverty and the need to protect and advance (rural) poor people´s land access and property interests".[6] Given this lack of "pro-poor orientation" in land grabbing, the communities in question resort to legal instruments, such as national and international law, in order to seek to protect their social rights.

5 GRAIN (2008). *Seized: The 2008 Landgrab for Food and Financial Security.* GRAIN Report, available at: www.grain.org/article/entries/93-seized-the-2008-landgrab-for-food-and-financial-security, last accessed 1 May 2015.

6 Saturnino Borras Jr. and Jennifer Franco, "From Threat to Opportunity? Problems with the Idea of a 'Code of Conduct' for Land-Grabbing", (2010) 3 *Yale Human Rights & Development Law Journal*, pp. 507–523, at 510.

This is the broader political context in which the two case studies presented in this chapter take place. Our arguments are divided into four sections. The first section briefly discusses some of the current interpretations of the expansion of the rights of cultural minorities, and based upon this debate, it proposes an analytical framework in which social and/or minority rights are understood as relays in asymmetrical power structures. The second section presents a case study of land conflict in the Pará State of the Brazilian Amazon, which involves the expansion of an area occupied by oil palm plantations for the production of biodiesel and its impact on negotiations of the *Quilombo* territories in the region. The third section is dedicated to the study of conflicts observed in the lower Atrato region on the border between Colombia and Panamá, specifically the issues involving the expansion of the cultivation of African palm trees on lands whose control is disputed by traditional rural oligarchies, new agrarian entrepreneurs, paramilitary groups, and indigenous, *mestizo*, and Afro-descendent communities. The final section explores different elements of these three arguments in order to show how minority rights – as related to transnational social rights in the sense of Andreas Fischer-Lescano and Kolja Möller, Chapter 2 in this volume – in some situations, can serve to strengthen the power of the local populations in their struggles to reach the guarantee of title and ownership of the lands that they occupy.

II. ANALYTICAL FRAMEWORK

The scope of this chapter is certainly not broad enough to discuss the vast multiplicity of analyses available within the specialised scholarship on the recent expansion of minority rights in the international political agenda and their incorporation into national and local legal and political frameworks. Nevertheless, delineating the extremes of the spectrum of analyses is a worthwhile and relevant endeavour that will contextualise our analytical-theoretical proposal within the existing debates. On the one hand, liberal multiculturalism sees the protection of cultural minorities as a necessary extension of individual rights. On the opposite extreme of the spectrum of interpretations are subaltern studies, which see social and minority rights as a dispositive that allows for the domestication and governmentalisation of differences.

Following the liberal multiculturalist position, as represented paradigmatically in the work of Will Kymlicka and his collaborators,[7] cultural

[7] See, for example, Will Kymlicka, *Liberalism, Community and Culture*, (Oxford-New York: Oxford University Press, 1989), idem, *Multicultural Citizenship: A Liberal Theory of Minority Rights*, (Oxford-New York: Oxford University Press, 1995), and idem, *Multicultural Odysseys: Navigating the New International Politics of Diversity*, (Oxford-New York: Oxford University

belonging corresponds to a fundamental space for the formation of choices and personal judgements. In this sense, the protection of cultural minorities is indispensable to individual autonomy, and conforms, for this reason, to a necessary extension of contemporary citizenship.

Historically, the constitution of modern nation states has implied the oppression of cultural minorities, which justifies, according to liberal multiculturalism, contemporary efforts to extend their rights:

> "This conception of [multicultural] citizenship attempts to replace or supplement nation-building policies with those that explicitly recognise and accommodate groups whose cultural differences have been excluded from the national imaginary, whether they be indigenous peoples, national minorities, racial groups, religious minorities, immigrants and refugees, or stigmatised groups such as gays and lesbians. This generates the familiar set of debates around minority rights and group representations that characterise multiculturalist literature."[8]

In this sense, the incorporation of minority rights into international law and into the agenda of international organisations observed in the past three decades, a process described by Kymlicka as "multicultural odysseys", represents what he considers to be a political and legal correction of the errors committed during the constitution of modern nation states.[9]

The analyses undertaken under liberal multiculturalism contain various analytical-theoretical deficiencies. They essentially involve, as discussed at greater length in other contexts,[10] the adoption of a pre-political and ahistorical concept of cultural identity, as if cultural belonging was constructed outside of the spaces of the dispute for resources and political and social power. These theoretical deficiencies aside, these analyses manifest a fundamental methodological limitation: in general, the studies linked to the field of liberal multiculturalism have a normative-prescriptive character. Therefore, they do not provide the instruments that allow for a discussion on the existing processes of negotiation, and of the reconstruction of cultural belonging observed in the specific contexts in which the implementation of rights and policies aimed at the protection of cultural minorities take place.

Press, 2007). See, also, Will Kymlicka and Bashir Bashir, "Introduction", in: idem (eds), *The Politics of Reconciliation in Multicultural Societies*, (Oxford-New York: Oxford University Press, 2008), pp. 1–24.

8 Kymlicka and Bashir, *The Politics of Reconciliation*, note 7 above, at 12.

9 Kymlicka, *Multicultural Odysseys*, note 7 above.

10 Sérgio Costa and Guilherme L. Gonçalves, "Human Rights as Collective Entitlement? Afro Descendants in Latin America and the Caribbean", (2011) 2 *Zeitschrift für Menschenrechte*, pp. 52–71. See, also, Sérgio Costa, "Freezing Differences: Politics, Law, and the Invention of Cultural Diversity in Latin America", in: Kathya Araujo and Aldo Mascareño (eds), *Legitimization in World Society*, (Farnham: Ashgate Publishing, 2012), pp. 139–156.

The analyses of the expansion of minority rights located at the opposite extreme of liberal multiculturalism, subaltern studies, recuperate a fundamental aspect completely absent from the formulations of authors such as Kymlicka, namely the nexus between power and cultural difference.[11] The work of Partha Chatterjee represents perhaps the broadest contemporary effort to build on the theoretical foundations offered by Michel Foucault;[12] an innovative analytical perspective on the expansion of rights and public policies in contemporary post-colonial societies. Based upon the concept of governmentality, as developed by Foucault in his lectures at the *Collège de France* in 1978, Chatterjee establishes the distinction between citizens and the bearers of rights on the one hand, and the population, that is, the target of control and of government policies and the bearers of entitlements, on the other:

> "Rights belong to those who have proper legal title to the lands or buildings that the authorities acquire; they are, we might say, proper citizens who must be paid the legally stipulated compensation. Those who do not have such rights may nevertheless have entitlements; they deserve not compensation but assistance in rebuilding a home or finding a new livelihood."[13]

Citizens and populations, according to Chatterjee, form two different genealogies and refer to opposite practices of and narratives about politics and social policies. While the citizen-narrative relates to the nation state and to a correspondent rule of law, as well as to a demographically small civil society populations represent the bulk of inhabitants of post-colonial societies like India, who only relate to the state as the governed and who interact with the public agencies in search of benefits and security.[14] Although the population groups constitute, from the perspective of governmentality, groups created by the administrative rationality of the state, their designation leads them to develop a correspondent collective identity:

> "Although the crucial move here was for our squatters to seek and find recognition as a population group, which from the standpoint of governmentality is only a

[11] This aspect is also emphasised by many Latin American authors identified with the fields of cultural and postcolonial/decolonial studies, such as Diana Bocarejo, "Legal Typologies and Topologies: The Construction of Indigenous Alterity and its Spatialization within the Colombian Constitutional Court", (2014) 39 *Law and Social Inquiry*, pp. 334–360; Arturo Escobar, *Territories of Difference: Place, Movements, Life,* Redes, (Durham NC: Duke University Press, 2008); and Eduardo Restrepo, "Ethnicization of Blackness in Colombia. Toward De-racializing Theoretical and Political Imagination", (2004) 18 *Cultural Studies*, pp. 698–715, among others.

[12] See Partha Chatterjee, "Beyond the Nation? Or within?", (1998) *56 Social Text*, 57–69, idem, *The Politics of the Governed*, (New York: Columbia University Press, 2004), and idem, "After Subaltern Studies", (2012) 47 *Economic & Political Weekly*, pp. 44–49.

[13] Idem, *The Politics of the Governed*, note 12 above, at 69.

[14] Idem, "Beyond the Nation? Or within?", note 12 above, at 61 *et seq.*

> usable empirical category that defines the targets of policy, they themselves have had to find ways of investing their collective identity with a moral content. This is an equally crucial part of the politics of the governed: *to give to the empirical form of a population group the moral attributes of a community.*"[15]

Chatterjee's reading of the relations between the state and the populations that are beneficiaries of its policies helps us to understand the impact of measures intended to protect cultural and ethnic minorities, in so far as these minorities are only constituted in most cases as communities that bear a common identity after they become potential targets of entitlements.[16] In addition, from a historical perspective, Chatterjee's findings apply to the important changes in the relationship between state and society observed in Latin America in recent decades. The national-populist import-substitution model which discursively integrated the entire population into universalising political categories of citizens and members of the nation, has disappeared. In its place emerges a heterogeneity of administrative categories that fragment citizenship into an endless set of groups of the governed and of beneficiaries of specific programmes and policies.

Nevertheless, the rigid separation established by Chatterjee between government and governed, civil society and population, citizenship and governmentality, limits the understanding of the effective shifts in the power relations in the cases studied in this chapter. That is, cultural and ethnic minorities can effectively make use of the instruments that the new minority rights offer them to influence the pattern of state interventions. These minorities come to relate not only to the agencies of the state as a target population for their benefits, but as citizens who demand rights and, in certain circumstances, who can initiate substantial changes in the quality of policies and of the state.

The less than rigid positions defined in distinct camps – on the one hand, the state and its citizens, on the other, the government and target groups – are borne out in the cases we studied, where we observe more dynamic power relations than a Foucauldian perspective would anticipate. Although new legal frameworks and policies do not in themselves immediately supersede brutal power asymmetries constructed throughout history, these new instruments contribute, in some cases, to a re-configuration of the ways in which power is negotiated and exercised. Therefore, it is an imperative analytical task to understand the specific circumstances that lead to shifts in power relations and the role that new rights, such as minority rights, perform in these changes. Ran Greenstein's tripartite distinction of powers is useful for the purposes of our

15 Idem, *The Politics of the Governed*, note 12 above, p. 72, italics in original.

16 Andrew Canessa, "Who is indigenous? Self-identification, Indigeneity, and Claims to Justice in Contemporary Bolivia", (2007) 36 *Urban Anthropology*, pp. 14–48. See, also, Costa, "Freezing Differences: Politics, Law, and the Invention of Cultural Diversity in Latin America", note 10 above.

analysis. Studying the political transition in South Africa, the author highlights three of the most relevant dimensions of power:

> "[S]*ocial power* (access by individuals and groups to resources and control over their allocation), *institutional power* (strategies employed by groups and institutions in exercising administrative and legal authority), and *discursive power* (shaping social, political and cultural agendas through contestations over meanings)."[17]

The struggles for land imply the exercise of – and disputes for – power on these three levels. However, the concrete results of the struggles always remain contingent. That is, the degree to which, for example, the exercise of discursive or institutional power can modify established forms of access to available resources, particularly land ownership, is something that cannot be pre-defined on a theoretical level. In addition, patterns of state intervention cannot be defined *a priori*. In some cases, the institutional power of the state is practically non-existent. There are other actors, such as paramilitary groups or local chiefs or guerrillas who may exercise the role of a political authority and, to some extent, an administrative authority. In other cases, the state effectively appears as the government of populations, or in other situations even as a promoter of citizenship.

The place that the law – and more specifically minority rights – occupies in these shifts of power relations is variable. In the case of socio-economic rights in South Africa, Greenstein identifies two distinct forms of mobilising the discourses and instruments offered by the law: the legal route which "seeks to use the courts to enforce compliance by the state with its constitutional obligations", and an activist route "that uses rights discourse as a mechanism to force the state to change its policies, but again without challenging the role of the state as such".[18] According to Greenstein, effective changes in the state intervention pattern and in power relations only occur when legal and activist strategies are combined. That is, the struggles to make the state comply with its obligation to guarantee access to certain resources are only successful when popular mobilisations are accompanied by initiatives that activate the instruments of the legal system itself to pressure the state.[19]

For our case studies, it is crucial to maintain a high level of analytical openness in order to understand empirical situations that are quite different from each other. In compliance with this open-mindedness, we do not pre-

---

17 Ran Greenstein, "State, Civil Society and the Reconfiguration of Power in Post-apartheid South Africa", *Centre for Civil Society Research Report 8*, (Durban: Centre for Civil Society, 2003), p. 1, italics in original.

18 Ibid., p. 37.

19 Ran Greenstein, "Socio-Economic Rights, Radical Democracy and Power: South Africa as a Case Study", in: Neve Gordon (ed), *From the Margins of Globalization: Critical Perspectives on Human Rights*, (Lanham MD: Lexington Books, 2004), pp. 87–126, *passim*.

establish a fixed correlation between the strategic uses of the new rights and their impact on power relations on the three levels mentioned above (that is: social, institutional, and discursive power). We understand that, as in electrical circuits, rights may function as "relays"[20] in circuits of political power. As such, they can operate in three alternative ways:

a) Rights serve as relays to modulate power, expanding the power of actors who previously had little political influence.
b) In extreme cases, rights, like electrical relays, can also function to block flows of power above the absorption capacity of a given circuit. This would be found, for example, in cases in which rights are mobilised to contain processes of violent removal of populations or those that protect the survival of a threatened group.
c) In other cases, neither the language nor the instruments associated with the new rights are mobilised, and therefore these remain innocuous, like electrical relays that are not activated if there is no electricity in the circuit.

III. COLLECTIVE TERRITORIAL RIGHTS IN THE CONTEXT OF GOVERNMENTAL AGROFUELS INITIATIVES – THE CASE OF THE *QUILOMBOS* IN PARÁ/BRAZIL

The high concentration of land property in Brazil, which began during Portuguese colonialism, was re-inforced after Brazil's independence. For instance, according to Law No. 601 of 18 September 1850, known as the Law of Land (*Lei de Terras*), public land could no longer be appropriated for agricultural use as before, but had to be purchased, instead. This was only possible for a privileged social class that was already in possession of vast areas of land. Hence, the high concentration of land was re-inforced and a lasting supply of labour on the plantations ensured. When slavery was abolished in 1888, the former slaves or resisting *Quilombolas* had no legal access to land. Today, most of their rural descendants are considered as landowners without title (*posseiros*, *i.e.*, occupiers).[21]

In the course of re-democratisation only 100 years later, the entitlement to land of rural Afro-descendant communities was recognised in Article 68 of

---

20 The image of relays entered the field of sociology through the work of Michel Crozier and Erhard Friedberg, *L'acteur et le système: Les contraintes de l'action collective*, (Paris: Éditions du Seuil [1977] 1996), who, upon studying organisations, identified relays as intermediary actors between organisations and their surroundings. As used here, the relays do not refer to concrete actors but to rights that can impact on power relations.

21 Girolamo D. Treccani, "Regularizar a terra: um desafio para as populações tradicionais de Gurupá", [Dissertation] (Belem: UFPA, 2006).

the 1988 Constitution.[22] In the aftermath, Brazilian black movements started fighting for the implementation of this law and the social recognition of cultural and territorial rights of *Quilombolas*. The new legal possibilities led to an ethnic re-identification of numerous communities of smallholder farmers, who now emphasise their common history of resistance against slavery in order to become legal owners of their land.[23] The category *Quilombo* implies a legal status: if their land is titled collectively, it cannot be commercialised and must be used in a "traditional manner".[24] Therefore, titled *Quilombo* territories have been effectively removed from the land market and are no longer available for agri-industrial uses.

After periods characterised by a noticeable growth of titles being issued to communities recognised as *Quilombo*, title proceedings have recently stagnated. The Brazilian government has 3,524 officially registered *quilombos*,[25] but as of 2012 only 192 communities had actually received their land titles, and in 2011 and 2012 only one collective title was issued *per annum*.[26]

There is considerable disenchantment among black movements. Political recognition of ethnic difference has been a critical milestone for the *quilombos* in terms of the re-construction of their missing history. But the legal enforcement of their territorial and political rights moves at a slow pace. The reasons are numerous: the inefficiency of the respective agencies, complicated property rights, lack of political commitment, as well as attempts to de-legitimise *Quilombo* communities with the allegation that rural black populations are falsifying their "real identities" as poor rural workers in order to profit from new rights.[27] In addition, agribusiness lobbying reaches into the parliament through the *Bancada Ruralista*,[28] thereby influencing directly the national debate on collective territorial rights. This lobby challenges aggressively the alleged "privileges" of traditional communities which supposedly impeded the development of Brazil into a global agro-energy-power.[29]

---

22 See José Maurício Arruti, "Direitos étnicos no Brasil e na Colômbia: Notas comparativas sobre hibridização, segmentação e mobilização política de índios e negros", (2000) 6 *Horizontes antropológicos*, pp. 93–123, at 101–107; idem, note 3 above, at 66 *et seq.*

23 Arruti, note 3 above. See, also, French, note 3 above, and Sérgio Costa, "Au-delà du métissage. Antiracisme et diversité culturelle sous les deux gouvernements Lula", (2010) 78 *Problèmes d'Amérique Latine*, pp. 91–112.

24 INCRA, "Territórios Quilombolas. Relatório 2012", (Brasília: 2012), p. 5.

25 SEPPIR, "Programa Brasil Quilombola" (Brasília: 2013) at: http://bit.ly/10SG30U, last accessed 20 June 2014).

26 Bianca Pyl, "Governo federal titulou apenas uma terra quilombola em 2012", (2012) *Brasil de Fato*, available at: http://bit.ly/QHnJ6s, last accessed 14 March 2013. See, also, Comissão Pró-Índio de São Paulo, (2012) *Terras Quilombolas*, available at: http://bit.ly/Wqalo9, last accessed 14 March 2013.

27 Arruti, note 22 above, p. 87.

28 This is a fraction of parliamentarians of various parties identified with the interests of the agro-élites and agri-business.

29 Henri Acselrad, "Agronegócio e povos tradicionais", in: *Le Monde diplomatique Brasil*, 2 February 2012, available at: http://bit.ly/Z1Vs80, last accessed 14 March 2013. Arruti,

THE GOVERNMENT FUNDED PALM OIL PROGRAMME IN THE AMAZON BASIN AND THE *QUILOMBOLAS*[30]

For several years, the Brazilian state has been promoting large infrastructural, mining and agribusiness projects in Pará. This includes the state "Programme for the Sustainable Production of Oil Palm" for the production of biodiesel.[31] Like the controversial Belo Monte mega-dam project, this programme resumes a large-scale project from the 1970s. The novelty here is the reframing of agro-industrial palm oil production as a green climate protection measure. A binding zoning plan is to ensure that the programme involves only areas de-forested before 2008.[32] The focus is supposed to be on the degraded grazing pastures in the north-east region of Pará and on capturing as much climate-harming carbon dioxide as possible in the growing oil palms. The programme has selected for this propose around six million hectares in 44 municipalities. Since the launching of the program in 2010, the area of oil palm plantations has been tripled to 180,000 hectares. The corporation employees interviewed predict a further growth of the plantations to up to four million hectares in the coming decades. The reservations and territories of traditional communities within the plantations are not supposed to be affected by this.

However, these expansions have had a massive impact on the access to land and on the land use conditions of the *Quilombo* communities. This accounts for the following:

(1) The issues of property rights remain mostly unresolved in the region.[33] The palm oil corporation project has fuelled aggressive land speculation. Frequent land sales and purchases through front men cause rises in prices. Interviewed agro-experts speak of a de-coupling of prices on the informal land market. This increases the pressure on *Quilombo* communities that have not yet obtained a land title to sell their land properties. For example, the *Taperinha* community

---

note 22 above, pp. 90–91; Alfredo W.B. Almeida and Rosa Acevedo, "Strategien der Landenteignung in Amazonien. Agrobusiness und Bodenkonflikte", in: Willi Bolle (ed), *Amazonien. Weltregion und Welttheater*, (Berlin: Trafo, 2010), pp. 151–170, and Alfredo W.B. Almeida, "Direitos territoriais e étnicos: as estratégias dos agronegócios na Amazônia", in: Andréa Zhouri and Klemens Laschefski (eds), *Desenvolvimento e conflitos ambientais*, (Belo Horizonte: Editora UFMG, 2010), pp. 382–387.

30 The section outlines the results of a qualitative survey on the impact of increasing palm oil plantations in two *quilombo* communities – one with and one without collective land title – in the municipalities of Moju and São Domingos do Capim in the north-east region of Pará.

31 Rosa Acevedo, "Territórios *Quilombolas* Face à Expansão do Dendê no Pará", in: Sandra Maria Franco Buenafuente (ed), *Amazônia. Dinâmica do Carbono e Impactos Socioeconômicos e Ambientais*, (Manaus: Editora da UFRR, 2010), pp. 165–184.

32 EMBRAPA, MAPA, "Zoneamento agroecológico do dendezeiro para as áreas desmatadas da Amazônia Legal", (Rio de Janeiro: 2010).

33 In all of Pará there are four times as many land claims as real existing land, which is why the state is referred to colloquially as "the state with four floors" (Treccani, note 21 above).

in the *Quilombo* territory of Povos do Aproaga in the municipality of São Domingos do Capim has been waiting for years for the claimed collective land title, while they see themselves increasingly surrounded by the oil palm plantations of the Brazilian mining corporation Vale and the dominant transnational American agricultural company ADM (Archer Daniels Midland Company). Without this title and in the light of the continuously growing land prices, it will be difficult for the 120 families to withstand the pressure from the growing oil palm plantations. Five families have already sold their parcels of land to a larger land owner. The *Quilombo* representative is concerned that the titling will be delayed until so many parcels of land have been sold so that a collective title can no longer be issued due to the lack of connected territories. Even titled *Quilombo* territories do not warrant a stop: the *Quilombolas* of the *São Bernadinho* community in the *quilombo* territory Jambuaçu[34] in the Moju municipality report attempts to purchase land belonging to single families. The promises of the corporations to use only degraded grazing pastures of large land owners thus hardly seem all too reliable.

(2) The expanding plantations affect the heterogeneous "traditional" systems of land use in the region. The region designated for oil palm plantations consists by no means merely of degraded grazing pastures. Since colonial times this has been namely one of the most populated and oldest settling regions in the Amazonian basin. In addition to various small farms and traditional communities, some untitled and 34 collectively titled[35] *Quilombo* communities live there. The territories of the *Quilombo* communities in *São Bernadinho* and *Taperinha* are located within the expansion areas of the oil palm plantations. The *Quilombolas* report deforesting initiatives in their neighbourhood for the conversion of these areas to homogeneous oil palm plantations. They also report the socio-ecological[36] impact of the plantations on their land and resources. The

34 Jambuaçu is an interconnected *quilombo* territory of 14 communities, of which 10 hold a collective land title. Joseline S.B. Trindade, "Território Quilombola de Jambuaçu: Conflitos socioambientais e as estratégias 'participativas' da mineradora Vale S.A.", (2012) [Paper presented at the "XI Congresso Luso-Afro- Brasileiro de Ciências Sociais"], at: http://bit.ly/13VsazR, last accessed 14 April 2013); Projeto Nova Cartografia Social da Amazônia, "Fascículo 3 – Nova cartografia social dos povos e comunidades tradicionais do Brasil. Quilombolas de Jambuaçu-Moju – Pará", (Brasília: 2007).

35 There are no reliable numbers regarding untitled *Quilombos* in the region. The number of titled communities is based upon an index by municipalities compiled by the NGO Pró-Índio (Comissão Pró-Índio de São Paulo 2012).

36 This term stems from political ecology, maintaining that the relations between society and nature are mutual, and that ecological experiences of crisis are always socially articulated and therefore embedded in power relations (Paul Robbins, *Political Ecology: A Critical Introduction*, 2nd ed., (Chichester: Wiley-Blackwell, 2010); Raymond L. Bryant and Sinéad Bailey, *Third World Political Ecology*, (London: Routledge, 2005); Richard Peet and Michael Watts (eds), *Liberation Ecologies: Environment, Development, and Social Movements*, 2nd ed., (London: Routledge, 2010).

use of pesticides contaminates rivers: this causes the fish to die, as well as skin irritation for those living near to the rivers. The decrease in harvestable fruit is also attributed to the contamination of the ground soil and the groundwater with pesticides. Monocropping cultivation changes flora and fauna: local game is crowded out and the cultivation of bees impeded. The oil palm fruit lures in rats and snakes. Interfering with natural stream courses, for example, to construct roads or to irrigate plantations, impedes access to water and irrigation.

State officials, in interviews, admit to the negative effects of the palm oil program. Nevertheless, they consider the palm oil programme to be a necessary development project for the region. They point to the jobs created by the oil palm plantations, which offer the *Quilombolas* a way to escape poverty. The *Quilombolas* interviewed disagree. In their experience, the work in palm plantations is poorly paid and precarious. Most of the workers' monthly salaries yielded less than the minimum wage (about 250 euros) – too little to sustain a family. Particularly young people whose land does not produce enough often have no choice. The *Taperinha* representative is quite clear on this point: "This is no development for us, this is semi-slavery". According to him, instead of turning people back into "semi-slaves", the government should protect and promote their land-use system:

> "We did not fight slavery only to return to plantations to work as slaves."[37]

(3) The *Quilombolas* hardly have a voice in the public debate on the palm oil programme. No studies have been commissioned to investigate their complaints. The reasons for this are complex. Socially, the *quilombolas* are marginalised throughout Brazil. They have low monetary incomes and only have precarious access to education, health, and agricultural credits.[38] In the case of Pará, numerous municipal offices and single trade unionists directly co-operate with the palm oil corporations. Unlike the situation in the 1980s, there are hardly any NGOs in the region today. The state palm oil programme has exacerbated their marginalisation. Not only the *Quilombolas*, but the entire rural population of the region has been circumvented by the programme implementation. As of today, the mandatory public hearings and environmental impact assessments for large-scale projects still have not been carried out.[39] Instead, (state) agro-experts as well as the palm oil corporations have expanded the discourse of degraded

---

37 Interview conducted by Maria Backhouse in 2011. All interview and text excerpts from Portuguese and Spanish were translated by the authors of this chapter into English.

38 José Maurício Arruti,, "Políticas públicas para quilombos. Terra, saúde e educação", in: Marilene de Paula and Rosana Heringer (eds), *Caminhos Convergentes. Estado eSociedade na Superação das Desigualdades Raciais no Brasil*, (Rio de Janeiro: Heinrich Böll Stiftung, 2009), pp. 75–110.

39 Resolutions CONAMA 01/86 and 009/87 mandate public hearings to enforce public participation in the process of environmental impact assessments. These were ratified in the state constitution of Pará in 1989.

grazing pastures by absorbing the old discourse of degrading traditional cultivation culture (shifting cultivation).[40] According to these experts, the agro-industrial palm oil production is a climate-friendly alternative to the traditional cultivation of manioc – an important crop for the *Quilombolas* and other smallholder farming cultures and main staple in the region. Thus, the *Quilombolas* are not only being spatially encapsulated or marginalised by the rapidly growing plantations, even their so-called traditional practices of land use are being questioned because of their ecological impact. The ambiguity of the term "traditional practice" is now being used against them; they are accused of promoting a system dating from the Stone Age that supposedly leads to land degradation.

Even the international environment politics closes the spaces of articulation for the so-called traditional communities, whose important impact on forest conservation is being emphasised in other contexts.[41] The widely endorsed strategy of conserving valuable primary forests and the climate by intensified monocropping of so-called degraded areas[42] proves, in the case of the *Quilombos*, that what seems to be a climate protection strategy may further undermine the access of already marginalised groups to vital resources. Through the technocratic narrowing down of climate change policies into the estimation of carbon capture and storage, monocropping cultivation is reframed as green in a region that, at the same time, is made out to be degraded. Through the naturalising definition of an entire region as degraded, the existing land-use systems are de-legitimised and destroyed.

IV. COLOMBIA'S LOWER ATRATO REGION: TERRITORIAL RIGHTS, POWER ASYMMETRIES, LAW AND RESISTANCE STRATEGIES

Concentration of land is one of the dimensions of historical inequalities in Colombia, whose far-reaching consequences include violence and social unrest. In this country, lands lend social prestige and regional political power. Historically, landowners have hoarded the best lands, in several cases even

---

40 Regarding the deconstruction of the agro-economical homogenising discourse and the supposedly degrading shifting cultivation in the Amazonas areas: Francisco Assis de Costa, "*Amazonien – Bauern, Märkte und Kapitalakkumulation*", (Saarbrücken: Spektrum, 1989); Thomas Hurtienne "Agricultura familiar e desenvolvimento rural sustentável na Amazônia", (2005) 8 *Novos Cadernos NAEA*, pp. 19–71.

41 See, for example, Article 8 (j) of the Biodiversity Convention.

42 World Bank, "The World Bank Group Framework and IFC Strategy for Engagement in the Palm Oil Sector", (Washington DC: World Bank, 2011), available at: http://bit.ly/13VtfYa, last accessed 14 March 2013. See, also, Rhett Butler, "Could Palm Oil Help to Save the Amazon?", (mogabay.com, 2011), available at: http://bit.ly/ihvJ4d, last accessed 14 March 2013.

leaving them unproductive, unused or employed for livestock. They have also refused to introduce agrarian reforms and resisted efforts towards them by political or violent means. In 2009, the Gini co-efficient of land concentration in Colombia reached 0.86, one of the highest in the region.[43] Land re-distribution has been demanded generally upon the basis of a class conflict between landowners and peasants without land. However, since the 1990s, racial and ethnic ties to land and territories have gained visibility with the introduction of minority rights and policies. Indigenous people and Afro-descendants inhabited mainly marginalised areas. Besides the struggles for land re-distribution demanded by peasants within the borders of the agrarian frontier, new territorial conflicts emerged as a consequence in the areas inhabited mainly by indigenous people and Afro-descendants. New sources of pressure have emerged from landowners and governmental neo-extractivist development policies, both of which aimed at grabbing land to expand agriculture frontiers and to exploit their resources. This has been the case of the lower Atrato region in Northwestern Colombia, near to the border with Panama. This region, inhabited mainly by Afro-descendants and *mestizos*, was included within the collective territories of black communities. It is also recognised at international and national level as a biodiversity hotspot. Its strategic location at the Darien Region has also attracted interest; the Americas Transversal Highway is planned to cross this area. Since 1996, paramilitary and military groups have displaced thousands of people, grabbing lands to introduce monocultures of palm oil.

However, several resistance strategies have been adopted by the communities, which now demand the recognition of their territorial rights and restitution. They have availed themselves of the new language and instruments supplied by Law 70 of 1993, demanding their minority rights to be respected, including their belief in the nexus between culture and nature.

A. AFRO-DESCENDANTS' TERRITORIAL RIGHTS (LAW 70 OF 1993), VIOLENCE AND LAND GRABBING

The most important recent developments in the situation of the inhabitants of the Pacific region of Colombia, and specifically in the lower Atrato, were the legal advances since the 1990s which defined collective territories of black communities and protected conservation areas. The Colombian government adopted institutional changes to grant rights to black populations. The Constitution of 1991 proclaimed Colombia to be a multicultural and pluri-ethnic nation. Social pressure and the support of several social sectors as well as of the

43 UNDP, Informe Nacional de Desarrollo Humano 2011. Colombia Rural, Razones para la Esperanza. Naciones Unidas (2011), p. 197.

indigenous representative at the Constitutional Assembly favoured the inclusion of the Transitory Article No.55 (AT-55).

The AT-55 forced the Colombian Congress to enact Law 70 of 1993, which defined territorial rights for black communities. Thus, the identities of these populations were, in certain way, essentialised, or "frozen",[44] by the Law. It defined "black communities", as "the groups of Afro-Colombian families who have their own culture, a shared history and their own traditions and customs in the village-rural side (*campo-poblado*) relationship, revealing and maintaining awareness of identity to distinguish them from other ethnic groups".[45] These populations lived in "collective occupations" among the river basins of the rural Pacific region, carrying out "traditional practices of production". Law 70 included aspects such as their cultural protection as an ethnic group and the promotion of their social and economic development, in respect of those traditional practices of production.[46] In turn, Decree 1745 of 12 October 1995 brought into effect Chapter 3 of Law 70 of 1993, which defined the process of recognition of their collective property rights, as well as the role of community councils (*consejos comunitarios*) as the local authorities in charge of the management of the collective territories.[47]

These community councils are composed of a General Assembly and a Junta. In 2001, the Constitutional Court ruled that the black communities in Colombia have the same international ILO status as indigenous populations.[48] Under this status, black communities would be consulted before the undertaking of any projects that would affect these territories.

A nexus was established between the recognition of collective territorial rights and the environmental preservation of these territories.[49] The black communities have lived mainly in areas with rich biodiversity, including conservation forests, rainforest, and wetlands. The legislation aimed to include the participation of these communities in the evaluation processes of economic projects planned for the region.[50] Historically, the Pacific region's use of its resources includes small-

44 Costa, "Freezing Differences: Politics, Law, and the Invention of Cultural Diversity in Latin America", note 10 above.

45 Republic of Colombia, Law 70 of 1993 (1993).

46 Ibid.

47 See Republic of Colombia, Decree 1745 of 1995 (1995).

48 See Constitutional Court of Colombia, Decision C-169 of 2001 on national special circumscription of ethnic groups, (2001).

49 Law 70 of 1993 includes as one of its principles "the recognition and protection of ethnic and cultural diversity and environmental protection, taking into account the relations established by black communities with nature", (Republic of Colombia, Law 70 of 1993, Article 3).

50 For example, Article 35 of Decree 1745 of 1995 established that a technical commission must evaluate proposals of projects for environmental licenses, concepts, permissions, and contracts for the exploitation of natural resources. Article 44 of Law 70 of 1993 established that black communities must participate in the design, elaboration, and evaluation of the environmental impact studies of the planned projects. Article 76 of Law 99 of 1993 claimed that the exploitation of natural resources should be carried out without affecting the cultural,

scale mining, logging, fishing, and gathering economies. Usually, megaprojects such as large-scale mining have been rejected by the respective communities, who garnered support from church representatives such as the *Verbitas del Verbo Divino.*[51] The legislation provided clear definitions of the collective property rights for Afro-descendants and *mestizos*, who had settled there decades and centuries ago.

Despite the recognition of territorial rights, these populations still have been affected by dispossession, mainly caused by to the introduction of monocultures. Paramilitary and military attacks were carried out in the lower Atrato because the area was a hiding place for guerrillas. Counter-insurgency activity drew the lower Atrato into armed conflict, with severe consequences for its local communities. The "Genesis Operation", which took place in February 1997, marked a breaking-point in the levels of violence. This "alleged" counter-insurgency operation against the 57th Front of the guerrilla fraction FARC was carried out by the 17th Brigade of the national army. Attacks by land and air were supported by paramilitaries of the Peasants' Self-defence Armies of Cordoba and Urabá (ACCU). Aerial bombings forced the displacement of thousands of people from the basins of the rivers Cacarica and Salaquí into the basins of the Truandó, Jiguamiandó, Curbaradó, and Domingodó rivers.

Those who stayed in the territory were advised by the paramilitaries to leave their lands because the war would continue and their lives would be at risk. However, those who returned found their lands cropped with oil palm monocultures.[52] After the people were forcibly displaced, paramilitaries and entrepreneurs began to occupy these territories.[53]

Dispossession and de-territorialisation have been introduced due to the asymmetries of power between external (military, paramilitary, and economic) actors and local communities. Governments, entrepreneurs, and paramilitaries have used violence to terrorise and displace communities, forcing them to accept the introduction of agro-industries. The government also promoted the policy of "Strategic Alliances" to forge the association between entrepreneurs

---

social, and economic integrity of indigenous people and black communities. In addition, Decree 1320 of 1998 enforced the process of prior consent from indigenous people and Afro-descendants to enforce Article 76 of Law 99 of 1993.

51 See Eduardo Restrepo, "Etnización y multiculturalismo en el bajo Atrato", (2011) 47 *Revista Colombiana de Antropología*, pp. 37–68.

52 The oil palm also arrived to lower Atrato because the Uribe government championed this sector, responding to the rise of global raw material demand for biofuels. See UNCTAD, *Challenges and Opportunities for Developing Countries in Producing Biofuels* (2006), available at: http://bit.ly/XLSWad, last accessed 14 March 2013, pp. 3 & 25.

53 There was a coalition between paramilitaries, functionaries of the INCODER, banana entrepreneurs, cattle ranchers, high range militias, and local chiefs, as well as unemployed peasants, drug traffickers, ex-guerrilla fighters, and retired soldiers. See Vilma Franco and Juan Restrepo, "Empresarios palmeros, poderes de facto y despojo de tierras en el Bajo Atrato", in: Mauricio Romero (ed), *La economía de los paramilitares: redes de corrupción, negocios y política*, (Bogotá: Nuevo Arco Iris, 2011), pp. 269–410, at 283.

and peasants to work for agribusiness, though the peasants could lose their property rights by being integrated as labourers in the plantations. In turn, agro-entrepreneurs have used their economic power to take advantage of the poverty of local communities, and "buy" or co-opt community leaders to enable the introduction of megaprojects.[54]

B. LAW AND RESISTANCE STRATEGIES AGAINST DISPOSSESSION AND DE-TERRITORIALISATION

There have been various social resistance movements in the lower Atrato. Historically, regional organisations chiefly demanded more adequate state attention and social policies as a response to the incursion of logging companies in the 1980s.[55] The resistance has also recently addressed violence, land grabbing, and the introduction of monocultures.

In the first place, Law 70 produced a change in the character and language of social organisations. Before Law 70, organisations such as the OCABA (Peasant Organisation of Lower Atrato) emerged from the Community Action Boards and the ACAMURI (Peasant Association of Riosucio Municipality). Law 70 created a shift in the identification and discourse of local populations. Struggles over the defence of forests were now subsumed under the notion of "territory". The peasant identity was incorporated into that of "black communities". Despite the partial victory that Law 70 embodied for the Afro-descendant rural populations, uncovering issues of discrimination and exclusion in urban populations,[56] one of its outcomes was the proliferation of social organisations in the rural Pacific, creating for the first time in history legal opportunities for national social movements to sustain their claims.[57] It also made social organisations established in the 1980s more visible.

Second, Law 70 gave the communities the possibility to achieve collective titling of the territories that they have inhabited for decades and centuries. In the lower Atrato, the populations were forcibly displaced before the achievement of collective titling between 1996 and 1997.[58] Even amid the violence, and as a defence strategy to preserve their rights, the communities applied for collective titling.[59] In the lower Atrato and in the Darien region, more than 720

54 Interview (J. Baquero), IIAP, October 2011 (all names of persons interviewed in Colombia are withheld for security reasons). Interviews translated from Spanish by J. Baquero.

55 Restrepo, note 51 above.

56 See Carlos Rosero, "Intervention", [Foro Regional IIAP. El Chocó Biogeográfico. 12 años después de la Ley 70 de 1993], IIAP 2005.

57 See Carlos Efren Agudelo, "Multiculturalismo en Colombia: política, inclusión y exclusión de poblaciones negras", p. 133, available at: http://bit.ly/YbV2A0, last accessed 14 March 2013.

58 It is relevant to remark that since these first episodes there have been several cases of forced displacement.

59 Interview (J. Baquero), inhabitant of Curbaradó, 2012.

thousand hectares were collectively titled for approximately 24 communities or community councils between 1999 and 2001.[60] The communities which benefited included the Afro-descendants who have been living in the region for several decades, and the *mestizo* peasants that arrived in the 1970s, having been displaced from the Sinú region by cattle ranchers. Although *mestizos* are not "black", as stated by Law 70, they have lived in harmony with the black communities. Thus, their collective rights have also been recognised, thanks to their productive practices and methods of land-use. In accordance with Law 70, they are "good faith occupants".

Third, many people have returned to their lands and have been resisting the actions of the paramilitaries and the agro-entrepreneurs. The populations created refugee areas such as the Humanitarian Zones, which are "fenced estates" that aim to provide security for the populations, upholding the International Humanitarian Law (IHL).[61] The local communities and NGOs cite the IHL in order to explain and point out that the Humanitarian and Biodiversity Zones are visibly marked with notices and warnings at their entrances, communicating to the armed actors the communities' decision to be neutral in the armed conflict. Thus, they avoid allying or collaborating with any of the armed groups, and demand that the armed actors abstain from fighting in these demarcated areas.[62]

After the international protest of several communities and NGOs, in 2003 the Inter-American Court of Human Rights granted the use of precautionary measures[63] to protect several threatened local leaders. Following Article 63.2 of the Inter-American Convention of Human Rights, the Inter-American Commission of Human Rights wrote on 5 March 2003 to the Inter-American Court of Human Rights, asking it to enact precautionary measures to protect the communities of *Curvaradó* and *Jiguamiandó*. Since 2003, the Inter-American Court of Human Rights has enacted several Resolutions. On 6 March 2003, the Court requested the state to adopt precautionary measures to protect the community councils and displaced families returning to the Humanitarian Zones. According to its requests, the Court:

> "i) Requires the State of Colombia to adopt, without delay, the measures necessary to protect the life and personal integrity of all members of the communities comprising the Community Council and families of Jiguamiando and Curbaradó; ii) Requires

60 Calculations made by Baquero (2012).

61 The International Humanitarian Law (IHL) is defined as a "set of rules, established by treaties or custom, applicable in international and non-international armed conflicts, which are also known as the 'law of armed conflicts' or the 'law of war'. Its goal is the reduction of the suffering of victims and the protection of essential resources for their survival, through limiting the adversaries' choice of war methods and means" (Peace Brigades International, 2011: 7).

62 Interview (J. Baquero) member of the CIJP (2012).

63 See Diego Rodríguez-Pinzón, "Precautionary Measures of the Inter-American Commission on Human Rights: Legal Status and Importance", (2013) 20 *Human Rights Brief*, pp. 13–18.

the State of Colombia to investigate the events that led to the adoption of these precautionary measures, in order to identify those responsible and impose the corresponding sanctions; iii) Requires the State of Colombia to adopt the necessary measures to ensure that the beneficiaries of these measures can continue living in their place of residence, without any coercion or threat."[64]

Furthermore, several resolutions were enacted to re-new those measures, some of them requesting the state of Colombia to maintain the precautionary measures in *Curbaradó* and *Jiguamiandó*: Resolution of 17 November 2004, Resolution of 15 March 2005, Resolution of 7 February 2006, Resolution of 5 February 2008, Resolution of 30 August 2010, and Resolution of 25 November 2011. Also, the Resolution of 17 November 2009 established that the state should determine the number of protected families.

These precautionary measures have been an important instrument for the protection of these communities. Nevertheless, this instrument is not infallible, and many risks remain in the region for many sectors of the communities that are not protected by these adoptions: "not all the people in the region are covered by those measures, and some of them have been murdered, including leaders that claim lands; several others have been displaced, or remain displaced".[65]

In July 2013, the Inter-American Court eliminated the precautionary measures in *Curbaradó* and *Jiguamiandó*.[66] In the Court's eyes, the country's government has made advances to ensure the rights of the local populations. However, the communities and NGOs have complained that the risks of being displaced or killed for demanding their rights still remain, due to the presence of paramilitaries, other armed actors, and multiple economic interests. The actions of INCODER, the state agency responsible for lands and agriculture policies in Colombia, the Constitutional Court, and the legal system have made further advances. The Inter-American Court has also mentioned that, if necessary, precautionary measures *can* be implemented again.[67]

At the same time, other legal processes have been mediated by the Inter-Ecclesial Commission of Justice and Peace NGO (CIJP), demanding, before the Inter-American Court of Human Rights, that investigations be carried out for the murder of Marino López[68] and for the Genesis Operation mentioned above.

64 Inter-American Commission of Human Rights, Resolution of 6 March 2003, p. 8.

65 See Inter-Ecclesial Commission of Justice and Peace, "Solicitud de precisión en el caso Curbaradó y Jiguamiandó", (2013), 3 July 2013.

66 *El Tiempo*, "Colombia gana 'round' en la Corte Interamericana", Bogotá, 2 July 2013.

67 See note 65 above.

68 This murder was particularly cruel. The paramilitaries cut his body into pieces and played football with his head in front of the population. The Marino López's case was reviewed by the Inter-American Commission and by Inter-American Court on Human Rights. See the Inter-American Commission of Human Rights, *Informe No 64/111 Caso 12.573 Fondo, Marino López y Otros (Operación Génesis), Colombia* (2011), Washington DC, March, 2011.

Biodiversity Zones were also created to procure environmental protection and stable food supplies, and have also been physically accompanied by the CIJP and Peace Brigades International (PBI) NGOs. The communities have claimed their rights given by Law 70, carrying out actions, such as cutting down oil palm trees, to implement their rights *de facto*. Various fields formerly cropped with oil palm now look like a sort of "palm cemetery".[69] In addition, several hectares of oil palm plantations in the Lower Atrato were affected by Butt Rot Disease (BRD). Even so, the entrepreneurs continue their own "counter-resistance" by cropping new products such as the cassava and plantains, as new proposals for cropping oil palm continue to arrive in the area.

Fourth, the NGOs have also begun criminal cases against the companies that cropped oil palm in the area. An attorney from CIJP who represented the civilian parties in proceedings against the agro-entrepreneurs pointed out the fact that investigations initially were focused on environmental harm. Article 19 of Law 70 stated that productive practices developed in these territories must guarantee the subsistence of populations instead of giving priority to agro-industrial activities. Furthermore, the introduction of agro-industrial projects in the lower Atrato is illegal, because Article 15 of Law 70 prohibits the purchase of land owned by the collective territories by external parties.[70] Accordingly, the Colombian Institute for Rural Development recognised the illegality of the plantations.[71]

INCODER stated that 93 per cent of areas with oil palm belonged to the collective territories of the black communities in *Curbaradó* and *Jiguamiandó*. Some companies showed purchasing contracts that they apparently signed with local people. Even so, the said contracts were illegal because they infringed Article 15 of Law 70. The companies tried to legalise their land-grabbing through several mechanisms. One of them was the enactment of false property titles, obtained from corrupt notaries; another was the enlargement of some estates that they bought from people that had legal titles before Law 70. Oil palm companies and cattle ranchers also bought private properties that were issued by the system of titling uncultivated land (*adjudicación de baldíos*) before the introduction of Law 70. These properties were excluded from the collective titling.

---

69 Interview (J. Baquero), NGO volunteer working in the region (2012).

70 Article 15 states that 'the occupation by parties external to the black communities of land issued as collective territories would not give these external parties the right to obtain titles or the recognition of improvements applied to the lands, and thus, they would be considered as "bad faith occupants"'. See INCODER, *Los cultivos de palma de aceite en los territorios colectivos de las comunidades negras de los ríos Curbaradó y Jiguamiandó, en el departamento del Chocó* (2005), Bogotá. The Law also states that areas could be sold, as a consequence of family dissolution, or depending on the procedures established by the communitarian councils. Privilege to sell the lands would be given to members of the same community or ethnic group.

71 INCODER 2005: 17. See note 70 above, at 17.

The courts have sided with the communities, showing that even part of the Colombian state, the judicial system, considers the entrepreneurs to have obtained their lands illegally and by force. These legal processes started after the accusations made by the local communities and the NGOs against oil palm companies. After the investigations performed in 2005, INCODER enacted a Resolution "recommending the suspension of crops and the return of 14,881 hectares, mostly cultivated with African palm, by 'bad-faith occupiers'".[72] By 2007, "a total of 23 entrepreneurs were charged with the crimes of land theft, forgery of public and private documents, harm to natural resources, the invasion of areas of ecological importance, and forced displacement".[73] Two agro-entrepreneurs of Antioquia (of the Pamadó S.A. Company) were recently sentenced to 10 years and five months of prison "for the crimes of aggravated conspiracy, forced displacement, and land grabs".[74] They were condemned for allying with paramilitaries in order to expand industrial palm crops in territories of the black communities. In these legal struggles, the proceedings have been mainly based upon national laws and regulations.[75]

Several hectares still remain under dispute. The government has used the cases of *Curbaradó* and *Jiguamiandó* as a model for restitution policies in Colombia. However, the government has been more focused on the "legal restitution" than in the real "material restitution". This involves the recovery and re-adaptation *(saneamiento)* of territories and the guarantee of security for peasants who return. The government initially planned to return the lands in May 2010 by giving the territory to a false legal representative who supported the interests of the agro-entrepreneurs. The Constitutional Court stopped the restitution by publishing the Decision of 18 May 2010, which forced the state to refine the process by conducting a population census within and outside the region, which would define the General Assembly that elects the Legal Representative of the community council. Currently, the process is still at a halt while the Constitutional Court defines the constitutional character of the census concluded in 2012. In addition, conflicts concerning the rights of the *mestizos* within the territories have arisen, such as the right to vote and to be elected as members of the Assembly. Nevertheless, the division has been created "from above" by entrepreneurs that "support" a sector of the Afro-descendants in the defence of their interests in the region.[76] Today the enterprises still remain in the

72 *El Tiempo*, "Es una investigación amparada en falsedades, dicen palmicultores", Bogotá, 22 December 2007.

73 Ibid.

74 *Noticias Uno*, "Empresarios de palma condenados por vínculos con paramilitares", 4 August 2013.

75 In a personal communication (Baquero, 2013) the CIJP was asked if they also invoked the international Law, but they did not respond. They emphasised the use of national, mainly environmental law, as the main strategy in legal actions against the companies.

76 Interview (J. Baquero), Lands Restitution Programme, Bogotá, 2012.

area, controlling big extensions of territories by bringing foreign workers in to occupy these lands, or by putting up enclosures and introducing livestock.

V. CONCLUSIONS

The struggles for land discussed in this contribution have been developed within a context characterised by improvements in the laws and policies designed to protect the ethnic and cultural minorities in Brazil and Colombia, following the multicultural turn[77] in international law. The studied cases of Brazil and Colombia reveal the interplay of resorting to diverse legal regimes in order to protect minority rights against processes of land grabbing. In both countries, there has been articulation of the legal instruments of ILO Convention 169 on land rights, the International Humanitarian Law, and cases presented before the Inter-American Court of Human Rights. These legal claims are part of the struggles of local communities, NGOs, activists, and some sectors of the government, to protect the rights of the Afro-descendant populations.

The contribution discussed to a greater extent the cases of Afro-descendent communities located in areas disputed by agri-industrial companies interested in expanding palm plantations for biodiesel production. In Brazil, the Constitution of 1988, as well as further legislation, has created the possibility to assign legal titles for the lands occupied by these communities. In the case of Colombia, the most important legal instrument has been Law 70 of 1993, which also prescribes the regularisation of lands occupied by the Afro-descendent communities.

The expansion of minority rights in the cases presented here does not have the impact described by liberal multiculturalism, namely, the preservation of the pre-existing cultural identities of minorities, so that the individual members of these minorities can develop a sense of personal autonomy within a culturally intact and coherent context. What we observe in north-east region of Pará in Brazil and in the Colombian lower Atrato, is a process of ethnic re-identification following the legal and political possibilities offered by new minority rights: groups previously engaged in struggles for land such as poor rural workers have re-articulated their interests as Afro-descendants. By doing so, they often differentiate themselves from other peasants who actually share similar life-forms and strategic interests with them, as in the case of the *mestizo* communities of the lower Atrato. Classificatory categories introduced by law and by policies have generated new loyalties and identifications, as suggested by Chatterjee in the passage highlighted in the first section of this chapter.

---

77 See Diana Bocarejo, "Legal Typologies and Topologies: The Construction of Indigenous Alterity and its Spatialization within the Colombian Constitutional Court", (2014) 39 *Law and Social Inquiry*, pp. 334–360, and idem, note 11 above.

Nevertheless, what the studied cases show is that the situation of the communities covered by the legal shift is more complex than the mere domestication and governmentalisation of differences as claimed by subaltern studies such as Chatterjee's. In Colombia as well as in Brazil, new minority rights have broadly re-configured local struggles for land. It is clear that the adoption of new rights does not abolish the existing power asymmetries. However, these rights re-frame the conditions under which struggles for land are conducted and negotiated. We can schematically confirm that the cases studied provided examples for all three types of impact produced by rights over power relations, as highlighted in the first section of this chapter. These are:

a) Minority rights serve to expand the discursive and institutional power of Afro-descendent communities and of their political allies, to the extent that claims for land, or better yet, cultural territories in both countries are now supported by the law and by specific policies. However, the impact of new rights over social power – *i.e.*, access to land – of Afro-descendants varies according to country and political circumstances. In Brazil, after a more favourable period during the 90s, when a considerable number of titles for the *Quilombo* communities were issued, we have observed a recent discursive and political counteroffensive of agri-industrial groups interested in using lands occupied by *Quilombos*. These actors try to reduce the discursive power of Afro-descendant communities, accusing them of falsifying their ancestry and of applying environmentally hazardous production techniques. These opponents also dispute the institutional power of the *Quilombolas* by working at parliamentary and governmental level to change legislations and policies that protect minorities. In Colombia, titling processes have been carried out since the middle of the 1990s, and, in the lower Atrato, took place amid violence. However, representatives of agribusiness have not yet disputed the discursive and institutional power of the Afro-descendent communities, as observed in the Brazilian case. Their preferred methods are violence and the co-optation of local leaders.
b) Minority rights functioned as a relay in the Colombian case, where oil palm farmers falsified titles to expropriate the Afro-descendant communities illegally. As shown above, the abuse of power led to a blockade in the power circuit: the courts condemned the farmers and confirmed the rights of the Afro-descendant to their territories.
c) In the case of extremely asymmetric power relations, minority rights cannot be implemented even if they exist formally. In the Colombian case, the application of minority rights had to be defended through the articulation of several international law regimes, such as ILO Convention 169, International Humanitarian Law, and the cases presented before the Inter-American Court of Human Rights. This was observed in the lower Atrato during the military

and paramilitary offensives between 1996 and 2004. Despite the legal protection guaranteed by Law 70, the local population was forced to leave their territories.

d) The cases studied in Brazil and Colombia show differing patterns regarding the interplay between national and international law.

What is particular about the case of the Brazilian Amazon region is that no such interplay takes place, due to the lack of political space and the lack of will to enforce the territorial rights of traditional communities.

In the case of the Colombian Lower Atrato region, on the other hand, diverse legal frameworks linked to national and international law are combined within the broader framework of transnational social rights. Communities and NGOs mainly used the expansion of land rights, introduced through the recognition of cultural rights that benefited the Afro-descendants and the *mestizos*, to demand the communities' rights to recover their land, and to avoid the introduction of agribusiness and infrastructure projects without their previous freely informed, and prior consent as stated by the ILO Convention 169 and the territorial rights. In this way, the communities defend their "lives, beliefs, institutions, and spiritual wellbeing" against the introduction of development projects.

The use of international law goes beyond the right to previous consent. The case before the Inter-American Court for the Genesis Operation in Colombia is another example of the use of the international law by local communities and NGOs to claim truth, justice, and reparation. Bearing in mind that the Colombian State ratified the American Convention, the communities demanded the investigation of the state's responsibility in forced displacement and the murders of local people.

In such cases, the Commission has remarked that the affected groups have been the Afro-descendants to whom the Colombian state legally gave collective territorial rights, and, at the same time, ratified the American Convention at international level. However, notwithstanding the potential positive effects of the Commission's intervention, new challenges emerge from the local inter-ethnic conflicts, due to the various interpretations of the Multicultural Law. Some local groups have stated that only black people have land rights, even though the *mestizos* have also inhabited and owned these lands. To date, the main mediator has been the Constitutional Court, which enacted the legislation defending the rights of the *mestizos* to the territory in question, despite the fact that the Law (national and international) addresses the black people.[78]

---

[78] See Constitutional Court of Colombia (2013), Auto 096 of 2013.

CHAPTER 11

THE ZAPATISTA STRUGGLE FOR THE RIGHT TO LAND: BACKGROUND, CONTEXT AND STRATEGIES

Judith Schacherreiter and Guilherme Leite Gonçalves

I. INTRODUCTION

Land rights are crucial factors in realising social rights. Their violation is a pre-requisite for the capital accumulation which precedes the expansion of capitalism and the emergence of new capitalist formations.[1] According to Karl Marx, money and commodities can be only transformed into capital when the peasant is expropriated from his land, separated from the factors of production, and left with nothing but his labour power to sell freely. In consequence, he is reduced to pauperism. This process is marked by expropriation, robbery and colonisation, all of which involve the integration of local, national or regional actors and areas into the global structures of domination.[2] Such integration transforms the spectrum of the struggle for the right to land: if resistance to the commodification of a particular territory is simultaneously an opposition to transboundary powers, then each peasant movement is part of a global process of critical meaning-making. Not only does this allow for the said movements to develop collective action connected to transnational networks, it also re-interprets the struggle for social rights as a struggle for transnational social rights.[3]

Under these circumstances, the pressure on land is increasing dramatically. As rural populations grow, cultivated plots are becoming smaller *per capita*

1 David Harvey, "The 'New' Imperialism: Accumulation by Dispossession", (2009) 40 *Socialist Register*, pp. 64 *et seq.*

2 This description relates to the analysis of primitive accumulation: Karl Marx, *Capital. A Critique of Political Economy*, Volume I, (London: Penguin Books/New Left Review, 1982), p. 874 *et seq.*

3 Andreas Fischer-Lescano and Kolja Möller, "The Struggle for Transnational Social Rights", Chapter 2 in this volume, p. 15.

and per household. The decline of the average farm size is combined with landlessness and compounded by erosion and soil depletion. In recent years, export-driven agricultural policies have further increased the pressure on land. In many regions, large-scale plantations have developed for the production of food, energy or cash crops. The switch to biofuels in transport has increased both the competition among the various uses of farmland and the risk that poorer groups will lose access to the very land upon which they depend. Under the heading "land grabbing", large-scale land acquisitions have become a contentious topic.[4]

These trends are linked with the food crises and threaten the right to adequate alimentation, as recognised by Article 25 (1) of the Universal Declaration of Human Rights 1948, and Article 11 of the International Covenant on Economic, Social and Cultural Rights 1966. In addition, they exacerbate conflicts over land and lead to the criminalisation of social movements that defend agrarian reforms from below. As a result, serious human rights violations occur, including the murders of the peasants connected to such activities.[5]

Since the 1990s, transnational financial institutions have promoted the individual titling of land and the creation of marketable land rights as the key to addressing rural poverty and food insecurity. According to this neo-liberal approach, land markets ensure efficient allocation and any land reform must aim to facilitate market transactions related to land.[6] Mexico followed this approach, adopting an agrarian counter-reform that abolished the agrarian law principles of the Mexican Revolution. Along with other neo-liberal measures, this reform provoked the uprising of one of the most important contemporary social movements: the *Ejército Zapatista de Liberación Nacional* (EZLN, also referred to as [Neo-] Zapatistas).

Against the backdrop of financialisation and free market expansion, this chapter analyses the significance of land rights for the Zapatistas as well as the inter-relation between their demands and the transnational claims regarding land as a transnational social right. Section II proposes an analytical framework to understand the historical Mexican struggle for the right to land, especially the Zapatista struggle, as an essential part of the struggle for transnational social rights. Section III describes the uprising of 1994 and the movement itself. Sections IV and V analyse the principles of Mexican revolutionary agrarian law and the break with these principles by the neo-liberal agrarian counter-reform. Finally, Section VI discusses the transnational dimension of the Zapatista struggle.

---

4 Olivier De Schutter, *Interim Report of the Special Rapporteur on the Right to Food*, submitted in accordance with General Assembly Resolution 64/159, 11 August 2010, p. 5 *et seq.*

5 De Schutter, note 4 above, p. 3 & 7; see the example below, Section IV.4.

6 Ibid., p. 9 *et seq.*

II. ANALITICAL FRAMEWORK: TRANSNATIONALISING THE MEXICAN STRUGGLE FOR THE RIGHT TO LAND

According to the hegemonic narrative of global history, all social innovations and evolutionary achievements are triggered by European peoples. Democracy was invented in Athens; bureaucracy in Rome; the modern state and the industry were invented in Western Europe. The list goes on and reveals a firm belief in Europeans "as the makers of history".[7] According to James M. Blaut, this belief is accompanied by the "super theory" of *Eurocentric diffusionism.*[8] Given their rareness, inventions are seen by diffusionist anthropology as historical products of very few communities, and for this reason most societies change over time due to the spread of foreign inventions, rather than due to inventions of their own. Based upon such scientific treatment, the belief in the European historical prerogative acquires the condition of empirical truth. The resulting world model thus considers Europe to be the centre that transmits transformations to the rest of the world, which, in turn, is reduced to a receiving periphery. In this context, any account of the struggles of Mexican social movements must allocate them in a place of historical subalternity.

This background explains, for instance, how the Mexican Revolution (1910–1917), one of the main events in the history of social struggles, was converted into a caricature in which the protagonists are represented as *bandidos.*[9] As part of his critique of *Orientalism*, Edward Said shows that this deformation is a European device to manufacture its own identity and superiority, which becomes a strategy of domination.[10] A culturalist elaboration which is disguised as universal, Eurocentrism is nevertheless anchored in objective conditions, namely, modern colonialism.[11] It is, as shown by Amin Samir, an ideology of world capitalism that allows for its expansion and occupation of regions across the globe.[12] In this sense, the Eurocentric diffusionism is a *coloniser's model.*[13]

7 James M. Blaut, *The Colonizer's model of the World: Geographical Diffusionism and Eurocentric History*, (New York: The Guilford Press, 1993), p. 1 *et seq.* The expression "Europe" is used in the same sense as Blaut uses it, that is, as a representation of a world region that monopolises the notions of rationality, civilisation and democracy. In this sense, it evidently includes Canada and the United States. It is, in other words, a synonym for the "West". Nevertheless, resorting to "Europe" is still valid for the purpose of binding or tying the image of the "West" to its historical-symbolic origin.

8 Ibid., p. 8 *et seq.*

9 Zuzana M. Pick, Constructing the Image of the Mexican Revolution: Cinema and the Archive, (Austin TX: University of Texas Press, 2010), p. 50 *et seq.*

10 Edward W. Said, *Orientalism*, (London: Penguin Books, 2003), p. 2 *et seq.*

11 Amin Samir, Eurocentrism: Modernity, Religion and Democracy: *A Critique of Eurocentrism and Culturalism*, (New York: Monthly Review Press, 2009), p. 152 *et seq.*

12 Ibid., p. 239 *et seq.*

13 Blaut, note 7 above, p. 17 *et seq.*

One version of Eurocentric diffusionism is the human rights paradigm. Its standard narrative describes a timeline of events in which Europe is the centre of legal innovation for the world:[14] the Declaration of the Rights of Man and of the Citizen and the French Revolution; the Holocaust and the Universal Declaration of Human Rights; the emergence of social human rights and the Constitution of Weimar; the liberal multi-culturalism of North America and cultural rights. This universalisation of a very specific experience is only possible because of the humanist discourse that presents the cited events as inherent values of human nature. Notwithstanding its universal representation, the human rights paradigm reflects the discursive framework of the nation state, which produces a provincial and nationalist interpretation of global legal history. According to Dipesh Chakrabarty, this global legal history is intended to project a "hyperreal Europe".[15] Therefore, even though the struggling experience of Mexican peasants and indigenous people is considered to be a human rights paradigm in several spaces,[16] this projection of a hyperreal Europe erases or exoticizes their potential, because Mexico is located beyond the frontiers of the European nation states. Allocated in a peripheral position, the non-European is thus locked in a "zone of non-being" of the global legal community,[17] reduced to either applying the rights conveyed by Europe or reproducing a nativist or tribalist understanding.

Accordingly, the human rights paradigm is an ideology that conceals the protagonist role of the non-European in modern legal achievement and therefore erases the non-European agency from the global legal history.[18] For this reason, as maintained by José-Manuel Barreto, human rights seem to arise solely from the resistance of (European) citizens against the violence of their national

14 Antony Anghie, "Finding the Peripheries: Sovereignty and Colonialism in Nineteenth-Century International Law", (1999) 40 *Harvard International Law Journal*, p. 20 *et seq*; R.P. Arnand, *Confrontation or Cooperation? International Law and the Developing Countries*, (The Hague: Kluwer Academic Publisher, 1987), p. 15 *et seq*; José-Manuel Barreto, "Decolonial Strategies and Dialogue in the Human Rights Field: A Manifesto", (2012) 3 *Transnational Legal Theory*, p. 3 *et seq*; Mohammed Bedjaoui, "Poverty of the International Order", in: Richard Falk, F. Kratochwil, and S.H. Mendlovitz (eds), *International Law: A Contemporary Perspective*, (Boulder CO: Westview Press, 1985), p. 153 *et seq*; Surya Prakash Sinha, *Legal Polycentricity and International Law*, (Durham NC: Carolina Academic Press, 1996), p. 15 & 35 *et seq*.

15 Dipesh Chakrabarty, *Provincializing Europe: Postcolonial Thought and Historical Difference*, (Princeton NJ: Princeton University Press, 2000), p. 27 *et seq*. This hyperreal Europe is projected both by the European imperialist historicism and by the nationalist narratives of the (former) colonies, which accept the idea of Europe as a bulwark of modernity and seek to establish national equivalents in their own countries (D. Chakrabarty, p. 7 *et seq*).

16 Paolo G. Carozza, "From Conquest to Constitutions: Retrieving a Latin America Tradition of the Idea of Human Rights", (2003) 25 *Human Rights Quarterly*, p. 304.

17 On the concept of "zone of non-being", see Frantz Fanon, *Black Skin, White Masks*, (New York: Grove Press, 1988), p. 2.

18 Samir, note 11 above, p. 180; B.S. Chimni, "Third World Approaches to International Law: A Manifesto", (2006) 8 *International Community Law Review*, p. 15 *et seq*.

states.[19] As a result, the human rights paradigm renders invisible five hundred years of legal knowledge and practice, from multiple source regions, of colonial domination, imperialism, hegemonic ethnicities, *etc.*[20] From this perspective, such a paradigm becomes an instrument of modern colonialism: by proclaiming Europe's alleged superiority on the civilising legal scale, and omitting the role of the non-European in the global repertoire of the struggle for rights, it produces the ideological conditions needed to expand the political and economic interests of the European élite.[21]

Among the instruments of resistance to this expansion, social and economic rights as well as cultural and minority rights no doubt occupy a prominent place. They are clearly part of the global fight against inequality. Yet their dominant account is not exempt from Eurocentric diffusionism: the second-generation human rights framework is attributed to the Weimar Constitution, while the consolidation of the said framework is associated with both the movement of European workers and the European welfare state.[22] At the same time, the human rights of minorities are seen as a decision made by Western democracies, which "'internationalize[d]' the treatment of national minorities"[23] in response to the ethnic wars in the post-Communist era. This line of thought ignores the fact that the Mexican Constitution of 1917 inaugurated the constitutional recognition of social and economic rights worldwide, decisively influenced the Universal Declaration of Human Rights (including Article 23), and inspired and still continues to inspire social constitutions in several countries.[24] Likewise, the said argumentation fails to recognise that the indigenous movements in Mexico played an important role in the development of ILO Convention 169, and that its re-appropriation by Zapatismo against neo-liberal reforms converted the

19 Barreto, note 14 above, p. 4.

20 Ibid., p. 3 *et seq.* See, also, Guilherme Leite Gonçalves and Sérgio Costa, "The Global Constitutionalization of Human Rights: Overcoming Contemporary Injustices or Juridifying Old Asymmetries?", (2016) 64(2) *Current Sociology*, pp. 311-331.

21 On the relationship between Eurocentrism and the power of the European élite, see Blaut, note 7 above, p. 10.

22 Jürgen Habermas, "The Concept of Human Dignity and the Realistic Utopia of Human Rights", (2010) 41 *Metaphilosophy*, p. 468; idem, "Why Europe Needs a Constitution", in: Erik Oddvar Eriksen, John Erik Fossum, and Agustín José Menéndez (eds), *Developing a Constitution for Europe*, (New York: Routledge, 2004), p. 21; Norberto Bobbio, *The Age of Rights*, (Cambridge: Polity Press, 1996), p. 66.

23 Will Kymlicka, *Multicultural Odysseys: Navigating the New International Politics of Diversity*, (New York: Oxford University Press, 2007), p. 52 *et seq.*, and p. 61 *et seq*; Will Kymlicka, "The Evolving Basis of European Norms of Minority Rights: Rights to Culture, Participation and Autonomy", in: John McGarry and Michael Keating (eds), *European Integration and Nationalities Question*, (New York: Routledge, 2006), p. 36.

24 Carozza, note 16 above, p. 303 *et seq*; Fernando Yllanes Ramos, "The Social Rights Enshrined in the Mexican Constitution of 1917", (1967) 96 *International Labor Review*, pp. 591–592.

indigenous issue into a global issue, contributing to the definition of cultural human rights.[25]

The parochial and Eurocentric narratives are problematical for two reasons. On the one hand, they conceal collective actions, insurgencies and revolutions brought by issues of re-distribution and recognition. As exemplified by the above-mentioned experience of Mexican people, these issues developed in non-European spaces and are a part of the global legal culture, both for their impact on (global) spheres of power and for their intervention in creating transnational organisations and legal norms. On the other hand, parochial narratives disregard the *entanglements* between the inequalities and struggles present in Europe and in other world regions – Europe's former colonies.[26] In a field as dependent on participation as that of social and cultural rights, Eurocentric diffusionism undermines any incentive for mobilisation in non-European sectors. After all, it ascribes to these sectors a condition of backwardness in the scale of rights, condemning them to reproduce a set of prescriptions to reach the stage allegedly reached by Western countries exclusively due to their own (rational) efforts. Further on, we will see that this is exactly the rhetoric employed by the neo-liberal ideology to set *the* ("rational") recipe for development, using institutions such as the World Bank. In the Mexican case, this discourse is used to undermine the alternative legal policies of peasants and indigenous people.

In order to render visible the decisive role of these Mexican struggles in building a global culture of social and cultural rights, it is necessary to adopt de-colonisation strategies that include the de-parochialisation and universalisation of the universal legal discourse.[27] Concretely, this de-colonising strategy of "universalising the universal"[28] involves elucidating the role of the Mexican Revolution and of Zapatismo in the global construction of social and cultural rights.

However, such an approach is conditioned to an analytical framework capable of overcoming the nationalist and provincial character upon which the legal Eurocentric diffusionism is based. This framework allows for the existence of a "hyperreal Europe" while simultaneously concealing the participation of non-European sectors – such as Mexican peasants and indigenous people –

25 Alison Brysk, *From Tribal Village to Global Village: Indian Rights and International Relations in Latin America*, (Stanford CA: Stanford University Press, 2000), pp. 158–159; Courtney Jung, "The Politics of Indigenous Identity: Neoliberalism, Cultural Rights, and the Mexican Zapatistas", (2003) 70 *Social Research*, p. 449 *et seq.*

26 Shalini Randeria, "Entangled Histories of Uneven Modernities: Civil Society, Caste Solidarities and Legal Pluralism in Post-colonial India", in: Yehuda Elkana, Ivan Krastov, Elisio Macamo and Shalina Randeria (eds), *Unraveling Ties: From Social Cohesion to New Practices of Connectedness*, (Frankfurt aM: Campus Verlag, 2002), pp. 284–311. See, also, Sérgio Costa, "Researching Entangled Inequalities in Latin America. The Role of Historical, Social and Transregional Inequalities", 9 *DesiguALdades.net Working Paper Series*, p. 6 *et seq.*

27 Barreto, note 14 above, p. 11 *et seq.*

28 Ibid., p. 12.

in global legal policy. Its nationalist character appears both in universalist European narratives and in nativist projects from the rest of the world:[29] in spite of the inverted signs (positive for the former, negative for the latter), both narratives relegate legal cosmopolitanism to the European spectrum. The question is therefore how to reverse this process and unveil the history of Mexican law in the global history of social and cultural rights.

The desired reversion can be offered by the *transnational approach*.[30] On the one hand, this approach implies a re-orientation of the observation field for non-state actors with transboundary constitution and operation, such as the global networks of social movements, multinational corporations, global financial systems and international institutions. On the other, it may allow a re-interpretation of the action of national governments in the light of their global interconnections. When it comes to the law, the transnational approach assumes that legal regimes are promoted from sector to sector by integrating several levels (from local to global), in multiple legal and political arenas that go beyond national frontiers.[31] By questioning the naturalisation of the nation state as an analytical unit, the said approach breaks with the nationalism that fosters the Eurocentrism present both in European provincialism and in the rest of the world's nativism.[32] From this perspective, the historical struggle of Mexican peasants and indigenous people for rights ceases to be a nationalist account – it is no longer an import of European ideas or a manifestation of a particular culturalism. In the light of their global impact, the protagonists of these struggles re-emerge as transnational political actors participating in the global production of law.

The concept of transnational law derives from a broader understanding of globalisation, according to which the recent increase in social relationships generates a world social order with multiple centres and levels. Though this order amplifies the importance of non-state actors and re-positions state actors as elements of global standardisation, the main players sustain their hegemony over the transnational legal policy, as shown by Andreas Fischer-Lescano and Kolja

29 Chakrabarty, note 15 above, p. 7 *et seq*.

30 This approach involves a multitude of schools of thought, such as dependency theory, world-system theory, post-colonial studies and theories of globalisation and world society. See, among others, Laura Briggs, Gladys McCormick and J.T. Way, "Transnationalism: A Category of Analysis", (2008) 60 *American Quarterly*, pp. 625–648; Linda Basch, Nina Glick Schiller and Cristina Szanton Blanc, *Nations Unbound: Transnational Projects, Postcolonial Predicaments, and Deterritorialized Nation-States*, (New York: Gordon and Breach Publishers, 1994), p. 1 *et seq*; Sarah J. Mahler, "Theoretical and Empirical Contributions Toward a Research Agenda for Transnationalism", in: Michael Peter Smith and Luis Eduardo Guarnizo (eds), *Transnationalism from Below: Comparative Urban and Community Research*, Vol. 6, (New Brunswick-London: Transaction Publisher, 2006), p. 64 *et seq*.

31 Fischer-Lescano and Möller, note 3 above, p. 24 *et seq*.

32 Andreas Wimmer and Nina Glick Schiller, "Methodological Nationalism, the Social Science, and the Study of Migration: An Essay in Historical Epistemology", (2003) 37 *International Migration Review*, p. 576.

Möller.[33] This hegemony derives from legal arrangements (such as contracts signed under the *Lex Mercatoria*) and judicial forums (such as the IMF, the WTO and the World Bank) designed to protect the free market and its interests.[34] In opposition to this scenario emerges the need for transnational social rights, that is, a counter-hegemonic agenda that creates alternative institutions and mobilises the available body of transnational social norms – such as the UN covenants and the Core Labour Standards of the ILO – to confront the inequalities inflicted by the liberal market regime.[35]

From the perspective of non-European peoples, this transnational context is hardly new. Instead, it occupies a determining space in the history of modern (neo-) colonialism. According to José-Manuel Barreto, non-state actors (such as enterprises) and their cross-border legal commitments have been "key figures" of this history.[36] While the occupation and looting of the colonies would not have been possible without conquerors and pirates acting as "quasi one-man enterprises", investor associations – such as the East India Companies or the East Africa Companies – truthfully inaugurated the colonial empires.[37] These companies were active in the global markets of spices, precious metals, opium, and human beings, establishing transnational rules invoked to promote trade wars and genocides.[38] Today, private conglomerates continue to be the key players in the expropriation of peasants and indigenous communities from their land, including the exploitation of natural resources.

These conglomerates are entirely committed to the neo-liberal accumulation. Since 1982, neo-liberal policies in Mexico have increased the concentration of wealth, eroded the purchasing power of workers and destroyed the peasant agriculture model of the 1917 Revolution.[39] This process is motivated by interests of US firms in Mexico as well as by the consolidation of NAFTA.[40] By opening the Mexican market to the US agribusiness, NAFTA led to the dismantling of the Mexican organism for coffee market control (INMECAFE), the withdrawal of subsidised corn prices and the erosion of the market power of the peasants' products.[41] When it comes to coffee, a sector in which 70 per cent of the producers were small farmers, the price fell by 50 per cent.[42] In the case of corn, the rise in input prices was accompanied by a fall in rural credits.[43] These effects

33 Fischer-Lescano and Möller, note 3 above, p. 24-25.
34 Ibid., p. 16.
35 Ibid., p. 13-14.
36 Barreto, note 14 above, p. 14.
37 Ibid., p. 14.
38 Ibid., pp. 14–15.
39 Richard Stahler-Sholk, "Globalization and Social Movement Resistance: The Zapatista Rebellion in Chiapas, Mexico", (2001) 23 *New Political Science*, p. 506 *et seq.*
40 Jung, note 25 above, pp. 439–440.
41 Stahler-Sholk, note 39 above, p. 507.
42 Ibid., p. 507.
43 Ibid., p. 507; Jung, note 25 above, p. 440.

are aggravated by the fact that international loans are conditioned to structural adjustments seeking to replace the agrarian model of the 1917 Revolution by financial liberalisation.[44] Since the state of Chiapas is particularly characterised by agricultural and peasant production, it was the most affected by neo-liberal policies.[45]

In the next sections, we detail the impact of neo-liberal policies on the right to land of peasants and indigenous people in Mexico. This process is conditioned by a global standard of capitalist development, according to which the accumulation of capital always depends on the appropriation of non-capitalist spaces – that is, the commodification of spaces that had hitherto not been commodified – to ensure its expansion. At the macro-sociological level, Klaus Dörre conceptualised this phenomenon with the abstract category of *Landnahme* or *land grabbing*.[46] From a concrete perspective, the phenomenon of land grabbing is connected to the investment opportunities for financial capital as well as to the opening of new markets as as a response to the 2008 financial crisis. David Harvey shows that this process (abstractly or concretely) reflects the permanent repetition of primitive accumulation.[47] This means that land grabbing happens through explicit non-economic violence, that is, through robbery, theft, (neo-) colonisation and legal-political-regulatory coercion.[48] In the Mexican case, such violence is clearly linked to the amendment of Article 27 of the Constitution,[49] which prescribed the possibility of an agrarian reform (which we will analyse subsequently). Such amendment was prepared by NAFTA and had the effect of concentrating land in the hands of foreign investors. Its impact was particularly felt in Chiapas, where 27 per cent of the (unanswered) claims for the right to land come from.[50]

The contemporary dynamics of accumulation by dispossession and land grabbing (as observed in peasant and indigenous lands in Mexico) highlight what Andreas Fischer-Lescano and Kolja Möller call the hegemonic disciplining character of transnational law.[51] This character is enough to prove that the project of de-colonising human rights may succumb to the naïve hope of liberal radicalism whenever it is disconnected from a comprehensive critique of the

---

44 Jung, note 25 above, p. 441 *et seq*; Neil Harvey, "Playing with Fire: The Implication of Ejido Reform", (1994) 11(2) *Akwe:kon Journal of Indigenous Issues*, p. 20 *et seq.*

45 Harvey, note 44 above, p. 20 *et seq*; Dan La Botz, *Democracy in Mexico: Peasant Rebellion and Political Reform*, (Boston MA: South End Press, 1995), p. 25.

46 Klaus Dörre, "The New *Landnahme*: Dynamics and Limits of Financial Market Capitalism", in: Klaus Dörre, Stephan Lessenich and Hartmut Rosa (eds), *Sociology, Capitalism, Critique*, (London-New York: Verso Books, 2015), p. 24 *et seq.*

47 Harvey, note 1 above, p. 74 *et seq.*

48 Ibid., note 3 above, p. 74; Marx, note 2 above, pp. 874–875.

49 Jung, note 25 above, p. 440; La Botz, note 45 above, p. 25; Harvey, note above 44, p. 20 *et seq.*; Stahler-Sholk, note 39 above, p. 507.

50 Stahler-Sholk, note 39 above, p. 507.

51 Fischer-Lescano and Möller, note 3 above, p. 24-26.

law, as if "purifying" the legal system from Eurocentrism was enough for its normative appeal to come unconditionally to fruition. On the contrary, the creation and application of human rights depart from highly unequal conditions (expressed, for example, by the IMF or the World Bank when using the discourse of rights to grant credits or execute free trade policies).[52] Contrary to the postulates of legal idealism, it is only within these highly unequal conditions that a legal-political subaltern struggle can emerge – a struggle capable of articulating the complaints against Eurocentrism, the opposition to neo-liberalism, and the orientation towards emancipatory concerns. This implies re-reading the role of human rights from the perspective of a social totality, in which economy, politics and law are intertwined in contradictory processes of exploitation and resistance.[53]

From this perspective, the struggle of peasants and indigenous Mexicans for their land is also a struggle for transnational social rights against the legal-political-regulatory violence of accumulation by dispossession and of land grabbing, as implemented by transnational economic conglomerates. From the 1917 Revolution to (Neo-) Zapatismo, this struggle confronts the global spheres of power and the expansion of transnational capitalism, either in the form of imperialism (from the nineteenth to the twentieth century) or in the form of financial globalisation in the turn of the twenty-first century. In these two moments, the Mexican struggle was immediately anchored in the contest for the right to land; this contest, in turn, ultimately spread to other dimensions of the transnational social rights. In its first phase, it served as the driving force behind social constitutionalism as well as behind the claims for social, economic and cultural rights in the international human rights system throughout the twentieth century.

The 1994 Zapatista uprising occurred because of the land.[54] Its main objective was the defence of the peasant model of agrarian organisation as defined in Article 27 of the Mexican Constitution of 1917 by Emiliano Zapata.[55] Along with the struggle for the right to land, the Zapatistas presented a series of demands concerning the rights of indigenous peoples (non-discrimination, self-

---

52 Ibid., p.

53 The concept of social totality has a Marxian origin. This concept is presented in various passages, amongst which, in particular, is Karl Marx, *Grundrisse: Foundations of the Critique of Political Economy*, (Harmondsworth: Penguin, 1973), p. 494: "Not only do the objective conditions change in the act of reproduction, e.g., the village becomes a town, the wilderness a cleared field etc., but the producers change, too, in that they bring out new qualities in themselves, develop themselves in production, transform themselves, develop new powers and ideas, new modes of intercourse, new needs and new language."

54 Jesús Antonio de la Torre Rangel, "Liberación y Derecho: Pluralismo Jurídico y Resistencia", in: 7. Coloquio Academico, "Ni una vida más para la toga, Homenage a Franz Fanon", (Puerto Rico: Facultad de Derecho Eugenio María de Hostos, 2009), p. 8.

55 Jung, note 25 above, p. 440; La Botz, note 45 above, p. 25; Harvey, note 44 above, p. 20 *et seq.*; Stahler-Sholk, note 39 above, p. 507.

governance and respect for their traditions, culture and dignity) as well as the rights to education, training, health care and basic needs. This set of demands reflects the claims made by the Zapatista delegation during the so-called *Jornadas por la paz y la reconciliación*, held in San Cristóbal de las Casas in late February and early March 1994.[56] The corresponding document pleaded for the conservation of Article 27 (demand no. 8) and the revision of NAFTA (demand no. 7). In addition, it called for free and democratic elections (demand no. 1); the political, economic and cultural autonomy of indigenous communities (demand no. 4); the construction of hospitals (demand no. 9), housing, recreational centres, supply of public services and essential goods (demand no. 11); the eradication of illiteracy through public and free education (demand no. 12); combating the discrimination against indigenous peoples (demand no. 15); administration of justice based upon traditional practices and customs (demand no. 17); fair labour with decent pay (demand no. 18); *etc.* This framework, which combines several human rights dimensions, was repeated in the Agreements of San Andrés[57] and in several other manifestations of Zapatismo.

Andreas Fischer-Lescano and Kolja Möller emphasise the trend in recent codifications of fundamental and human rights of re-inforcing the conception of indivisible human rights.[58] The above-mentioned Zapatista claims confirm this tendency and show that the divisibility makes no sense from the point of view of social struggles and necessities, given that the various forms of precariousness are intertwined. However, the particular experience of Zapatismo re-conceptualises the terms of the discussion on the interdependence and the universality of human rights. According to this experience, the right to land is the radiating and unifying basis of all other rights. As shown by Jesús Antonio de la Torre Rangel, this right is the condition for the material support that enables the social development of the community and the maintenance of their cultural identity.[59] From this perspective, the Zapatista struggle against dispossession and land violation cannot be reduced to the state-society conflict upon which the dominant (and European) conception of human rights is based. Not only does the Zapatista perspective reveal another type of conflict based upon (neo-) colonialism, it also challenges the notion of a universal subject of rights. Franz Fanon summarises this re-orientation in the values of social struggle as follows:

> "For a colonized people the most essential value, because the most concrete, is first and foremost the land: the land which will bring them bread and, above all, dignity.

---

56 See the communiqué of the EZLN from 1 March 1994 "Las Demandas Torales del EZLN", (The EZLN Demands Torales), available at: http://palabra.ezln.org.mx/comunicados/1994/1994_03_01_a.htm, last accessed 4 June 2015.

57 See *infra*.

58 Fischer-Lescano and Möller, note 3 above, p. 28-31.

59 Rangel, note 54 above, p. 8.

But this dignity has nothing to do with the dignity of the human individual: for that human individual has never heard tell of it."[60]

The land of Mexican peasants and indigenous people has been historically invaded, dispossessed, violated and plundered by global spheres of power, such as imperialism, colonialism and financial speculation. Zapatismo has become a model for collective transnational action, connected to different networks,[61] and mobilising a set of transnational rights to ensure its autonomy over the land. The prime example of such action was the successful claim to implement ILO Convention 169 in Mexico – a guarantee of autonomy for indigenous communities.[62]

Zapatismo proposes the re-conceptualisation of human rights, binding them to an autonomous project that radically differs from the hegemonic legal regime.[63] In the next sections, we will analyse in detail the various historical stages in which this struggle has been carried out by peasants and indigenous peoples in Mexico.

III. THE UPRISING OF THE EZLN AND THE RIGHT TO LAND

On 1 January 1994, the same day that the NAFTA entered into force, a social movement dominated by Chiapanecan indigenous people started an armed uprising in Chiapas, one of the poorest states of Mexico. Presenting themselves as the *Ejército Zapatista de Liberación Nacional*, they marched from the Lacandon Jungle to one of the larger cities of Chiapas, San Cristóbal de Las Casas, occupied government buildings and other towns nearby,[64] and pronounced the "First Declaration of the Lacandon Jungle" with the title "*¡Hoy decimos basta!*" ("Today we say: Stop!").[65] The following excerpts of the Declaration summarise the critique of the EZLN and their demands, which mainly refer to social rights:

60 Franz Fanon, *The Wretched of the Earth*, (New York: Grove, 1963), p. 44.

61 Thomas Olesen, "Globalising the Zapatistas: From Third World Solidarity to Global Solidarity", (2004) 25 *Third World Quarterly*, p. 259 *et seq.*

62 Brysk, note 25 above, pp. 158–159; Gemma van der Haar, "The Zapatista Uprising and the Struggle for Indigenous Autonomy", (2004) 76 *European Review of Latin America and Caribbean Studies*, pp. 100–101; Jung, note 25 above, p. 445 *et seq*; Rangel, note 54 above, p. 15 *et seq.*

63 Shannon Speed, *Rights in Rebellion: Indigenous Struggle and Human Rights in Chiapas*, (Stanford CA: Stanford University Press, 2008), p. 39.

64 Gloria Muñoz Ramírez, *20 y 10 – el fuego y la palabra*, (Mexico City: La Jornada Ediciones, 2003), p. 85 *et seq*; Carlos Tello Díaz, *La Rebelión de las Cañadas*, reprint, (Mexico City: booklet, 2006) p. 15 *et seq.*

65 Primera Declaración de la Selva Lacandona: "*¡Hoy decimos basta!*" in: Subcomandante Insurgente Marcos, *Nuestra arma es nuestra palabra*, (Mexico City: Siete Cuentos, 2001), p. 13 *et seq.*

> "[The élite] have been extracting the wealth of our country and don't care about the fact that we have nothing, absolutely nothing, not even a roof over our heads, no land, no work, no health care, no food, no education. Nor are we able to elect our political representatives freely and democratically, nor is there independence from foreigners, nor peace, nor justice for ourselves and our children. [...] We, men and women, sincere and free, are conscious that the war that we are declaring is our last resort, but also that it is a just one. The dictators have been waging a non-declared war of genocide against our people for many years, and therefore we ask for your uncompromising participation to support this plan of the Mexican people which struggles for work, land, housing, food, health care, education, independence, freedom, democracy, justice and peace. We declare that we will not stop fighting until these basic demands of our people are satisfied [...]."[66]

Formed in the 1980s as a small guerrilla group in the Lacandon Jungle, the EZLN was initially dominated by left-wing students. They were gradually joined by indigenous people, who had been struggling for their rights for decades and possessed significant practical experience of a political organisation. In consequence, the struggle against being marginalised and against the poverty of indigenous people became the central engagement of the EZLN; indigenous approaches towards nature and indigenous communalism were united with a socialist critique on hegemonic neo-liberal politics and individualism; communal political and social structures influenced their organisation and decision-making processes.[67]

For many years, the EZLN continued its political work in the shadows of the Lacandon Jungle and was continuously joined by more activists. In 1992, the social and political conflicts in Chiapas intensified with the NAFTA negotiations and the neo-liberal Agrarian Counter-Reform of 1992. In huge manifestations, peasants and indigenous peoples criticised the privatisation of agrarian land and the abolition of land re-distribution as an attack on their most important right: the right to land, as laid down in Article 27 of the 1917 Mexican Constitution. Although reality had always lagged the aims of Article 27, this provision had given the peasants a legal possibility of receiving land and insisting on their demands. The Agrarian Counter-Reform brought these possibilities to an end and definitely rejected the peasants' most elementary needs. In this context, social protests increased, the EZLN gained more and more support, and the state repression against the protests brought forth the increasingly insistent idea that an armed struggle was necessary to defend their interests.[68]

---

66 In this article, all English versions of the original Spanish are translated by the authors.

67 Tello Díaz, note 64 above, p. 110 *et seq*; Subcomandante Marcos, quoted in Carlos Montemayor, *Chiapas: La rebelión indígena de México*, reprint, (Mexico City: Debolsillo, 2009), p. 156 *et seq.*

68 Tello Díaz, note 64 above, p. 168 & 179 *et seq*; Subcomandante Marcos, quoted in Montemayor, note 67 above, p. 159.

As noted, the neo-liberal Agrarian Counter-Reform of 1992 was one of the main reasons for the uprising of 1994. Among other social rights, the demand for land is repeatedly mentioned in their Declarations of the Lacandon Jungle.[69] The EZLN demands to re-establish Article 27 of the Mexican Constitution in accordance with its original version, which was generated by the Mexican Revolution and was still in force before the 1992 Reform. Furthermore, they demand that the indigenous territories be protected in accordance with Convention 169 of the ILO.[70]

IV. RIGHT TO LAND IN REVOLUTIONARY AGRARIAN LAW

A. REVOLUTIONARY AGRARIAN LEGISLATION

The EZLN continues the struggle of social-revolutionary groups, which, at the end of the Mexican Revolution, had not prevailed against the liberal-*bourgeois* movements in military terms, but nevertheless had a strong influence on the revolutionary agrarian legislation.[71] Specifically, the EZLN refers to the agrarian programme of the indigenous peasant leader Emiliano Zapata.[72] In accordance with this programme, after the Agrarian Counter-Reform of 1992, they demanded that Article 27 should "retake the spirit of the struggles of Emiliano Zapata which may be summarised in two demands: 'The land belongs to those who cultivate it!' and 'Land and Freedom!'"[73] Thus, Adolfo Gilly argued that "Zapatismo is still the programme, direction and inspiring myth for the

69 They have issued six Declarations of the Lacandon Jungle, all available at: http://enlacezapatista.ezln.org.mx, partly published also in Marcos, note 65 above.

70 See the communiqué of the EZLN from 15 February 1996 "Diálogo de San Andrés y los Derechos y Cultura Indígena", (Dialogue in San Andrés on indigenous rights and culture) available at: http://palabra.ezln.org.mx/comunicados, last accessed 7 December 2012, and part B.1 of the Acuerdos de San Andrés of 16 February 1996, in: Luis Hernández Navarro and Ramón Vera Herrera (eds), *Acuerdos de San Andrés*, 2 reprint, (Mexico City: Era Ediciones, 2004), p. 53 *et seq*. Regarding their critique on the Agrarian Counter-Reform 1992 in the context of international neo-liberal politics, see the Sixth Declaration of the Lacandon Jungle, (Sexta Declaración de la Selva Lacandona, June 2005), available at: http://enlacezapatista.ezln.org.mx/2005/11/13/sexta-declaracion-de-la-selva-lacandona, last accessed 5 January 2013.

71 As to the revolutionary movements, processes and results, see Adolfo Gilly, *La revolución interrumpida*, 2 reprint, (Mexico City: Ediciones Era, 2009).

72 Martha Chávez Padrón, *El derecho agrario en México*, 17 edn., (Mexico City: Porrúa, 2005), p. 257 & 260 *et seq*; Eduardo López Betancourt,*El derecho en México*, (Mexico City: Porrúa, 2007), p. 37.

73 See the communication of the EZLN from 15 February 1996, "Diálogo de San Andrés y los Derechos y Cultura Indígena", available at: http://palabra.ezln.org.mx/comunicados, last accessed 7 December 2012, and part B.1 of the Acuerdos de San Andrés of 16 February 1996, in: Hernández Navarro and Vera Herrera (eds), note 70 above, p. 53 *et seq*.

struggles of peasants and indigenous people in today's Mexico".[74] In 2011, rural and indigenous organisations commemorated Zapata's "Plan de Ayala of 1911", and insisted on the need to realise this plan.[75]

Revolutionary agrarian law was developed upon the basis of the Agrarian Law of 6 January 1915[76] (later elevated to constitutional level)[77] and Article 27 of the Constitution of 1917.[78] As noted above, the Constitution of 1917 was the first to guarantee social rights.[79] According to Gilly, it was the world's most progressive constitution at the moment of its adoption.[80]

The constitution strongly curbed liberal freedoms, particularly the freedom of contracts through labour law (Article 123) and the freedom of property through agrarian law (Article 27).[81] Given these provisions, the 1917 Constitution is not deemed to be a mere reform of the liberal 1857 Constitution, but is considered to be a new constitution.[82] According to Pastor Rouaix Méndez – a member of the constitutional assembly and of the commission that elaborated Article 27 and the first president of the National Agrarian Commission after 1917 – it was impossible to realise the necessary "radical modifications" of agrarian law within the framework of the 1857 Constitution, as this framework gave almost unlimited guarantees and protection to property rights according to classic liberalism and individualism. After the Revolution, a new legal basis was needed to implement a "revolutionary transformation". The leading idea of this transformation was that individual property rights were subject to the superior rights of the society: social distribution and sustainable use of land. Indeed, the central aim was social justice.[83]

---

74 Adolfo Gilly, in an interview on the occasion of the 100th anniversary of the Mexican Revolution in the Mexican daily newspaper *La Jornada*, 8 May 2010, p. 32.

75 See the reports of the Mexican newspaper *La Jornada* of 29 November 2011, p. 10: "López Obrador y unas 30 organizaciones firman el *Plan de Ayala para el siglo XXI*", and p. 14: "Calderón traicionó los ideales de la Revolución: Campesinos." The "Plan de Ayala" of 25 November 1911 is reprinted in Jesús Silva Herzog, *Breve historia de la Revolución Mexicana*, Vol I, 19 reprint, (Mexico City: Fondo de Cultura Económica, 2007), p. 309 *et seq*.

76 Law of 6 January 1915 which declares void all transactions over land, water and mountains of rural communities, which were granted contrary to the Law of 25 June 1856, reprinted in Jesús Silva Herzog, *Breve historia de la Revolución Mexicana*, Vol II, 18 reprint, (Mexico City: Fondo de Cultura Económica, 2004), p. 203 *et seq*.

77 Article 27, Part VII, Paragraph 3, Constitution 1917 (original version).

78 Constitución Política de los Estados Unidos Mexicanos que reforma la de 5 de febrero del 1857, Diario Oficial Federal, 5 February 1917. In general, the cited constitutional articles in Section II describing revolutionary agrarian law refer to their original version; with regard to its main principles, this version did not change until the Reform of 1992.

79 Marco Antonio Díaz de León (ed), *Historia del derecho agrario mexicano*, (Mexico City: Porrúa, 2002), p. 324, 330, 478 & 884 *et seq*; Chávez Padrón, note 72 above, p. 256.

80 Gilly, note 71 above, p. 256.

81 Díaz de León, note 79 above, p. 493.

82 Gilly, note 71 above, p. 256.

83 Pastor Rouaix Méndez, "Génesis de los Artículos 27 y 123 de la Constitución Política de 1917, 1945", in: Díaz de León (ed), note 79 above, pp. 303–310, at 308 *et seq*.

The centrepieces of revolutionary agrarian law and of the EZLN's agrarian demands are land re-distribution by expropriation and communal forms of land tenancy, which are termed "social property". An important legal concept in this regard is the "original property of the nation" in terms of land and water. This concept extends the principle of *dominio eminens*, known in Mexican land law since colonial times. It means that all land and water originally belong to the Crown, the Republic and, finally, to the nation; hence, in general, they belong to the sovereign. In revolutionary agrarian law, the highest right to the land of the sovereign is considered to be the legal basis for expropriating and limiting property rights for social purposes.[84] In sum, property was declared to be deduced from the nation, and the nation holds the right to place limitations on it and make modifications to it.[85]

At first glance, the revolutionary Constitution of 1917 seems to protect property in the same way as the liberal Constitution of 1857. This, however, is an illusion. According to Article 27, Paragraph 2, expropriation is allowed only for public benefit and against indemnification. However, realising socially just land distribution was considered a public benefit and could therefore justify expropriation. Thereby, the Constitution of 1917 made expropriation and land re-distribution possible for social purposes. Accordingly, Article 27, Paragraph 3 conferred on rural communities the right of *dotación*, which meant that they were entitled to receive both the land and the water that they needed as a means of existence. If necessary, the land could be taken from huge land holdings by expropriation. The wording of this article reads as follows:

> "Article 27. Paragraph 3. The nation has at any time the right to apply modalities to private property which public interest demands, [...] in order to realise a just distribution of public wealth and its protection. This aim requires measures to break up large land holdings, to foster small property, to create rural communities with the necessary extent of land and water, to promote agriculture and avoid the destruction of nature [...]. The towns and communities which lack the land and water necessary for their people are entitled to receive land by *dotación*. The required land shall be taken from adjacent estates, but small properties[86] must be protected at all time. [...]"

---

84 Commentary to the proposal for Article 27, submitted to the constituent assembly, reprinted in Díaz de León, note 79 above, p. 504; referring to this commentary are Chávez Padrón, note 72 above, p. 296, and Mario Ruiz Massieu, *Derecho Agrario Revolucionario*, (Mexico City: Porrúa, 1987), p. 214 *et seq*.

85 Article 27, Paragraph 1 and 3, Constitution of 1917.

86 The term "small property" (*pequeña propiedad*) refers to land property, the extent of which does not supersede a certain limit. These limits are determined by the quality, characteristics and cultivation of the respective land. See, for example, Article 14 of the Reglamento Agrario de 10. Abril 1922, Diario Oficial Federal of 18 April 1922, reprinted in Díaz de León, note 79 above, p. 360 *et seq*; Article 105 of the Ley de dotaciones y restituciones de tierras y aguas, Diario Oficial Federal of 27 April 1927, reprinted in Díaz de León, note 79 above, p. 396 *et seq*; Article 51 Código Agrario 1934; Article 173 Código Agrario 1940; Article 104 Código Agrario 1942; and Article 249 Ley Federal de la Reforma Agraria 1971. According to a constitutional

Based upon the proceedings of *dotación*, land was assigned to a rural community that did not possess any land title – an aspect that distinguished the *dotación* from the *restitución*, another legal institution introduced by Article 27. By *restitución*, rural (above all, indigenous) communities received the land of which they had been illegally dispossessed in the decades before the Mexican Revolution. If a demand of *restitución* was not allowed because of the lack of a valid title, the proceedings were automatically converted into the proceedings of *dotación*.[87]

New legal concepts of tenancy called "social property" emanated from the proceedings of restitution and re-distribution provided by Article 27. Land, wood and water exploited in common by rural communities were all subject to "social property". Typically, these communities had received the respective land by *dotación* or *restitución*. They were considered associations with legal personality and had a democratic organisation. Revolutionary agrarian law identified two community types: the *ejido* (a product of a *dotación*) and the *comunidad* (a product of *restitución* or, if communities had not been dispossessed previously, of a confirmation act).[88]

Furthermore, the Constitution of 1917 stipulated that only Mexicans were entitled to acquire land and water. Foreigners could obtain such permission provided they "waived their nationality" in relation to the land. This meant that they would not call upon their home country to protect their land. In no case could foreigners acquire land within 100 kilometres of the frontier or 50 kilometres of the coast.[89]

In the first years after the Mexican Revolution, the agrarian legislation was casuistic and unsystematic.[90] After the short-lived Law of Ejidos of 1920,[91] the first codification aiming at a comprehensive and systematic regulation of agrarian law was implemented in 1934 (*Código Agrario* 1934). Further codifications followed in 1940, 1942 and 1971 (*Código Agrario* 1940, *Código Agrario* 1942, *Ley Federal de la Reforma Agraria* [LFRA] 1971),[92] and Article 27 of the Constitution of 1917 was reformed several times. However, the main structures and principles of revolutionary agrarian law, which are the subject of this chapter, remained unchanged until 1992.

reform of 1934 (Diario Oficial Federal of 10 January 1934), small property was protected only if it was actually cultivated (see Article 27 Part XV Paragraph 3 after this reform).

87 Article 27 Part VII Paragraph 3 Constitution of 1917, Article 1 Ley Agraria 1915.

88 For more information on *ejidos* and *comunidades* and the respective references, see Section III.2.

89 Article 27, Part I, Constitution of 1917.

90 Overview in Díaz de León, note 79 above, p. 314 *et seq.*, 325 *et seq.*, & 346 *et seq.*

91 Ley de Ejidos of 30 December 1920, reprinted in Díaz de León, note 79 above, p. 346 *et seq.* This law was in force for only 11 months. The law with which it was abrogated is reprinted in Díaz de León, note 79 above, p. 358 *et seq.*

92 All codifications are reprinted in Díaz de León, note 79 above, p. 586 *et seq.*

B. SOCIAL LAW AND LEGAL "SOCIALISATION"

Revolutionary agrarian law was developed upon the basis of revolutionary agrarian legislation and became an autonomous branch of law. This field of law is considered a part of the so-called social law ("*derecho social*"), which emanated from the Mexican Revolution. Apart from agrarian law, it comprises labour law and social security law. The constitutional basis of labour law (Article 123) resulted from the labour movement that participated in the Mexican Revolution and guaranteed fundamental rights such as the eight-hour day and the prohibition of child labour.[93]

Mexican legal literature describes social law as a branch of law that regulates relationships between different social groups, focusing on the interests of socially weaker groups and thereby protecting them. The main aim is to achieve social justice. Individuals are not abstract, but are, instead, considered parts of concrete social groups, such as peasants or workers. Thus, social law highlights any inequalities that might be disguised by the liberal conception of the isolated individual. In view of these inequalities, social law tries to transform the contradiction between the interests of different social groups in order to create social justice and freedom.[94]

Mexican legal doctrine places social law outside the classic distinction between private law and public law.[95] Hence, agrarian law goes beyond this dichotomy. Once land enclosure converted land into property, land property became a subject of private law, and private law was considered a sphere of private dispositions and free from state intervention. Limitations to the freedom of property became part of public law and had to be justified. This system had been adopted in Mexico after independence and was set aside by revolutionary agrarian law.

To solidify the characteristics of social law, Mexican literature refers to Gustav Radbruch,[96] who generated the concept of social law in opposition to "individualistic law". The point of reference of individualistic law is an isolated and abstract human being who actuates individually, self-interestedly and rationally, and thereby corresponds to the *homo economicus* of classic economics. Judicially, this concept becomes manifest in the legal subject, an egalitarian concept that comprises the poor and the rich, the weak and the strong. It annihilates all differences between persons, and connects the resulting

93 López Betancourt, note 72 above, p. 62 & 101 *et seq.*

94 Isaís Rivera Rodríguez, *El nuevo derecho agrario mexicano*, 2nd edn., (Mexico City: McGraw Hill, 2000), p. 4 *et seq*; Lucio Mendieta y Nuñez, *El Derecho Social*, (Mexico City: Porrúa, 1953), p. 49; Ruiz Massieu, note 84 above, p. 111, 114 *et seq.*, & 117 *et seq.*, with further references.

95 López Betancourt, note 72 above, p. 62 & 108; Chávez Padrón, note 72 above, p. 295; Ruiz Massieu, note 84 above, p. 113 & 116 *et seq*; Rivera Rodríguez, note 94 above, p. 4 *et seq.*

96 See, for example, Ruiz Massieu, note 84 above, p. 111.

"equality" with the freedom of property and contract. In social reality, this system allows for the interests of the socially stronger party to prevail over the interests of the socially weaker party. Material inequality is maintained and reproduced. In contrast, social law refers to persons in their social position, for example, as workers. The concept's point of reference is one's social status, rather than the idea of equality. In contrast, equality in the form of equalisation is the aim of social law. Accordingly, social law limits the rights of freedom and attaches different obligations to these rights.[97]

In the drafting history of the new agrarian law itself, no explicit reference to a foreign doctrine or law can be found.[98] On the contrary, the political actors involved were eager to stress the autochthonous origin of agrarian law and criticised the liberal legislation of the nineteenth century for having adopted foreign legislation and allegedly universal legal ideas (such as property) without taking the Mexican reality into consideration.[99] However, as seen above, the constitution of social rights, as triggered by the Mexican Revolution, is intertwined in the spheres of global inequalities and is a driver of the conception of transnational social law that was historically consolidated during the twentieth century. Amongst the many contributions to the formation of the so-called second-generation human rights, the Mexican experience emphasises the struggle for the right to land as a universal condition for the acquisition of social rights. In Section II, we have seen that this experience as a whole influenced many international treaties and constitutions worldwide.

Accordingly, revolutionary agrarian law forms part of the general "legal socialisation", a post-revolutionary process that was definitely inter-related with transnational developments. Pastor Rouaix Méndez argues that the new Constitution of 1917 expresses the ideas of social law in accordance with the new thinking of social and economic justice promoted throughout the world.[100] Similarly, in the 1920s, the commission in charge of drafting a new civil code argued that the aim of the new code was to "socialise" the individualistic character of civil law in accordance with the ideas of the Mexican Revolution and international legal developments. Thus, property should no longer be understood as an individual right, but as a social function. In this regard, the commission explicitly referred to the Constitution of Weimar and to the theories

97 Gustav Radbruch, "Vorschule der Rechtsphilosophie", in: idem (ed), *Gesamtausgabe Band 3, Rechtsphilosophie III*, (Heidelberg: C.F. Müller Verlag, 1990) (1948), p. 96 *et seq.*

98 Diario del Congreso Constituyente de Querétaro del 29, 30, 31 de enero 1917, Volume II, Nr 79, 80 (debate sobre el artículo 27); Rouaix Méndez, note 83 above, p. 303 *et seq.*

99 Proyecto de la Comisión de Diputados sobre el Artículo 27 de la Constitución, in Díaz de León, note 79 above, p. 502, at 504); Luis Cabrera (deputy and lawyer with strong influence on the revolutionary agrarian law), speech to the parliamentary assembly of 3 December 1912, in Díaz de León, note 79 above, p. 260 *et seq.*, at 265.

100 Rouaix Méndez, note 83 above, p. 308 *et seq.*

of the León Duguit.[101] Nevertheless, this openness to transnational dialogue on the part of the Mexican experience was not reciprocal, as it was not followed by the recognition of the Mexican struggles in promoting legal innovation for the transnational social law. On the contrary, as stated in Section II, this role was rendered invisible by a Eurocentric perspective on the development of rights.

C. SOCIAL PROPERTY: *EJIDOS* AND *COMUNIDADES*

1. *Characteristics*

The idea of property as a social function also determines the two central institutions of revolutionary agrarian law: the *ejido* and the *comunidad*. The *ejido* is a rural community arising from the proceedings of *dotación*, which expropriates land from large holdings and assigns it to a rural community in need.[102] The term "*ejido*" refers both to the community and to its communal land. Only Mexican citizens can be members of the *ejido*, and are called *ejidatarios*.[103]

The existence of *comunidades*, in turn, can be traced to earlier (typically pre-Hispanic) times. If these communities were dispossessed of their land after the liberal counter-reforms of the nineteenth century and have had it restored subsequently (*restitución*), they form a *comunidad* in terms of agrarian law.[104] If they still possess land, they may have it confirmed and may also be recognised as *comunidades*.[105]

---

101 Rodolfo Batiza, "Las fuentes de la codificación civil en la evolución jurídica de México", in: José Luis Soberanes Fernández and Instituto de Investigaciones Jurídicas de la Universidad Nacional Autónoma de México (eds), *Memoria del III Congreso de Historia del Derecho Mexicano* (1983), (Mexico City: Universidad Nacional Autónoma de México, 1984), pp. 155–162, at 158; Juan Carlos Marín in: Juan Carlos Geneyro, Antonio Azuela and Juan Carlos Marín (eds), *¿Por qué leer a Durkheim hoy?*, (Mexico City: Fontamara, 2009), pp. 103–130, at 103 *et seq.*, 119 & 123; Sara Montero Duhalt, "La Socialización del Derecho en el Código Civil de 1928", in: Jorge A. Sánchez-Dávila and Instituto de Investigaciones Jurídicas de la Universidad Nacional Autónoma de México (eds), *Libro del cincuentenario del Código Civil*, (Mexico City: Universidad Nacional Autónoma de México, 1978), pp. 157–176, at 161 *et seq*; Ernesto Gutiérrez y González, *El Patrimonio*, (Mexico City: Porrúa, 2008), p. 272 *et seq.*

102 Article 27, Paragraph 3, Constitution of 1917; Article 21, Código Agrario of 1934; Article 62, Código Agrario of 1940; Articles 50 ff, Código Agrario of 1942; Articles 195 ff, LFRA of 1971; Ruiz Massieu, note 84 above, p. 235 *et seq.*

103 Article 44 a Código Agrario of 1934; Article 163 I Código Agrario of 1940; Article 54, I Código Agrario of 1942; Article 200 I LFRA of 1971.

104 Article 27, Part VII, Paragraph 3 Constitution 1917; Article 20 Código Agrario 1934; Articles 59 ff Código Agrario 1940; Articles 46 f Código Agrario 1942; Articles 191 f LFRA 1971; Ruiz Massieu, note 84 above, p. 235 *et seq.*

105 Article 35 Código Agrario 1940; Article 33 Código Agrario 1942; Articles 356 ff LFRA 1971; Ruiz Massieu, note 84 above, p. 235 *et seq.*

Ejidos and *comunidades* are associations with legal personality[106] and legislative, administrative and controlling bodies of their own. According to the literature and the wording of the laws, "property"[107] in the land of *ejidos* and *comunidades* belongs to the communities as legal persons and not to individual members.[108] In fact, collective cultivation was the sole option envisioned by agrarian laws in the immediate aftermath of the Mexican Revolution. Only over time did legislation allow for individual cultivation.[109] Even in these cases of individual use, the land remains a property of the community.[110] The rights of the individual *ejidatarios* and *comuneros* are considered rights of usage and *usus fructus*, referring to the ideal parts of communal land or – if the land has been divided into individual parcels – to specific lots of land. Such lands cannot be rented and must be cultivated personally by the *ejidatarios* and *comuneros*.[111] A member who tries to sell, mortgage or rent his or her plot of land loses all his or her parcel rights.[112] The same applies if he or she leaves the parcel uncultivated for more than two years.[113]

Apart from the individual parcels, the *ejido* comprises different types of land that serve different purposes. For example, the *tierra de agostadero para uso común* (land for common pasture) cannot be cultivated and necessarily remains subject to common use. This also applies to woods and mountains.[114] The *parcela escolar* (school plot), in turn, provides research and teaching in the fields of general education, agriculture and rural economics.[115] The land specially

106 In the beginning, they were granted legal personality by federal agrarian laws and, in 1934, also by constitutional law (Article 27, Part VII, implemented by the constitutional reform published in Diario Oficial Federal of 10 January 1934); Chávez Padrón, note 72 above, p. 302.

107 The term "property" might lead to misunderstandings. This will be explained below, Section III.3.b.

108 Ruiz Massieu, note 84 above, p. 236 & 237; Raúl Lemus García, *Derecho Agrario Mexicano*, 7 edn., (Mexico City: Porrúa, 1991), p. 343 *et seq.* Article 120 Código Agrario 1940; Article 130 Código Agrario 1942; Article 51 LFRA 1971.

109 Primera ley reglamentaria sobre repartición de tierras ejidales y constitución del patrimonio parcelario ejidal de 19 de diciembre de 1925 (First law on the re-distribution of ejidal land and the constitution of the ejidal parcel of 19 December 1925), Diario Oficial Federal of 31 December 1925; Chávez Padrón, note 72 above, p. 335.

110 Article 52 LFRA 1971.

111 Article 123 Código Agrario 1940; Article 140 Código Agrario 1942; Articles 55, 76, 85 I LFRA 1971.

112 Article 140 V a Código Agrario 1934; Article 139 I Código Agrario 1940; Article 85 V LFRA 1971.

113 Article 140 VI b Código Agrario 1934; Article 139 II Código Agrario 1940; Article 169 Código Agrario 1942; Article 85 I LFRA; Ruiz Massieu, note 84 above, p. 246 *et seq.*, & 292 *et seq.*

114 Ruiz Massieu, note 84 above, p. 255 *et seq*; Article 147 Código Agrario 1934; Articles 85 I, 86 II, 138 Código Agrario 1940; Articles 77, 80 I, 206 Código Agrario 1942; Articles 138, 221 LFRA 1971.

115 Article 133 II Código Agrario 1934; Articles 145 ff Código Agrario 1940; Articles 185 f Código Agrario 1942; Articles 102 f LFRA 1971.

dedicated to women helps guarantee a certain income and thereby economic independence.[116]

These are the most important characteristics that distinguish social property from civil law property. To protect land as a means of existence for the rural population, they remove land from the free market, so that land ceases to be a commodity.

2. *Legal Form*

As mentioned, the Mexican legal literature classifies the land of the *ejidos* and *comunidades* as "property" (*propiedad*) of the community. However, the literature notes that agrarian law "property" differs strongly from civil law property.[117] This difference is expressed by the term "social property" (*propiedad social*), as opposed to "private property" (*propiedad privada*). Sometimes, the "property" of the *ejidos* and *comunidades* is also called "property *sui generis*".[118] The commission that elaborated Article 27 of the Constitution of 1917 uses the term "*propiedad privada plena/perfecta*" (full/perfect private property) for civil law property and "*propiedad privada restringida*" (restricted private property) for the agrarian law "property" of the *ejidos* and *comunidades*.[119] Agrarian laws generally qualify the *ejidos* and *comunidades* as the "proprietors" (*proprietarios*) of their land.[120]

Although the term "property" is used for agrarian land communities, the characteristics of the *ejidos* and *comunidades* force the literature to modify the concept of property in this context. For example, Ruiz Massieu argues that the "property rights" of the *ejidos* and *comunidades* are not absolute rights, as the communities cannot dispose freely of their land.[121] Furthermore, the legal literature employs the term "relative property",[122] and argues that the "property *sui generis*" of agrarian communities does not correspond to the concept of property in Roman and natural law, as adopted by the Declaration of Human Rights and the Napoleonic Code.[123]

In addition to the dominant idea that the *ejidos* and *comunidades* have property rights to their land, we also find approaches in the literature and legal texts that do not use the concept of property. Instead, they use the notions of

---

116 Articles 103 ff LFRA 1971; Ruiz Massieu, note 84 above, p. 250 *et seq.*

117 See Ruiz Massieu, note 84 above, p. 273 *et seq*; Lemus García, note 108 above, p. 343 *et seq.*

118 Carlos Humberto Durand Alcántara, *El Derecho Agrario y el Problema Agrario en México*, (Mexico City: Porrúa, 2009) p. 261 *et seq.*

119 Commentary to the proposal for Article 27, submitted to the constituent assembly, reprinted in Díaz de León, note 79 above, p. 505.

120 Article 139 Código Agrario 1934; Article 120 Código Agrario 1940; Article 130 Código Agrario 1942; Article 51 LFRA 1971.

121 Ruiz Massieu, note 84 above, p. 276 & 315.

122 Díaz de León, note 79 above, p. 622.

123 Durand Alcántara, note 118 above, p. 262 & 272, footnote 8.

dominio directo and *dominio útil*, which have their origins in feudal land regimes. Carlos Humberto Durand Alcántara describes the *ejido* as a regime of simple land tenancy and possession ("*regimen de tenencia de la tierra*";"*simple posesión del suelo*") for purposes of use and exploitation, in which the nation keeps the *dominium directo* and assigns to the *ejidatarios* the rights of *usus fructus*.[124] Similarly, the National Agrarian Commission explained in 1921 that the *dominio* in the land was divided into two parts. First, the *dominio directo* is the right to control dispositions of land, in which the land remains with the nation to prevent the communities from losing the land by contract, prescription or other legal acts. Second, the *dominio útil* is the right to use and exploit the land which belongs to the communities.[125]

The dominant classification of the land of *ejidos* and *comunidades* as "property" is somehow misleading, above all because the respective land can neither be sold, nor rented, nor mortgaged. As the so-called "proprietor", the community cannot dispose of "its" land and is obliged to use it according to the pre-ordained purposes.

D. RIGHT TO LAND AS A FUNDAMENTAL SOCIAL RIGHT

Revolutionary agrarian law entitles rural communities to receive land according to their social and economic needs. The respective rights of the communities are social and collective rights which have their roots in the revolutionary demand "*¡Queremos tierra para todos, para todos pan!*" ("We want land for all, bread for all!"). The Constituent Assembly considered this slogan – originally proclaimed by the anarchistic revolutionary Ricardo Flores Magón – to be a utopia, but accepted it as a directive for constitutional legislation.[126] One of the members of the Assembly argued that the demand "Land for all!" had been the central device of the Revolution.[127]

Revolutionary aims included the social liberation of the people and the guarantee of a life lived with dignity. Flores Magón pointed out that "the French Revolution achieved the right to think, but not the right to live".[128] Indeed,

124 Ibid., p. 272, footnote 8, p. 273 & 274.

125 Circular Number 28 of 1 September 1921, quoted in Chávez Padrón, note 72 above, p. 334.

126 Ricardo Flores Magón, "Vamos hacia la vida", (1910) 5 *Regeneración*, p. 3; the original versions of the journal *Regeneración* are available at: www.archivomagon.net, last accessed 7 December 2012. (1910). Bojórquez, deputy and member of the constituent assembly, refers to this slogan in his speech in the constituent assembly, Diario del Congreso Constituyente of 29, 30 and 31 January 1917, Volume II, Nr 80, p. 785 & 786.

127 See the speech of the deputy Bojórquez, Diario del Congreso Constituyente of 29, 30 and 31 January 1917, Volume II, Nr 80, p. 785, and of the secretary Lizardi, ibid., Nr 79, p. 774 *et seq*.

128 Flores Magón, note 126 above.

with the term "living", he referred to a life with dignity that should include an appropriate economic and social basis. According to Pastor Rouaix Méndez, the constitutional principles of revolutionary agrarian law were based upon giving the peasant the "life of the citizen".[129] Similar arguments were advanced in the Constituent Assembly itself, for example, when it was argued that "rural workers who become proprietors achieve the independence and ease which they need to develop their intellectual and moral conditions".[130]

At transnational level, the struggle of Mexican peasants imported two fundamental consequences for expanding the horizon of the notion of rights. On the one hand, it denounced the limits of the liberal legal model and explained its inability to deal with re-distributive issues. In this fashion, it contributed decisively to creating the legal social model and conceiving transnational social law. On the other hand, it challenged the notion of a universal individual by exposing that material inequalities are re-produced from the power asymmetries already in existence, under the veil of formal freedom and equality between all people. The legacy of the Mexican struggles consists in emphasising that the fulfilment of a revolutionary agrarian programme is a fundamental condition for the affirmation of social transnational rights. There are no social rights without rights to land.

IV. THE NEO-LIBERAL REFORM OF 1992 AND NEW FORMS OF LAND-GRABBING

A. POLITICAL BACKGROUND

The realisation of the revolutionary agrarian programme has always been difficult because of the political and economic relationships of power. Nevertheless, in the early 1990s, when the neo-liberal agrarian reform was adopted and abrogated the re-distribution of land, over 50 per cent of agrarian land and more than 70 per cent of the woods were subject to the regime of the *ejidos* and *comunidades*.[131]

The background of the 1992 Agrarian Reform was dominated by the economic and debt crises of the 1980s. The productivity of the Mexican agrarian sector had decreased and most of the alimentation formerly produced by Mexican peasants had to be imported.[132] The government argued that the

129 Rouaix Méndez, note 83 above, quoted in Díaz de León, note 79 above, p. 310.

130 Speech of the secretary Lizardi, Diario del Congreso Constituyente of 29, 30 and 31 January 1917, Volume II, Nr 79, p. 775.

131 Ana de Ita, "Land Concentration in Mexico after PROCEDE", in: Peter Rosset, Raj Patel and Michael Courville (eds), *Promised Land: Competing Visions of Agrarian Reform*, (Oakland CA: Food First Books, 2006), pp. 148–164, at 149.

132 José Luis Calva, *La disputa por la tierra*, (Mexico City: Fontamara, 1993), p. 13 *et seq.*

decrease in production was due to the "rigid property regime" of the *ejidos*, which did not allow for investment.[133]

Critics of the Agrarian Counter-Reform reject this explanation and argue that it was a mistake to hold the *ejidos* responsible for the agrarian crises. The *ejidos* were also the basis of agrarian production in the past, when the Mexican agrarian sector was referred to as the "Mexican miracle" due to its high productivity. Hence, the tenancy structure of *ejidos* does not prevent productivity *per se*.[134] The decrease in agrarian production in the 1980s occurred due to general economic developments, in particular the decline of public agrarian support and the price erosion of agricultural products on the world market.[135] Also, a working paper by John Richard Heath of the World Bank (1990) argues that there is no evidence that the *ejidos* are less productive *per se* than agrarian land subject to private property. The decisive factors affecting the productivity of both forms of agrarian production are price and subsidy policies.[136]

In contrast, the Mexican government under President Salinas de Gortari insisted on the need to "modernise the agrarian sector". The notion of "modernisation" meant de-regulation, privatisation and opening the agrarian sector to transnational trade and competition. Accordingly, reforming the tenancy structures of agrarian land meant privatising agrarian land and subjecting it to the free market.[137]

These policies were closely connected to the NAFTA negotiations, to Mexico's public debt and the resulting influence of the transnational financial institutions, mainly the World Bank.[138] Hence, the Reform was also an adaptation of Article 27 of the Mexican Constitution of 1917 to the transnational normative order dominated by the neo-liberal politics of free trade and protecting investments.

The NAFTA liberalised the agrarian sector by eliminating tariff and non-tariff barriers. This resulted in severe competition problems for the Mexican agrarian sector, which was flooded by highly subsidised agrarian products from

---

133 Iniciativa de Reformas de 1992 al Artículo 27 Constitucional, reprinted in Díaz de León, note 79 above, p. 918 *et seq.*

134 Calva, note 132 above, p. 13 *et seq*; Durand Alcántara, note 118 above, p. 419.

135 Calva, note 132 above, p. 13 *et seq*. With regard to the adverse effects of reduced agrarian support, see, also, Alicia Puyana and José Romero, *Diez años con el TLCAN. Las experiencias del sector agropecuario mexicano*, (Mexico City: Flacso México/Colegio de México, 2005), p. 21, and Díaz de León, note 79 above, p. 870.

136 John Richard Heath, "Enhancing the Contribution of Land Reform to Mexican Agricultural Development", Working Paper of the Agriculture and Rural Development Department and Latin America and the Caribbean Regional Office of the World Bank, February 1990; World Bank Working Paper (1990) p. 1, 7, 45 *et seq.*, & 56.

137 Díaz de León, note 79 above, p. 868 *et seq*; Durand Alcántara, note 118 above, p. 414 & 418 *et seq*.

138 Durand Alcántara, note 118 above, p. 346 *et seq.*, 411 *et seq*; Calva, note 132 above, p. 73 *et seq*; Willem Assies, "Land Tenure and Tenure Regimes in Mexico: An Overview", (2008) 8 *Journal of Agrarian Change*, pp. 33–63, at 49 *et seq*; Chávez Padrón, note 72 above, p. 395 *et seq.*

the United States. The situation was aggravated by the fact that the Mexican government had started to reduce agrarian support even before the NAFTA was enacted.[139] Although the NAFTA does not include rules regarding the agrarian property regime, it influenced the Agrarian Counter-Reform in several ways. First, the opening of the agrarian sector to transnational trade and competition, and the privatisation of agrarian land stemmed from the same neo-liberal agrarian politics. Second, the agrarian property regime was actually an issue during the NAFTA negotiations. The United States in particular questioned the possibility of expropriating land for purposes of social re-distribution, the inalienability of the land of the *ejidos* and *comunidades*, and the strong restrictions on foreign investors acquiring agrarian land.[140] The long story of US interventions against Mexican revolutionary agrarian law continued; indeed, since 1917, Washington had been pressuring Mexican governments again and again to protect the landed property of US citizens and enterprises.[141]

The World Bank also influenced the Agrarian Counter-Reform of 1992. Heath's 1990 working paper includes a list of "recommendations" for the Mexican agrarian sector. According to this publication, the central problem of the *ejidal* land regime is the legal uncertainty caused by the prohibition of selling and renting of the land – a prohibition often infringed in practice.[142] Another problematical aspect is that many *ejidatarios* do not possess land titles, which prevents them from investing in improvements of their land.[143] Furthermore, Heath makes the criticism that the *ejidos* do not have access to the commercial credit market and depend on public credit systems that are allegedly paternalistic and inefficient.[144]

In this context, Heath criticises common use according to the typical argument advanced against the commons: the individual *ejidatario* does not feel responsible for the land used in common and exploits it according to his or her egoistic interests as much as he or she can, which leads to over-exploiting and exhausting the land. Hence, compared to land that is cultivated upon the basis of private property, productivity decreases. The same argument had already been brought forward by the defenders of the enclosure system against the commons in feudal England, and, following Garrett Hardin's "Tragedy of the Commons",[145] it still dominates the debate about the commons today. In all

---

139 Díaz de León, note 79 above, p. 868 *et seq*; Puyana and Romero, note 135 above, p. 21.

140 Calva, note 132 above, p. 76 *et seq*. See, also, Assies, note 138 above, at 49, and Chávez Padrón, note 72 above, p. 307 *et seq*.

141 Gilly, note 74 above, p. 259 *et seq*., & 351; Sergio Reyes Osorio, Rodolfo Stavenhagen, Salomón Eckstein and Juan Ballesteros, *Estructura Agraria y desarrollo agrícola en México: Estudio sobre las relaciones entre la tenencia y uso de la tierra y el desarrollo agrícola de México*, reprint, (Mexico City: Fondo de Cultura Económica, 1979), p. 27 *et seq*.

142 Heath, note 136 above, p. 4, 6, & 22 *et seq*.

143 Ibid., p. 44.

144 Ibid., p. 5, 35 *et seq*.

145 Garret Hardin, "The Tragedy of the Commons", (1968) 162 *Science*, pp. 1244–1247.

of these contexts, the defenders of private property allege that common land is over-exploited and treated without diligence, and that the users do not invest in the land due to lack of incentives.

Notwithstanding this, according to Heath's working paper, there is no evidence that an *ejido* would be less productive *per se* than private property,[146] except that *ejidal* land divided into parcels is preferred to land used in common. Heath also stresses the symbolic significance of the *ejidos*. They represent the Mexican Revolution and its heroes as well as the government's historical obligation towards the rural poor. Therefore, the total abolition of the *ejidos* could provoke resistance. As a result, he recommends not abolishing the institution, but substantially de-regulating it.[147] For this purpose, Heath concretely suggests issuing documents that prove the titles of the *ejidatarios* to their parcels, to permit the renting and leasing of *ejidal* land, as well as transferring the rights to the parcels from one *ejidatario* to another.[148] However, the expansive privatisation of agrarian land fulfilled by the 1992 Reform went well beyond these recommendations.

B. PRIVATISATION AND END OF LAND RE-DISTRIBUTION

The 1992 Reform brought about fundamental changes to Article 27 of the 1917 Constitution, including a new agrarian law (*Ley Agraria* 1992) that abrogated the LFRA 1971. The changes were so extensive that the agrarian law post-1992 was no longer called the "revolutionary agrarian law". In general, the agrarian law moved from social to civil and commercial law, as directly reflected in Article 2 *Ley Agraria* 1992, which stipulates the subsidiary application of civil and commercial law rules.

One of the most important and disputed changes refers to the re-distribution of land. The 1992 Reform abolished the possibility of expropriating land from large land holdings for the purposes of re-distribution. Concretely, it abolished the previously mentioned *dotación*. Hence, since the Reform of 1992, the limits to the so-called "small properties" are relevant only with regard to the general constitutional aims of fostering small properties and breaking up large land holdings.[149] These aims, however, are no longer accompanied by a legal entitlement either for individuals or

146 Heath, note 136 above, p. 1, 7, 45 *et seq.*, & 56.

147 Ibid., p. 55 *et seq.*

148 Ibid., p. 1, 6, 7 *et seq.*, 22, & 57 *et seq.*; Calva, note 132 above, p. 73 *et seq.*

149 See Article 27, Paragraph 3 of the Constitution of 1917 in the version of the Diario Oficial Federal of 6 January 1992 (which is still in force) in contrast to its original version (which corresponds to the version in force before the Reform of 1992. This was the version of the Diario Oficial Federal of 10 August 1987).

communities. Hence, they are hardly effective and do not bring about social re-distribution.

The second important change was the opening of social property to the transnational free market. With the Reform, different legal options to sell, rent, mortgage and prescribe *ejidal* land were implemented. Furthermore, *ejidal* land could now be converted to civil law property and detracted from the agrarian law regime.[150] The respective provisions of the *Ley Agraria* 1992 refer explicitly to the *ejidos* but, in large part, also apply to *comunidades*.[151] In detail, they stipulate that third persons (meaning persons who are not members of the community) can acquire rights of usage for both common land and in the parcels of an *ejido*.[152] This involves abolishing the obligation of the *ejidatarios* to cultivate the land personally.[153] Furthermore, the right of *usus fructus* in the *ejidal* land used in common and in the *ejidal* parcel can be transferred or pledged as security.[154] Thereby, the *ejidos* gain access to the private credit market, whereas, formerly, they could only receive public credits specially provided to the agrarian sector.[155]

Theoretically, the principle that the "property" in *ejidal* land is inalienable and imprescriptible, and that it cannot be subject to a mortgage, still applies.[156] In practice, companies can now acquire communal land, provided that the *ejido* and/or the *ejidatarios* acquire shares in the respective company in return.[157] Correspondingly, an individual *ejidatario* can assign his or her rights of use and *usus fructus* in his or her parcel to a company if, with this assignment, he or she acquires shares in this company.[158] All these assignments involve a change in the regime for the respective land. The rights held by companies in the land must also be rights of civil law or commercial law. After all, a company is a legal "person" not of agrarian law but of general civil and commercial law. Hence, the companies acquire civil law property rights or civil law rights of use. These rights are subject not to agrarian law but to civil and commercial law, and the

---

150 Article 27, Part VII, Paragraph 4 in the version of the Diario Oficial Federal of 6 January 1992 (version still in force at this writing).

151 The relevant articles in particular are Articles 20, 45, 46, 60 & 74 together with Articles 75, 79, 80 & 100 regarding the freedom of disposition and Articles 20, 48 *Ley Agraria* 1992 regarding the prescription. The wording of these articles mentions only *ejidos*; with regard to their application to *comunidades*, see Article 107 *Ley Agraria* of 1992.

152 Articles 45 and 79 *Ley Agraria* 1992. According to Articles 100, 107 this also applies to *comunidades*.

153 Armando López Nogales and Rafael López Nogales, *Ley Agraria Comentada*, (Mexico City: Porrúa, 2008), p. 132.

154 Article 46 *Ley Agraria* 1992.

155 López Nogales and López Nogales, note 153 above, p. 133.

156 Article 74 *Ley Agraria* 1992.

157 Article 75 *Ley Agraria* 1992. In accordance with Articles 100 and 107, this also applies to *comunidades*.

158 Article 79 *Ley Agraria* 1992.

ejido and/or the *ejidatarios* become(s) shareholders.[159] As a further possibility of disposition, the Reform of 1992 allows an *ejidatario* to transfer his or her rights in the parcel to another *ejidatario*.[160]

Moreover, the 1992 Reform enables the conversion of *ejidal* land into civil law property. In this context, the agrarian law provisions refer to civil law property as "*dominio pleno*" (full property). With this conversion, the respective land is also detracted from the agrarian law regime. Two proceedings can be distinguished: first, the conversion of an *ejidal* parcel into property by a decision of the *asamblea* and an application to the National Agrarian Register by the *ejidatario* concerned;[161] and second, the termination of the *ejidal* regime for the entire *ejido* by a decision of the *asamblea*, whereby the *ejidatarios* acquire the *ejidal* land proportionally in the form of civil law property.[162]

In addition, the Reform brought new rules to facilitate foreign investment. Companies can now acquire a land surface 21 times larger than the limits of the so-called "small property"; with regard to the shareholder, this applies different rules of proportionality.[163] Foreign shareholders must not hold more than 49 per cent of the capital, which represents the agrarian property of a company.[164]

Finally, the Agrarian Counter-Reform of 1992 was accompanied by programmes of land certification, entitled *Procede* and *Procecom*.[165] With these programmes, certificates are issued for common land and for parcels in order to guarantee legal certainty, facilitate dispositions over the land, and attract foreign investment.[166]

C. THE EXPLANATIONS AND AIMS OF THE GOVERNMENT

According to the Mexican government,[167] the 1992 Agrarian Counter-Reform is a response to the extreme poverty of the rural population and the low

159 López Nogales and López Nogales, note 153 above, p. 188 *et seq*. The authors use the term "*derecho común*", which, in this context, means the general private law in the sense of a law that is applied in general and not only to the agrarian land.

160 Article 80 *Ley Agraria* 1992.

161 Article 81 ff *Ley Agraria* 1992.

162 Article 29 *Ley Agraria* 1992.

163 Article 27 Part IV Constitution 1917 in the version of the Diario Oficial Federal of 6 January 1992; Articles 126, 129 *Ley Agraria* 1992.

164 Article 130 *Ley Agraria* 1992.

165 "Programa de Certificación de Derechos ejidales y Solares Urbanos", (Procede, Programme for the Certification of *ejidal* rights and *solares urbanos*); "Programa de Certificación de Derechos Comunales", (Procecom, Programme for the Certification of the rights of *comunidades*).

166 de Ita, note 131 above.

167 Iniciativa de Reforma de 1992 al Artículo 27 Constitucional, reprinted in Díaz de León, note 79 above, p. 918 *et seq*.

productivity of the agrarian sector. Specifically, the government notes that the rural population often violated the prohibitions of agrarian law in the past, renting and selling *ejidal* land in reaction to social misery. In fact, this practice often happened with the complicity of the responsible state authorities. Therefore, it should be legalised so that the peasants can dispose of their land upon a legal basis and with legal protection.[168] Moreover, the government argues that previous demands for land could no longer be satisfied due to population growth, therefore justifying the need for an agrarian counter-reform.[169]

In the end, these arguments are directed towards prompting poor peasants to transfer their land to those who are supposed to exploit the land more efficiently according to the capitalist and neo-liberal logic of profit – above all, because they have more capital and technology. Although it is not stated explicitly, this aim implies that the peasants, having sold their land, are subsequently to maintain themselves by wage labour, perhaps even by working on the land that was formerly theirs, and that thereby both the quality of their life and the agrarian productivity will increase. This idea is not new. As stated above, it had already been advanced by the defenders of enclosure against the commoners in feudal England. Privatised land was to become the property of those who were both able and willing to cultivate it according to capitalist standards, and the landless commoners should convert themselves into agricultural or industrial workers. This was also deemed to be a factor of modernisation and progress.[170] In Section II, we showed that this process implies the repetition of primitive accumulation, in terms of what Harvey labels "accumulation by dispossession". It is a fundamental mechanism for the cross-border expansion of neo-liberalism.

In truth, the government's argument that the sale and rent of the *ejidal* land had already been a common practice is weak. The government itself argues that the reason for this practice was the peasants' lack of technology and capital. Yet this problem could be solved with specific support, in particular regarding machinery and irrigation systems. Furthermore, with regard to the low education level and the widespread illiteracy of rural people, it is doubtful whether they would find any work that could guarantee a means of subsistence once they had lost their land. Moreover, the reform goes far beyond the alleged practice of *de facto* selling and renting when it allows the mortgaging and the conversion of the *ejidal* land into private property.

168 Díaz de León, note 79 above, p. 924.

169 Iniciativa de Reforma de 1992 al Artículo 27 Constitucional, reprinted in Díaz de León, note 79 above, p. 924 & 926 *et seq*; Comments of the parliamentary commission, reprinted in Díaz de León, note 79 above, p. 941 *et seq.*, & 946.

170 J.M. Neeson, *Commoners: Common Right, Enclosure and Social Change in England, 1700–1820*, reprint, (Cambridge: Cambridge University Press, 1996), p. 21 *et seq.*

D. THE CONCENTRATION OF LAND AND LAND GRABS

Abolishing land re-distribution by *dotación* ended a process that was still a work in progress at that time. Because of the economic and politic power of the large landholders, and because governments and local politicians often did not support the revolutionary agrarian programme, its realisation lagged far behind its ambitious aims. This is particularly true for the south of Mexico. In Chiapas, for example, the social and economic situation in the early 1990s was still dominated by land conflicts between the large land holders and the rural (above all, indigenous) poor, who had either insufficient or no land to enable them to survive.[171] The Agrarian Counter-Reform of 1992 legalised these conflictual structures of distribution.

In addition, the special rules for land acquisition by companies created further possibilities of land concentration.[172] José Luis Calva criticises the huge properties which, in the wake of the Reform, can be acquired by stock companies as modern share-based *latifundio*. Economically, these large land holdings are unjustified, as no proof exists that they are more productive than smaller land holdings when provided with the same technological equipment.[173] Moreover, critics of the reform argue that the allowed percentage of foreign capital participation in agrarian land is too high and threatens both territorial and food sovereignty.[174]

The new possibilities of disposing of the *ejidal* land and of converting it into private property have brought about a phenomenon that may be described as "legitimised land grab". This term refers to the problem that economic and sometimes political pressure, the low education level of the rural population, and the corruption of local authorities lead to situations in which apparently legal transactions over land disguise new forms of fraudulent and violent land acquisitions. There is thus a clear pattern of accumulation by dispossession, exactly as described in Section II.

The NAFTA aggravates this problem by opening the agrarian sector to the highly subsidised products of the United States, against which Mexican products cannot compete.[175] Thereby, further economic pressure on Mexican peasants ensues. This pressure, coupled with the low level of education and the scant

---

171 Calva, note 132 above, p. 27; de Ita, "México: Impactos del Procede en los conflictos agrarios y la concentración de la tierra", note 131 above, p. 24 & 27 *et seq.*

172 Durand Alcántara, note 118 above, p. 440 *et seq*; Calva, note 132 above, p. 81.

173 Calva, note 132 above, p. 63, 152 *et seq.*

174 See the critique of the parliamentary opposition in *Gaceta Parlamentaria* of 16 June 2000, p. 5.

175 See Timothy Wise, "Agricultural Dumping under NAFTA. Estimating the Costs of U.S. Agricultural Policies to Mexican Producers", Working Paper 2009, available at: www.ase.tufts.edu/gdae/Pubs/wp/09-08AgricDumping.pdf, last accessed 7 December 2012; in the context of the Agrarian Counter-Reform of 1992, see, also, Díaz de León, note 79 above, p. 869, and Assies, note 138 above, p. 56 *et seq.*

economic experience of the rural population, leads to contracts regarding the *ejidal* land being concluded with national or transnational investors in situations of extremely unequal bargaining power.[176]

The media has reported many cases of highly unfair contracts between *ejidatarios* and transnational enterprises. In many cases, the purchase price or the rents paid to the peasants were much lower than the true value of the acquired land. Many of these contracts benefited international mining companies.[177] Furthermore, cases came to light in which the interested buyer – sometimes in collaboration with state authorities or the *ejidal* administrative bodies – exerted enormous pressure on the *ejidatarios*, sometimes using threats and violence,[178] or concluded contracts without the necessary approval of the *asamblea*.[179] Moreover, dispositions over the *ejidal* land can provoke severe conflicts within the *ejidal* community between those who want to sell or rent and those who do not.

For illustration purposes, one example of these new forms of "legitimised land grabs" is described in more detail. This land grab occurred in San José del Progreso, a municipality in the southern state of Oaxaca, and provoked an explosive conflict that peaked in early 2012 when one of the leading activists was murdered. The parties involved are an *ejido* of San José del Progreso and the mining company Cuzcatlán, a subsidiary of the Canadian mining company Fortuna Silver. The conflict arose from contracts concluded between the

---

176 Calva, note 132 above, p. 23, 68 *et seq.*, 81 *et seq.*, & 157 *et seq.*

177 See, for example, the contracts between *ejidatarios* of the state of Oaxaca and Spanish enterprises, *La Jornada*, 6 November 2008, p. 19: "Buscan sacar a firmas españolas de Oaxaca", and *La Jornada*, 17 November 2008, p. 13: "Apoyo del gobierno al Corredor Eólico." Furthermore, the contracts between *ejidatarios* and a Canadian mining company in San José del Progreso, Oaxaca, *La Jornada*, 8 August 2011, p. 9: "Mentiras y traiciones, estrategias de trasnacionales para obtener ganancias", and *La Jornada*, 8 August 2011, p. 8: "Se alista minera canadiense a explotar ejidos en Oaxaca; temen grave contaminación"; for further cases that also involve mining companies: *La Jornada*, 26 June 2009, p. 34: "Ejidatarios de Chihuahua demandan a minera renegociar precio de tierras"; *La Jornada*, 26 May 2009, p. 30: "Habitantes de tres ejidos en Zacatecas exigen a minera canadiense cumplir compromisos"; *La Jornada*, 23 April 2009, p. 36: "Firman ejidatarios de Zacatecas acuerdo con la minera Goldcorp."

178 See, for example, the case of the *comunidad* Santa Rosa Jáuregui in Querétaro, *La Jornada*, 8 August 2008: "Ejidatarios queretanos denuncian presiones para vender tierras"; the legal dispute between the *ejido* El Quince and the company Coppel, *La Jornada*, 8 December 2008, p. 40: "Amenazan a ejidatarios de Sinaloa", and *La Jornada*, 9 December 2008, p. 38: "Investigan anomalías en desistimiento de juicio campesino contra Coppel en Sinaloa"; the contracts between a Canadian mining company and the *ejido* San José del Progreso in Oaxaca, *La Jornada*, 8 August 2011, p. 9: "Mentiras y traiciones, estrategias de trasnacionales para obtener ganancias", and *La Jornada*, 8 August 2011, p. 8: "Se alista minera canadiense a explotar ejidos en Oaxaca; temen grave contaminación"; a case of threats and pressure towards ejidatarios is reported in *La Jornada*, 17 March 2009, p. 31: "Ejidatarios denuncian hostigamiento". Many cases are mentioned in a report in *La Jornada*, 25 July 2011, p. 17: "Obliga la Procuraduría Agraria a ejidatarios a vender sus tierras a empresas particulares: Cocyp."

179 Report in *La Jornada*, 24 May 2009, p. 33: "Poladores de El Monteón, Nayarit, denuncian despojo de playa y represión por defenderla."

ejidatarios of this *ejido* and the enterprise Cuzcatlán. According to background reports,[180] Cuzcatlán was granted a public licence for mining activities in the region of San José del Progreso. Because the corresponding land was an *ejidal*, the exercising of mining activities also required the acquisition of the appropriate land rights (the property rights or rights of usage) from the *ejido* and the *ejidatarios*. The then-governor of the state of Oaxaca and the *Procuraduría Agraria* intervened in the *ejido* so that individual parcels were converted into property. Furthermore, the governor took action against a resistance movement that arose from within the *ejido*, which tried to prevent the assigning of rights to Cuzcatlán. Ultimately, Cuzcatlán concluded contracts with 32 *ejidatarios*, earning the rights of *usus fructus* for 30 years. However, it seems that these *ejidatarios* neither knew of the intentions of the mining company nor about the gold and silver deposits on their land. One of them argued in an interview that he "had no idea what this was all about" and that only after concluding the contract did he learn that Cuzcatlán was interested in the gold and silver. He had assigned the right of *usus fructus* for eight hectares of land for 30 years and received 40,000 Mexican pesos (about 2,270 euros) per hectare. "Never in my life had I seen so much money! I got carried away." Cuzcatlán, in contrast, alleges that, in general, it had paid per hectare between 160,000 and 180,000 Mexican pesos (between about 9,000 and 10,200 euros). The affected *ejido* forms part of a semi-arid zone, its land is of low fertility and production has served, above all, to meet the needs of its own population. "Therefore, the contracts with the mining company gave many of us hope." Within the *ejido*, violent conflicts erupted between those who had concluded contracts with Cuzcatlán and the opponents of these transactions. In total, Cuzcatlán acquired *usus fructus* rights to 92 hectares of land. The company argues that its project will benefit the community, because it will create 650 jobs.

The conflicts regarding the affected land continue at the time of writing. In early 2012, a leading activist of the movement against Cuzcatlán was murdered. The *ejidatarios* who have assigned the rights of their land to the company have thereby lost their means of subsistence. It was a poor livelihood, but when the money received from Cuzcatlán ends, they will be left with nothing and will be dependent on wage labour. Perhaps they will work in Cuzcatlán's mines or migrate to larger cities in Mexico or to the United States. In general, the communities of San José del Progreso fear contamination of the environment and the water because of the mining operations, but Cuzcatlán denies such risks.

---

180 See the background report in *La Jornada*, 8 August 2011, p. 9: "Mentiras y traiciones, estrategias de trasnacionales para obtener ganancias", and *La Jornada*, 8 August 2011, p. 8: "Se alista minera canadiense a explotar ejidos en Oaxaca; temen grave contaminación." Further reports on this case are available at: www.educaoaxaca.org.

V. FORMS OF STRUGGLE AND THEIR TRANSFORMATION DIMENSION

A. TRANSNATIONAL RESONANCE

With the privatisation of agrarian land, Mexican neo-liberal politics reached their peak with intense and escalated rural social protests. On the day NAFTA entered into force, at a time when rebellions seemed to have passed and the neo-liberal order seemed to have become the only alternative at global and transnational level, the EZLN's "*¡Ya basta!*" fundamentally opposed this restriction of perspectives.

The enormous resonance of the Zapatista uprising among leftist movements and with intellectuals worldwide was not only a result of solidarity, but also – and this is even more interesting – of identification. Although the living conditions in European cities, for example, differ from those in the Lacandon Jungle, the "*¡Ya basta!*" of the Zapatistas expressed an unease also felt by many European urban people.

Aware of the transnational dimension of its struggle, the EZLN consistently addresses an international audience, in particular with their communiqués and organising of transnational political events. For example, two years after the insurrection, the EZLN called the "First Intercontinental Meeting for Humanity and against Neo-liberalism" (*Primer Encuentro Intercontinental por la Humanidad y contra el Neoliberalismo*).[181] In the Sixth Declaration of the Lacandon Jungle,[182] they argue that "the neo-liberal globalisation is a global war of conquest, a world war, a war made by capitalism in order to enforce its domination worldwide".

B. TWO COMPLEMENTARY STRATEGIES

1. *Building their own World beyond the Existing Order*

On the one hand, the EZLN turns its back on the state, the political institutions, political parties and laws, building "its own world". The occupation (re-conquest) of land and the establishment of the *municipios autónomos* form a central part of this strategy. They have enacted several "laws" to be applied throughout their autonomous territory, for example, a "Revolutionary agrarian

---

181 This information is available at: http://palabra.ezln.org.mx, last accessed 7 December 2012.

182 Sexta Declaración de la Selva Lacandona, June 2005, available at: http://enlacezapatista.ezln.org.mx/2005/11/13/sexta-declaracion-de-la-selva-lacandona, last accessed 5 January 2013.

law"[183] based upon the principles of the revolutionary agrarian legislation of 1917.

John Holloway describes the Zapatista autonomies as the "other side of saying that we want to change the world without taking power". This form of struggle fights the dominant neo-liberal order by creating space and time beyond the capitalistic logic. Thereby, neo-liberalism suffers fractures and disruptions. According to Holloway, this strategy might serve as a source of inspiration for other social movements.[184] It "is the revolutionary challenge at the beginning of the twenty-first century: to change the world without taking power. [...] The Zapatistas have said that they want to make the world anew, to create a world of dignity, a world of humanity, but without taking power".[185] The EZLN describes its strategy as "building from below and for below an alternative to neo-liberal destruction".[186] Based upon their autonomous municipalities, they aim to build a "non-institutional alternative".[187]

In this context, the poetic language and artistic images used by the Zapatistas are not just a matter of form, but rather a central part of their struggle, because:

> "[they] offer a different way of seeing the world, a vision that breaks with the dominant logic of there-is-no-alternative. Poetry (and indeed other forms of artistic expression) has come to play a central role in the anti-capitalist struggle: poetry not as pretty words but as struggle against the prosaic logic of the world, poetry as the call of a world that does not yet exist."[188]

2. *Struggling within the Existing National and Transnational Order*

Although the EZLN focuses on creating its own element beyond the existing order, we should not ignore, in contrast, that it also struggles for the realisation of reforms within the existing legal system to gain as much room as possible in order to establish an alternative world. Accordingly, the Zapatistas negotiated with the government, proposed concrete reforms of the Constitution, in

---

183 Ley Agraria Revolucionaria 1993, in: Carlos Monsiváis and Elena Poniatowska (eds), *EZLN. Documentos y comunicados*, Vol. 1. (Mexico City: Era, 2003), p. 43 *et seq.*

184 John Holloway, "Die zwei Zeiten. Lieder von Unschuld und Erfahrung", in: idem (ed), *Die zwei Zeiten der Revolution. Würde, Macht und die Politik der Zapatistas.* 2nd edn., (Vienna: Turia + Kant, 2007), pp. 69–74. (2007) p. 72; idem, "Zapatismo Urbano", (2005) 29 *Humboldt Journal of Social Relations*, pp. 168–178, at 172.

185 Holloway, "Die zwei Zeiten. Lieder von Unschuld und Erfahrung", note 184 above, p. 20.

186 Sexta Declaración de la Selva Lacandona, June 2005, http://enlacezapatista.ezln.org.mx/2005/11/13/sexta-declaracion-de-la-selva-lacandona, last accessed 5 January 2013.

187 Comunicado del Comité Clandestino Revolucionario Indígena – comandancia General del Ejército Zapatista de Liberación Nacional, 30 de diciembre de 2012 (Communiqué from the Indigenous Revolutionary Clandestine Committee – General Command of the Zapatista Army of National Liberation, 30 December 2012), http://enlacezapatista.ezln.org.mx/2012/12/30/el-ezln-anuncia-sus-pasos-siguientes-comunicado-del-30-de-diciembre-del-2012, last accessed 15 January 2013.

188 Holloway, "Zapatismo Urbano", note 185 above, at 176.

particular of Article 27, and still insist on the constitutional implementation of the Agreements of San Andrés.[189]

At transnational level, the Zapatistas refer mainly to ILO Convention 169. They pose the social question as a transnational social question, and many of their demands correspond to transnational social rights that are protected in international agreements such as the Declaration of Human Rights and the International Covenant on Economic, Social and Cultural Rights, including, for example, the right to food, health, housing, education, *etc.* Hence, the EZLN is just one of the social movements "joining in the call for transnational social rights and global commons".[190]

This is specifically true for the agrarian problem. Although there is no international consensus that land rights are human rights, particularly due to the dominant Eurocentric perspective on human rights, it cannot be disputed that tenure rights – which provide access to land, fisheries and forests – are essential for the realisation of human rights, in particular, the right to a standard of living adequate for health and well-being, including food and housing. Tenure systems are thus increasingly discussed in the context of international human rights,[191] and some experts even argue that land should be recognised and protected as a human right.[192]

Indeed, several international human rights' provisions offer a legal basis for land claims. Primarily, access to land is closely related to the right to adequate food, as recognised under Article 25 of the Universal Declaration of Human Rights and Article 11 of the International Covenant on Economic, Social and Cultural Rights. Indeed, the right to food does not automatically translate into a right to land because governments may pursue its realisation through policy interventions in other areas. However, not taking appropriate steps to tackle resource access violates the right to food if it results in insufficient access to adequate food because of a lack of alternative livelihood sources.[193]

Consequently, the right to food requires that states refrain from taking measures that may deprive individuals of access to the productive resources upon which they depend when they produce food for themselves (the obligation

---

189 See, for example, the reports in the Mexican newspaper *La Jornada*, 2 January 2013, p. 6 & 7, ("*Los comunicadoes del EZLN, mensaje de vigencia y visión de la realidad nacional*", "Demanda el gobernador de Chiapas cumplir los acuerdos de San Andrés") and the recent *Comunicado del Comité Clandestino Revolucionario Indígena – comandancia General del Ejército Zapatista de Liberación Nacional, 30 de diciembre de 2012*, note 230 above.

190 Fischer-Lescano and Möller, note 3 above, p. XXX.

191 FAO, "Voluntary Guidelines on the Responsible Governance of Tenure of Land, Fisheries and Forests in the Context of National Food Security", (Rome: FAO, 2012); De Schutter, note 4 above.

192 De Schutter, note 4 above, p. 4 & 5.

193 Lorenzo Cotula, "The Right to Food and Access to Natural Resources: Using Human Rights Arguments and Mechanisms to Improve Resource Access for the Rural Poor", (Rome: FAO, 2008), p. 23 & 59.

to respect). When a community has settled on a piece of land and depends upon that land for its livelihood, the obligation to respect the right to food thus requires that eviction of the community from that land be prohibited and, should prevention fail, it should provide effective remedies to those whose human rights have been violated. Furthermore, states are obliged to protect such access from encroachment by other private parties (the obligation to protect). Finally, the state must pro-actively engage in activities intended to strengthen people's access to resources to ensure their livelihood(s), including food security (the obligation to fulfil).[194] Thus, if landless groups have no alternative means of producing or purchasing food, the state has to make access to resources possible – for example, through re-distributive programmes that may result in restrictions on others' rights to property. In these cases, the realisation of the right to food constitutes a public purpose which justifies the taking of property.[195]

The right to property[196] is a double-edged sword. On the one hand, it may be used by private proprietors against landless groups to constrain re-distributive reform efforts. On the other, it may also be used to protect marginalised groups, because it extends to forms of land occupation that are not formally recognised through a legal title or that are based only upon customary tenure. For example, the Inter-American Court of Human Rights and the African Commission on Human and Peoples' Rights consider that indigenous people's traditional possession of their lands has effects equivalent to those of a full property title. Thus, states may have to recognise the customary systems of land tenure that protect communal property rights.[197] In this sense, the struggles of Mexican peasants and indigenous people put pressure on the transnational legal order not only to adopt the principle of the social function of property, but also to re-define this principle as communal property.

Clearly, the situation of indigenous people is specific in so far as the land rights of such peoples are explicitly recognised under international human rights law. In particular, ILO Convention 169 (Articles 13–19) and the UN Declaration on the Rights of Indigenous Peoples [Articles 8 (2) (b) and 10] protect the relationship of indigenous communities with their lands, territories and resources.

Neo-liberal agrarian policies that promote individual titling, propertisation and the creation of marketable land rights have not been able to fulfil the obligations arising from transnational social rights. In fact, they have been an

194 Committee on Economic, Social and Cultural Rights, General Comment 12 on the right to adequate food, 12. May 1999 (E/C. 12/1999/5), paragraph 15; De Schutter, note 4 above, p. 3.
195 Cotula, note 193 above, p. 59; De Schutter, note 4 above, p. 4.
196 The right to property is protected under Article 17 of the Universal Declaration of Human Rights, Article 14 of the African Charter on Human and Peoples' Rights, Article 1 of the First Protocol to the European Convention for the Protection of Human Rights and Fundamental Freedoms, and Article 21 of the American Convention on Human Rights.
197 De Schutter, note 4 above, p. 8.

obstacle. Olivier De Schutter, the Special Rapporteur on the Right to Food, argues that, for groups living upon the basis of common land usage, the formalisation of property rights is the problem, not the solution: it may cause them to be fenced off from the very resources upon which they depend. In addition, individual titling can become a source of conflict and legal insecurity if it conflicts with customary rules and communal land ownership. Finally, the creation of a market for land rights may have a series of undesirable consequences. The primary justification for the establishment of such a market is that it facilitates the re-allocation of land towards more efficient users, thus providing an exit route from agriculture for rural residents for whom farming is not sufficiently profitable. However, experience shows that land sales tend to favour not those who can make the most efficient use of land, but those who have access to capital and whose ability to purchase land is greatest. In fact, the creation of a land-rights market can cause land to be taken out of production in order to be held as an investment by speculators, resulting both in decreased productivity and in increased landlessness among the rural poor.[198]

Fortunately, the neo-liberal approach is being increasingly challenged by alternative policies that link agricultural policies with transnational social rights and the concept of the global commons. Accordingly, customary rights and systems of common use will increasingly come to be recognised and protected in order to provide effective security and favour long-term investments. The requirements applicable to indigenous peoples are to be extended to certain traditional communities that entertain a similar relationship with their lands and are centred on the community rather than on the individual. This will encourage the management of common-pool resources at local level by the communities directly concerned, which is deemed to work better than top-down prescriptions or privatisation of the commons.[199] In the presence of the sometimes highly unequal distribution of land in rural areas, land re-distribution for the benefit of smallholders is considered to be necessary.[200]

VI. CONCLUSION: A WORLD WHERE MANY WORLDS FIT

In conclusion, the Zapatista struggle operates at two levels in its quest to realise an alternative to neo-liberalism and obtain the right to land. On the one hand, the protesters occupied land against the existing legal rules in order to realise the pre-conditions for their autonomies – namely, cultivating their own land and growing their own most basic food. By establishing their autonomies on

198 Ibid., p. 10 *et seq.*
199 Ibid., p. 13; FAO, note 191 above, p. 8 & 11 *et seq.*
200 De Schutter, note 4 above, p. 14 *et seq*; FAO, note 191 above, p. 15 *et seq.*

occupied land, they create their own world "from below" and turn their back on the existing (legal and institutional) order. After a long period of silence, in December 2012, they re-appeared in public with a spectacular march of silence and a *communiqué* which re-affirmed that they aim to build up a "non-institutional left alternative" both in Mexico and in the world, and to co-operate with other social movements worldwide.[201]

On the other hand, their struggle is effective within the existing legal (national and transnational) order. Here, together with other counter-movements, it may help to extend this order so that establishing counter-models (such as the Zapatista autonomies) can be pushed forward as far as possible. In this context, relying on the legal provisions of the existing (national and/or transnational) legal system may be considered as an attempt to gain as much room as possible to establish an alternative world. It only complements the first form of the struggle, which aims to create another world beyond that of the capitalist logic.

---

201 Comunicado del Comité Clandestino Revolucionario Indígena – comandancia General del Ejército Zapatista de Liberación Nacional, 30 de diciembre de 2012, note 230 above.

INDEX

I

L

M

N

O

P

Q

R

S

T

www.ingramcontent.com/pod-product-compliance
Ingram Content Group UK Ltd.
Pitfield, Milton Keynes, MK11 3LW, UK
UKHW051920100926
8556IPUK00021B/1290

9 781780 683966